BRADFORD W.G. PUBLIC LIBRARY

3328 00200400 6

P9-DMF-637

BOOK SMART

FEB 1 3 1996

BOOK SMART

*How to Develop and Support
Successful, Motivated Readers*

Anne E. Cunningham
and Jamie Zibulsky

OXFORD
UNIVERSITY PRESS

Bradford WG Public Library
425 Holland St. W.
Bradford, ON L3Z 0J2

OXFORD

UNIVERSITY PRESS

Oxford University Press is a department of the University of Oxford.
It furthers the University's objective of excellence in research, scholarship,
and education by publishing worldwide.

Oxford   New York
Auckland   Cape Town   Dar es Salaam   Hong Kong   Karachi
Kuala Lumpur   Madrid   Melbourne   Mexico City   Nairobi
New Delhi   Shanghai   Taipei   Toronto

With offices in
Argentina   Austria   Brazil   Chile   Czech Republic   France   Greece
Guatemala   Hungary   Italy   Japan   Poland   Portugal   Singapore
South Korea   Switzerland   Thailand   Turkey   Ukraine   Vietnam

Oxford is a registered trademark of Oxford University Press
in the UK and certain other countries.

Published in the United States of America by
Oxford University Press
198 Madison Avenue, New York, NY 10016

© Oxford University Press 2014

All rights reserved. No part of this publication may be reproduced, stored in a
retrieval system, or transmitted, in any form or by any means, without the prior
permission in writing of Oxford University Press, or as expressly permitted by law,
by license, or under terms agreed with the appropriate reproduction rights organization.
Inquiries concerning reproduction outside the scope of the above should be sent to the
Rights Department, Oxford University Press, at the address above.

You must not circulate this work in any other form
and you must impose this same condition on any acquirer.

Library of Congress Cataloging-in-Publication Data
Cunningham, Anne E.
Book smart : how to develop and support successful, motivated readers / Anne E. Cunningham,
Jamie Zibulsky.
pages cm
Includes bibliographical references and index.
ISBN 978–0–19–984393–0 (pbk.)
1. Oral reading.   2. Storytelling. 3. Children—Books and reading.   4. Children—Language.
5. Language acquisition—Parent participation.   I. Zibulsky, Jamie, author.   II. Title.
LB1573.5.C96 2014
372.45'2—dc23
2013022810]

1 3 5 7 9 8 6 4 2
Printed in the United States of America
on acid-free paper

CONTENTS

DISCARDED
BRADFORD WG
PUBLIC LIBRARY

ACKNOWLEDGMENTS

We first started talking about the idea for this book three years before we penned this acknowledgments page. So many people have helped us turn those conversations into the book in your hands now, and we owe them all a great deal of gratitude. Our graduate students have tirelessly assisted us throughout this process and provided helpful edits, activities, and background knowledge that fundamentally improved our final product. At University of California, Berkeley, many thanks go to Anne's research group, including: Yi-Jui Chen, Kelly Campbell, Andrea Golloher, Neil Hasser, Stevie Jeung, Jerred Jolin, Catherine Lipson, Alejandra Ojeda-Beck, Mary Requa, and Gat Harussi Savaldi. And at Fairleigh Dickinson University, we thank Jamie's research group, including Jasmine Davis, Courtney Santucci, Chelsea Schubart, and Veronica Slaght. We've also received a great deal of support from our editor at Oxford, Abby Gross, as well as the rest of her team, and we thank everyone at Oxford University Press for their support.

We also appreciate the support of our friends and colleagues who read drafts of the book along the way, offered helpful critiques, and shared their own knowledge of this topic. We have too many wonderful cheerleaders to name here, and we thank each one of you. Special thanks to Dr. Ruth Nathan, Molly O'Connell, Robyn Becker, Kelly Boyle, and Dr. Katie Raher who not only shared their expertise, but also adorable anecdotes and videos of themselves, their children, and their grand-children engaging in just the sorts of activities we discuss in this book. Their enthusiasm for this project helped us keep going. Thank you also to Theresa MacArthur at the West Milford Township Library in New Jersey, who helped us tremendously when we compiled our recommended book lists.

As we hope will be clear throughout this book, we are both passionate about the field of reading development and fascinated by many aspects of this complex process. Anne's enthusiasm for this field was first fueled by her mentor, Keith Stanovich, who has continuously helped her think about research, refine her ideas, and be a confident scholar for more than 30 years. Similarly, Jamie's academic trajectory has largely been shaped by taking a class with Anne in her first semester of graduate school and the advice and support Anne has provided since then. Becoming a successful, motivated academic is similar to becoming a successful, motivated reader in that one cannot do it alone—we depend on our role models to shepherd us through each step in the process. Our deepest gratitude goes to Keith for beginning this mutigenerational model of mentorship that has served us both so well.

Our inspiration to write this book came, in large part, from our own families. Without her parents, Pat and Herb Zibulsky, who helped her become a successful, motivated reader, Jamie would not be the person she is or in the field she is in. And although Anne's expertise in reading development preceded her son Michael's birth, helping him learn to read enriched her understanding of the joyful role that parents can play in developing successful, motivated readers. Thank you, Michael, for helping a mother see the world more vividly through the eyes of a child. Of course, Anne's initial understanding of this shared process came from her own mother, Carol Cunningham, who always took the time to read to and with her, and did so much more. We both want to deeply thank our husbands, Conor and Gary, who could probably write their own books on reading at this point, and who helped with the editing and formatting of this book tremendously, as well as taking care of the feeding and stress level of its authors. We know now that it takes a village to write a book, and we couldn't have done it without you all—thanks!

PREFACE

About This Book

Any time you pick up a book from the shelf of the library, or decide to purchase one at your local bookstore, you do so because the book inspires some sort of curiosity in you or promises to provide answers to questions you have been asking. We suspect you have picked up this particular book because you have heard about the importance of reading with your child and want to develop strategies for reading together. Perhaps you love reading and want to make sure that your son or daughter does, too. Or maybe you never get around to reading yourself, but know it is important to figure out how to spend more time reading together. Either way, we are glad you are here, and we have written this book to help parents like you. We want to congratulate you for taking the time to embark on this journey with us, and with your child. Developing strategies for reading with your child can seem complicated at first, but our goal is to show you a number of ways to read together, and talk about reading, that are is easy to fit into your daily routine. In fact, we know that reading this book will help you realize how much you are already doing to foster your child's language and literacy development. The strategies we provide in each chapter should help you build on the great work you are already doing.

Although many parents know that reading aloud to children is an important activity for building later literacy and life skills, why this is the case is rarely explained clearly to them. Understanding the specific benefits of reading together will help you deepen and enrich your relationship with your child while supporting his or her academic development. Increasingly, daycare centers and preschools provide early literacy instruction that complements parents' efforts to help children make progress toward learning basic reading skills, but our education system does not consistently focus on developing the skills that will help children comprehend text and think critically about what they read. We believe we need to do more to support long-term reading success in all aspects of literacy.

You have the power to help, because parents can develop responsive and engaging ways to read at home so that their children become motivated, critical readers. However, too many parents are either unaware of the importance of these strategies or unsure of how to specifically use them. And that is the real reason we have written this book: we believe that educating parents about the benefits of reading aloud as a family, from cradle to college, has the power to boost academic performance and social-emotional development.

In terms of academic performance, reading together over the years will help your child develop his vocabulary, learn to sound out new words, and begin to comprehend and remember details of written stories. As we will discuss throughout this book, researchers know that children's reading abilities in early elementary school predict their reading abilities in high school. Even things that your child does during her preschool years, like the way she plays rhyming games or holds a book, can indicate what her later reading skills will be like. The seemingly simple act of reading together builds a wide variety of academic skills, and we will discuss these skills in the first several chapters of this book.

But another aspect of reading that makes it so critical is that it has the potential to change the way your child thinks, relates to others, and understands the world. We often overlook the fact that reading can help young children develop critical thinking skills and social-emotional skills, but it is one of the most important points we want to make in this book. Reading can help children learn to be introspective. Katherine Paterson, the author of wonderful, award-winning children's books including *Bridge to Terabithia* and *Jacob Have I Loved*, sums up the lofty goals that most parents have for their children as growing readers. She says:

> It is not enough to simply teach children to read; we have to give them something worth reading. Something that will stretch their imaginations—something that will help them make sense of their own lives and encourage them to reach out toward people whose lives are quite different from their own.[1]

It takes a lot of time and care to ensure that your child develops the capacity for reflection that Paterson talks about here, and we will share strategies for building this type of knowledge in the latter chapters of the book. But neither teaching children to read nor stretching their imaginations can happen overnight. In each chapter of this book, we will talk about the gradual unfolding of your child's reading skills, and we hope you will see how these different sets of skills—academic and social-emotional—both develop over time. Just as your child learned to ride a bicycle in many stages, reading is a process, not a one-time event.

Even before you buy your toddler a plastic tricycle, you play games and encourage activities that help him develop many important motor skills that will make riding the new trike easier for him. You make your home and yard feel like safe places to explore, and you help your child to be confident about his abilities. It will be years until you begin practicing with him on a two-wheeler, running down the street with one hand on the handlebars and another hand steadying your child or gripping the seat, but you are already preparing for that day. And shortly after that, you know the day will come when you no longer need to keep holding on. But you will keep on being watchful and helping him develop more advanced skills, like learning how to signal when he wants to make a turn.

Reading is no different. Even before your child became enthralled with the early board books you read with her, the one-sided conversations you led as you walked around the house and responded to her actions had already stimulated her language processing skills, which become so important to reading development. But soon afterwards, your interactions could become more dynamic. Sharing those first board books together creates a situation where you read and watch, pause to listen and respond to your child, and demonstrate a give-and-take between what the books says and what you and your child have experienced together. Reading those board books will help her think of reading time as a special part of the day, and let her begin to understand how to hold a book and turn the pages. Eventually, your child will begin to share her own ideas about the pictures you look at and the stories you read, and you will begin to see her gain her balance as a reader. But even when she begins reading fluently, your work is still not done. Reading requires reflection, responding to new situations, and letting your background knowledge interact with the text to create its meaning. Children must learn to do all this as readers, so imagine the benefits afforded to children who have had responsive parents.

Using the book. Each chapter in this book focuses on a specific step in the process of reading development, from building oral language skills, to emergent reading skills and the path of writing development, to the many skills needed for reading comprehension and engagement, and finally, to the social-emotional skills cultivated by reading. Moreover, each chapter highlights activities and strategies that will allow your child to build these skills while furthering his or her special bond with you and ensures that reading time becomes highly valued by you both. We explain how reading aloud together can develop each of these skills and, in turn, how each of these skills will help your child become a successful learner, as well as a lifelong, motivated, and confident reader. In Appendix E, we recommend a variety of books that may help you build the many skills we discuss throughout each chapter.

We hope that you first pick this book up when your child is an infant, and that you page through it to get a clear sense of the amazing developments he or she will make with your help over the next several years. As your child matures, we picture particular chapters in this book becoming well worn and dog-eared, as you focus more intently on skills that are appropriate to build at that time. This is not a book to read cover to cover and then put away, but a tool and reference guide that we hope will continue to provide you with useful information and strategies as your child becomes a toddler, a preschooler, enters elementary school, and eventually becomes a fluent and avid reader.

For this reason, we want to be sure to explain that the activities and strategies we recommend in this book are just that—recommendations. You should pick and choose between these recommendations to select the ones that make most sense for you and your child, and should not try to simultaneously tackle all of the recommendations in one list or chapter. In fact, trying to do too many new things at the same time might feel overwhelming for you and your child, which would be counterproductive. The activities we suggest are designed to make language and literacy a fun, shared experience for you and your child. Setting a goal for yourself of trying out one new activity a week may be a good way to start incorporating these strategies into your daily life.

To aid you in selecting appropriate activities and strategies, you will see that all of the recommendations we make are followed by an icon indicating if the activity suggested is best for 0–3-year-olds (a rattle) , 4–7-year-olds (alphabet blocks) , or children 8 and older (a reader) . Many activities are appropriate for more than one age group and these age guidelines are approximate ones. You know your child best, so use your own judgment in determining if an activity will be fun and at the right level of challenge for him or her. If your son has a very sophisticated vocabulary as a 3-year-old, you may select some of the activities that are listed as appropriate for 4–7-year-olds. If your 8 year-old daughter is still working hard to keep track of the details of the stories she reads, you might continue to select some of the activities that are listed as appropriate for 4–7-year-olds. Again, the most important thing to do is to select activities that you think will be engaging to your child. If you do that, you can't go wrong.

As you read through the book, you will see that each chapter includes recommendations appropriate for each of the three age groups, because most of the language and literacy skills that we discuss take several years to unfold. So, although you can read across chapters and focus on the activities that are suited to 0–3-year-olds in each chapter, we think it is also important for you to understand which skills—within each chapter—your child will be working on as he or she gets older. Preparing for the next stage in your child's development in advance by reading about the skills he or she will need to focus on next can help you anticipate how to support your child in the months and years to come. For this reason, a new topic is discussed in each chapter and subsection of the book. For example, you might choose to read just one subsection of the book at a time—perhaps focusing on the phonological awareness section when your child is in the second year of preschool—or you might choose to skim across chapters, looking for activities focused on a variety of skills that seem appropriate for your four-year-old. Either approach can work well and the most important thing is to pick activities that allow you and your child to bond while building important reading skills.

Another big idea that we focus on throughout the book, and that Katherine Paterson points out in the quotation at the beginning of this preface, is that reading gives us a glimpse into the lives of others, who may think and act very differently from us. By providing this insight into the broader world, reading can help children become more empathetic people. The interpersonal skills that children acquire through shared reading with a parent, combined with the knowledge that children gain through reading, together coalesce to play a powerful role in the way that they approach tasks and people. It is truly astonishing that children can develop so many different types of knowledge through book reading, as they learn about unfamiliar worlds and the perspectives of other people, and explore their own emotional reactions to poignant moments in stories. As Katherine Paterson suggests, we need to find books and stories that can awaken children's understanding of the world around and beyond them. However, to become this sort of responsive reader and use literacy as a tool for perspective-taking, children need to possess many basic reading skills, which we hope to help you foster through the activities and strategies provided throughout the book. The early chapters of this book provide strategies to ensure that your child can develop a robust vocabulary, gain access to and play with the sounds in words, express himself in writing, and read simple words and sentences. The later chapters in this book will explain how your child can begin to read between the lines and use background knowledge to make sense of stories at a deep level, how you can ensure that reading is a favorite pastime, and how books can be tools for understanding oneself and others. These later chapters should help you see how your child will begin to ride that two-wheeler without much assistance at all. We hope you enjoy this ride towards independence as much as your child does!

About Activities and Strategies on Other Topics of Interest

Before continuing to the next section of this preface, we would like to take a moment to discuss two additional important matters that relate to the goals of this book. Our world today is becoming increasingly technology oriented and multilingual. In response to this diverse landscape, and in the interests of providing a more comprehensive account of children's literacy development, we will share some advice and strategies on the topics of selecting educational technology and learning English as a second language. However, given the already comprehensive nature of this book, we will not have the privilege of going into great detail on the two subjects. Instead, we will provide tables at the conclusion of each chapter that offer credible resources to help you be a more informed consumer of educational technology and summarize research-based strategies shown to facilitate the development of two languages simultaneously. To ignore these topics would be both a great disservice to you, our reader, and a naive appraisal of an increasingly diverse and technological society. The following brief introductions to these topics will orient you to relevant background information in these critical areas.

Tech Tips. In each chapter of this book, we will include a small section focused on how technology can help you build the skills that we discuss in that chapter, as well as how to ensure that technology does not negatively affect your child's development of these skills. As we write this book, our society is in the midst of a transition from relying primarily on print to digital information, and this new phenomenon affects all families. In the past decade, an increasing amount of research has been conducted that explores how parents are integrating new technologies into their households and how these new media are influencing learning and reading together in the home environment. The launch of the iPad in 2010 helped this phenomena hit a tipping point. Parents, educators, and researchers are working hard to identify the ways in which digital books, games, and other content shape household interactions, as well as the types of opportunities children have to learn outside the home—in schools, museums, libraries, and in the car. These new tools provide parents with many ways to use digital media and apps appropriately to promote literacy.

However, there are also many concerns people have about these new technologies, from determining the appropriate content and amount of screen time for children of a particular age to making sure that children are safe when using the Internet. Some of the big questions parents have include:

- **How Much Screen Time Do Children Log Per Day?**
  - A recent large-scale study by the Kaiser Family Foundation[2] found that children ages eight to eighteen spent more than seven hours a day using some form of digital media. By multitasking (for example, watching a movie while playing on the computer), children actually managed to view almost eleven hours of media content during that time. The amount of screen time that children log each day continues to increase as smartphones and tablets make it easier to access media content at any time.
- **How Much Screen Time Do Experts Say Children Should Get Per Day? Why?**
  - The American Association of Pediatrics (AAP) discourages television watching and the use of other digital media for children younger than two years old and suggests limiting screen time for older children to less than one to two hours per day.[3] The AAP found that for each hour that children younger than two years old spent watching television alone, they spent close to the same amount of time not interacting with parents or siblings during the day and lost out on valuable opportunities

for vocabulary development. This finding makes sense—we have a limited number of hours in each day, so time spent using technology can easily end up being time spent not interacting with people. And as we will discuss throughout this book, many of the most important activities for language and literacy development require play, conversation, and shared book reading between a child and caregiver...all activities that can best be accomplished when the television is turned off and the smartphone is put away.

That said, it is very common to see families using technology tools in ways that are not consistent with the recommendations of the AAP and other organizations who provide such guidelines. Our goal in writing this book is to meet you and your child where you are right now and to help you do more to support your child's reading development. We assume you may already be using technology tools with your child, and therefore, although we respect the recommendations made by these governing bodies, we want to help you find more effective ways to use those technology tools to which your child has already been introduced. A general rule of thumb is that technology can be helpful as a *supplement* to the language and literacy activities you already engage in with your child, and harmful as a *replacement* for the language and literacy activities you already engage in with your child.

You can also make decisions about when to use technology and when to stick with old-fashioned methods. Some language and literacy skills may make sense to foster in your older toddler or elementary school age child by using technology tools, and other skills may best be developed solely through interpersonal interactions. Here are some major benefits of these technology tools:

- **They allow for immediate access to the materials you want to watch or download.**
  - These tools can allow your child access to materials that might be hard to find otherwise or as quickly. Technology allows you to "strike while the iron is hot" and get your child engaged in a language or literacy activity when he's in the mood for one.

- **Your child can learn through repetition.**
  - Repetition can be both helpful and harmful, and the ability to watch or play the same thing repeatedly is also a common concern parents have about technology. That said, there is variability in the skills that children need to learn and some, like learning to recognize and pair letter sounds and letter names, require more exposure and practice to acquire. Technology is a way to supplement the number of exposures your child needs, especially when your time is limited. When your child does need practice with a particular skill and you do not have the time to help him, technological tools can be useful.
- **Educational computer games or applications can be highly motivating for children.**
  - Children often stay engaged in academic activities because of the interesting graphics, opportunities to win points, rewards, or praise, and interactive feedback. High-quality technology tools are capable of being responsive to your child by providing individualized feedback and tailoring the difficulty level of questions and materials as appropriate. Lower-quality technology tools, while also easily accessible, do not take your child's needs and abilities into account in the same way as the tools that have been developed to serve a true educational purpose. It is important for you to monitor what your child is watching and playing to make sure that the technology tools he uses are high quality.

Although we are reluctant to provide references to online tools because we have no way of knowing how long these websites and applications will be accessible to readers, we do so sparingly in the **Tech Tips** section in each chapter in order to provide you with clear examples of technology tools that might be useful. We have tried to pick only those websites and applications that we think will be accessible over time, and will update this information on our website regularly. We will also share some guidelines that you can use to select appropriate applications and websites independently. After reading this book, you will understand which language and literacy skills are most important to acquire and why, which will make you a more informed consumer of educational technology and understand that there is high value in some, but not all, of these tools.

English Language Learners. This section in each chapter is focused on children learning English as a second language (L2) and how parents can support their development of language and literacy skills in both it and their first language (L1). If your child is on the road to multilingualism, we want to congratulate you and tell you about the benefits that come along with fluency in multiple languages. As a parent, you play an important role in helping your child acquire English language skills and in fostering the development of his home or first language. We also want to assure you that you and your child can still use all of the tips and strategies described in this book in your first language. Researchers have demonstrated that the same skills that predict reading success in monolingual English speakers also play an important role in the literacy development of children learning English as a second language.[4] These skills are highlighted in each chapter of this book, such as oral language and vocabulary development, phonological awareness, and print knowledge. Some of these language and literacy skills transfer easily across languages (like phonemic awareness), while other skills are less directly connected (like vocabulary). By focusing on the development of these skills in both languages, you will certainly help your child become a better reader, writer, and speaker because scores of research studies show that strengthening abilities in your child's first language will help him become a better reader, writer, and speaker in both languages.[5] Below, we include an overview of the research looking at the development of multilingualism.

Contrary to what many believe, exposing your child to a new language will not impede her development of her first language.[7] Initially, developing two languages simultaneously may be more challenging or emerge more slowly for your child than developing just one,[8] but ultimately this challenge will be beneficial for her in the mastery of both languages.[9] In fact, research has demonstrated that learning two languages actually fosters brain development, such that areas of the brain dedicated to language, memory, and attention are significantly different in monolinguals and bilinguals.[10] This positive influence on brain development will promote children's cognitive development and flexibility, especially in language processing.[11] Thus, helping your child acquire L2 will not have negative effects on her language development; instead, she will acquire both languages with time. An important point to emphasize is that, in developing proficiency in L2, your child will actually be improving her skills in reading, spelling, and writing for both L1 and L2. We will tell you a bit more about how second language development can affect these specific literacy skills.

Specialists in the domain of multilingualism have demonstrated a cross-language transfer of reading comprehension ability in individuals who are bilingual.[12] What this means, according to these researchers, is that the ability to understand written information can transfer across languages for children of all ages and from both L1 to L2 and L2 to L1. Cross-language transfer, then, may be thought of as a "cognitive tool" that activates and then transforms a child's background knowledge; which is helpful in the development of both languages.[13] The instructional strategies we provide will help you to expand your child's background knowledge and language skills in L1, as well as to promote the transfer of this information to L2. As you will read in the chapter on Story Comprehension, background knowledge is critical for reading comprehension.

Word recognition is closely associated with successful reading comprehension, because we need to be able to identify words quickly and accurately in order to focus on making meaning out of the words we read.[14] There are several steps involved in successful word recognition: first, an oral form (the spoken word) is mapped onto a visual form (the written word), while at the same time meaning is assigned to both the spoken and written word. Fluent readers complete this mapping process rapidly, which supports reading comprehension. Individuals who are learning multiple languages have an advantage because word recognition skills in one language have been shown to transfer to another language.[15] In this way, fostering your child's word recognition skills in a second language will enhance her word recognition ability, which in turn facilitates her reading comprehension in both languages.

The evidence for cross-language transfer is not limited to reading and word recognition, but also is evident in writing.[16] Knowledge of writing in a bilingual child's first language can carry over to the second, thereby promoting the emergence of writing in the new written language.[17] Moreover, learning another language can enhance knowledge of English structure and vocabulary,[18] two critical elements in the endeavor to write proficiently in English. For example, several studies have demonstrated that an individual's literacy level in Chinese can predict abilities to write in a second language.[19] Finally, as in the case of language-specific strategies transferring between languages, general writing strategies acquired in the first language, such as generating ideas, backtracking, or planning, can be used when writing in a second language.[20] Therefore, developing your child's second language writing will be an amazing investment both in your child's first and second language.

One of the specific challenges for a beginning L2 writer is accurately spelling words. Researchers have suggested that proficiency in spelling translates into proficiency in writing and phonology, both critical in understanding, remembering, and being able to efficiently retrieve words from memory.[21] Complicating the situation, however, is the fact that English is not a "transparent" written language. This means that multiple letter patterns can represent the same sounds (for example, rain and reign) and similar patterns represent sounds differently based on the letters that come before or after them in a written word (for example, can and cane). This issue makes spelling particularly difficult for English language learners, as well as for students whose first language is English. However, children who learn to be aware of both the regular patterns and irregular deviations from them in English will have a better opportunity for learning the language. For the child learning English as a second language, an early focus on developing accurate spelling may have a strong impact on the development of reading comprehension.[22]

In addition to these academic benefits of your child learning a second language, maintaining your home language has invaluable social, emotional, and cultural benefits. Staying connected with members of your family who primarily speak this language strongly contributes to your child's developing sense of cultural and community identity. Not speaking to your child in your home language (when you want him to learn English over the home language) has the potential to break down the natural communication parents have with their children and create a rift between home language/culture and the outside world. The ability to speak two languages offers your child experiences with both cultures and the connections between them. Knowledge of more than one language opens the door to a wider array of music, literature, poetry, and history found across cultures. This wide exposure sets the stage for your child to develop greater compassion, empathy, and appreciation of different customs and values. Also, the need to consider a conversational partner's primary language gives bilingual children more opportunities to develop perspective-taking skills (or the ability to "step into someone else's shoes" and appreciate that person's thoughts and feelings) than their monolingual peers. For a child raised in a Spanish-speaking household in the United States, it's likely that she'll speak with Spanish- and English-speaking friends, family, and community members every day. Understanding that others have different backgrounds allows a child to modify her expectations depending on whom she is speaking with. Developing this understanding will serve your bilingual child well as she considers the perspective of others in the complexities of human interaction.

As a parent of a blossoming bilingual child, you will find myriad ways to successfully engage your child in learning two languages. Our goal is to provide you with the ability to encourage and implement reading and writing activities in two languages so that the journey toward bilingual literacy will be less daunting and much more enjoyable for you both.

About Us

Our desire to write this book comes from two places. First, we are both passionate readers. Books have been a source of inspiration, solace, and escape for us, and we think that a love of literature enhances one's life and want to be sure that no child misses out on the chance to become someone who reads for pleasure. Just as important, though, we are driven by our professional experiences in schools and clinics. We have both seen children who are frustrated and disengaged readers—because reading is difficult for them, because reading makes them feel stupid, because parents and teachers pushed them too much or not enough or just not the right way—and parents who are confused about how to help their children most. Even though these experiences are quite common, we often neglect to think about the fact that reading is an emotional experience for children and their caregivers. It always has been for us.

Jamie's interest in the field of reading development, and her decision to become a school psychologist, was propelled by a photograph that hung in her bedroom throughout college. The moment captured in this picture, of Jamie's father sitting on the beach and reading intently—and 18-month-old Jamie perched in her own chair next to him, studying her own picture book with fervent interest, is the perfect illustration of the type of early exposure to books that jumpstarted Jamie's lifelong love of reading. A precocious reader who began reading independently during kindergarten, Jamie received a great deal of attention and praise from the adults in her life for her love of books. These behaviors—of opening a book, talking about stories, and learning to sound out words—had been reinforced even from the time Jamie was still wearing diapers. Reading side-by-side with her parents, on the beach or on the couch, was a frequent and magical part of Jamie's childhood.

Although Jamie began reading to spend time with and receive attention from her parents, she began to derive her own intrinsic pleasure from reading as she became a more sophisticated reader. In elementary school, when Jamie had a disagreement with her friends or bickered with her sister, diving into a book was the best way for her to make herself feel better. She remembers devouring playful books by authors like Gordon Korman (who wrote the *Bruno and Boots* series) and Ann M. Martin (who wrote *The Baby-sitter's Club* series), while also adoring more serious books by Patricia MacLachlan, Natalie Babbit, and Katherine Paterson. For someone who catches the reading bug, books become friends in times of joy and in times of annoyance. To this day, one of the best ways that Jamie knows how to cope with sadness or frustration is to pick up a familiar book and visit with characters she adores. And in good times, selecting books to bring to the beach or on a vacation is one of the great pleasures of her life.

Similarly, when Anne thinks back on her childhood, she remembers a family that thrived on print: books, newspapers, and magazines. Reading played a large role in her upbringing and both parents modeled the joy that they derived from reading literature, history, and newspapers. Anne could always rely on the comfort of reading a book with one of her parents after an evening bath. Because her family shared a love of literature, her mother often read two, three, and four books out loud to her and her siblings every day. Growing up, her family visited the library each week. Anne recalls poring over all the options available to her at the library. Patrons were limited to taking out twelve books at a time, and Anne would always take out the maximum possible, leaving the library with a stack of books that reached her chin. Novels such as *Misty of Chincoteague* opened up new and magical places and allowed her to enter a world that satisfied her love of horses. Reading the *Nancy Drew* series gave Anne an outlet—a place where she could read about the challenges other people experienced and the solutions that they found—and where she could invariably find comfort and excitement. To this day, Anne likes to borrow and buy as many books as possible, because digging into stories and learning new information continue to bring her a great deal of comfort and delight.

As a parent, Anne has passed along this enthusiasm for reading. Sharing books with her son, Michael, has always been a joyful experience and an opportunity to introduce him to the worlds and characters that have meant so much to her. When Michael was a baby, Anne would cuddle with him on her lap in the rocking chair and read board book after board book with him. Michael liked *The Very Hungry Caterpillar* the best, perhaps because of the silly voices and sounds that Anne made while reading. Anne was particularly excited when Michael, as a toddler, began to pick up books and "read" them on his own. Sometimes the book was upside down, and he certainly didn't yet know that it was the letters on the page that told his mother what to read, but he looked at the pages intently and turned them until the end.

One of Anne's favorite activities as Michael continued to grow older was during the calm before bedtime, when it was just the two of them away from the busy and hectic aspects of their day, and they could snuggle up together and read a few of Michael's favorite books. By the time he was three years old, he was hooked, and would bring book after book to Anne wherever she was and ask her to read with him. She often had things to do, but how could she say no to reading a book? Let's just say cooking dinner wasn't a very efficient process in their household for a couple years. Many of you can probably relate.

Our belief that reading is so important does not simply stem from our personal experiences as readers. We also know this as professionals. Jamie is a school psychologist by training, and her interest in the area of reading research developed over time, as she was frequently asked to evaluate older elementary school children and adolescents for special educational services or to provide these students with social skills or anger management training. Almost always, when she looked through their cumulative records, she would see that all through elementary school, often starting in kindergarten, their teachers had warned that they were struggling as readers. But because help was not given soon enough, these children began to have incredible difficulty making sense of the information that was presented throughout each and every school day—because reading is an essential part of math, science, and social studies learning, too—and they began to misbehave instead of trying to learn. For Jamie, once she knew of their reading difficulties, their frustration seemed quite understandable.

This observation, that so many children who needed help in reading at an early age were not getting it, is what inspired Jamie to become a professor. By training the next generation of educators, she hopes to help change the school system so that these students get help sooner. She also continues to work with children and parents at Fairleigh Dickinson University's Center for Psychological Services. Her work with families has shown her that teaching parents to serve as their children's teachers and therapists is tremendously powerful, because parents have the opportunity to help children learn and practice new skills many times every day. She hopes, as does Anne, that this book allows you to think of yourself as your child's first teacher and guide.

As a young college student, Anne realized she loved sitting on the stoop of Michigan State University's Laboratory Preschool and interacting with four- to five-year-old children. It became clear to her that a career teaching young children would be ideal, and Anne turned her energy toward becoming the best preschool and elementary school teacher she could become. For almost a decade, Anne taught preschool through elementary age students. During that time, Anne helped many beginning readers unlock the magic of books, many kindergarteners and first graders excitedly recognize new words, and second and third graders begin to comprehend the stories they read on their own. But in those years she also witnessed firsthand how different students' experiences with reading and writing can be and how learning to read is actually one of the most challenging and frustrating educational accomplishments for a number of children.

Anne's curiosity about these differences and desire to prevent reading difficulties caused her to embark on her career in research. Anne was trained as a developmental psychologist at the University of Michigan and for the next 20 years she conducted groundbreaking research that contributed to our current understanding of the ways that children learn to read and the ways in which parents and teachers can support them. Anne's research demonstrated that learning to perceive and hear the sounds of the English language is a causal factor in determining who will become a skilled or less-skilled reader, and that kindergarten through second grade children spontaneously "self-teach" spelling patterns of words when reading. In a series of carefully conducted studies with Dr. Keith Stanovich from the University of Toronto, she also demonstrated the relationship between reading volume and the development of student's reading ability, vocabulary and general knowledge about the world. As a professor at the Graduate School of Education of the University of California, Berkeley, she has also been able to accomplish her goal of preventing reading difficulties on a large scale because of the many opportunities to translate this research to families and practitioners and affect policy at local, national, and international levels.

Indeed, as a former classroom teacher, Anne was, and still is, very interested in how the support adults provide to a child early on can affect the development of the skills that cultivate long-term achievement and motivated readers. Although Anne studies the development of reading throughout the lifespan, she has become more and more focused on the earliest years of children's lives, because of the substantial evidence that these years provide the greatest (but not only) window of opportunity to support a child in becoming a capable, confident, and avid reader. Her current research with early childhood educators has focused on the information that young children need to develop the building blocks of language and literacy required to become lifelong readers. As their children's first teachers, it is important for parents to have this information as well.

We wanted to share this background information with you so you had a sense of how we have both helped parents and teachers use this type of information most effectively. It has been such a privilege for us to work with parents who are passionate about education and child development, and we have always been gratified when our perspective can help someone build on the great work they are already doing at home. It is our hope that this book will help you master a full set of practical tools and interpersonal strategies to help build your child's foundation as a reader.

Conclusion

As we wrote this book, we thought about what type of interaction you, as a parent, would want to have with this text. There are some basic principles that come up in each of the following chapters that can help guide reading time with your child. In the next section of this book, *Introduction to Shared Reading: Definitions and Practices,* we want to describe to you exactly what shared reading is and how to engage your child in his or her zone of proximal development (a term we promise to define!) while providing scaffolding and praise. These ideas are so important to what we are talking about throughout the book that we want to emphasize them here. They are core practices we will talk about again and again.

As you move on to read the first three chapters of this book, our hope is that the information provided will ensure you feel confident helping your child learn to read, a challenging task in its own right. In those chapters, we will focus on oral language games you can play with your child, letter recognition activities, and the unfolding of writing development. But, if we focused on just the reading skills that your child will need to learn, without talking about the interpersonal relationship between the two of you or the relationship we hope your child develops with books, we might fall short of our goal—to help you support a motivated, enthusiastic, lifelong reader. The last three chapters of the book focus on what happens after children learn to read and use reading to learn by beginning to reflect on the characters and situations in books and developing an emotional connection with texts. We hope that, in particular, the latter three chapters in the book inspire you to work toward these broader aims.

We want your child to become an accomplished reader, because reading sets the stage for academic and occupational success. But as we have said, we think there is a deeper and more important element of reading that you as a parent can foster. Let's not forget that reading also provides models for coping with difficult situations, opportunities for understanding the lives of people who are very different from us, and an escape valve when times get tough. This book will also focus on the ways that reading together can foster social-emotional skills like persistence and confidence in your child, and the ways that stories themselves can help your child acquire a new understanding of the world.

Notes

1. Paterson, K. (1990). *The Spying Heart*. New York: Puffin, p. 163.

2. Rideout, V. J., Foehr, U. G., & Roberts, D. F. (2010). *Generation M²: Media in the Lives of 8- to 18-Year-Olds. A Kaiser Family Foundation Study*. Retrieved from http://kff.org/other/poll-finding/report-generation-m2-media-in-the-lives/.

3. Council on Communications and Media. (2011). Media use by children younger than 2 years. *Pediatrics, 128*(5), 1040–1045.

4. August, D., & Shanahan, T. (Eds.). (2008). *Developing Reading and Writing in Second Language Learners: Report of the National Literacy Panel on Language-Minority Children and Youth*. Mahwah, NJ: Lawrence Erlbaum.

5. Lindsey, K. A., Manis, F. R., & Bailey, C. E. (2003). Prediction of first-grade reading in spanish-speaking english-language learners. *Journal of Educational Psychology*, *95*(3), 482–494; Roberts, T. A. (2008). Home storybook reading in primary or second language with preschool children: Evidence of equal effectiveness for second-language vocabulary acquisition. *Reading Research Quarterly*, *43*(2), 103–130; Stewart, M. R. (2004). Phonological awareness and bilingual preschoolers: Should we teach it and, if so, how? *Early Childhood Education Journal*, *32*(1), 31–37.

6. Winsler, A., Díaz, R. M., Espinosa, L., & Rodríguez, J. L. (1999). When learning a second language does not mean losing the first: Bilingual language development in low-income, Spanish-speaking children attending bilingual preschool. *Child Development*, *70*(2), 349–362.

7. Espinosa, L. M. (2008). *Challenging Common Myths about Young English Language Learners*. New York: Foundation for Children Development.

8. Chiappe, P., & Siegel, L.S. (1999). Phonological awareness and reading acquisition in English-and Punjabi-speaking Canadian children. *Journal of Educational Psychology*, *91*, 20–28; Kuhl, P. K. (2004). Early language acquisition: Cracking the speech code. *Nature Reviews Neuroscience*, *5*(11), (2004), 831–843; Lesaux, N. K., & Siegel, L. S. (2003). The development of reading in children who speak English as a second language. *Developmental Psychology*, *39*(6), 1005–1019.

9. Espinosa (2008).

10. Kovelman, I., Bakers, S., & Petitto, L.A. (2006, October) "Bilingual and Monolingual Brains Compared: An fMRI Study of a 'Neurological Signature' of Bilingualism." Paper presented at the annual meeting of the Society for Neuroscience, Atlanta, GA.

11. August & Shanahan (2008); Jimenez, R. T., Garcia, G. E., & Pearson, P. D. (2011). The reading strategies of bilingual latina/o readers: Opportunities and obstacles. *Reading Research Quarterly*, *31*(1), 90–112.

12. Cummins, J. (2011). The intersection of cognitive and sociocultural factors in the development of reading comprehension among immigrant students. *Reading and Writing*, *25*(8), 1973–1990.

13. Adams, M. J. (1990). *Beginning to Read: Thinking and Learning About Print*. Cambridge, MA: MIT Press, p. 3.

14. Duyck, W. (2005). Translation and associative priming with cross-lingual pseudohomophones: Evidence for nonselective phonological activation in bilinguals. *Journal of Experimental Psychology: Learning, Memory, and Cognition*, *31*, 1340–1359; Lagrou, E., Hartsuiker, R. J., & Duyck, W. (2011). Knowledge of a second language influences auditory word recognition in the native language. *Journal of Experimental Psychology: Learning, Memory, and Cognition*, *37*(4), 952–965; Van Assche, E., Duyck, W., Hartsuiker, R. J., & Diependaele, K. (2009). Does

bilingualism change native-language reading? Cognate effects in a sentence context. *Psychological Science, 20,* 923–927.

15. Wolfersberger, M. (2003). L1 to L2 writing process and strategy transfer: A look at lower proficiency writers. *TESL-EJ: Teaching English as a Second or Foreign Language, 7*(2), 1–15.

16. Aidman, M. (2002). Early bilingual writing: Some influences of the mother tongue on written genre learning in the majority language. *Australian Review of Applied Linguistics, 25*(1), 1–18.

17. Li, T., McBride-Chang, C., Wong, A., & Shu, H. (2012). Longitudinal predictors of spelling and reading comprehension in Chinese as an L1 and English as an L2 in Hong Kong Chinese children. *Journal of Educational Psychology, 104*(2), 286–301; Titone, D., Libben, M., Mercier, J., Whitford, V., & Pivneva, I. (2011). Bilingual lexical access during L1 sentence reading: The effects of L2 knowledge, semantic constraint, and L1–L2 intermixing. *Journal of Experimental Psychology: Learning, Memory, and Cognition, 37*(6), 1412–1431.

18. Wang, L., & Wen, Q. (2004). Influences of L1 literacy on L2 writing: A study of Chinese tertiary EFL learners. *Foreign Language Teaching and Research, 36*(3), 205–212.

19. Beare, S., & Bourdages, J. S. (2007). Skilled writers' generating strategies in L1 and L2: An exploratory study. In G. Rijlaarsdam (Series Ed.) & M. Torrance, L. Van Waes, & D. Galbraith (Vol. Eds.), *Studies in Writing, Vol. 20, Writing and Cognition: Research and Applications* (pp. 151–161). Amsterdam: Elsevier; Jones, S., & Tetroe, J. (1987). Composing in a second language. In A. Matsuhashi (Ed.), *Writing in Real Time: Modeling Production Processes* (pp. 34–57). Norwood, NJ: Ablex; Manchón, R. M., Roca de Larios, J., & Murphy, L. (2000). An approximation to the study of backtracking in L2 writing. *Learning and Instruction, 10,* 13–35.

20. Burt, J. S., & Tate, H. (2002). Does a reading lexicon provide orthographic representations for spelling? *Journal of Memory and Language, 46,* 518–543.

21. August, B. (2011). Spelling facilitates good ESL reading comprehension. *Journal of Developmental Education, 35*(1), 14–24.

Introduction to Shared Reading

When people talk about reading *to* their children, reading *with* their children, or engaging in "shared reading" (a term that researchers often use), they can mean many different things. Defining what we mean when we talk about reading together is necessary to do early in this book, because we want you to understand how to foster shared reading experiences that will be most beneficial to your child. Although it is always important to read with your child frequently and to make the experience fun, the specific strategies you will use change as your child gets older. Each chapter of this book will detail strategies that can be used with different age groups and reading levels.

Figuring out the best way to engage in shared reading with your child gives you an opportunity to use cuddle time together as a way to also help your child understand a book more deeply, and to simultaneously teach specific reading skills. Perhaps as important, children who have an enthusiastic reader as a role model may stay determined to learn to read, even when facing challenges, rather than becoming easily discouraged.[1] The magic of shared reading comes from this combination of warm, interpersonal experiences, playful and captivating storytelling, and opportunities for learning. This winning combination helps children not only learn to read, but learn to love and value reading.

Throughout this book, we will use the terms *shared reading, reading aloud together, joint book reading,* or *reading with your child* to discuss any reading strategy that includes an adult or good reader and a child reading together. Shared reading may help children learn how to open a book and turn the pages, identify where the title or author's name is usually written, learn new vocabulary words, discuss rhyming words or pictures, make predictions about what will happen next in the story, or make connections between the book and their own lives. Shared reading is beneficial regardless of which of these skills a child is learning, but the benefits of shared reading change as the focus of reading time together changes. Picking the right focus for your child's age and skill level can maximize learning and fun and minimize frustration during shared reading time.

Keep this idea—that the way we read together is dependent on many factors—in your mind. It may help you picture shared reading time a bit differently, or more flexibly, than you have in the past. Many people think that the best way to read with a child is to make sure that he sits quietly and listens carefully while the adult reads the text word-for-word, stopping only to ask basic questions (like, "Do you see the puppy in the picture?"). But actually, when children play a more active role in shared reading, they build their vocabularies and begin to identify letters and words more quickly.[2] Although it may seem counterintuitive to take less control of what shared reading looks like, allowing children to have more of a voice leads to the development of many language and literacy skills.

The most widely known and researched strategy for engaging children in interactive reading experiences is called *dialogic reading,* and we talk about this strategy in much more depth in chapter one. In dialogic reading sessions, the adult reader encourages the child to participate actively in the reading experience by asking specific types of questions and making instructive comments.[3] This type of shared reading helps children build stronger language skills than shared reading where the adult reader does all the work.[4] Other shared reading strategies help children become familiar with the relationship between letters and sounds and the usual structure of written stories.[5] In later chapters of the book, we will talk about these other strategies as well.

These experiences can provide children with opportunities to feel like competent readers even before they are able to decode text. Through shared reading experiences, young children learn how to hold a book, turn its pages, and experiment with "reading" the story from memory or by adding their own embellishments to a familiar story.

Parent-Directed Shared Reading	Child-Directed Shared Reading	Joint Reading
• Parent reads story to child without interruption.	• Child tells story to parent, relying on his own imagination—as well as picture clues and memory of the story, to tell the story as he wants to . . . perhaps with few similarities to what is written.	• Parent and child take turns "reading" pages of the story, using whatever imaginative or literacy skills are appropriate.
• Parent reads story to child, pausing to ask questions about the pictures on the page. ("Oh, what do you think is happening here? What is the gorilla going to do?")	• Child tells story to parent, relying on text clues, along with picture clues and memory of the story, in order to approximate the story as it is written.	• Parent takes the lead in reading the story, often pausing to ask the child to supply a word or idea, or flexibly allowing the child to take over telling the story whenever he wishes to do so.
• Parent reads story to child, pausing to ask *Wh-* questions about the text on the page. ("What letter does this word start with? Who was sleeping?")	• Child reads story to parent with some degree of fluency, largely telling the story as it is written, but occasionally substituting some words for others.	• Child takes the lead in reading the story, and parent scaffolds as appropriate (by helping to sound out words, reading a difficult word for the child, and pointing out information the child overlooked).
• Parent reads story to child, pausing to ask open-ended questions about what the child thinks will happen on the next page or in the future. ("So the gorilla let other animals out of their cages. What do you think all of the animals are going to do now?")	• Child fluently reads story to parent.	
• Parent reads story to child, pausing to ask open-ended questions about how the story relates to the child's own life and experiences. ("Does anything about this story remind you of when we went to the zoo?")		

If you take one thing from this book, we hope it is the idea that children begin to identify themselves as readers and take pride in reading, even at a very young age. Shared reading experiences are not only valuable for their potential to influence learning, but also because they can be a vehicle for developing and sustaining interpersonal relationships, creating opportunities for talk about a variety of topics together, and helping children see reading as an enjoyable and social process.

As we have said, there are many different shared reading strategies, and each builds different language and literacy skills. In this book, we won't tell you that there is one right way to read together. Instead, we will focus on finding just the right strategies for you and your child to use at different points in time—based on the skills your child has already developed, the skills you want her to develop next, and her interest in the story you are about to read. We've listed a number of the different activities that can be described as shared reading on page 3. As you will see, there are many ways to read together!

It can certainly be challenging to begin reading with your child in these ways. Letting your child become an active participant in the reading process requires you to do more listening and reflecting than merely reading the book would require. For that reason, we want to give you a few tips that can be applied when engaging in a wide variety of language and literacy activities with your child. While you are reading together, you are simultaneously thinking about what your child knows and how you can help your child acquire new knowledge. Rather than providing your child with the right answers, or instructing him very directly, we will encourage you to scaffold him through reading experiences and to praise his efforts. These tips are not specific to any one chapter in this book or limited to reading time, but rather general principles to keep in mind as you read and practices that can be useful when engaging in many different types of activities with your child.

> **Tips to Remember**
> - Scaffold your child's reading
> - Work within the zone of proximal development
> - Praise your child

Scaffolding Your Child's Reading

The scaffolding on a building allows the workers to reach heights that they could not reach on their own and complete work on the building in a safe and efficient way. Similarly, instructional scaffolding is a way of providing support to children so that they can complete tasks with which they need assistance. You already provide support all of the time, in many different domains of your child's life. When scaffolding, though, parents, teachers, or other people who understand the task well provide a specific type of support. This support helps the child solve the problem in a way that allows her to feel competent and to learn from the situation, but also lets the adult to guide the child through the problem-solving process. Scaffolding also allows the child to successfully experience tasks she would not have been able to tackle alone, or that would otherwise make her become frustrated and give up.

Scaffolds are used to:

- Motivate the child's interest in the task.
- Simplify the task to make it more manageable and achievable for a child by breaking it into smaller parts.
- Provide an appropriate amount of direction to help the child focus on achieving his or her goal. One approach is to *notice* what your child seems to be interested in ("You really like that picture"), *nudge* her to explore further and build knowledge about the topic ("What do you think she is going to do with that big red ball?"), and then *narrate* to expand upon and praise her response. ("Great job remembering that red is her favorite color. I think we also know something about her favorite place to play. I wonder if that's where she'll go next.")
- Reflect on differences between the child's current ability level and the desired goal in order to move the child closer to that goal.
- Reduce frustration and the risk associated with giving a wrong answer.
- Model and clearly define the expectations of the activity to be performed
- Highlight the child's successes, even if the end goal was not achieved, so that the next time a similar activity is attempted, you can remind the child of those successes.

Throughout the book, we will provide you with many different suggestions for ways to scaffold your child's reading as you focus on aspects of the reading process.

Working Within the Zone of Proximal Development

Through scaffolding, children learn to approach tasks more independently, and scaffolding is one particular technique associated with the broader idea that each child has what is called a *zone of proximal development*. This term refers to the area of growth and change that exists between Point A, what a child can do independently, and Point B, what a child can do with the assistance of a more capable peer or adult. This zone refers to the growth that can occur from one day to the next; the reason the word *proximal*, meaning *close to*, is used here is to reflect the idea that the changes we are expecting to see are small. Providing experiences within this zone allows children to enhance their learning capacities. If you think about almost any activity you expect your child to complete, you can probably think back to a time when you completed that activity for her. Gradually, over time, she took more responsibility and was able to do more of the task independently. This is not only true for activities like getting dressed and tying shoes, but also for language and literacy tasks, as well as tasks that require memory and concentration.

For example, think about a time when you crossed the street with your young toddler. You probably held her hand and said aloud, "Now, we need to look both ways before we cross the street." A year or two later, when crossing the street, you probably still held on to your daughter's hand, but may have prompted her to cross safely in a slightly more independent way by saying, "Now, what do we need to do before we cross the street?" The type of scaffolding you provided changed along with your goal for her. Initially, looking both ways after a prompt was a task within her zone of proximal development and later, looking both ways with a smaller prompt was a goal within her grasp. By the time she was in the middle of elementary school, although you stayed close, perhaps you no longer felt like you needed to hold her hand. You could likely count on your daughter to say, "We need to look both ways!" when she came to a crosswalk, even before you gave the prompt. Older children and adults remind themselves to look both ways, too, but they usually do it silently. They have internalized the cues and information that others used to provide to them. Your fourth grader has likely mastered the art of crossing the street, but there are other tasks that now fall within her zone of proximal development, and are achievable when she gets support from you.

Reading with your child is not all that different than crossing the street with your child. Each time you want to teach a new skill—identifying a letter, predicting what will happen next, sounding out a word—you will give most of the directions, at first. But by interacting with you, your child will start to display that skill more independently. Throughout this book, we offer many different activities and strategies that can help you foster your child's reading development, but we want to emphasize now that we do not expect every one of these activities to be appropriate for you or your child. Nor do we expect you to attempt seven of them at a time. When working within your child's zone of proximal development, you will pick those activities that seem to be the best fit for her current ability and interest level, and only those activities that you think will be manageable to work on, because they are activities she is almost able to do independently. You—better than anybody—know what your child is capable of doing. By thinking carefully about how to scaffold your child, and focusing on just one skill at a time, you will help her become a more self-sufficient and confident reader.

Praising Your Child

Another way you can help your child become a more self-sufficient reader is by keeping him motivated. Praise and encouragement from parents is a powerful motivational tool. Because shared reading is such a social activity, much of your child's initial pleasure in reading together may come not primarily from the stories that he hears, but from the joy of sitting in your lap and spending time together. When you spend this time together, it is likely that without even thinking about it, you will give him verbal praise—perhaps focusing on how quietly he is sitting, how quickly he realized what would happen next in the story, or how well he identified a picture or read a word. These comments are a big part of what makes shared reading time special.

However, it is important to make sure that the type of praise you give encourages your child to be persistent, rather than increases his fear of failure. It might sound implausible that praising a child could have negative effects, but some types of praise are more helpful than others. The most helpful type of praise is very specific and highlights the effort your child put into a particular task. For example, specific praise might sound like, "Great job taking your time while you sounded out that word. I really like the way you moved your hand along the page, said each sound slowly, and then blended them together. Wow!" This type of praise identifies for your child exactly what behavior you are proud of and encourages him to exhibit the same type of effort in the future. It teaches him that hard work pays off.

In contrast, global praise like, "You're a great reader!" conveys to him that that he possesses an unchangeable trait that has made him successful. Kids who are told that they are smart or great athletes and that they possess these stable traits feel wonderful—until the day comes that they have some trouble in school or miss a goal in a big soccer game. All of a sudden, they begin to think about that global praise, suspecting it is no longer true. Your son may think, "Well, I was a great reader before, when I sounded everything out perfectly. But today I stumbled over so many words; I'm not a great reader anymore." Thinking that way can be defeating, because your child has no idea how to gain that trait back and may believe that success is not within his control. As far as he knows, people are either good readers or poor readers, and there is not much they can do about that. But a child who has received specific praise will remember, even when facing a tough task, the strategies that help him move toward success. So as you read through this book, you will see that we frequently remind you of how motivating praise can be, and how important it is to make sure that your praise is specific.

We hope that this brief introduction to the book makes it clear that the role you play in your child's reading development should not be underestimated. The time that you spend reading together, in varied ways, will help build all of the skills we talk about in the chapters that follow. And using these tips—scaffolding, working within the zone of proximal development, and praising—should make reading time exciting and productive. Have fun and happy reading!

Notes

1. Snow, C. E., Burns, M. S., & Griffin, P. (1998). *Preventing reading difficulties in young children*. Committee on the Prevention of Reading Difficulties in Young Children. Washington, DC: National Academy Press, p. 143.

2. Justice, L. M., & Ezell, H. K. (2002). Use of storybook reading to increase print awareness in at-risk children. *American Journal of Speech-Language Pathology*, *11*, 17–29; Whitehurst, G. J., Falco, F. L., Lonigan, C. J., Fischel, J. E., DeBaryshe, B. D., Valdez-Menchaca, M. C., et al. (1988). Accelerating language development through picture book reading. *Developmental Psychology*, *24*, 552–559.

3. Whitehurst, G. J., Falco, F. L., Lonigan, C. J., Fischel, J. E., DeBaryshe, B. D., Valdez-Menchaca, M. C., et al. (1988). Accelerating language development through picture book reading. *Developmental Psychology*, *24*, 552–559

4. National Center for Family Literacy (NCFL). (2009). *What works: An introductory teacher guide for language and emergent literacy instruction. Based on the National Early Literacy Panel Report.*

5. Bus, A. G., & van IJzendoorn, M. H. (1995). Mothers reading to their three-year-olds: The role of mother-child attachment security in becoming literate. *Reading Research Quarterly*, *30*, 998–1015.

Chapter 1

The Role of Oral Language in Reading Development

How Language Skills Lead to Literacy Skills

You may think the most important activity you are engaging in when reading together with your child is reading, but the comments you make spontaneously during shared reading time are just as important as the words you read from the page. Although most parents know that talking and reading are skills that are broadly connected to one another, many parents are not familiar with the specific ways that early oral language development affects later reading development. In fact, even many people who work in the fields of education and psychology do not fully recognize the critical importance of early oral language skills. We designed this chapter to enhance your knowledge of the crucial role that oral language skills play in supporting specific reading skills and to help you develop strategies to build your child's use and understanding of spoken language. We hope that the stories shared throughout the chapter help you reflect on your child's own amazing language discoveries and that the suggested activities listed are flexible enough to let you have fun strengthening your child's skills.

Talking and Reading: Some Similarities

Adults tend to see speaking as a very natural process, and something that young children begin to do on their own, without any direct instruction. In contrast, adults see reading as a difficult task that children cannot embark upon before they are ready. Parents often think of reading as a skill that children begin to acquire in elementary school, while sitting at desks and working hard to make sense of new information. This distinction between the way that we learn to talk and the way that we learn to read is an important one, and people aren't necessarily wrong to think about these processes differently.

However, one of the main ideas we want to convey in this book is that the process of reading acquisition is an all-encompassing part of a child's development. In the same way that a baby progresses through physical milestones—rolling over before crawling, crawling before walking—young children need to develop certain prerequisite language skills in order to become proficient readers. It would be incredibly difficult to try to make sense of written language if the words on the page did not convey meaning to you already.

Just as children begin to develop reading skills long before they decode their first written word independently, they also begin to develop their language skills long before they utter their first spoken word. Linguistic development is often described as a transactional process, meaning that children's innate skills and their home and school environments affect one another during the process of language acquisition. What children learn, and how quickly they learn, is not entirely dependent on them or on their caregivers. However, there is a great deal that you can do to make sure that a child's environment provides all of the support he or she needs. And the good news is that simple and enjoyable things like playing with your child, singing silly songs, and reading books are the foundation of language and reading development. These activities, which prepare children for school success, also give you opportunities to bond with your child and to support his social development. Reading aloud to and with your child is one of the most effective ways to build his language skills and has many other benefits as well. However, even the conversations you have with your child—no books involved—help foster later reading success.

The Importance of Everyday Conversations

Because talking with your child is such a spontaneous and natural part of your daily routine, you probably don't spend much time thinking about how the conversations you have in the bathtub or in the car help support reading development. You talk to your toddler all the time—to convey information, to let him know how much you love him, to prepare him for what is about to happen—but these conversations are spontaneous, not premeditated. No parent has the time to write out a script before going out to do some errands! But more importantly, trying to plan a lesson for your child would take a lot of the joy out of the conversations that you have with each other. In this chapter, we want to share with you the reasons that these natural conversations are so vitally important for reading development, and also give you some ideas about how to pepper your conversations with new activities to support the development of linguistic components like semantics, syntax, and pragmatics (terms we will define in more depth just a few pages from now). However, we don't want you to feel like you need to start watching your words. The most interesting conversations you will have with your children, and the ones that they will likely learn the most from, are ones that you never expected. The impromptu and seemingly inconsequential discussions that come up naturally each day often help children understand new ideas about which they are actually curious, and will be more interesting to your son or daughter than any scripted conversation we could suggest.

When Jamie was in graduate school, she stumbled across an old audiotape that her family had saved, filled with conversations she had with her mother as a two- and three- year-old. During one of these conversations, Jamie and her mother discussed the fact that Jamie's cousin, who was around her age, had broken the mobile that hung above his crib.

"How did Danny feel when his mobile broke?" Jamie asks her mother. (They should have known then that she would become a psychologist!)

"Well, I think that Danny was sad," replies her mother.

"Was Danny happy?" Jamie then asks tentatively. Clearly, she knows that people have *feelings* and understands that happiness is an emotion that a person can experience. But apparently, happiness is the only emotion she can really call to mind right then, or the only one that she can identify by name. Jamie's new question let her mother know that she needed more information about the different feelings people can have, and that any other emotion she talked about needed to be compared with happiness.

"No, he wasn't happy. He was sad. He cried, but then his mother got him another mobile." They continue talking, and it is clear that this answer satisfies Jamie. You can almost hear the *Ah-hah!* All of a sudden, because happiness is contrasted with sadness for her, she understands that they are opposites. But Jamie's mother seemed to know that she was still lacking a real definition for sadness, so she added a description of someone behaving as if they were sad that would make sense to her: sad people cry. Then, to further help Jamie understand how sadness fit into the world she knew, her mother explained that after sad people cry, their mothers resolve the problem. For a three-year-old's understanding of the world, that definition was what Jamie needed to know about sadness in order to navigate future social situations, preschool, and story books.

You may not have time to analyze every conversation you have with your child in such depth, but if you did, we think you would see that many of them lead to these types of *Ah-hah* moments. By talking with your children and reading books aloud with them, you help them understand word meaning, sentence structure, and social language. In turn, this greater understanding of language helps prepare them to make sense of complicated stories by using their prior knowledge to puzzle out tough new words and confusing new phrases. In the next section, we will tell you more about why oral language skills are so important for later reading development.

The Domino Effect

It is often not until third or fourth grade, when children begin to read complicated stories on their own, that the effect these oral language skills have on reading development becomes obvious. Many of these oral language skills are only indirectly related to early reading skills but they eventually exert a stronger influence on children's ability to comprehend text in later elementary school.[1] In other words, a child's ability to use and understand language as a toddler has a domino effect on her reading skills throughout elementary school—the first domino helps knock down the later ones, but only indirectly.

Let's take a moment to think about the first domino in this line and how it starts a process that continues for many years. A child's capacity to understand and use new vocabulary words directly affects phonemic awareness (the ability to perceive and manipulate the speech sounds in words, a skill we'll talk about much more in the next chapter). Phonemic awareness significantly affects children's alphabetic knowledge (the ability to pair letters with the sounds they represent) and ability to sound out new words. This ability to sound out new words marks a turning point in the development of reading skills; we tend to think of children as "becoming readers" when they can sound out words independently, often early in first grade. So, looking at first-grade readers, we might think that strengthening young children's phonemic awareness is the most important thing we can do to make them become better readers later in life.

But if we look at children in late elementary school or middle school, we realize how important the vocabulary words they learned as toddlers are in their own right. By then—when the goal of reading is not just to sound out individual words, but instead to make sense of the information presented across pages and chapters—oral language skills like vocabulary size become a direct predictor of these later reading skills.[2] Because oral language skills have this sort of "sleeper effect" on reading development, their importance is often underestimated. But no matter how accurately a middle school student can sound out new and difficult words like *omniscient* or *prejudice*, his ability to understand these words in context will depend on how often he has talked about these words and the concepts related to them. Each new word that a child acquires verbally becomes a word that he will eventually be able to recognize and make sense of when he sees it in print, so early vocabulary development is an essential skill for later reading success. For this reason, we've started this book by talking about oral language development.

> **SPEECH**
> The ability to express oneself orally, using language.
>
> **ORAL LANGUAGE**
> The many different components of spoken words that help us understand others (our *receptive* skills) and share our own thoughts (*expressive* skills).

Important Elements of Oral Language Development

Before we describe the process of oral language development and provide strategies for fostering it, it is important to make sure that we define the many oral language skills that children possess. First, we must establish what we mean by *oral language*. People often talk about speech and language interchangeably, but they refer to different skills. Speech is the output of language, the ability to express oneself orally. It refers to your child's ability to produce spoken words—how she articulates each word that she says, whether she speaks fluently or haltingly, and how she sounds when she speaks (loud or soft, nasal or raspy).

Oral language, in contrast, refers to all the different components of those spoken words and phrases that help us understand others and express ourselves. As Figure 1-1 shows, language functions at different levels, including the **translexical** level (which allows us to understand the meaning of sentences), the **lexical** level (which allows us to understand the meaning of individual words), and the **sublexical** level (which allows us to understand the meaning of parts of words). Language includes your child's choice of words and the meaning of the words he says. As children build their ability to understand what people are saying to them (**receptive language skills**) and their ability to share their own thoughts and feelings (**expressive language skills**), they build strong foundations for later reading success.

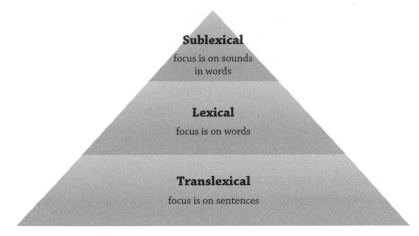

Figure 1-1 Levels of language.

When children are using their receptive and expressive language skills, they draw from many different components of language. In this chapter, we're going to describe three important aspects of language development and then explain how each one paves the path for later reading success.

These skills include translexical and lexical aspects of language like **semantics,** word meaning, including vocabulary development, such as using synonyms and antonyms; **syntax,** the rules that govern sentence structure; and **pragmatics,** the social aspect of language. In the sections below, we will give you information about what to expect your child to know about word meaning, sentence structure, and social language, as well as tips for helping those skills develop. In later chapters, we will also talk about two other important aspects of language development, **phonology,**

FIVE MAIN COMPONENTS
OF LANGUAGE
- **Semantics:** word meaning
- **Syntax:** sentence structure
- **Pragmatics:** social language
- **Phonology:** sounds that make up words
- **Morphology:** an aspect of language that dictates word formation; morphemes like *–s, –ed,* and *–un* are the smallest meaningful units of language.

the sounds that make up words and the sublexical level of language, and **morphology,** the smallest meaningful units of language.

Semantic Development

What Is Semantic Language?

You likely have most often heard the word **semantic** being said in exasperation, like when somebody says, "Oh, stop arguing about semantics!" The semantic aspect of language refers to the meaning of words and the links that children form between words. For example, your daughter may have learned that the objects she sees up in the sky can be called "sun" and "moon." She may know that there are similarities between these two objects, like the fact that they are the two big things in the sky that make light for us. But she may link different words to each of these objects, describing the sun as "hot" and struggling to find a descriptor for the moon other than saying that it comes out as night, when it is dark. At this stage in semantic development, she can compare and contrast these two objects, and the words she associates with them. With so many words to recognize, and so many different links that can be made between them, you can probably see this topic is much broader and more complicated than one might think. But before we delve deeper into how children learn new words, let's explore the idea of words and their meanings in order to better understand how children begin to make these links.

An early step in the process of semantic development requires the ability to understand that every word has a definition. And in order to understand that a word means anything at all, or that a word can be paired with a longer definition, children must be able to understand that words are representational or symbolic. The word *cat*,

> **SEMANTIC DEVELOPMENT**
> The ability to understand the meaning of words and make connections between words, including finding a word's synonyms and antonyms.

for example, means "a small domesticated mammal that has soft fur, sharp claws, pointed ears, and usually, a long furry tail."[3] A young child may know that the family pet is called a "cat" through context clues (like the fact that his father asks him if he sees the cat on the couch, or calls out, "Hey, kitty cat"), but not yet realize that all such animals are also called cats. Once your child has reached that stage of semantic development, she will be able to conjure up an image of the neighbor's cat when she hears that word; she won't need to wait to see a real cat to remember what the word means or to make the connection between the cat and the symbol used to refer to it (the written or spoken word *cat*). With more exposure, she will go on to acquire a deeper understanding of each word she learns and will eventually be able to connect that word with many others.

Over time, children begin to make connections between these symbols and to build semantic webs, meaning that they begin to construct links between words that refer to similar objects or concepts, or that refer to particular features of the same object or concept. For example, by contrasting words with one another, the way that Jamie's mother did with sadness and happiness, children can also begin to build semantic webs and to recognize that the two words in question belong to the same word class.[4] Figure 1-2 shows what Jamie's semantic web might have looked like, after that conversation.

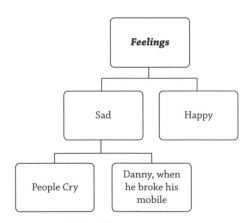

Figure 1-2 Jamie's semantic web for *feelings*.

Why Are Semantic Skills Important for Reading Development?

This increasingly sophisticated understanding of words and their meanings is crucial for reading development. Think about how often your child asks you what a new object is named, what purpose it serves, and where it comes from. These questions are natural for children to ask as they begin to learn about the world around them. But as we all know, these questions can also be quite distracting! It can be hard to finish a conversation, or a picture book, when your child is asking questions about everything that is new. Right now, though, it is more important to answer your toddler's questions and satisfy her curiosity than it is to get through all of the pages in a book. And answering these questions should pay off later, because then your child will be able to read through more complicated passages without having to stop and ask questions. The stronger the language foundation that you build now, the easier and quicker it will be for your child to make sense of all the new topics being discussed in school and in textbooks when she is older.[5]

By strategically helping your child build his semantic vocabulary over time, you can help him acquire vocabulary knowledge and other new reading skills as he proceeds through elementary school and beyond. Ordinary conversations, particularly those focused on children's books, are one of the best ways to introduce your child to unfamiliar and less frequently used words. As children learn these new words, they build more semantic webs and begin to understand the connections between an increasingly wider set of words, connections that they would not be able to make without exposure to these less familiar words. For example, as a toddler, Jamie began to build a semantic web for *feelings*—like the one we drew earlier—on the day that she had the conversation about mobiles with her mother. Once she understood that *feelings* included a whole category of words and could place *happy* and *sad* on opposite sides of that category, it became easier for her to place similar and often more complex words she learned later in their appropriate place in the semantic web. As children build their vocabularies and place more and more words into their appropriate categories, it becomes easier to make sense of broader concepts.[6] We will discuss this idea in greater depth when we move on to talk about writing development and reading comprehension.

Oral language skills are also important for reading development as children move through elementary school because fluent reading is dependent upon recognizing many words and being able to understand their meaning very quickly. In fact, researchers have found that a child's vocabulary size at two years old is a significant predictor of a child's reading skills through fifth grade.[7] Why would that be? Well, think about how frustrating a process it can be to read over legal or medical documents, or anything that includes a lot of jargon that is unfamiliar to you. You probably read through those types of documents very slowly, maybe even with the help of a dictionary, in order to make sure you can comprehend what you are reading. What if you had to do the same thing in order to read the sentence "The cat sat on the bed"? You would need to say to yourself, "So, okay, the furry mammal was resting his haunches on furniture for sleeping." A young child's vocabulary size is a good proxy for later vocabulary size, and as this example illustrates, being able to automatically comprehend the meaning of individual words makes it easier to understand a whole sentence or passage.

Here's another example.[8] Take a look at this brief quote from a newspaper below, and try and explain the passage in your own words.

> The Batsmen were merciless against the Bowlers. The Bowlers placed their men in slips and covers. But to no avail. The Batsmen hit one four after another along with an occasional six. Not once did their balls hit their stumps or get caught.

Although you might be able to make an educated guess about what is going on here (two teams are playing against one another), you would likely be at a loss if someone asked you to explain the nuances of the story—unless you were a follower of British cricket, in which case this story would be very easy to follow. As you read through this passage, you probably reread sentences more than you would normally. You also probably read a bit more slowly than you typically would and asked yourself questions as you read through the passage (unless, feeling frustrated by something that didn't make much sense, you stopped reading entirely). You may have tried to relate the game you were reading about with baseball, since they seem to have some similarities. This laborious process of reading comprehension is the one that children engage in all the time when they are faced with new words and new topics. The more background information someone has about a topic, the more easily she can make sense of written information. If you had the good fortune to chat with someone about cricket yesterday, you probably did not find that paragraph terribly difficult to read. But think about how many conversations we need to have with children to make sure that new topics in their science or social studies books are not too challenging for them!

If you know the meaning of all the words in a sentence, have developed the decoding skills needed to read text, and can use your background knowledge and context clues to interpret those words correctly, you are immediately able to make sense of what you have just read. If there is just one word that is unfamiliar to you, it is likely that you'll still be able to get the gist of the sentence and continue building your knowledge about that story or conversation. But if too many of the words are unfamiliar to you or presented out of context (like in the example about cricket), it will become very difficult to understand what is going on. You may also start to feel incompetent and become convinced that no matter how hard you try, you'll never understand. In contrast, if you have an understanding of a word or concept, it will be easier for you to make sense of its synonyms and antonyms. You'll be able to puzzle your way through a difficult passage without doubting yourself too frequently. The larger a child's receptive and expressive vocabulary, the more likely it is that when he sees a word in print for the first time, he'll be able to recognize it and understand its meaning. We will also talk more about building background knowledge later in the book, but the first strategy you should use for supporting later reading comprehension is building your child's vocabulary.

The rich language that you use at home with your child will also make it easier for her to enter into a school environment, where new words—spoken or in written—are presented all the time. One of the most important and challenging tasks that young children encounter when they begin their formal schooling is listening to directions, and children who can make sense of the requests or directives they receive are likely to fare better than students who need more time to decipher a sentence and determine the meaning of an unfamiliar word.

How Children Learn New Words: Beyond Asking for Definitions

Young children possess a number of tools they can use to decipher words that are new to them, even though asking parents for more information may be their favorite strategy. Children also use logic and recall to define unfamiliar words. Linguists use several different principles to explain how children learn new words and why understanding the meaning of an unfamiliar word can be so difficult.[9] First, since children are aware that all objects only have one name, they will not associate unfamiliar words with familiar objects. That is, they understand that each name of a word is exclusively used to describe just one person or object. This principle helps guide them in guessing what a new word might mean. For example, David is a three-year-old boy who loves goats. When he and his mother go to a petting zoo together, they see a peacock standing next to a goat. When David's mother says, "That peacock is such a beautiful, colorful animal," David is likely to know which animal she was referring to, even if he has never heard of a peacock before, because he is familiar with the word *goat*. Since David knows the name for the goat is already in place, he then assumes the new word he has just learned must be associated with an unnamed object. By process of elimination, or through what scientists call *fast mapping,* children can determine what object or aspect of an object an unfamiliar word refers to, presuming that there are not too many unfamiliar words in any particular sentence. When most children fast-map a word, they create a rudimentary definition of the word after hearing it just once, but they also continue to develop more nuanced definitions of the word with repeated exposure.[10] So, after that visit to the zoo, David would have a very simple semantic web for peacock in his mind. However, it might not be until his next trip to the zoo or even the following year until he learns that peacocks very rarely fly, even though they are birds.

Children are also likely to assume that any new word they hear refers to the object itself or its most prominent feature, rather than small details about the object. For example, David will know that the new word *peacock* refers to the whole animal, rather than just its feathers or feet. Once he is familiar with the word for the object itself—peacock— David will begin to map any additional new words that his parent uses to describe it (like saying that the bird's *plumage* is colorful) onto the bird's most salient features. In this way, prior to and during the vocabulary spurt that children experience during their second year of life, they begin to learn increasingly more sophisticated words.

They also begin to group these objects into categories by creating a more sophisticated type of semantic web called a *taxonomy*. When we organize items into a taxonomy, we categorize them by type and subtype. For example, as shown in Figure 1-3, a child might begin a semantic web by defining the word *vehicle* and then move on to describe the different types of vehicles that can be used on land and on water. By kindergarten, children who are able to easily retrieve semantic information from memory tend to provide information organized in this way, first listing all land vehicles and then all water vehicles.

A child who becomes interested in the topic of vehicles will take this taxonomy even further, naming models of cars or types of planes. As a child becomes more sophisticated cognitively, her ability to group objects in this way increases. So, once a child is taught the word *peacock* and asked to find another one at the petting zoo, she will be more likely to identify other species of birds as peacocks, rather than selecting other types of animals. This demonstrates a developing understanding of what type of animal the peacock is.

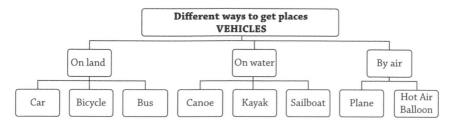

Figure 1-3 A semantic web for *vehicles*.

All of these tools—the ability to fast-map, to identify the object or part of the object being named, to group similar objects together—help children make more educated guesses about the meanings of new words. But how educated their guesses are depends on all of the background knowledge and past conversations that help them make sense of the other words in the sentence. Think of how often you have been surprised by the phrases your child parrots back at you after she hears them come out of your own mouth. Being exposed to the words and phrases that you use in conversation is one way that she builds background knowledge. Although children will begin to use these linguistic principles when building their vocabulary over time, several groups of researchers have found that children go through several months in which they begin to use new words at a relatively slow rate—approximately three to five words per week—and then, once they have an expressive vocabulary of around 150 words, experience a vocabulary spurt that leads to gains of approximately eight to ten words per week.[11] On average, children hit this point by the age of three, which allows them to express themselves in new ways and engage in more interactive shared reading activities. All the while, though, they are also building their receptive vocabulary (the words they understand when others say them), which far exceeds their spoken language.

What Is the Role of Parents in the Development of Semantic Language Skills?

By now, it must seem apparent that conversations are an important way of building children's knowledge and vocabularies. Many researchers have demonstrated that the more often parents use a particular word in their own speech, the sooner their children will begin to use that word as well.[12] They have also found that, in the English language and many other language systems, children's early vocabularies contain more nouns than verbs. They hypothesize that this is because the relationship between nouns—concrete objects like *tables, bowls,* and *shoes* that parents can point at—and the symbols that represent them is easier for children to understand than the relationship between verbs—which, like *running, bowling*, or *talking*, occur only for a moment of time—and the symbols that represent them.[13] In other words, parents talk more about objects than actions with young children, and children find it easier to understand the meaning of these more concrete nouns. When adults describe the world around them to young children, they are more likely to label objects, saying, "Look at your teddy bear!" than to explain what is happening by saying something like, "Your teddy bear is laughing." These findings might sound like common sense, but they have very important implications for children: the amount of language that children hear each day can vary astronomically from home to home. The number of new words that children hear each day, and the types of words that they hear, have a large effect upon their developing vocabulary skills and later reading skills.

The word gap. One famous research study, conducted in the 1980s, illustrates the importance of parents' talk very clearly and also helps illustrate the idea that both children's innate skills and their environment play important roles in language development. Two researchers, Betty Hart and Todd Risley, embarked upon a three year project to examine the types of conversations that went on every day in the homes of parents with young children.[14] These researchers found that the most important factor in determining the effect of parent language on child language was just the sheer *amount* of talking that parents did. Parents who kept up running monologues with their child, or in their child's presence, about the daily activities that they were completing exposed their children to both new words and multiple opportunities to become more familiar with old words, whereas parents who were quieter did not provide their children with such opportunities. Of course, beyond just talking at your child and defining words, it is important to make conversations as relevant and interactive as possible.

Consider one parent who, when feeding his young child, talks constantly. He says, "Mmmmm ... you're going to have some sweet potatoes. Look how orange they are—that's a bright color! Almost as orange as the pumpkin we got at the farm stand last weekend." Another parent, in the same situation, may just say, "It's time for dinner!" Both of these parents are meeting their child's basic needs by getting dinner on the table, but that first parent is enriching his child's vocabulary and knowledge base at the same time. If you were not exposed to this type of chatter in your home growing up, it may feel strange to talk at a child who can't respond with a full sentence. But this type of talk is exactly what will help build your child's vocabulary.

The families Hart and Risley studied differed from one another in terms of socioeconomic status, and the type and amount of language used in these families was associated with that status. It is not that family income, in and of itself, was so important to consider. But measuring family income is often a quick and easy way to assess more complicated variables, such as how much time a parent has to spend with a child, how much stress the parent is under, or how many books are available in the home. Some parents in this study had professional or "white-collar" jobs, and on average, these parents spoke 2,100 words per hour to their children. Other parents had working class or "blue-collar" jobs, and on average, they spoke 1,200 words per hour to their children. In contrast, those parents who were living in poverty spoke only 600 words per hour to their children. What does this finding mean over time? By the age of four, the average child in a working class family would have heard 13 million more words of language than the average child in a poor family. When you think about what that figure means for children's eventual language and literacy development, the implications are staggering.

These findings do not mean that low-income parents are destined to speak less to their children, or that all middle-class parents speak to their children with adequate frequency. Even within each of these groups, the researchers found that parents spoke to their children with varying frequency. Perhaps even more important, they found that parent education or income level was less critical than the amount of language used at home in predicting children's gains over time. This study underscores the need to encourage parents to actively engage their children in conversation, even—and perhaps especially—about mundane issues, like the color of sweet potatoes, which they can chat about casually. We are focusing on the relevance of these seemingly insignificant comments because distracted parents are less likely to provide their children with opportunities for conversation.[15] As technology such as smartphones and iPads becomes a part of everyday life in many households, this notion of stay-ing engaged and talking with children is even more crucial.

Hart and Risley's study also illustrates how important these very early interactions are for children. They found that children spoke more and more frequently until they matched the amount of talking that their parents did. Once they reached this level, their parents started to speak to them less frequently, and children began to make vocabulary gains more slowly. When they were three years old, the amount that children spoke was very similar to the amount that their parents spoke to them when they were first learning to talk.[16]

We find this pretty amazing: no matter how much any particular par-ent said, their child matched it . . . for better or for worse. These findings highlight the importance of talking to your infant or toddler, not just for its immediate language and social benefits, but also because of how it can affect academic development over time.

Developing Semantic Skills: How Can I Support My Child's Individual Needs?

The processes of fast mapping (forming a simple definition of a word after hearing it just once) and vocabulary acquisition can differ from child to child.[17] Some children have more difficulty remembering new words immediately after they've been presented and then retaining this information over time. You may need to repeat the same informa-tion multiple times to familiarize your child with the name for that bird with the long tail at the zoo, or remind him of that word (or scaffold his memory by sharing just the first sound in its name) when you return to the zoo. If your child seems to have significant trouble maintaining joint attention—for example, looking where you are pointing when you point to the peacock or sharing your focus on another object or activity—or remembering many of the words he has learned, it may be beneficial to discuss your concerns with a pediatrician or a speech and language pathologist. But it is natural for children to sometimes not listen to you when you provide a definition or to forget newly acquired words, so be sure to concentrate on getting your child's attention, using the word multiple times if necessary, and connecting the new word to other familiar words.

What Activities and Strategies Can I Use to Support Semantic Development?

You are already introducing your child to new words naturally, through your regular conversations at home. But if you are reading this book, you want to know more about the strategies that you can use to boost your child's vocabulary and reading level. In your everyday conversations with your child, you probably use many of the conventional words that we tend to use in our informal, spoken language. Doing so is very important, because these are the words that teachers assume children will already be familiar with when they enter school.

When discussing the words that you should focus on at home, there are distinctions that we can make between different types of vocabulary words.[18] Some words—like *baby, dog,* and *eat*—are relatively easy for children to acquire, because they are commonly used in everyday conversation, and their meanings are concrete and easily understood. Because it is assumed that children will learn this first tier of words through exposure, researchers suggest that teachers in elementary schools focus on teaching more abstract and sophisticated words in their classrooms, so that children can make sense of words like *reluctant, analyze,* and *difference.* Then there are even more challenging words, a third tier, that are usually specific to a particular domain. For instance, a student will likely only talk about *parallelograms* in math class and *isthmuses* in social studies class. When we talk about reading volume in chapter 5, we will talk much more about the importance of building one's vocabulary throughout elementary school and provide you with some tips for ensuring that your child begins to recognize these more challenging words.

But before we get to these more sophisticated skills, your goal prior to your child's entering kindergarten is to help her acquire the simple, but essential, words in that those first two tiers. Remember, teachers focus on more sophisticated words because they assume that children already have an understanding of many words before they enter school. In fact, research has shown that, before second grade, school experiences have a negligible effect on children's vocabulary size. In contrast, the volume and diversity of language that a child hears at home during these early years predicts a child's vocabulary size very well.[19] Helping your child develop an adequate vocabulary is one of the most important early steps you can take towards reading success. Reading books and taking field trips (even down the block!) are great ways to get into the practice of talking to your child about new things and introducing her to new words within the lower tiers.

Labeling and elaborating during shared reading. It is probably no surprise to you that there are many different styles of shared reading. Researchers have found creative ways to explore what types of shared reading experiences are most beneficial to children. It is important to highlight that, although the amount of time a parent spends reading with his or her child is related to later reading success, the quality of their interactions is also a significant factor. Quality and quantity do not always go hand in hand, so make sure that you are reading frequently *and* engaging in high quality conversations that employ many of the types of questions and comments we have discussed throughout this chapter, rather than focusing on only one of these important aspects of shared reading experiences. A considerable body of literature supports the idea that reading aloud with your child impacts the development of later reading skills.[20]

The relationship between these two variables, quality and quantity, is illustrated well in one particular study that explored which styles of shared reading are most likely to promote skill development.[21] In this study, four-year-olds were asked to engage in a joint book reading task, but from a book—*Frog on His Own* by Mercer Mayer—that originally included only pictures and no text. The researchers who designed the study wrote an original story to accompany this picture book, and included ten nonsense words in the story. (The reason that nonsense words are used in scientific studies is because they allow for researchers to examine the process of new word acquisition without worrying about whether some students already know the real word that is being presented, or another word that shares the same root.) In this story, the nonsense word *browling* was used in the story to mean *leaping*.

In this particular study, students were split into several groups. In each group, students were to read *Frog on His Own* three times. In one group, the story was simply read aloud to the child during each session, and each child had three opportunities to learn each of these new words. In other groups, after reading each nonsense word, the adult reader either made a comment that also used the word, saying "Oh no! Leroy is browling towards the boat" or asked a question designed to have the child identify the nonsense word, saying, "What is Leroy doing?" So, in these other groups, children had more opportunities to learn these new words.

After reading the story on those three occasions, children were then tested to see whether they recognized words like *browling* when they were presented and whether they were able to independently name them. When the children were tested, everyone performed better than they would have by chance. Children who were just read the story three times, on average, accurately identified five words and were able to independently name two words. But, hearing these unfamiliar words more than three times helped children recognize more words (on average, seven words) and name more words (on average, four words). This study, along with several others, demonstrates that repeated readings of a story accompanied with word explanations lead to vocabulary gain.[22] These results give us a clue about how much time we need to spend making sure that children are repeatedly exposed to new words. Taken together, they suggest that *making comments* and *asking questions* about new words are effective strategies for parents to employ. Making comments, in particular, was especially helpful for building children's expressive language skills.

Other studies have demonstrated that the type of conversations parents engage in during shared reading activities can affect children's later language and reading abilities. In one study, parents and their 27-month-old children were observed while they engaged in shared reading activities.[23] The observers kept track of what each of the parents

BOX 1-1. STRATEGIES FOR TALKING TO PRESCHOOLERS DURING SHARED BOOK READING

Several years ago, researchers began to develop a technique called *dialogic reading* that parents and teachers could use to help toddlers develop language and literacy skills. This technique is based on the idea that even before children are able to read independently, they are ready to be active participants in book reading experiences. Two acronyms were developed to guide adults through these dialogic reading interactions. The first is:

P Prompt or initiate a conversation about the book.

E Evaluate the child's response.

E Expand upon the child's response.

R Repeat the initial question to ensure that the child comprehended the information you shared during expansion.

For example, if you were reading *Goldilocks and the Three Bears* with your child, you might ask her why Papa Bear seemed so upset. If she says, "Because Goldilocks was in their house!" you can take a moment to evaluate her response and then respond to her statement, adding in an additional detail or new vocabulary word. You might say, "You're right! She was in their house, and she did not ask permission. She wasn't allowed in there." or "Yeah, she went right into their house and touched things that weren't her property. Those beds didn't belong to her." Then, through asking the same question again—perhaps in a different form, like "Why do you think Momma Bear was so upset?"—you will provide your child with an opportunity to use a new word like *permission* or *property* on her own.

One of the difficult parts of this process is often figuring out how to prompt your child, and coming up with new ways to do so throughout the book. A very simple prompt might be to ask the child to describe what is happening in the picture that accompanies a page of text. You can also ask your child what just happened in the story, or what he predicts will happen next. You can even ask him if what is happening in the story reminds him of anything that has happened to him. The specific questions that you ask are not particularly important, because the most important thing about dialogic reading is for you and your child to talk together and enjoy the experience. As children's vocabularies grow and their comprehension of the material becomes more sophisticated, beginning to ask more open-ended questions becomes appropriate.[31] It is absolutely okay to ask silly questions or talk about something that is not related to the book itself. Your goal is to make reading time a fun experience for your child, so once this activity starts to feel like work, it is time to take a break!

To help you think of prompts, there is another helpful acronym that the dialogic reading researchers created:

C **Completion questions**, in which you ask your child to finish a sentence by filling in the blanks. You might say, "Papa Bear was mad because Goldilocks did not ask..." and wait for your child to say "permission!"

R **Recall questions**, in which you ask your child to share details from the book to demonstrate that she understood the plot and kept track of the sequence of events. You might ask your daughter, "Can you tell me what happened when Papa Bear walked into his bedroom? And then what happened?"

O **Open-ended questions** that allow your child more freedom in discussing any aspect of the book that piqued his interest. Asking questions that your child can't answer with a single word will lead to richer conversations and may give your child the opportunity to ask you a question, too. You might ask, "How do you think Goldilocks felt when she walked home?"

W **Wh- questions** (using the words *who, what, when, where, why*) to teach your child new vocabulary words and focus on details of the story.

D Distancing questions that distance your discussion from the book itself and help your child make connections between the story that you read and his own life. You might ask, "Is there ever a time that you have wanted to use something that wasn't yours?"

Using both of these acronyms to guide your shared reading time may help you let your child take a more active role in the process. To help you get started, we'll give you some examples of how each of these prompts could be used when reading a few different books aloud with your child. Although asking these types of questions might feel artificial at first, we know you will become more and more comfortable with these strategies over time. Remember, having fun and letting your child take the conversation in the direction that interests him is the most important part of this process. Over time, you should begin to ask more directed questions about the story and the features of the text, but you always want the activity of reading together to be enjoyable for your child. It is better to have a fun time together and ask fewer of these questions than ask a ton of questions, but have a child who doesn't want to read together again tomorrow. The following examples may help you brainstorm questions about your own favorite books!

Caps for Sale: A Tale of a Peddler, Some Monkeys and Their Monkey Business, by Esphyr Slobodkina,[32] is a lively picture book that tells the story of a man who sells caps throughout the countryside. On a slow day, he decides to take a nap while balancing all his caps on his head, and monkeys steal them. He is unsuccessful at persuading the monkeys to return the caps until he throws down his own cap in frustration. Then, in a case of "monkey see, monkey do," they return all of his caps. Here are some examples of ways you could apply PEER and CROWD to this story:

P **Prompt or initiate a conversation about the book**

You can prompt a conversation just by looking at the illustration on this book's cover. You can say, "Hey, look at this picture! There's a man who climbed all the way up a tree. What else do you see in this picture?"

E **Evaluate the child's response**

When your child mentions that monkeys are hiding behind the tree, and there are lots of cushions in front of the tree, you have the opportunity to teach him some <u>new vocabulary words</u> and to clarify that the cushions are really caps.

E **Expand upon the child's response**

You can say, "You're right. Those monkeys look like they're hiding. Maybe they're up to something... they look like they are being <u>sneaky</u>. The title of the story is "Caps for Sale" and the man is holding one of those cushions, too. I think the cushions are actually floppy <u>hats</u> or <u>caps</u>. What do you think?"

R **Repeat the initial question**

You can then repeat and expand upon your initial question, saying "So what do you see in this picture that helps explain the title of the story "Caps for Sale"? This question will give your child a chance to use the new words he learned and elaborate upon his initial response.

C **Completion questions**

As the peddler says his signature line, "Caps! Caps for sale! Fifty cents a cap!" you can leave out some key words and have your child fill them in. As he gets older and pays more attention to the written words on the page, you can point to the omitted words as he says them.

R **Recall questions**

In the story, the peddler makes sure to walk with very good posture so that his caps do not fall off his head. Several pages after this fact is mentioned, you might ask your child why the peddler stands up so straight and when he started to do so. His response can help you evaluate how well he is able to recall and describe the sequence of events in the story.

O Open-ended questions

You can ask your child, "If you were the peddler, where would you put your caps while you napped?"

W Wh- questions

After the peddler took his nap, you can ask, "Why do you think he felt so rested and refreshed?"

D Distancing questions

You can ask your child, "Has there ever been a time when walking away from an argument helped you get what you wanted?" You might also say, "The monkeys acted just like the peddler—they wanted the caps when he did, too, and gave them up once he gave up his. Have you ever been around someone who did exactly what you did?"

There's a Nightmare in My Closet, by Mercer Mayer,[33] tells the tale of a young boy who is afraid of what lurks in his closet—until he learns that his nightmare may be just as afraid of him as he is of it! It is a great story to read with your child to help her talk and laugh about her fears. Here are just a few of the ways you could begin to talk about this book.

P Prompt or initiate a conversation about the book

The very first page of this book says, "There used to be a nightmare in my closet" and the boy in the picture looks very worried. What do you think this story is going to be about?

E Evaluate the child's response

Your child might say that the book will be about how scared the child is of nightmares, without realizing that the story refers to his fears in the past tense.

E Expand upon the child's response

You can say, "I think you are right. This is a story about how the boy used to feel about going to sleep at night. He says, 'There used to be a nightmare in my closet so I bet he doesn't think that anymore."

R **Repeat the initial question**
You might ask, "So, if he used to be scared of nightmares and he isn't anymore, what do you think will happen in this book?" If she needs an additional prompt, you can say, "How do you think he will stop being so afraid?"

C **Completion questions**
The boy in the story tells us, "One night I decided to get rid of my nightmare once and for all." After reading this story together a few times, you can help familiarize your child with common phrases by saying "once and . . ." and looking expectantly at your child.

R **Recall questions**
You can ask, "Where in the room did the nightmare go when he came out of the closet?" As your child answers, you can flip back to the page where this happens and run your fingers under the words "sitting at the foot of my bed." You can then ask, "What happened next?" to see if your child remembers the order in which things happened.

O **Open-ended questions**
You can ask, "How do you think the boy is going to get rid of this nightmare?" Even if she notices the boy's arsenal, you can ask, "What are other ways you could get rid of a nightmare?"

W **Wh- questions**
To help your child focus on print cues, you can ask, "What letter does nightmare start with?" and then point to the "N" on the page.

D **Distancing questions**
You might want to ask, "Have you ever been afraid of something that turns out to be afraid of you, too?" or "Are there times when you acted brave and it helped you stop being afraid?"

Ladybug Girl and Bumblebee Boy[34] is one in a series of books by David Soman and Jacky Davis, a husband and wife team who write books that help children think about the social situations they encounter by following along with the adventures of young Lulu and her alter ego, Ladybug Girl. The story introduces children to metaphorical language and keeps them entertained with the imaginative play of children who want to be playground superheroes. As Lulu and her pals learn to compromise, they also get the chance to conquer playground menaces. There are many different aspects of this book that you could talk about with your child, but here are just a few ideas to get you started.

P   **Prompt or initiate a conversation about the book**

Early in the story, Lulu and a frend are having trouble deciding what to play together. As the situation unfolds, you can ask, "How do you think Lulu feels when Sam wants to play different games than her?"

E   **Evaluate the child's response**

When your child says that Lulu is mad, you have the opportunity to teach her a synonym for this word.

E   **Expand upon the child's response**

You can say, "You're right. Lulu looks mad. I think she's frustrated *that he doesn't want to play the same thing as her, just like you get frustrated when your sister doesn't want to play board games with you."*

R   **Repeat the initial question**

You can then repeat and expand upon your initial question, saying, "So now look at the next page! Sam still doesn't want to do the same thing as Lulu—he won't go on the seesaw. How do you think she feels?" This question will give your child a chance to use the new word she learned and elaborate upon her initial response.

C   **Completion questions**

When Ladybug Girl is in action, she lifts a bag that is "as heavy as a boulder." You can leave off the last word in this sentence and let your child guess, so that she can build her semantic web of heavy objects. Even if her answer isn't correct, you can say, "You're right—a bulldozer is really heavy!! In this story, they said 'as a boulder,' but I think the sentence would sound just as good if it said bulldozer!"

R **Recall questions**

Ladybug Girl and Bumblebee boy pretend that a squirrel is a scary monster and that the tire swing is a mean robot. You can ask your child what the superheroes pretended these things were. You can also ask what happened in the story before and after they started playing, to see how easily your child can recount the full sequence of events.

O **Open-ended questions**

You can ask your child, "How do you think they felt when the whole Bug Squad wanted to play with them?"

W **Wh- questions**

Lulu is very attached to her dog, Bingo. You can ask your child her name, and then sing your own version of the song about a dog by that name, saying "There was a Lulu who had a dog, and Bingo was her name-o. B-I-N-G-O..."

D **Distancing questions**

This book provides you with a great, organic opportunity to ask your child the question, "Have you ever had a hard time getting along with other kids at the playground?"

Keep using these strategies with the books you regularly read with your child, and you will be amazed at the new words and issues you end up discussing during book reading time. As you will see in the next few chapters, these shared story times build much more than just oral language skills.

said during the book reading session and differentiated between simple prompts (for instance, to point to a picture, to turn a page, or to answer a yes/no question) and more sophisticated prompts that assisted the child in further exploration of the story. For example, some parents defined new vocabulary words for their children or asked their children open-ended questions that allowed the children to respond in many different ways. These same children were then tested at the age of 30 and 42 months, and the researchers found a significant relationship between the frequency with which parents made sophisticated comments during these early book reading sessions and children's later expressive and receptive vocabulary skills.

The key to helping your child build semantic skills during any of these experiences is to focus on just the conversation that you are having with your child and the questions that come up naturally, rather than worrying too much about whether you are reading every word to her right away. *Your* story, rather than the story that is already written, is most important. You can always go back and read the same book several times, for several different purposes, and it is likely that your child already requests the same favorite books over and over again. Take a look at the examples in Box 1-1 to see what questions you might want to ask about familiar stories.

Selecting themed books and building children's knowledge base.
One way to naturally help your child begin a conversation about semantics, or the meanings of words, is to choose a book with one theme, because many of the words within this book will fall into a particular category. A great resource for selecting themed books is **www.readingrockets.org/ books/booksbytheme/**

Reading a book all about the different animals that live on a farm or at the zoo or a book about different jobs people have can help you develop and expand your child's semantic webs. When Jamie's niece and nephew were four years old, she observed them chatting in the car about the animals they had seen during that day's trip to the zoo.

"Lions eat meat," said Max. "They're carnivores."

"Yes," replied Madeleine. "They're predators."

How is it possible that these two little kids were able to have this sophisticated conversation about lions' eating habits? Well, adults shared important information with them at the right time and started off with words that made sense to them already. Max and Madeleine had, in fact, seen lions at the zoo during feeding time and had also been read many books that talk about all sorts of animals and their eating habits. So, their initial semantic web for animals included two categories: animals who eat meat, and animals that don't eat meat. From spending lots of time talking about dinosaurs, they then learned that a fancy name for an animal that eats meat is a *carnivore*. And then, from hearing more stories about animals and how they interacted with one another, they learned that carnivores had to go out and hunt for their food, whereas herbivores just grazed on nearby plants. And a fancy way to describe an animal that goes off hunting is a *predator*.

Jamie's niece and nephew learned these new words because they engaged in deep conversations about the books they read and the things that they did. However, one of the best reasons to read a book about these new topics, rather than just relying on the conversations that would happen naturally, is that all books, including children's literature, contain more novel words, forms of grammar, and styles of conversation than do many other sources.[24] Especially if you are a parent who happens to be less talkative, or if you do not have the time or money to take your child on frequent field trips, books can be a vehicle for talking about any new topic you want and for introducing children to written language, including how it sounds (phonology) and how it is structured (syntax). Young children with small vocabularies face the same conundrum as inexperienced workers entering the job market, who often feel frustrated that they can't get hired without past experience, but can't gain experience without getting hired. If no one will read books with them and teach them new words, how will they ever build their skills?

> **Young children with small vocabularies face the same conundrum as inexperienced workers entering the job market, who often feel frustrated that they can't get hired without past experience, but can't gain experience without getting hired. If no one will read books with them and teach them new words, how will they ever build their skills?**

Labeling and elaborating throughout the day. These types of conversations do not need to happen just during joint book reading, but can also occur when you and your child are in the car together, watching television, or looking at a billboard. In fact, these types of conversations can happen almost any time. Part of the reason that talking about new words during book reading is a simple and structured way to build your child's vocabulary is that the new words are already included there for you, and storybooks provide helpful visual support so that children can begin to pair words and the objects those words represent. But, while you are out in your neighborhood every day, you can also find new objects to label and discuss.

For example, you might pass a bulldozer or a dump truck while driving on the highway in your own, much smaller car. Asking clarifying questions and helping your child name these objects will eventually help her understand that all vehicles share common characteristics, but are different in many ways (for example, some vehicles transport people, and other vehicles transport supplies). As you and your child come across new things, ask questions about how this object compares to one she already knows well. How are they similar? How are they different? When you really think about it, there is a tremendous amount of information you can convey as you do something fun, like reading together, visiting the park, or going grocery shopping. Focusing these conversations on objects or situations that interest your child can motivate her to talk about these things with you.

Another way to help your child develop semantic skills is to play some version of *the association game* or *categories* while you are driving in the car. In its simplest form, you can play the association game by selecting someone to pick a word first, and then taking turns coming up with associated words. For example, your youngest child might say the word *red*, which causes you to think of "rubies." This might remind your older child of the ruby slippers in the *Wizard of Oz*, so then she would say "slippers," leading your youngest child to say "pajamas." This fun and sometimes silly way to pass the time can help widen semantic webs. To make the game more structured, you can pick any category, such as "things that are blue" or "fruits" and work together to find as many examples as possible. This game helps your child in many ways. If you add a word to the list that he is not familiar with, such as blue jay, you've given him an opportunity to learn a new word. Similarly, you can ask your child to define the words that he adds to the list, so that he can build his vocabulary in this area and discover synonyms for his chosen word. This activity also helps children begin to categorize people and objects. As you work together to name as many zoo animals as possible, for example, your child begins to learn that both zebras and alligators are animals, although not all animals are alligators. Beginning to grasp this idea of class inclusion and developing a taxonomy is important for overall cognitive development.

Helping children build their vocabularies also has social and motivational benefits. Children take pride in knowing and using new words, and those who are read to and with by their parents frequently have more motivation when faced with reading tasks later in life.[25] Researchers have found that children who often engage in language and literacy activities with their parents seem more interested in reading and more willing to attempt to read challenging materials. Because young children are developing skills related to autonomy and initiative during their toddler and preschool years, allowing them to show you what they know when completing the types of activities discussed in Table 1-1 should be gratifying for them.

Praise for their attempts will also motivate children, and it is important to provide your child with specific reinforcement for the task he just engaged in, rather than global praise for being good at that type of task. For example, if you and your child are taking turns coming up with synonyms for *cold* and he says "freezing," you would want to say something like, "Great job thinking hard about another word for cold!" instead of saying, "You have such a big vocabulary." Providing this specific praise is important because it will encourage him to think hard about other synonyms in the future, whereas giving the global praise might actually discourage him from persisting when he's asked a tough question. "Hmm," he might think, "If I have such a big vocabulary, why is this so hard for me?" The most likely conclusions for him to draw, then, are that the task is too hard or that he doesn't really have a large vocabulary, both of which might discourage him from being persistent. As you begin to use the strategies below, and those throughout the book, keep in mind the importance of providing praise that is very specific.

TABLE 1-1. SEMANTIC DEVELOPMENT: STRATEGIES FOR PARENTS

What to Do	How to Do It	Age(s)
Label and Elaborate on New Words During Shared Reading	Make comments and ask questions to draw your child's attention to new vocabulary words and new ideas during shared reading. For example, when reading a book about a *schooner*, first label this boat by pointing at its picture and saying, "This kind of boat is called a schooner." Then elaborate by saying things like, "Look how tall the schooner is compared to those other boats!"	
Label and Elaborate on New Words Throughout the Day	Make comments and ask questions about the things you see or people and situations you encounter during shared activities such as driving in the car, watching television, or looking at a billboard. Word association games are another good way to introduce new vocabulary.	
Select Themed Books	Choose a book with a theme (for example, a day at the beach, or a visit to the zoo), which will help your child learn many words that fall into a particular category. A great resource for selecting themed books is www.readingrockets.org/books/booksbytheme/	

continues

TABLE 1-1. CONTINUED

What to Do	How to Do It	Age(s)
Play a Synonym ID Game	Make a game out of identifying synonyms by asking your child, "What's another word for *big*?" Take turns, so that your child needs to pick the word, as well as identify the synonym. Your child may choose words for which she can't identify a synonym, in which case you get a chance to teach her a new word. You can play the same game using antonyms and asking your child to pick words that are the opposite of the word you stated.	
Make a Word Web	Help your child make a word web, using a large piece of paper to create a graphic showing the connections between related words (e.g., things you do in summer, things you see on a farm, or things that make a superhero powerful). Your child can draw pictures, find photos from a magazine, or select stickers depicting each word she thinks of. Once items are pasted, taped, or stuck to the web, you can label the objects. Save the word webs you create so you can add to them over time or review them together!	
Play Prepositional Simon Says	Play a game of Simon Says with your child. Give increasingly complex directions that require him to make sense of prepositional phrases. For example, "Simon says, 'Put the ball under the chair behind the table.'"	

Syntactic Development

Syntax refers to the rules that govern language. These rules help us make sense of sentences in many different ways. These rules make it clear what happened (described by the verbs, adjectives, and adverbs in the sentence), who made it happen (that is, the subject of the sentence), and to whom it happened (that is, who the object of the sentence is). With the help of morphemes like *–ed* and *–ing,* these rules help us understand whether something already happened, is happening right now, or will happen in the future (that is, whether the sentence is in past, present, or future tense). Syntax, an important aspect of grammar, involves recognizing that the words we select to include in any particular sentence can change its meaning and that the order of the words also has the potential to change the sentence's meaning. Understanding these rules allows children to realize that sentences follow a formula and that they can use the clues provided by a sentence's syntax to make meaning from it. Thus, these syntax skills make comprehension easier—first, in conversations, and then when applying the same rules to written sentences. We generally learn these rules through exposure to spoken and written language, although some direct instruction in syntax is also necessary. The examples in Box 1-2 may help you see how important syntax is to making meaning.

> **SYNTACTIC DEVELOPMENT**
> The ability to understand the structure of a sentence, including its tense, subject, and object.

BOX 1-2. WHY DOES SYNTAX MATTER?

The boy is sad	vs.	The boy was sad
Naturally, we talked	vs.	We talked naturally
The tired man was quiet	vs.	The quiet man was tired

Word choice and order change the meaning of sentences!

Why Is Syntax Important for Reading Development?

The process of acquiring this understanding of syntax is somewhat mysterious, as most adults can't remember being taught all of the rules of grammar that they know and can't even articulate why certain phrases are right or wrong—we'll often say "it just sounds right." To a large degree, children begin to understand syntactic structure by being immersed in language and literature.

Understanding sentence structure may sound like a dreary task for a young child, and perhaps a topic that would not be introduced until much later in a child's academic career. But even young children have a remarkable capacity to understand the nuances of spoken language. For example, think about the different meanings conveyed by the sentences *I want to get a dog* and *A dog wants to get me*. Just a small change in word placement leads to sentences that mean quite different things. Even children who are too young to generate those complete sentences understand what the small words mean, and the different implications of those two phrases. Understanding syntax helps readers glean the meaning of spoken or written sentences, so that we know that a child is excited to pick out a new pet, rather than fearing an attack from a neighbor's dog.

Studies have shown that even children under two years of age will spend more time looking at a picture that matches the sentence than one that does not.[26] For example, if a toddler were read the sentence *I want to get a dog* and shown one picture of a person picking out a new puppy in a pet store and another picture of a dog chasing a person, the toddler's eyes would linger on the first picture. From studies like these, it is clear that humans are hard-wired to understand syntax—the rules that guide sentence creation—even before they are able to produce syntactically correct sentences.

How Do Syntactic Skills Grow Over Time?

Table 1-2 outlines the developmental progression of these syntactic skills, although it is important to recognize that there is natural variation

TABLE 1-2. LANGUAGE DEVELOPMENT OVER TIME

Child's Age	Average Sentence Length, in Number of Words	New Words	New Ideas
1–2 years	1–2 words	• Most words are nouns • Learns to say "no"	• Understands the possessive ("Mommy shoe")
2–3 years	3–4 words	• Begins to use more verbs and verb forms ("walk**ing**, walk**ed**")	• Asks simple questions ("Cat here?") • Uses pronouns to refer to self and one other person ("I," "you")
3–4 years	4–7 words	• Begins to use "'s" to show possession ("Mommy**'s** shoe") • Learns to say "because"	• Uses "Is" at the beginning of simple questions ("Is cat here?") • Uses "and" to form compound sentences • Uses pronouns "he," "she," and "it" • Begins to ask *wh-* questions
4–5 years	5–8 words	• Learns to say "if" and "so" • Learns to say "could" and "would"	• Begins to use passive voice ("The bird was fed by Mom") • Uses pronouns "our," "they," and "their"
5–6 years	6+ words	• Continues to use more sophisticated language	• Understands superlatives ("hot," "hotter," "hottest")
6–7 years	7+ words	• Continues to use more sophisticated language	• Understand irregular superlatives ("good," "better," "best")

Source: Adapted from Gard, A., Gilman, L., & Gordon, J. (2012). *Speech and Language Development Chart*, 3rd ed. Austin, TX: Pro-Ed.

in the age and rate at which children acquire these skills.[27] Some children may learn new words and ideas somewhat earlier than others, but most children who are progressing more slowly catch up with their peers by late toddlerhood. If your child's language development seems to be significantly slower than that of his peers, it may be a good idea to talk to your pediatrician or a speech and language pathologist about your concerns. But also know that the information presented in Table 1-2 includes rough estimates, and we can't expect all children to pick up new skills on a strict schedule.

Although you will probably always remember your child's first word very clearly, you may find it even more amazing when she first strings two words together to explain what she wants, saying something like, "Mom go" or "Dad cookie" (meaning, respectively, "I want you to come here" and "I want you to give me a cookie"). These utterances are often called **telegraphic speech** because your child is, essentially, sending a brief telegram communicating her needs. Such telegraphic speech, which emerges around two years of age, indicates a burgeoning understanding of sentence structure. Children at this age tend to talk mainly about objects (like *bed*) or actions (like *go*), and to pair these words with the agents who might interact with them (like *my bed* or *Dad go*). They also begin to describe objects with attributes (like *soft bed*). When using these simple and novel phrases that they create independently, children are already following simple rules of syntax and placing words in their correct order.[28]

> **TELEGRAPHIC SPEECH**
> The type of speech that emerges around two years of age in which children often use two words to communicate their needs (for example, "Mom go," or "Dad cookie").

After mastering this first stage of syntactic development, children begin to create longer and more complicated sentences by combining elements of prior telegraphic phrases. For instance, a toddler might discuss an action and an object at the same time, saying something like, "Dad come my bed." At this age, children also begin to utilize small words and word endings called grammatical morphemes that are not meaningful on their own but alter the meaning of the sentence in which they are used. These morphemes include prepositions like *by* or *on*, articles like *a* and *the*, and verb endings like *–ing* and *–ed*. Researchers have established that children begin using these morphemes in a fairly predictable order.[29] As they begin to utilize these additional units of sound, children form their first true sentences, like "Dad, come *to* my bed." Around this same time, when they are approximately two to four years old, children begin to understand how to use the different tenses—in sentences like "Dad *came* to my bed," "Dad *comes* to my bed," and "Dad *will come* to my bed"—to discuss and interpret language in a more sophisticated way.

With this increased ability, children begin to express their questions and statements in a grammatically correct way, and to understand sentences that use the passive voice (like, "At night, the dog was walked," as compared with sentences in the active voice, like, "At night, Mom walked the dog."). As children's command of syntax increases, they can also utilize this skill to help them make sense of unfamiliar words, and thus, boost their semantic development. For instance, if a child who was unfamiliar with what a guitar looked like heard someone say, "My guitar is heavy!," it is likely that he would be able to use the syntactic clues in the sentence, like the fact that the possessive *my* precedes the new word and a verb follows it, to surmise that a *guitar* is an object. This example illustrates that language growth in one area can facilitate language growth in other areas as well and that syntactic skills can help children fast map new words.

What Is the Role of Parents in the Development of Syntactic Language Skills?

Techniques like imitation, modeling, and expanding upon a child's sentences allow children to become comfortable generating more complete and sophisticated sentences. When they are very young, children usually concentrate on only the most salient words in a sentence needed to convey meaning, moving from saying, "milk!" to "want milk" to "me want milk" as their capacity for expression develops. Our job is to help them add in the more incidental words, correctly, as they get older. We can do this by imitating the words that they said accurately, expanding upon their statements to include those incidental words, and then modeling a complete sentence for them. In the example above, you might do that by saying something like, "Want milk?" and then looking at your child. After making eye contact, you might say "Oh, *you* want milk. I'll get it for you. I like milk, too." Scaffolding your child's development in this way can foster syntactic language development.

What is most important for parents to understand about this developmental progression is how to help your child move along to the next natural point. In the above example, if your son says, "Want milk" and you say, "Oh, *you* want milk?" or "Who wants milk? The dolly?" to prompt him to say, "No, I want milk!," your expansions will help him begin to understand the importance of pronouns. Rather than immediately correcting your child, the goal is to naturally restate or expand upon what he or she said, using correct language.

Developing Syntactic Skills: How Can I Support My Child's Individual Needs?

All children go through the process of learning grammatical rules slowly and apply them imprecisely when they are young. At times, learning a new rule can actually make life more confusing. A child who previously knew to say that her family *grew* tomatoes in the backyard when talking about something that happened last summer may begin to formally learn about the past tense and then begin to say that her family *growed* tomatoes in the backyard. She will only begin to correctly say *grew* again when learning that the rule of adding *-ed* to the end of verbs, in order to signify that they occurred in the past, only applies to certain words. Be patient as these rules click into place, and scaffold your child's language development without correcting too many things at the same time. Restating what your child wanted to communicate using the correct syntax in a nonchalant, supportive manner seems to be the most helpful way to boost these skills.

What Activities and Strategies Can I Use to Support Syntactic Development?

We said earlier that people learn about syntax most often through exposure to properly structured sentences. Although you may remember diagramming sentences in school, few teachers today pay such close attention to grammar instruction, while still expecting children to speak and write in accordance with the rules governing language. We certainly don't expect you to take on the job of diagramming those sentences, but exposing your child to correct sentence structure playfully and through children's literature will help him begin to make sense of these syntactic rules.

Labeling and word play during shared book reading. Because books often include more formal and sophisticated sentences than everyday conversation, exposure to storybook language can have an important influence on children's syntactic development. And, of course, discussing the books that you read with your children can provide limitless opportunities for expanding upon their own speech, helping them to understand the meaning of prepositional phrases and pronouns, and differentiating between what already happened in a story and what is going to happen. Parents are more likely to incorporate sophisticated aspects of adult speech into the conversations that they have with their children about storybooks than into discussions of other common topics, so book reading again becomes a vehicle for language development. It is not that children have no other methods for acquiring syntactic knowledge, but that shared book reading is an incredibly effective tool for allowing them to do so.

As you read with your child, you have the opportunity to highlight and label different parts of speech by turning grammar into a fun game. For example, you might read the sentence "The boy was running" and ask your child, "Who is this sentence about?" Depending on how your child responds, you have a chance to help clarify by saying, "Who is this sentence about—the boy or running?" or to define a subject for him, by saying, "The subject is the person, place, or thing that is doing something in the sentence." Once your child understands the idea that each sentence has a subject, you can move onto the next sentence and again ask him to identify who the sentence is about, and then begin to help him identify other parts of the sentence, including objects, verbs, and adjectives. Because young children enjoy demonstrating their new skills and autonomy, this game can become an engaging part of shared reading time.

You can also begin to play with words in order to help your child understand which words are of the same word class. Think of this as if you were creating your own *Mad Libs* out of any book you read with your child. You might use the same sentence from the prior example and ask your child to think of other characters from the story that could take the place of "the boy" in that same sentence, or other verbs besides "running" that could be used to describe the boy's actions. Creating many similar sentences will help your child understand these parts of speech and sentence structure. Just as with all the strategies we have discussed, this game should be played sparingly, so that it continues to seem fun to your child and does not detract from the book reading experience.

Labeling and elaborating throughout the day. Another way to help your child develop syntactic skills is to build sentences together, using refrigerator word magnets or your own tangible materials (such as stuffed animals or Lego people). Narrating stories and adding in the descriptive and incidental words that enrich passages is a great way to model skills for children. As these stories become more sophisticated, you can help your child combine two short sentences into one longer sentence. If that is difficult for your child, you might choose to model this increase in syntactic complexity or have your child repeat a longer sentence after you say it.

There are many ways repetition can be a fun and informative teaching tool for young children. Playing verbal games when you are in the car or running errands can also increase syntactic skills. Any games that always start with the same sentence, such as Simon Says or Twenty Questions ("I am thinking about a person who...." or "I am thinking about a movie that...."), will help your children learn that particular sentence structure. Take a look at Table 1-3 for a summary of strategies that you can use to build syntactic skills in fun ways.

TABLE 1-3. SYNTACTIC DEVELOPMENT: STRATEGIES FOR PARENTS

What to Do	How to Do It	Age(s)
Label Parts of Speech During Shared Book Reading	Highlight and label different parts of speech by turning grammar into a fun game. For example, you might read the sentence "The boy was running" and ask your child, "Who is this sentence about?" If your child can identify who the sentence is about, give her specific positive feedback, "Great! 'The boy' is the subject of the sentence. He's the one who is running." As she begins to understand the game, you change the question to "Who is the subject of the sentence?" Once your child understands the idea that each sentence has a subject, you can move on to verbs, objects, and adjectives in the sentence. You may be surprised by how quickly your child starts to shout her answers triumphantly.	
Create Your Own Mad Libs	Help your child understand parts of speech by creating your own *Mad Libs* modeled after the popular fill-in-the-blank game. Use any book you read together to create many similar sentences in order to help your child to understand nouns, verbs, adjectives, and adverbs!	
Build-a-Sentence Using Objects	Build sentences with your child by using your own tangible materials (such as stuffed animals or Lego people). For example, you could line up a baby doll, a spoon, and a bowl of cereal and "read" the sentence "The baby eats cereal." This is a fun, interactive way to build skills together!	

continues

TABLE 1-3. CONTINUED

What to Do	How to Do It	Age(s)
Make Sentences Using Objects and Flashcards	Using tangible objects and flashcards, help your child build full sentences. Choose a few nouns (for example, a stuffed animal, a baby doll, flashcards with names of family members, and then some toys, snacks, or other objects), a few verbs (for example, the written words *loves, runs,* and *eats*), and a few adjectives (for example, *shiny, delicious*). Swap words to make new sentences that highlight different parts of speech: "The baby eats cookies" becomes "The baby loves cookies" or "The baby loves delicious cookies" or "The baby loves shiny toys."	
Make Sentences More Complex Using and, but, or Changes in Tense	Using the same objects from the previous tip, connect two short sentences using the words *and* or *but*. The two sentences "The baby eats cookies" and "The baby eats apples" can become "The baby eats cookies and apples." You can also play with tense. For example, ask "Yesterday, what did the baby eat?" Then help your child construct the sentence "She ate cookies and apples."	
Label Prepositions and Pronouns During Shared Book Reading	As you read together, point out pronouns and prepositional phrases. For example, if you are reading the book *We're Going on a Bear Hunt,* you might comment that "We" is a pronoun that refers to the family. Or you can play a game focused on identifying all of the prepositions in this book, such as *through, over,* and *under*.	
Read Books That Focus on Grammar and Parts of Speech	Read books that explicitly address grammar and parts of speech, such as Brian P. Cleary's *Words are Categorical* series or other fun grammar books.	

Pragmatic Language Development

What Is Pragmatic Language?

The **pragmatic** aspects of language refer to how we use language to express meaning and connect with other people. Pragmatic skills are different than semantic skills in that they are a marker of how well we can communicate with others, not just how accurately we can communicate. Young children use pragmatic language to make requests (e.g., "Can I please have that book?") and to refuse what others offer or tell them (e.g., "No! I won't eat that spinach"). As children get slightly older, they begin to make assertions (e.g., "I already asked for the book.") and provide denials (e.g., "No—we went to the pool on Tuesday, not Wednesday"). Eventually, they also rely on the pragmatic aspects of language to speak in metaphorical ways (e.g., "He's a real bruiser") or express themselves through idioms (e.g., "It's raining cats and dogs"). In other words, we use pragmatic language skills both to socialize with others and to discuss practical information. And the pragmatic language that we use is developed by the culture in which we live—to know the right way to ask someone to pass the pepper or the best way to make a joke, one needs to be aware of the social norms that govern that country, region, culture, or sleepover party. Sorting out these unspoken and shifting rules of language can be very challenging.

> **PRAGMATIC DEVELOPMENT**
> The ability to use language for social communication, including requests, refusals, assertions, denials, as well as using metaphors and idioms.

Why Are Pragmatic Skills Important for Reading Development?

Much of what we read highlights the interactions between people, so pragmatic language is a key component of the dialogue in any story. Being able to comprehend what is happening in a book requires your child not only to understand what the characters are thinking and feeling, but also the reasons why characters may have a misunderstanding or disagreement. Moreover, your young reader will need to grasp the social aspects of language well so that he can understand how these nuances of the way we speak befuddle others. In order to appreciate the humor and the problems posed by the actions of storybook character Amelia Bedelia, the reader (or listener) must understand that when someone asks you to "put the lights out," she doesn't mean to hang them on the clothesline outside, or when you "draw the drapes," you are closing them, rather than drawing a picture of them. The desire to communicate with others, and the exciting and sometimes confusing outcomes of these interpersonal exchanges, is the driving force of most narratives, so it stands to reason that children's enjoyment of texts is enhanced when pragmatic language makes sense to them.

How Children Develop Pragmatic Language Skills

Before the age of nine months, infants begin to vocalize sounds to other people in order to get attention and to imitate sounds that they have heard others make. Even these simple vocalizations are considered pragmatic language milestones, because they demonstrate that infants recognize their own capacity to connect with other people through making noise. Many children this young are already capable of maintaining joint attention with a parent by looking at an object in which a parent has expressed interest, engaging in social interactions even without words. Shortly afterwards, infants begin to recognize that they can use nonverbal cues to learn language and may begin to point at new objects in hopes that adults will provide labels for them. Similarly, children may hold out their hands as a signal that they want to be picked up and then begin to accompany this gesture with the word *up*! This pairing of verbal and nonverbal expression is an aspect of pragmatic language that persists over time, as adults often convey the meaning of their words through facial expression and body language, as well as through the tone and literal meaning of their words.

Between the ages of one and two years, young children may begin to use a few social words (like *hi, bye-bye, please,* and *thank you*) in conversation, and to recognize that *wh-* questions (that ask about the *who, what, when, where, why,* and *how* of a story) require a response. As a child begins to use two-word telegraphic speech, the repertoire of phrases she uses to get her needs met will continue to grow. Between the ages of two and three, toddlers will begin to use language to express emotion (as you observed when reading about Jamie and her mother's conversation earlier in this chapter). Children of this age will also begin to use language in more creative ways and find a means of getting attention through language, like by beginning sentences with an exclamation such as "Hey!"

As pragmatic skills continue to develop, children begin to focus not only on their own words, but also to convey that they understand the words of others. Between the ages of three and four years, children begin to indicate that they are listening to what their partner in conversation is saying by increasing their own short utterances like "mm hmm" and "okay." They can carry on a dialogue for approximately three turns and maintain appropriate eye contact during conversation. From this point forward, children continue to build their pragmatic capacities, engaging in longer reciprocal conversations and answering questions promptly and completely.

What Is the Role of Parents in the Development of Pragmatic Language Skills?

As we said earlier, some of the important early pragmatic skills that children develop include the ability to make requests, refusals, assertions, and denials. More sophisticated skills involve understanding metaphorical language, idioms, and social situations. Many children require some level of assistance to make sense of the social and idiomatic aspects of language. For example, as part of Jamie's job as a school psychologist, she counseled students who have social and emotional difficulties. Many students with whom she worked, for a variety of reasons, had not developed the pragmatic language skills we would expect a child of their age to exhibit. Jamie will always recall the day that two middle school boys

ran to her office during their recess, pounded on the door, and franti-
cally asked, "How can you fix a sandwich? Why would a sandwich ever
be broken?" At lunch, when explaining why he wasn't going to wait in
the line with them for hot lunch, a friend of theirs had mentioned that
his mother had fixed him a sandwich to bring to school that day. Totally
unfamiliar with that idiom, the boys racked their brains to try and make
sense of what they had heard. Although these boys both had adequately
developed semantic skills and could formally define *fix*, it was extremely
difficult for them to understand how this word could be used informally
to mean something other than *mend* or *repair*.

Some children understand language very literally, but most children
begin to understand that we use language in less concrete ways as well,
through exposure to these terms and conversation about them. Even
though many six-year-olds would not be able to verbalize clearly why
we might say that someone has "fixed us a sandwich," most would be
able to use this phrase functionally, knowing that—in this context—
fix is a synonym for *make*. As we said earlier, children develop oral language skills through imitation and modeling, so a child who is asked if
he wants someone to fix him a sandwich will likely ask someone to fix
him a sandwich in the future. You can help your child make sense of the
pragmatic aspects of language by encouraging him to think about how
we use words, saying something like, "Hey, isn't it funny that we talk
about fixing a car and fixing a sandwich? What's the difference between
doing those two things?" By talking about this term together, your child
may begin to realize that, in both cases, someone is putting something
together, although in very different ways. At any age, helping your child
reason about new and strange pragmatic phrases can make their meaning clearer.

Developing Pragmatic Skills: How Can I Support My Child's Individual Needs?

While it may surprise you to read that some middle school students still
struggle to understand colloquial or social language, it is perhaps more
expected that young children will have questions about unfamiliar and

nonsensical phrases that they hear for the first time. Because pragmatic language skills are social in nature, it stands to reason that children learn these skills through their interactions with other people. Although the same can be said of all language skills, the rules of social language are even more arbitrary than the rules that govern other aspects of language. Parents are the first guides that children have to help them navigate the social world. Being a guide involves not only interacting with your child, but also practicing social skills and language with him, as well as teaching him idioms and other phrases that require explanation.

It may be appropriate to explain social situations and social language in a very direct way with your child. Beyond defining terms like *fix* in multiple ways, you may focus on explaining to your child how to engage in everyday social interaction and then helping him understand the nuances at a later date. For example, when one of Anne's friends was young, her parents instructed her to answer the phone by saying, "Hello. How are you?" For years, she blurted out these two parts of the greeting immediately upon picking up the phone. It was only when she was in later elementary school that she began to understand it was important to pause between these two statements and to find out who was on the phone before asking how that person was feeling. The prompts you give your child will become more sophisticated as he gains the skills to understand what others are thinking and feeling.

It is important to note again, although we have said it before, that children develop at different rates, and that it is natural to see individual differences in the speed at which children acquire these particular skills. The age guidelines discussed in this section are rough approximations of when children are expected to exhibit particular skills and are not set in stone. However, if your child does not exhibit interest in conversing or maintaining eye contact with others, or has a great deal of difficulty expressing his or her needs, consult with your pediatrician. Children with delayed pragmatic language skills are at risk for a number of other issues, and early intervention is the best way to alleviate future problems.

What Activities and Strategies Can I Use to Support Pragmatic Language Development?

Why would we expect a child to understand what we mean when we say that it is "raining cats and dogs" or that someone is "pulling your leg?" Virtually the only way to help someone understand these types of linguistic riddles is to familiarize them with such phrases and to help them understand that not all language is meant to be interpreted literally. It takes years for children to recognize that many words have multiple meanings, some of which are context or culture dependent or metaphorical. To make sense of the phrase "every cloud has a silver lining," one cannot interpret "silver lining" literally. Through conversation, a parent needs to unpack such a phrase, explaining that a "cloud" is a big bad thing, but a "silver lining" is a small nice thing that comes along with it. For example, a parent might say, "Remember how miserable you felt when you got the flu last month? That was really awful. But you and I were so happy that we got to finish reading the big *Winnie the Pooh* book together, and that was a real silver lining!" The following strategies can help encourage these types of conversations about the meaning of words and how to use them in social contexts.

Labeling and elaborating during shared book reading. Beginning to make sense of social language and idiomatic phrases adds new threads to a child's semantic web. Being able to interpret these types of statements accurately, however, helps children not only understand many of the conversations that take place around them, but also a wide variety of books. As you read with your child, you can help her decipher some of these phrases that may be puzzling to her.

Sometimes it is not the content of the book that helps children develop these pragmatic language skills. Instead, they acquire them through having the opportunity to spend time talking with an adult, particularly when they get the chance to discuss new and sophisticated topics, instead of run-of-the-mill issues. Children's books, even those written for very young children, often include conflicts and dilemmas that need to be resolved. Using these books as springboards for conversations about how to handle a bully or what to do to make a sad person feel better is a natural way to broach these topics with your child. Books can also provide you with an excellent way to prepare your child for new experiences—there are wonderful stories that talk about the first day of school or camp, becoming a big brother or sister, as well as going to events as varied as parties and funerals. These stories can serve as scripts that help children learn what might be expected of them in these situations and find out that their questions and concerns about these experiences are totally normal. Books can be great avenues into talking about these social issues because they provide a way to decipher idioms and discuss tough issues—like being unkind or scared—without having to talk about personal examples. We will talk more about this idea in the chapter on the social and emotional benefits of reading together at the end of the book.

Labeling and elaborating throughout the day. Every day, we all use social language and encounter complicated social situations. Helping your child make sense of these situations, through conversation or acting them out together, can be very beneficial. If your son is nervous about going to a birthday party where he won't know many people, you can set up a fake birthday party at your house—attended by yourself, other family members, and some stuffed animals. Helping him strategize about what to say when he walks in, how to pick a chair to sit in, and how to wish the host happy birthday may make him feel much more comfortable about the day.

It can also be helpful to model this type of behavior for your child. If you have a difficult conversation coming up at work, writing down some talking points and practicing what you want to say with your spouse, partner, or a friend can demonstrate to your child that we all need to work on our pragmatic skills from time to time. Similarly, sharing the ways that you have misunderstood idiomatic language can help your child recognize how quirky and funny the English language can be. Exemplifying how we solve problems by using language "out loud" within hearing distance of our children can be an extremely effective tool for teaching them some of the nuances of pragmatic language.

Even very young children display early pragmatic language skills when engaging with others. You can begin to help your child develop pragmatic language skills through the types of activities listed in Table 1-4. Many

TABLE 1-4. PRAGMATIC DEVELOPMENT: STRATEGIES FOR PARENTS

What to Do	How to Do It	Age(s)
Elaborate on Figures of Speech During Shared Reading	As you read with your child, help her decipher any puzzling phrases by encouraging her to think about nonliteral meaning. For example, say something like, "Isn't it funny we talk about fixing a car and fixing a sandwich? What's the difference between those two things?" By discussing this concept, your child may realize that the same word has different meanings in different contexts.	
Choose Books Focused on Social Interactions	Read books that focus on social situations relevant to your child. Picking these types of books will give you the opportunity to engage in a conversation about these topics. For example, books about the first day of school, how to handle a bully, or how to be a good friend can allow your child to express his feelings about the subject. You can then have a conversation with him about different solutions and what to expect.	
Talk about and Act Out Social Situations	Help your child get ready for unfamiliar social situations (e.g., starting school, going to her first sleep-over party). First, talk with her to find out if she has any questions or concerns. Then, explain what will happen at this event. You can also act out the scenario so she can practice how to behave in this new situation.	

What to Do	How to Do It	Age(s)
Model Coping Strategies	Model the coping strategies you use in stressful situations so your child can observe how you deal with them. For example, if you are nervous about having a new boss at work, you can let your child know how you will approach this situation. For example, you might engage in thinking aloud and problem solving, and then practice what you want to say to this new boss with your spouse, partner, or a friend, while your child is present.	
Play Pretend Games	Play pretend games with your child, taking these opportunities to embellish upon the social aspects of language. If your child is pretending to be the cashier at a store, you can remind him to greet you at the beginning of your exchange and to say "Thank you very much!" at the end. Pretending to talk over the telephone is another fun way to help your child practice structuring a conversation.	
Act Out Challenging Situations	Make a specific point to act out situations that are more challenging for your child. You can say, "Remember when you got really angry at your brother last week because he wouldn't share with you? Let's pretend that I'm him, and you can remind me that these toys are for both of us. Maybe you can ask me to share this doll after I've played with it for five more minutes!"	

continues

TABLE 1-4. CONTINUED

What to Do	How to Do It	Age(s)
Write a Script & Act It Out	Develop oral or written scripts for the situations that you act out. For instance, a script for going to a birthday party might include (1) saying hello to the birthday girl, (2) saying hello to the other guests and deciding who to sit near, (3) singing "Happy Birthday" and sharing cake, and (4) saying thank you at the end of the party. These scripts can help a child know what to anticipate in a new social situation, and acting them out together will make your child more comfortable when she is actually faced with that situation.	
Explain Idioms	Read books that explicitly explain the meaning of idioms, like Marvin Terban's *In a Pickle: And Other Funny Idioms* and Fred Gywnne's *A Little Pigeon Toad*.	

of these activities are playful and interactive—you don't need to start giving your child formal lessons in pragmatic language development! All of these skills are learned best when they are infused into daily life and games.

Conclusion: The Bigger Picture

A recap. In sum, we hope that this chapter has helped you recognize how much your child is already learning everyday, through the conversations you have while reading, in the car, and over supper. With increased attention to the natural conversations that you have regularly, you can focus on deliberately enhancing your child's vocabulary, awareness of word choice and sentence structure, and ability to use language socially. Not all at once, of course! These ideas, all of which are grounded in empirical research, are intended to be used in meaningful and fun ways. Not all of these skills should be used at the same time nor addressed in every conversation. With this knowledge, however, you can pick and choose, in a way that makes sense to you in the moment, when to expand on what your child has said or to make a correction. Remember that asking questions and making comments, during book reading or conversation, is an excellent way to give your child several opportunities to hear the same word said, defined, and put into context.

> Not all of these skills should be used at the same time nor addressed in every conversation. With this knowledge, however, you can pick and choose, in a way that makes sense to you in the moment, when to expand on what your child has said or make a correction. Remember that asking questions and making comments, during book reading or conversation, is an excellent way to give your child several opportunities to hear the same word said, defined, and put into context.

Most children fast-map a new word after hearing it just once, but repeated exposure enriches their understanding of that word and broadens their semantic web. Think of your job as helping to build that web so wide that it begins to connect with another web, and then another, until your child's vocabulary becomes crowded with new ideas. If you use the strategies outlined in this chapter, you have the skills to spin this type of web.

Where do we go from here? Remember, there are three levels of language that are important for us to consider when discussing the process of language development and its relationship to later reading skills.[30] *Translexical* aspects of language are those that help us make meaning across words, *lexical* aspects of language refer to the meaning of individual words, and *sublexical* aspects of language include awareness of parts of words. We have talked mainly about the first two levels of language within this chapter. We talked about the levels that begin this pyramid, translexical and lexical aspects of language, because this strong foundation helps children engage with others and prepare to be readers.

Children learn to process both small and large chunks of language, whether this information is presented verbally or in writing. When you think about teaching your child to read, you most likely think about the *translexical* aspects of language development—making meaning across words—that allow children to make sense of phrases and sentences. Of course, doing so also requires *lexical* awareness, or recognition of words themselves. We hope that this chapter has helped you think of new strategies, like elaborating on stories you have read, to support translexical understanding, and new strategies, like naming synonyms, to support lexical understanding.

And at the most nuanced level, children also need to develop *sublexical* skills, or the awareness of parts of words. These word parts include syllables, some grammatical morphemes, individual speech sounds or phonemes in words, and the word's *onset* (the initial consonant sound in a word, for example the /c/ in *cat*) and the word's *rime* (the vowel and remaining parts of the word, for example the /at/ in *cat*). Throughout the book we will denote these speech sounds by putting a slanted bracket around the pattern, like /a/ or /at/. In the following chapter, we will discuss the development of these sublexical skills in great depth, because the development of phonological awareness is a crucial prerequisite skill for reading development. As you keep reading, you will learn more about how children use all three of these levels of language simultaneously and how all three are necessary components of reading success.

TABLE 1-5. TECH TIPS FOR PARENTS: ORAL LANGUAGE

Tech Tips: Oral Language

Listed below are several tips explaining how you can use technology to support oral language development. But before you look them over, we also want to provide a reminder that technology use can also negatively affect oral language development. How? Parental access to technology, like the smartphones that have become so ubiquitous, can decrease opportunities for interaction and shared learning.[35] Distracted parents miss out on chances to expand on what a child has just said or to ask questions about what is happening in the moment. Similarly, the rise of online searching often means that when a child asks a question, an adult goes to the Internet to get the correct answer as quickly as possible, instead of launching an investigation with the child to learn more about the broader topic. The studies we discussed in the Preface found a negative association between the amount of time children spend using technology and their vocabulary size.

What to Do	How to Do It	Age(s)
Listen to Audiobooks in the Car and Then Talk About Them	Listening to audiobooks in the car (or while doing chores) can allow you an opportunity to ask many of the same questions you would ask during a dialogic reading session. This is a great example of when technology can *supplement* what you already do with your child, because most families spend their long car rides doing things other than reading together. Anything you do to make your time in the car more interactive can facilitate language development. If your children normally watch DVDs in the car, with headphones on, then getting everyone to agree to watch the same movie with the audio being played throughout the car gives you a wonderful opportunity to build language skills. Listening to audiobooks is also valuable because it allows your child to be exposed to vocabulary words that may be more sophisticated than the words in a book he could read independently.	

continues

TABLE 1-5. CONTINUED

What to Do	How to Do It	Age(s)
Use Technology Tools to Create Semantic Webs	Online tools like *The Visual Thesaurus* (www.thevisualthesaurus.com) create semantic webs for you, which you can use to expand upon the brainstorming you and your child have already done, to see what words you can add to your own webs. Additionally, many basic word processing programs and tools like PowerPoint allow you to create graphics, so that you can make your own semantic webs electronically. If your child is excited by chances to use the computer or tablet, it may be easier to encourage her to create a semantic web electronically than by hand.	
Get Online Practice with Syntactic Skills	Although we highly encourage syntax learning just through everyday exposure to language, there may come a time when you feel like your child needs more direct practice understanding sentence structure. Because practicing this skill can be one of the drier ones, applications like *Syntax City* (from www.smartyearsapps.com) can make the process fun.	
If Watching TV and Movies, Make Selections Carefully and Interact with Your Child as You Watch Together	Television and movies provide us with vivid examples of what different social situations look like, and—if selected appropriately—can help children learn about how to act in many different scenarios. If you are letting your child watch television, be sure to stay aware of what is happening on the screen and talk with your child about what is happening in particular scenes.	

What to Do	How to Do It	Age(s)
Sing Songs	Listening to music helps children build many important language and literacy skills, from developing a sense of rhythm to processing small and large chunks of sound (like phonemes and sentences). Listening to music can help children make sense of language at many different levels—translexical, lexical, and sublexical. The words that children learn while singing a song can help build vocabulary and comprehension. Whether we are talking about old technology (a record or cassette player) or new technology (using Spotify to play songs on an iPod), these tools can help children access material that may motivate them to learn words.	

TABLE 1-6. ENGLISH LANGUAGE LEARNER TIPS FOR PARENTS: ORAL LANGUAGE

English Language Learner Tips: Oral Language

As we discussed throughout this chapter, oral language skills refer to the many different components of spoken words that help us understand others (our receptive skills) and share our own thoughts (expressive skills). As a parent of an English Language Learner (ELL), you have probably asked yourself how oral language development is affected by exposure to two languages (L1, her first language, and L2, the new language she is learning). Research suggests that being raised bilingually supports the development of important cognitive skills that will benefit your child throughout her lifespan, including benefits in the area of attention, working memory, metalinguistic awareness (or the awareness of different parts of language and how they fit together), and the ability to represent symbols and abstractions mentally.[36] However, how bilingual children acquire and develop language varies, depending on their environment and exposure to both languages,[37] and there may be times in your child's development when it appears that she is developing language more slowly than her monolingual peers. Despite this perception, when taking both of her languages into account, she is making good progress when compared to her monolingual peers. This is because children who are developing more than one language are learning more than children who are acquiring only one language![38] As a parent, you can support your bilingual child's development of oral language skills using the following tips.

What to Do	How to Do It	Age(s)
Build Vocabulary in Both L1 and L2	Build your child's learning of new vocabulary words in both L1 and L2. There may be some ideas that can be expressed more eloquently in one language, and that are difficult to translate to another language. By speaking two languages, your child has a richer repertoire to choose words from when trying to express a new idea. Play synonym and antonym games in both languages.	

What to Do	How to Do It	Age(s)
Anticipate the Blending of Two Languages	Bilingual individuals may use two languages in the same conversation, an act called "code switching".[39] For example, a Spanish-speaking child who is learning English may say, "*Abuela, este es mi favorite book,*" blending the vocabulary of both languages. This is a common step on the path to full bilingualism for both children and adults. Although you want to model proper vocabulary and syntax, you don't need to correct each misstep your child makes.	
Notice Pragmatic Differences Between L1 and L2	Promote social interaction with friends who speak both languages to help your child learn the cultural norms for how language is used in social situations. For example, conversational roles such as taking turns and making eye contact as well as how to address authority figures like teachers may differ between two cultures. Give your child more time or more interaction with English language speakers to become familiar with the unique, social aspects of the English language.	
Connect Words to Categories Using Both L1 and L2	A semantic web is a model for how we organize words and concepts. Categories are one way to build semantic webs. You can play verbal games with categories to help you child develop rich semantic webs. Choose categories, such as *animals, toys,* or *food,* that interest your child. Ask him to come up with as many examples that fit in that category as he can. Play this game in L1 and L2.	

continues

TABLE 1-6. CONTINUED

What to Do	How to Do It	Age(s)
Play Language Games in Both L1 and L2	Oral language develops similarly in many languages. We encourage you to use the activities and strategies we discussed in this chapter using both L1 and L2.	

Notes

1. Sénéchal, M., & LeFevre, J. (2002). Parental involvement in the development of children's reading skills: A five-year longitudinal study. *Child Development, 73*, 445–460; Sénéchal, M., Ouellette, G., & Rodney, D. (2006). The misunderstood giant: On the predictive role of early vocabulary in future reading. In D. K. Dickinson & S. B. Neuman (Vol. Eds.), *Handbook of Early Literacy Research, Vol. 2* (pp. 173–184). New York: Guilford; Sénéchal, M., & Young, L. (2008). The effect of family literacy interventions on children's acquisition of reading from Kindergarten to Grade 3: A meta-analytic review. *Review of Educational Research, 78*(4), 880–907; Neuman, S.B. & Dwyer, J. (2011). Developing vocabulary and conceptual knowledge for low-income preschoolers: A design experiment. *Journal of Literacy Research, 43*(2), 103-129.

2. Sénéchal, Ouellette, & Rodney (2006); Snow, C. E., Burns, M. S., & Griffin, P. (1998). *Preventing Reading Difficulties in Young Children*. Committee on the Prevention of Reading Difficulties in Young Children. Washington, DC: National Academy Press.

3. Pinker, S. (2008). *The Stuff of Thought*. New York: Penguin.

4. Karmiloff, K., & Karmiloff-Smith, A. (2001). *Pathways to Language: From Fetus to Adolescent*. Cambridge, MA: Harvard University Press; Neuman & Dwyer (2011).

5. Hirsch Jr., E. D., Kett, J. F., &; Trefil, J. S. (1988). *Cultural literacy: What every American needs to know*. New York: Random House Digital; ; Neuman & Dwyer (2011).

6. Hirsch Jr., E. D. (2006). *The Knowledge Deficit: Closing the Shocking Education Gap for American Children*. New York: Houghton Mifflin.

7. Lee, J. (2011). Size matters: Early vocabulary as a predictor of language and literacy competence. *Applied Psycholinguistics, 32*, 69–92.

8. This example is taken from Daniels, H., & Zemelman, S. (2004). *Subjects Matter: Every Teacher's Guide to Content-Area Reading.* Portsmouth, NH: Heinemann, p. 21.

9. Karmiloff & Karmiloff-Smith (2001).

10. Biemiller, A. (2006). Vocabulary development and instruction: A prerequisite for school learning. In D. Dickinson & S. B. Neuman (Eds.), *Handbook of Early Literacy Research* (Vol. 2, pp. 41–51). New York: Guilford.

11. Karmiloff & Karmiloff-Smith (2001).

12. Naigles, L., & Hoff-Ginsberg, E. (1998). Why are some verbs learned before other verbs? Effects on input frequency and structure on children's early verb use. *Journal of Child Language, 25,* 95–120.

13. Pease, D. M., Gleason, J. B., & Pan, B. A. (1993). Learning the meaning of words: Semantic development and beyond (pp. 115–149). In J. B. Gleason (Ed.), *The Development of Language.* New York: Macmillan.

14. Hart, B., & Risley, T. R. (1999). *The Social World of Children Learning to Talk.* Baltimore: Paul H. Brookes.

15. Scelfo, J. (2010). The risks of parenting while plugged in. *New York Times,* June 9, 2010. Retrieved from www.nytimes.com/2010/06/10/garden/10childtech.html

16. Hart & Risley (1999), p. 39.

17. Alt, M., & Plante, E. (2006). Factors that influence lexical and semantic fast mapping of young children with specific language impairment. *Journal of Speech, Language, and Hearing Research, 49*(5), 941–954; Wilkinson, K. (2007). Effect of "missing" information on fast mapping by individuals with vocabulary limitations associated with intellectual disability. *American Journal on Mental Retardation, 112*(1), 40–53.

18. Beck, I. L., McKeown, M. G., & Kucan, L. (2002). *Bringing Words to Life: Robust Vocabulary Instruction.* New York: Guilford.

19. Biemiller (2006).

20. Cunningham, A. E., & Zibulsky, J. (2010). Tell me a story: The benefits of shared book reading. In D. K. Dickinson & S. B. Neuman (Eds.), *Handbook of Early Literacy Research:Vol. 3* (pp. 396–411). New York: Guilford.

21. Ard, L. M., & Beverly, B. L. (2004). Preschool word learning during joint book reading: Effect of adult questions and comments. *Communication Disorders Quarterly, 26*(1), 17–28.

22. Biemiller. (2006).

23. Deckner, D. F., Adamson, L. B., & Bakeman, R. (2006). Child and maternal contributions to shared reading: Effects on language and literacy development. *Applied Developmental Psychology, 27*(1), 31–41.

24. McKeown, M. G., & Beck, I. L. (2006). Encouraging young children's language interactions with stories. In D. Dickinson & S. B. Neuman (Eds.), *Handbook of Early Literacy Research* Vol. II, (pp. 281–294). New York: Guilford.

25. Baker, L., Scher, D., & Mackler, K. (1997). Home and family influences on motivation for reading. *Educational Psychologist, 32*(2), 69–82.; Baker, L., Mackler, K., Sonnenschein, S., & Serpell, R. (2001). Parents' interactions with their first grade children during storybook reading and relations with subsequent home reading activity and reading achievement. *Journal of School Psychology, 38*, 1–24; Home and family influences on motivations for reading. *Educational Psychologist, 32*(2), 69–82; Klauda, S. L., & Wigfield, A. (2012). Relations of perceived parent and friend support for recreational reading with children's reading motivations. *Journal of Literacy research, 44*(3), 3–44; Sonnenschein, S., & Munsterman, K. (2002). The influence of home-based reading interactions on 5-year-olds' reading motivations and early literacy development. *Early Childhood Research Quarterly, 17*(3), 318–337; Weigel, D. J., Martin, S. S., & Bennett, K. K. (2006). Contributions of the home literacy environment to preschool-aged children's emerging literacy and language skills. *Early Child Development and Care, 176*(3–4), 357–378.

26. Golinkoff, R., Hirsh-Pasek, K., Cauley, K. & Gordon, L. (1987). The eyes have it: Lexical and syntactical comprehension in a new paradigm. *Journal of Child Language, 14*, 23–45.

27. Adapted from Gard, A., Gilman, L., & Gordon, J. (2012). *Speech and Language Development Chart*, 3rd ed. Austin, TX: Pro-Ed.

28. Tager-Flusberg, H. (1993). Putting words together: Morphology and syntax in the preschool years (pp. 151–193). In J. B. Gleason (Ed.), *The Development of Language*. New York: Macmillan.

29. Ibid.

30. Berninger, V. W. (1994). *Reading and Writing Acquisition: A Developmental Neuropsychological Perspective*. Madison, WI: Brown & Benchmark.

31. Reese, E., & Cox, A. (1999). Quality of adult book reading affects children's emergent literacy. *Developmental Psychology, 35*(1), 20–28.

32. Slobodkina, E. (1968). *Caps for Sale: A Tale of a Peddler, Some Monkeys and Their Monkey Business*. New York: Harper Collins.

33. Mayer, M. (1986). *There's a Nightmare in My Closet*. New York: Dial.

34. Soman, D., & Davis, J. (2009). *Ladybug Girl and Bumblebee Boy*. New York: Dial.

35. Turkle, S. (2012). *Alone Together: Why We Expect More from Technology and Less from Each Other*. New York: Basic Books.

36. Adesope, O. O., Lavin, T., Thompson, T., & Ungerleider, C. (2010). A systematic review and meta-analysis of the cognitive correlates of bilingualism. *Review of Educational Research, 80*(2), 207–245.

37. Hoff, E. (2009). *Language Development*, 5th ed. Belmont, CA: Wadsworth.

38. Ibid.

39. Cromdal, J. (2005). Bilingual order in collaborative word processing: On creating an English text in Swedish. *Journal of Pragmatics: An Interdisciplinary Journal of Language Studies, 37*(3), 329–353.

Chapter 2

Emergent Literacy

The Roots of Reading

As you now know from chapter 1, where you learned about the importance of early language development for later reading success, even before entering kindergarten, children develop concepts, behaviors, and attitudes that are the developmental foundation for later skilled reading and writing.[1] Like the roots of a plant, these early skills are critical for supporting and nurturing future development. This is still true even though these skills may look different than the final product they produce, which is "reading" in the conventional sense of sounding out and understanding printed words. Although some of these skills involve looking at letters and words in print, others—like the language skills we already discussed—often do not. These varied "roots" of reading development are often collectively referred to as *emergent literacy skills,* because they emerge simultaneously and are the first visible evidence that your child is beginning the process of learning to read. Like the roots of a tree or plant, most people don't pay much attention to these skills, noticing only when a flower pops up out of the ground. But taking a closer look reveals that each root serves a specific function, and each works together to help the flower blossom. In this chapter, we want to tell you more about the skills that need to be in place before all the conventional reading skills can be developed.

A great deal of research has been dedicated to identifying which of these foundational skills are most important for reading success,[2] and it is these most important emergent literacy skills that we discuss in this chapter. An essential tool for "breaking the code" of reading is phonological awareness (the ability to perceive and manipulate sounds), which includes skills such as being able to rhyme.[3] In chapter 1, we mentioned that there are three levels of language that children learn to perceive and think about: meaning across words (*translexical*), identification of words themselves (*lexical*), and sounds within words (*sublexical*). Sublexical phonological awareness is a primary focus of this chapter, and being able to manipulate the sounds in words eventually helps children recognize that the letters they practice writing and the alphabet song they sing have meaning. We talk about reading as "breaking the code" because reading requires a key, or a set of tools to use when deciphering words and phrases. Children break the code when they can match letters to sounds, and phonological awareness comprises half of the key they need to do that.

The language-based skills that foster reading development are not its only hidden roots. Concepts of print, another important element of emergent literacy, allow children to effectively interact with books and print and include skills such as understanding that the words in books have meaning.[4] Through familiarity with books acquired from shared book reading sessions or by observing a parent or older sibling engaged with a great story, children learn how to look like readers. They know where to look for information—glancing at the title page, concentrating on the words as well as the pictures in their books, and recognizing the power of the written words "The End" on the last page even before they can decode them independently.

There is one other skill that we will discuss in this chapter: alphabetic knowledge, which includes being aware of the relationship between sounds and letters that represent them, is one of the most significant predictors of later literacy.[5] In contrast to the other emergent literacy skills we have just discussed, this important root of reading development is not hidden out of view. Alphabetic knowledge is a skill that most people already see as clearly connected with reading success. As children acquire alphabetic knowledge, mapping letters to the sounds they represent, they begin to "break the code" of reading by using their developing skills in all of the areas outlined above. The English language is not a simple code to break, though, and we will tell you more throughout the chapter about the process that children go through as they learn to decipher simple and then complex words.

When all of these skills develop, we see the beginnings of a flower sprouting from the ground, because the roots have grown strong and provided all the nutrients necessary for the flower to blossom. This chapter will provide more detail regarding each of these key building blocks of emergent literacy and the ways in which each supports the future development of reading skills. These are the basic skills that your child needs to acquire to become a reader. We will talk in more depth at the end of the chapter about research that highlights the importance of these emergent literacy skills, but want to share with you now that the skills described in this chapter lead to growth in different areas of reading than the skills described in the chapter on oral language. Both are very important, but the conversational skills we discussed in the previous chapter may seem more natural to you. The skills discussed in this chapter require you to focus on nitty-gritty aspects of reading, like letters and sounds. Although you might not think of yourself as the type of parent who would coax your child into this type of "unnatural" activity, children can take pleasure in and get very excited about acquiring this new knowledge. For that reason, in addition to sharing details about the developmental course of the key emergent literacy skills, we will also provide you with a number of fun and engaging research-based strategies and activities that you can use to promote your child's foundational skills throughout the day, including playtime and errands. We will also provide specific information about how your child's skills in each of these areas develop over time, so that you can keep track of your child's progress. By using a range of strategies to support your child's emergent literacy development and understanding how these skills grow, you can help your child build emergent literacy skills and inspire a love for reading that will help propel him or her to future success as a lifelong reader and learner.

Phonological Awareness

When Anne was a kindergarten teacher, she spent a great deal of time encouraging her students to play with words. The activities they completed in her classroom did not feel like work to them, and in fact, were often the same types of activities the children played with their parents at home or in the car. Anne introduced these activities in her classroom because she knew they would facilitate skill development, and parents independently used them at home because their kids just found them to be fun. Many parents, over the years, told Anne that their children loved to sing songs such as "The Name Game" ("Ella, ella bo-bella, banana-fana fo-fella, me-mi-mo-mella..."), but that they—as parents—had no idea that they were doing more than making up a silly song when they chanted it with their children. Without even knowing it, these parents were helping their children take early steps toward reading development. As children sing such songs, clap the syllables in the word *di-no-saur,* or notice that *pickle* and *pepper* start with the same sound, they are building an important foundation in literacy.

What Is Phonological Awareness?

By experimenting and playing with the sounds of language, children are developing their **phonological awareness.** Phonological awareness is the ability to perceive and manipulate sounds. As language development progresses to include mastery of sublexical skills, children must focus on the complex task of paying attention to the *sounds* of speech rather than concentrating on the meaning of speech. For example, when the word *river* is broken down into syllables, *ri* and *ver* have no meaning on their own, but being able to break the word down into its component sounds is essential to future reading success. Fortunately, phonological

> **PHONOLOGICAL AWARENESS**
> The ability to perceive and manipulate sounds.

awareness abilities exist on a continuum, from simple skills, such as recognizing individual words within spoken sentences (which is still a lexical skill), to very complex sublexical skills, such as being able to perceive and manipulate individual sounds in words. Therefore children are initially able to use their broader oral language skills, which involve knowledge of words, to make sense of the cognitive gymnastics involved in more simple phonological awareness tasks (e.g., *cup + cake = cupcake*) before moving to very complex tasks that solely involve individual sounds (e.g., /k/ + /ŭ/ + /p/ = *cup*).[6]

You may be thinking that being the ability to separate out all of these individual sounds, like the three sounds that make up the word *cup,* would be difficult for a child who hasn't yet started to read or spell. But pure phonological awareness does not involve the knowledge of letters. In other words, it is important for children to initially develop knowledge of word sounds and sound structures in a separate context from their developing knowledge of letters, meaning that simple phonological awareness activities should not involve printed materials, although more advanced phonological awareness activities can include print. Like the language games you learned about in chapter 1, you can play early phonological awareness games with your child in the car, while waiting on line, or in the bathtub—the location doesn't matter because you do not need to have any materials with you. Phonological awareness games only require your voice, because they are oral language activities—no letters or writing required. This brings up an important distinction between phonological awareness and **phonics** (the alphabetic principle), a topic we'll talk about in depth later in this chapter. Whereas phonological awareness is the ability to perceive and manipulate *sounds,* phonics instruction fosters the ability to connect the sounds of spoken language to printed letters. One way to discern the difference is that instruction in phonological awareness can be done in the dark, whereas phonics instruction requires light in order to see letters and letter patterns. Again, phonological

PHONICS
An approach to teaching beginning reading that emphasizes letter–sound relationships as the path to efficient word recognition.

awareness is, in essence, an oral language skill, whereas phonics involves printed text—two separate roots that grow together over time.

Why Is Phonological Awareness Important for Future Reading Development?

The significance of phonological awareness has surfaced in the research field only over the last few decades and is still in the process of becoming mainstream knowledge. Although we spent much of the last chapter describing how to maximize the development of oral language, its development is largely natural, such that all children are hard-wired to learn to understand and express themselves with spoken language. In contrast, reading and writing entail understanding the relationship between language and printed texts. Once all the roots of early reading take hold, the child who recognized the three sounds in *cup* would also need to realize that those sounds—/k/ + /ŭ/ + /p/ – are represented by letters *c* + *u* + *p* when the word is written down. In order to connect language and printed texts, children need to develop conscious awareness of the structures that underlie oral language. Therefore, the development of phonological awareness is instrumental in helping children achieve the extraordinary challenge of understanding this mapping between language and printed text, learning to write, and learning to read.[7]

After children become aware that language is something that can be analyzed, they begin to recognize how language is structured and can be manipulated at more and more fine-grained units of language (words, then syllables, then onsets and rimes, and finally phonemes, the smallest unit of language; we will discuss this in more detail shortly). This awareness supports them as they are simultaneously confronted with the task of understanding how each level of language is represented *in print*. Developing this sophisticated awareness of language structures, and its connection with print, enables children to "break the code" and understand that words are composed of letters that represent sounds. In other words, promoting phonological awareness in the early years of children's lives helps them to understand that words are made up of smaller sounds and develop a good understanding of these sounds of language so that they can eventually connect printed symbols (for example, *B*) to the corresponding sounds (for example, /b/), and in turn acquire the ability to decode or read words.[8]

> **Children who have well-developed phonological awareness are much more likely to learn to read quickly and be good readers over time.**

In addition to the role that phonological awareness plays in supporting children's ability to break the code, phonological awareness also plays an ongoing role in children's attempts to read and spell every word they encounter early in their formal reading career.[9] Imagine a child in the beginning of elementary school who comes across the word *ham* in a book. The child's phonological awareness may have supported his knowledge that this printed word represents sounds in language, and he may also know that the letter *h* says /h/, the letter *a* says /ă/, and the letter *m* says /m/. However, if the child's phonological awareness is not yet well developed, he may be unable to blend, or put together, those sounds, as needed to determine that the printed word says *ham*. Even though he may be able to identify each of the sounds in this word, because smoothly blending them into a coherent whole is too difficult for him, he will be unable to completely break the code and make meaning out of that printed word.

Having poorly developed phonological awareness not only makes decoding printed text difficult, but it also makes the act of writing and spelling (encoding speech to print) difficult. Imagine that the same child now wants to write a story about a big dog. Despite his understanding that words represent spoken sounds and knowledge of all the letter–sound correspondences for the letters he needs to write, the child will not even be able to start his story if he is unable to segment, or break apart, the sound /b/ from the beginning of the word *big*.

> **Without well-developed phonological awareness, receiving the common suggestion to "sound it out" will make little sense to a child who is attempting to read or spell words.**

Although he may know that he needs to put letters down on the page to tell his story, his inability to isolate the /b/ sound will keep him from getting started. In fact, without well-developed phonological awareness, receiving the common suggestion to "sound it out" will make little sense to a child who is attempting to read or spell words.

Overall, children who have well-developed phonological awareness are much more likely to learn to read quickly and to be good readers over time than children who struggle to play with the sounds of language.[10] Furthermore, children with the most well-developed phonological awareness at the start of kindergarten are likely to continue to have the most well developed phonological awareness and reading skills through-out school, whereas those with the most poorly developed phonological awareness at school entry are likely to consistently lag behind their peers in phonological awareness and reading.[11] In fact, weaknesses in phono-logical awareness are at the core of reading difficulties, including dys-lexia.[12] Given that phonological awareness is one of the *most* significant skills needed for your child to develop beginning reading and spelling skills, it is critical that parents do all they can to cultivate phonological awareness in time for children to take full advantage of the formal read-ing instruction they will receive in elementary school.[13] Of course, if chil-dren do have difficulties in elementary school, many effective strategies exist to help develop phonological awareness and hence reading skills,[14] but the development of phonological awareness is more flexible during the early years before elementary school.[15] That is, with appropriate sup-port, preschool-aged children with weaker than average phonological awareness can get back on track at a much quicker pace.

How Does a Child's Phonological Awareness Develop Over Time?

Regardless of their age and skill level, supporting the development of phonological awareness with fun and developmentally appropriate activ-ities will help all children progress toward learning to read.[16] To help you select activities that are most appropriate for your child, you'll need to consider how phonological awareness develops. Overall, children's

TABLE 2-1. LEVELS OF PHONOLOGICAL AWARENESS

Skill Level	Description	Example
Word Awareness	Sentences are made up of words.	*I + want + milk =* *I want milk.*
	Compound words are made up of smaller words.	*pop + corn = popcorn*
Syllable Awareness	Words are made up of syllables.	*nap + kin = napkin*
Onset–rime Awareness	Syllables and one-syllable words are broken into a part that precedes the vowel (onset) and the remainder.	/f/ + *ork = fork*
Phoneme Awareness	Words are broken into individual sounds.	/f/ + /ĭ/ + /sh/ = *fish*

awareness of the structure of language develops along a continuum, moving from large to increasingly smaller segments of language. For additional insight into how activities can look across this developmental continuum, refer to Table 2-1 for numerous examples of phonological awareness strategies parents can use with their children.

As children advance along these levels of the phonological awareness continuum (word awareness, syllable awareness, onset–rime awareness, phoneme awareness), they do not need to fully master a certain level before progressing to the next; rather, phonological awareness of different levels can be developed simultaneously.[17] Similarly, no matter where children's initial skill levels fall along the continuum, they can benefit from a range of phonological awareness activities.[18] Therefore, to help a child make progress *along* the continuum, parents can select various activities that seem to meet their child's needs.

To develop children's skills *within* each level, parents can also vary the difficulty level of the activities and strategies they use.[19] You can scaffold your child by alternating between activities that will be fairly simple for her to complete, giving her a chance to show off her well-developed

TABLE 2-2. TYPES OF PHONOLOGICAL AWARENESS ACTIVITIES

Type of Task	Description	Example
Identifying	Counting or identifying units of language	"Let's clap for each word in the song: *row, row, row your boat . . .* "
Blending	Putting together units of language to form a meaningful whole	"What word am I trying to say: *di* – (pause) *–no–* (pause) *–saur*?"
Segmenting	Taking apart a meaningful whole into smaller units, which may be abstract	"Tell me all the sounds you hear in the word *cat*."
Deleting	Taking a unit of language away from a meaningful whole	"Say *rainbow* without *rain*."

skills, and initiating activities that are more challenging and that enable you to praise her for her effort and development. Pick tasks that will allow her to gain new skills on this continuum, but at a slow enough rate that she isn't frustrated by being asked questions that go over her head. The hierarchy of task difficulty (described in more depth in Table 2-2) is the same for each level of awareness, and moves from identifying, to blending, to segmenting, and then deleting sounds.

Word awareness. As we mentioned earlier, young children initially focus mostly on the meaning of language. When children shift their focus to the sound structure of language, it is easiest to first become aware of individual words in sentences or compound words, because these units of language are still, in fact, meaningful.[20] For instance, young children often hear meaningful sentences as one long string (for example, *Let'sreadthebook*) and think that meaning is conveyed by the whole string as a unit, without being attentive to the meaning of the individual words. Even though a child might know that "Let's read the book" describes the act of sitting down together to page through a story, he wouldn't be able to identify the subject of the sentence, or know that "read" is the action being described. As phonological awareness becomes more advanced, though, children can become aware that sentences are made up of individual words that also have meanings. Similarly, children learn that compound words (for example, *airplane*) can be broken down into individual words, and the units of language that remain are still meaningful (for example, *air + plane*).

Although word awareness as a whole is the easiest level on the phonological awareness continuum, we recommend that parents vary the difficulty level of the activities and strategies they use to develop their child's skills *within* this level.[21] Table 2-3 provides some examples of identifying, blending, segmenting, and deleting tasks at the word awareness level. The words you use as part of your activities can also affect the level of difficulty for your child. It may be easier to begin by using one-syllable words for your sentences (for example, *I played with my doll*) and compounds (for example, *snowman*). Selecting words with more than one syllable (for example, *computer* or *Spiderman*) can confuse children, as they may mix up the concept of word and syllable; for instance, rather than segmenting Spiderman into *Spider – man* (which is correctly separated by words), they may segment it into *Spi – der – man* (which is first separated by syllables and then a one-syllable word). Eventually, however, it will be important that your child understand the difference between words and syllables, so using words with varying numbers of syllables can help you at that point.

Syllable awareness. Because syllables can be easily heard and made and correspond to the rhythm of our language, they can help children become attuned to the sublexical aspect of language. However, because many syllables are not meaningful on their own (for example, *basket* is meaningful, but *bas* and *ket* are not), children typically have a bit more difficulty with activities at this level than at the word awareness level.[22] Further, the concept of a syllable will be foreign to children at first, so it can be helpful for parents to explain how words are made up of parts called syllables. It will also be difficult for a child to recognize that the number of syllables in words differs between words (for example, *cat* versus *caterpillar*), so it can be helpful to draw your child's attention to this fact. In general, parents can adjust the difficulty level of syllable awareness activities for their children by (a) using words with different numbers of syllables, with more syllables being more difficult, and (b) selecting different types of tasks. Table 2-4 provides some examples of

TABLE 2-3. WORD AWARENESS EXAMPLES

	Identification
Words within Sentences	**Parent:** I'm going to clap for each word in a sentence, and then I want you to do the same. Listen... *We went to the zoo.* [While clapping for each word] **Child:** We went to the zoo. [While clapping for each word]
	Blending
Words within Sentences	**Parent:** Let's play a guessing game. I'm going to say some words and I want you to guess the sentence I'm trying to tell you. Listen... *I* (pause) *love* (pause) *pizza.* **Child:** I love pizza.
Words within Compound Words	**Parent:** What word do you get if you put together *cup* (pause) *cake?* **Child:** Cupcake.
	Segmenting
Words within Sentences	**Parent:** I'm going to say a short sentence. I want you to break apart the sentence and tell me every word you hear. Ready? *The balloons are red.* **Child:** The (pause) balloons (pause) are (pause) red.
Words within Compound Words	**Parent:** I'm going to say a compound word. I want you to break apart the compound word and tell me both words you hear. Ready? *Baseball.* **Child:** Base (pause) ball
	Deletion
Deleting the Initial Word in a Compound Word	**Parent:** Say *lunchtime.* **Child:** Lunchtime. **Parent:** Now say it without *lunch.* **Child:** Time.
Deleting the Final Word in a Compound Word	**Parent:** Say *lunchtime.* **Child:** Lunchtime. **Parent:** Now say it without *time.* **Child:** Lunch.

Increasing Difficulty →

Increasing Difficulty →

Identification

Two-syllable Words	**Parent:** Do what I do and tell me how many syllables we hear. [Claps while saying *ba – by*] [Claps while repeating parent] . . . Two syllables. **Child:** [Claps while repeating parent] . . . Two syllables.
Three-syllable Words	**Parent:** Do what I do and tell me how many word parts we hear. [Claps while saying *va – ca – tion*] **Child:** [Claps while repeating parent] . . . Three syllables.

Blending

Two-syllable Words	**Parent:** What do you get when you put together *ta – ble?* **Child:** Table.
Three-syllable Words	**Parent:** What do you get when you put together *po – ta – to?* **Child:** Potato.

Segmenting

Two-syllable Words	**Parent:** I'm going to say a word. I want you to tell me the syllables that make up the word. *Window.* **Child:** Win – dow (says pause between the syllables).
Three-syllable Words	**Parent:** I'm going to say a word. I want you to tell me the syllables that make up the word. *Spaghetti.* **Child:** Spa – ghe – tti (says pauses between the syllables).

Deletion

Deleting the Initial Syllable in a Word	**Parent:** We're going to take away syllables from words and see what we have left over. Say *napkin.* **Child:** Napkin. **Parent:** Now say it without *nap.* **Child:** Kin.
Deleting the Final Syllable in a Word	**Parent:** Say *simple.* **Child:** Simple. **Parent:** Now say it without *ple.* **Child:** Sim.

* Note: The (–) symbol represents a pause.

> **ONSET**
> The sounds that come before the vowel in a syllable
>
> **RIME**
> The rest of the syllable that is left over
>
> b - ug
> onset – rime

identifying, blending, segmenting, and deleting tasks at the syllable level.

Onset–rime awareness. Moving beyond syllable awareness, onset–rime awareness is more difficult, because children must now become consciously aware that language can be broken down into even smaller pieces, such that syllables can be broken down into onsets and rimes. The onset is what comes before the vowel in a syllable, and the rime is what is left over in a syllable. These terms may be unfamiliar to you, and we certainly don't expect your children to learn their meanings—we just want to be sure you understand how to use these ideas in practice. The one-syllable word *bug* can be broken down into its onset (/b/) and rime (*–ug*), although you want to be very careful to pronounce that onset as crisply as possible (like "bb") without adding an extra sound with it (turning it into "buh"). Adults often do add in this extra sound when exaggerating letter sounds for children, but doing this makes it complicated for a child to sound the word out accurately, because they end up pronouncing the word with that extra sound (as "buh-ug"). This notion of onset and rime gets a bit more complicated, though, because words with multiple syllables have multiple onsets and rimes. For example, the word *chimney* has two syllables: (1) *chim-* is made up of the onset /ch/ and the rime *–im*, and (2) *–ney* is made up of the onset /n/ and the rime *–ey*.

Although identifying each syllable's onset and rime may seem fairly simple, there are many words that make this issue more complicated. Consider the word *envelope*. The final syllable in the word, *–lope*, has a traditional onset (/l/] and rime (*–ope*). However, many syllables are not so straightforward. Some syllables do not have an onset, such that noth-ing comes before the vowel; for example, in *envelope*, the first syllable *en–* does not have an onset. Further, the rimes in some syllables are only made up of the vowel itself; for example, in *envelope*, the middle syllable *ve–* has the onset /v/ but the rime is only made of the vowel *–e* without anything following it. As you can see, this can become very complicated!

We provide the example of *envelope* as an illustration of how a single word may have many onsets and rimes depending on the syllables within it, but there is no reason to start playing with such a tricky word with your young child. With your child, you will probably use much simpler words for activities at this level. For example, we suggest using one-syllable words for onset–rime activities. To help children slowly increase their onset–rime awareness skills, you can adjust the difficulty level of the tasks they use, just as with word and syllable awareness. Table 2-5 provides some examples of blending, segmenting, and deletion tasks at the onset–rime awareness level.

The issue of rhyming. Even infants and young toddlers seem to enjoy listening to a rhyming songs and books, finding their sing-song quality

TABLE 2-5. ONSET–RIME AWARENESS EXAMPLES

Increasing Difficulty	**Blending**	
	One-syllable Word	**Parent**: What word you get when you put together /s/ – /it/? **Child**: Sit.
	Segmenting	
	One-syllable Word	**Parent**: "I'm going to say a word. I want you to tell me the first sound and the rest of the word: *cat*." **Child**: /c/ – /at/.
	Deletion	
	Deleting the Onset from a Spoken Word	**Parent**: Say *big*. **Child**: Big. **Parent**: Now say it without /b/. **Child**: /ig/.
	Deleting the Rime from a Spoken Word	**Parent**: Say *fun*. **Child**: Fun. **Parent**: Now say it without /un/. **Child**: /f/.

* Note: The (–) symbol represents a pause.

to be fun and soothing, and such rhyming activities should be used often to help them become excited about and tuned in to language. Although participating in and enjoying rhyming activities comes relatively easily to most children, it is more challenging for them to consciously understand what "rhyming" means, or to independently produce a word that rhymes with another. In the developmental continuum of phonological awareness, rhyming is actually a type of onset–rime awareness.[23] (Yes, as if this wasn't confusing enough already, rhyme and rime rhyme!) Perhaps a simple way to explain and remember the relationship between these similar words is that for words to *rhyme,* they must end in the same *rime*, or in more simple terms, they must *sound* the same at the end. Another aspect of rhyming that can be confusing is that words do not actually have to look the same in print to rhyme, such as *bear/hair* and *fly/tie*. Therefore, when teaching young children about rhyming, it is best to focus on words sounding the same at the end, rather than looking the same. When first asking your child to pay attention to the issue of rhyming, it can be helpful to begin with activities that simply require rhyme identification. Rhyming word puzzles and rhyming bingo are some examples of activities that will allow your child to match pictures of words according to rhyme (for example, *king/ring* and *cat/bat*).

Asking your child to *produce* rhymes will be more difficult. In fact, children can become frustrated if asked to generate rhyming words on their own before they have developed some more basic phonological awareness. Consider how many steps are required to produce rhymes. Perhaps you have been singing "Down by the Bay" with your child and your favorite verse is, "Have you ever seen a whale with a polka-dotted tail down by the bay?" You have decided to ask your child to come up with a new word that rhymes with *whale*. To do so, your child must (a) figure out that *whale* sounds like *–ale* at the end, which requires that he or she delete the /wh/ sound at the beginning of the word, and (b) then add different sounds at the beginning to find a new, real word, which requires blending of onsets and rimes, as well as knowledge of alternative sounds and a large vocabulary. For example, after deleting the /wh/ sound, your child could begin to go through the alphabet letter by letter, thinking systematically about what words might rhyme with whale (although many young children will not think to approach this task systematically). Even if your child does, he may not be familiar with the words *ale* (or *ail*) or *bale* (or *bail*). When he gets to the letter c, for *cale*, he may not realize that he could use a /k/ to represent that first sound, and create the word *kale*. As you can see, rhyme production is not as easy as one might suspect! For this reason, and because any rhyming activity can support the development of later reading skills like decoding, encouraging your child to think up new, made-up rhyming words can be fun and helpful too. Once your child develops the ability to produce rhymes (even nonsense rhymes like *The whale sat on the fale waiting for lale*), you will have vast new opportunities for creating silly games with your child and supporting the growth of her phonological awareness.

Phoneme awareness. Phoneme awareness (also commonly called *phonemic awareness*) is the most difficult level of phonological awareness (note that *phonological awareness* refers to being aware of the sounds of language at any level of complexity from words, to syllables, to phonemes, whereas *phoneme awareness* refers specifically to an awareness of sounds at the phoneme level).

> **PHONEME (OR PHONEMIC) AWARENESS**
> The ability to perceive and manipulate phonemes, or the smallest units of sound within words.

At the level of phoneme awareness, children must become aware that every word is made up of a sequence of phonemes (i.e., individual sounds), the smallest unit of language. A major reason that this is so difficult is that we generally overlap the sounds we say in speech, making it nearly impossible to separate phonemes fully. Consider the words *tea* and *top*. Because you anticipate the next sound you are going to make with your mouth as you say the initial /t/ sound, you move your mouth differently as you finish up that sound and move onto the vowel that follows it, and thus, produce the /t/ sound in a subtly different way in each of those words. If you are not convinced, say *tee* and *ta* over and over to yourself a few times in a row. Because we cannot segment sounds in words purely, phoneme awareness activities are the most abstract and difficult for children. Nevertheless, the support that you will have already provided your child by engaging in phonological awareness activities at the easier levels will make it more likely that your child will successfully develop skills at the phoneme level, and therefore be more likely to learn to read and spell.[24]

Although you can engage in phoneme awareness activities anywhere that is convenient, such as in the car or at the grocery store, once your child is ready to practice these more advanced phonological awareness skills, it is also helpful to start using letters as part of your activities whenever possible. Earlier we said that initial phonological awareness activities should be conducted without any thought to the printed word, but it is at this level of complexity that the roots related to phonological awareness and the alphabetic knowledge become forever intertwined. Your child is actually more likely to develop both phoneme awareness and alphabetic knowledge at a quicker pace when letters are used than if you were to do phoneme awareness activities without letters.[25] That is, by engaging in the phoneme awareness tasks, children increasingly understand that sounds of language are connected to printed symbols, and using letters helps children mentally represent the sounds that must be put together to form a word. Indeed, all of the "roots" of reading that are discussed in this chapter develop together and work as a team to bring your developing reader all of the essential "nutrients" he needs.

To pair letters with your phoneme awareness activities, you can use letter tiles (which can simply be made of squares of paper or borrowed from a board game) to help represent the phonemes that you are asking your child to manipulate. For example, when asking your child to blend the sounds *t + o + p* to form the spoken word *top,* you could use three letter tiles to represent each phoneme and initially place each tile an inch away from the next. You could then point at each tile and say the sound that it represents, pausing after each sound. Finally, you could push the tiles together and slide your hand fluidly across the tiles while blending the sounds together into a coherent word. Doing the activity in this way will help your child recognize how these three sounds and represented in print.

Since phonemes do not always have a one-to-one correspondence with letters in the English language (for example, the two letters *sh* together make one sound; the long *a* sound can be spelled a variety of ways, such as in *cake, hay, sleigh, bait*), it may be easiest to start with words that have the phoneme represented by only one letter (for example, *H–A–M*) when you use letters to represent phonemes for your child. When you select words that have a vowel that is spelled various ways, you can create a letter tile that symbolically demonstrates what it is, such as a very tall *A* for the long *a* (that says its own name, "ay") and a very small *A* for the short a (which does not say its name), so that the tiles might be *H–A* for the word *hay*, which is made up of only two phonemes. Furthermore, when you do move on to use words that have phonemes represented by more than one letter, you may create letter tiles that include both. For instance, if you are blending *F–I–SH*, where the letters *S* and *H* together make only one sound, you can put the letter combination *SH* on one tile. To help you get started, and keep track of those phonemes that are represented by more than one letter, take a look at appendix A. This worksheet includes letter tiles for phonemes that are represented by just one letter, as well as for those that are represented by more than one letter.

To help scaffold your child's progress through this complex level of phonological awareness, you can use tasks that slowly increase in difficulty; examples of identification, blending, segmenting, and deletion phoneme awareness activities can be found in Table 2-6. As can be seen in the table, identification tasks are easiest if you focus on the initial phoneme, more difficult if you focus on the final phoneme, and the most difficult if you focus on the phoneme in the middle of a word. When presenting your child with a list of words, some of which share initial, middle, or final phonemes, it is also easier to ask him to identify two words that share the same phoneme rather than two words that have different phonemes. You can make the manipulation tasks easier or more challenging for your child by adjusting the number of phonemes in the words that you use for your activities.

TABLE 2-6. PHONEME AWARENESS EXAMPLES

		Identifying
Increasing Difficulty →	Initial Phoneme: Same	**Parent:** [Shows child picture of a ball, and then a row of pictures (dog, coat, bear)]. Point to the one that starts with the same sound as ball.
	Initial Phoneme: Different	**Parent:** [Shows child four pictures (ball, cup, bear, bell).] One of these words starts with a different sound than the others. Point to the one that starts with a different sound.
	Final Phoneme: Same	**Parent:** [Shows child picture of a fan, and then a row of pictures (hat, phone, cake)]. Point to the one that ends with the same sound as fan.
	Final Phoneme: Different	**Parent:** [Shows child four pictures (bat, nut, mitt, sun). One of the words ends with a different sound than the others.] Point to the one that ends with a different sound.
	Middle Phoneme: Same	**Parent:** [Shows child picture of a mop, and then a row of pictures (rug, cat, cot)]. Point to the one that has the same sound in the middle as mop.
	Middle Phoneme: Different	**Parent:** [Shows child four pictures (cap, pan, dig, bat). One of the words has a different sound in the middle.] Point to the one that has a different sound in the middle.
		Blending
		Begin Using Letters During Phoneme Awareness Activities
	Two-Phoneme Word (Consonant-Vowel)	**Parent:** What word you get when you put together /t/ – /ea/? **Child:** Tea

		Increasing Difficulty →

Three-Phoneme Word (Consonant-Vowel-Consonant)	**Parent:** What word you get when you put together /m/ – /u/ – /g/? **Child:** Mug.

Segmenting
Continue to Use Letters During Phoneme Awareness Activities

Three-Phoneme Word (Consonant-Vowel-Consonant)	**Parent:** I'm going to say a word. I want you to tell me all the sounds you hear in the word. *Red.* **Child:** /r/ – /e/ – /d/.

Deleting
Continue to Use Letters During Phoneme Awareness Activities

Delete Initial Phoneme	**Parent:** Say *rat.* **Child:** Rat. **Parent:** Now say it without /r/. **Child:** /at/.
Delete Final Phoneme	**Parent:** Say *rat.* **Child:** Rat. **Parent:** Now say it without /t/. **Child:** /ra/.

*Note: The (–) symbol represents a pause.

Beyond phoneme awareness. Although phonological awareness develops along a continuum, children are certainly not done developing phonological awareness before they enter elementary school. In fact, during the beginning stages of reading, the very act of sounding out words will foster the development of more advanced levels of phoneme awareness.[26] Consequently, these advanced phoneme awareness skills can help children sound out more difficult words.

Once children become fluent, skilled readers, they begin to focus more on print, and the phonological awareness that once required conscious attention becomes automatic. Whereas a young, nonreading child who is asked how many sounds are in "ship" will only rely on how the word sounds (and, with the support of strategies from this chapter, should hopefully be able to correctly respond that there are three sounds), someone who has become a skilled reader may visualize the four letters in the printed word and mistakenly indicate that there are four sounds. Therefore, if, as a parent, you are finding it challenging to do phoneme awareness activities, know that this is because you are such a skilled reader, and you must relearn to have an explicit and conscious focus on the manipulation of sounds rather than letters.

What Is the Role of Parents in Fostering Phonological Awareness?

Research suggests that the literacy experiences a child has at home, including shared book reading and parent coaching and teaching, can have a significant impact on children's phonological awareness.[27] Much of the research in this area has been focused on comparing children from low-income backgrounds, who tend to have fewer literacy experiences and fewer literacy materials in the home, to more advantaged children, leading some to assume that beyond a certain threshold of socioeconomic status, variability in home literacy activities doesn't matter.[28] However, one study found that even within middle-class families, the amount of exposure to literacy activities does matter: children whose parents provided them with greater exposure to literacy activities demonstrated stronger phonological awareness than children whose parents engaged less frequently in these activities.[29] Furthermore, this study found that for children's phonological awareness development, a particularly important part of children's home literacy experience was the age at which their parents started reading to them. Children who had greater cumulative exposure to language through books developed greater sensitivity to the sound and structure of language.

Another study found that different elements of the home literacy environment are linked to different levels of children's phonological awareness development.[30] This is such an important finding because it demonstrates that as a parent, you need to have a lot of tricks up your sleeve to help your child develop all of the important skills he needs to become a reader. For example, parents' familiarity with a broad range of children's books, suggesting that they read a lot with their children, was associated with children's rhyme awareness skills but not with their phoneme awareness. In contrast, the frequency with which parents engaged in teaching emergent literacy concepts (for example, teaching about words, letters, and sounds) was related to children's phoneme awareness, but not their rhyme-awareness skills. This suggests that although activities like shared reading can support the development of less advanced aspects of phonological awareness such as rhyming, in order for children to develop the most sophisticated aspects of phonological awareness, parents may need to engage in activities like the ones described in all three sections of this chapter that more explicitly draw children's attention to the individual sounds of language.

Developing Phonological Awareness: How Can I Support My Child's Individual Needs?

Because becoming aware of the sound structure of our language is not easy for many children, there are a number of tricks that will allow you to boost your child's understanding of phonological-awareness concepts while also keeping him interested and motivated.[31] Remember, we

always want children to have opportunities to show off their developing skills and demonstrate that they are competent, so it is important
to pick activities that allow them to grow but are not too frustrating.
The strategies described in this section, which make phonological awareness more concrete and allow you to provide clues and praise along the
way, can be helpful for all children, but may be especially beneficial for
young children, children with language and/or developmental delays, or
English Language Learners who are doing phonological awareness activities in English. Once your child becomes more and more successful at
a certain phonological-awareness level, it is still important to practice
skills without the use of these strategies to help your child think about
phonological awareness at a more abstract level and take steps toward
skilled and independent reading.

Using blocks. While playing phonological-awareness activities that
require manipulating the sounds in words (like the blending, segmenting,
and deleting tasks we described earlier), children often have difficulty
understanding what they are being asked to do. Using colored blocks
or other physical objects can make phonological-awareness activities
more concrete. For example, you can show your child how to blend the
syllables in a two-syllable word (for example, *pencil*) by putting out a
blue block to represent *pen–* and a red block to represent *–cil* with a little
space between them. Then you can physically put the blocks together
to show your child you want her to blend the syllables to make a whole
word. You can also do the reverse to support segmenting. Give your child
the same number of blocks as there are syllables in a word, and ask her
to use the blocks to represent the syllables in the word. Blocks can be
used to support more advanced levels of phonological awareness as well.
Given that young children's abstract thinking is still developing, physical,
concrete objects can help them better visualize what is being asked of
them, and can increase their interest in such games. Remember to praise
your child for her efforts and her progress. If she is ready to move on to
a more advanced task, you can say something like, "Nice job blending
those syllables together! I know that you are ready to try something
tougher, because you did so great." If she continues to struggle, praise is

just as important. You can say something like, "I am so impressed with how hard you are working! Blending syllables together is really tough. Let me show you how I'd blend those two syllables together and then you can try again."

Physical gestures. Using physical gestures can also help your child understand what is being asked of him during phonological awareness activities. For example, you can make an onset–rime blending task easier for your child by adding hand gestures: "What do you get when you put together /b/ (hold one hand up) –*ag* (hold the other hand up)?" Then physically put your hands together to demonstrate that you want your child to blend the onset and rime. You can have your child join you in making the physical gestures as well.

Pictures. Pictures and visual props help reduce the amount your child has to remember and allows her to focus primarily on the phonological awareness task. For example, to help your child develop syllable awareness, you can print pictures of different items and cut them into the number of pieces that there are syllables in the words you have chosen (for example, cut a picture of a banana into three parts, since there are three syllables, *ba – na – na*). Then say each syllable while touching the parts from left to right. Next, have your child push the picture pieces together and tell you what the whole word is. Pictures can be used to facilitate your child's understanding of segmenting and deletion as well, and they can be used at the other levels of the phonological awareness continuum (for example, for phoneme awareness, you could use a picture of a cow cut into two pieces [/k/ + /ow/] or a pig cut into three pieces [/p/ + /ĭ/ + /g/]).

Providing choices as answers. Before your child is able to verbally produce answers, he or she may be able to successfully select an answer from a few choices you provide. For instance, if you are singing "Down by the Bay" again, you can ask your child which one rhymes, "Have you ever seen ants wearing purple pants?" or "…ants wearing purple shirts?" You can provide similar choices when you are reading rhyming books to your child and you leave off the final word for your child to guess the rhyme.

Motivating topics. Selecting topics and words of interest to your child can be an effective motivational technique. For instance, parents can clap out the syllables of words that are particularly interesting to their child, such as their own name and names of friends and family (for example, *Jor – dan, Me – li – ssa, Do– mi – nic, Aun – tie*). Your child may also enjoy playing with different units of language in other highly interesting words, such as names of zoo animals (for example, *mon – key, el – e – phant, bear*) or dinosaurs (for example, *tri – cer – a – tops*).

Specific feedback. Throughout all tasks at all levels of the phonological awareness continuum, it is most helpful to give feedback that is specific. Rather than simply saying "good job," your child is more likely to have more and more success if you say something like, "That's right! *Lunchtime* without *time* is just *lunch*." By giving the specific feedback, you are not only supporting your child's motivation to learn, but also providing your child an additional opportunity to practice being aware of language.

What Activities and Strategies Can I Use to Support Phonological Awareness?

Keeping in mind your child's unique needs, we will now consider activities and strategies that will help support your child's development of phonological awareness. These strategies and activities include encouraging vocabulary development; developing print-rich environments; engaging in shared writing activities; and using play-based word, syllable, onset–rime, and phoneme awareness activity ideas.

Vocabulary development. Phonological awareness does not naturally develop in the same way that most aspects of translexical and lexical aspects of spoken language do and therefore requires explicit practice to be developed fully. However, research does suggest that supporting consistent and substantial vocabulary growth can help children become phonologically aware.[32] More specifically, by helping to develop your child's vocabulary in the ways discussed in the previous chapter of this book, you are essentially compelling your child's brain to reorganize how words are stored, in part according to different units of language. For example, if the only words a two-year-old knows that start with /b/ are *bear, ball, bat,* and *baby,* it is easy for these to be stored or "filed" in their entirety. However, once the child develops knowledge of hundreds of other words that either start with /b/ or are similar to those initial words in other ways (for example, *put* and *bat* end in the same sound; the second syllable in *ruby* and *baby* are the same), the child's brain is forced to come up with a new "filing" system that allows the increasingly complex connections to be stored (for example, words that have matching syllables; words that have the same sound at the beginning, middle, or end; words that rhyme and sound the same at the end). Although a child may not be able to explicitly describe these connections right away, a growing vocabulary volume can help a child become more and more aware of the units of sounds in our language. Therefore, parents' efforts to cultivate vocabulary development simultaneously boost their children's phonological awareness development. This is another example of how all of these skills work together.

Print-rich environments. Providing children with a literacy- and print-rich environment can also support the development of phonological awareness, as well as a general fondness for the patterns in our language. As part of this print-rich environment, nursery rhyme books are an excellent beginning tool for parents. Nursery rhymes can help children become attuned to the rhythm of language and language play, such as rhyming or alliteration (repetition of the same sounds at the beginning of words, for example, *buzzing baby bumblebees*). For example, "Hush Little Baby"[33] is a traditional rhyming lullaby that parents can read or sing to their child, and *Henny Penny*[34] is a classic book that uses rhyming names for the characters Henny Penny meets as she worries that the sky is falling. There are also numerous books with collections of nursery rhymes and Mother Goose rhymes that can provide ideas for parents. In addition to reading nursery rhyme books, singing nursery rhymes (for example, "I'm a Little Teapot" or "Twinkle, Twinkle Little Star") throughout the day, such as during car rides and bath time, provides additional opportunities for children to begin having fun with components of our language.

Parents should provide their children with predictable books as well. Because of the repetition and patterns of language in predictable books, you can easily encourage your child to make guesses about the words, phrases, or refrains that might come next. Moreover, your child is likely to quickly memorize predictable books and enjoy demonstrating his or her ability to "read." Predictable books can take a number of forms. *The Napping House*[35] and *Today is Monday*[36] are examples of cumulative stories, in which each page of text includes new information as well as repetition of the same text from all previous pages. Predictable stories can also be framed around repetitive phrases (for example, *The Important Book*[37]), question-and-answer patterns (for example, *Brown Bear, Brown Bear, What Do You See?*[38]), story patterns (for example, *The Runaway Bunny*[39]), or familiar sequences (for example, numbers in *Moo, Moo, Brown Cow*[40]). *If You Give a Mouse a Cookie*[41] is an example of a circular story, another type of predictable book in which the sequence of events eventually circles back to the beginning. Books that use rhymes throughout (for example, *Is Your Mama a Llama?*[42]) or familiar song phrases (for example, *Over in the Meadow*[43]) are some additional examples of predictable books.

In addition to helping children develop enthusiasm for and awareness of the structure of our language, predictable books provide parents an opportunity to cultivate the concept of a word. Young children do not automatically understand that sentences are made up of separate words and can therefore benefit if their parents draw their attention to how our written, and spoken, language is organized. Because your child will be very familiar with her favorite predictable books, you can use a type of print referencing that entails pointing to each individual word in text as you or your child tells the story. Occasionally reading at a slower pace while pointing can also help your child understand that sentences are broken down into words. Although the concept of words typically develops around four to five years of age,[44] parents' use of print referencing is likely to maximize their children's development in this regard.

Shared writing activities. Parents can also use shared writing activities as an opportunity to help develop phonological awareness.[45] First, writing activities can help you teach your child certain concepts (for example, *first, last, same, different, word, sound, letter*) that are needed to be successful with various phonological awareness activities. Additionally, your child is more likely to become phonologically aware if he or she regularly observes you modeling how to break apart our spoken language into smaller units.

When you must use writing as part of your daily activities, such as when making a grocery list or notes for yourself, modeling how you think through the process can be helpful for your child. The following example demonstrates how you might develop a child's phonological awareness at the word level as well as his concept of words. You may need to write *post office* on your list of errands for the day. You can think aloud, "Okay, I have to mail a letter at the post office today. I'm going to write down *post office*. I'll write the first word, *post* (write it down). Now I need a little space between my words. The next word I'm going to write is *office* (write it down)." After completing the entire errands list, you could then read through it while pointing to each corresponding word.

If you model how to sound out words aloud, your child can also develop other levels of phonological awareness, along with alphabetic knowledge, during shared writing activities. For example, if you are going to write *milk* on your grocery list, you could model how you figure out the first sound and then translate this sound to the writing itself, "Hmm, what is the first sound I hear in the word *milk*? Mmmmmilk? Mmm–ilk? Oh, I hear *mmm*. And I know that the letter *m* says *mmm*, so I'll write down the letter *m*." You can also engage in these types of "think alouds" when helping your child get his thoughts on paper, such as when you take dictation for your child as he writes thank you notes or stories to correspond with pictures he has drawn.

When children become interested in writing words on their own, parents have another meaningful opportunity to focus on the sounds of language and help support their children's phonological awareness. For example, a child may want to write *Mom*, because she is trying to write a note addressed to her mother (an activity that may be as exciting and motivating for Mom as for the child!). When attempting to write the word, the child may ask for a parent's help. Rather than simply providing the letters to the child, it will be more beneficial to encourage the child to notice the sounds that make up the word. The parent can elongate or repeat the first sound, "Mmmm—om, what sound do you hear at the beginning? *Mmm. Mom*"? Once the child is aware that the first sound is /m/, the parent can then help her determine which letter corresponds to that sound. Of course, parents can and should adjust the amount of support they provide to their children based on their developmental needs and phonological awareness and alphabetic knowledge skill levels. Regardless of how much support children may need, it can be valuable to display their writing samples in visible places like the kitchen, as parental recognition of children's efforts is likely to motivate children to persist with writing attempts.

Play-based word awareness activity ideas. You can design your word awareness activities to meet the developmental needs of your child and to be as fun and silly as you and your child would like. Rather than clapping, you could have your child stomp, hop, tap, drum, or use any other creative movement to identify words in sentences. For instance, you could put out paper plates to represent lily pads, and your child can be a frog who hops along the lily pads for each word he or she hears you say in a sentence. Your child would also probably enjoy seeing you have a turn as the frog! Additionally, you could play *I Spy* with your child using a picture book or other pictures you have that contain pictures of compound words. For example, *I spy with my little eye a snow* (pause) *man*. When your child finds the snowman picture, she is practicing blending words to make compound words.

Play-based syllable awareness activity ideas. Although becoming consciously aware of units of our language will require support from parents and teachers, children's awareness of rhythm in songs will come more naturally. Parents can use this to their advantage. While singing songs that separate the beat at the syllable level, parents can clap along with their children. For example, you might clap along with "Twinkle, Twinkle Little Little Star" by clapping out, "Twin – kle, twin – kle, li – ttle star, how I won – der what you are." Parents can also turn many other common activities into fun guessing games. For instance, while playing "house" with your child, you could ask for a *Klee – nex* or say that you want *spa – ghe – tti* for lunch. Ask your child to guess the word you are saying. While at the grocery store, you can also have your child help you get items by giving them clues in syllables, such as *carr – ots* or *yo – gurt*.

Play-based onset–rime awareness activity ideas. As with the easier levels of phonological awareness, you can be as creative as you would like with the onset–rime activities you use with your child. For instance, you could pretend to be a "robot" (or use a puppet) who speaks in silly, choppy language. Invite your child to ask questions to which you can respond in onsets and rimes. Your child will have to determine what you, the robot, are trying to say. If your child asks the robot what it wants for breakfast, you could respond with *t – oast*. Once he has aquired the ability to perceive onsets and rimes, your child should be able to tell you that the robot wants *toast*. In addition to using this activity to teach blending, you could support your child's segmenting skills by giving him or her words and asking how the robot would say it.

Play-based phoneme awareness activity ideas. Phoneme awareness activities can also be built into your playful, yet busy, day with your child. While at the grocery store, you can have your child search for items that start or end with the same sound. If you really want to give your child a challenge that will occupy time, ask him or her to find items that have the same sound in the middle (like *cheese* and *beets*)! To keep him from wandering away, make sure to specify that all the items need to be ones that he can see while sitting in the cart or staying in the same aisle as you. You can also use common household items to create fun phoneme awareness activities. You can cut an empty egg carton so that the number of empty egg spots matches the number of phonemes in the words you will be using. Then give your child beans or macaroni noodles, and ask him to drop a bean or noodle in a hole for each sound heard in a word. This is a fun and appropriate way to "play" with food. Many more suggestions for developing phonological awareness are provided in Tables 2-7 through 2-10, and each table provides strategies pertinent to a specific level of phonological awareness skill.

TABLE 2-7. WORD AWARENESS

What to Do	How to Do It	Age(s)
Encourage Vocabulary Development	Cultivate your child's vocabulary, because the more words your child knows, the more this facilitates his phonological abilities. For example, when describing the color of a strawberry, describe it as "crimson" and "scarlet."	
Promote Awareness of Individual Words In Text	Point to each individual word in the text while you or your child read a story to demonstrate that sentences consist of many individual words.	
Segment and Blend Words within Stories	Practice making compound words while reading. When reading a book with a picture of a snowman. You might say "*I spy with my little eye a snow* (pause) *man.*" When your child finds the snowman picture, she can practice blending words to make a compound word.	
Elongate Sounds	Encourage your child to notice the sounds in a word. For example, when reading the word "Mom," you can elongate or repeat the first sound, "Mmmm—om, what sound do you hear at the beginning? *Mmm. Mom*?" Once your child is aware the first sound is /m/, you can then help him determine which letter corresponds to that sound.	

What to Do	How to Do It	Age(s)
"Hop Out" Sentences	While waiting in line at the grocery store or post office, give your child a sentence and ask him to "hop it out." Your child should hop one time while saying each word in the sentence.	ABC
Make a Sentence Segmenting Board Game	Play a homemade board game to help your child segment sentences into words. Draw a game board with a start and finish and invite a couple of family members to play. Have each player move a game piece along a square for each word in a given sentence. If your child makes a mistake, model the correct way to segment the sentence and encourage him or her to try that one again on the next turn.	ABC
Play Compound Word Games	Put pictures of items that are compound words (for example, *baseball, popcorn, rainbow, cupcake, mailbox, snowman, airplane*) into a shoebox. Have your child take out a picture and give you clues such as *rain* (pause) *bow* to guess the word *rainbow*. Or you could pull out the pictures and give your child the clues. This is a great game for car rides.	ABC

TABLE 2-8. SYLLABLE AWARENESS

What to Do	How to Do It	Age(s)
Play Syllable Awareness Games	Clap along with "Twinkle, Twinkle Little Little Star" by clapping out, "Twin – kle, twin – kle, li – ttle star, how I won – der what you are." Or choose certain words from your shared reading and separate them into their syllable parts. You can also turn common activities into fun guessing games. While playing "house" with your child, ask for a *Klee–nex* or say that you want *spa – ghe – tti* for lunch. Ask your child to guess the word you are saying.	A B C
"Feel" the Syllables by Keeping Your Hand Under Your Chin When Talking	Help your child understand the concept of syllables by "feeling" the syllables. Put your hand under your chin and slowly say a few words with different numbers of syllables (for example, *giraffe, computer*). Your child can have fun "feeling" the syllables in words on his own chin, or perhaps even feeling syllables on your chin!	A B C
Play "Syllable Catch"	Play a game of "Syllable Catch" in which you say the syllables of a word and toss the ball to your child. She has to guess the whole word when catching the ball. You can also play in the reverse direction, so your child gives you the clues and tosses you the ball to catch and guess.	A B C
Sort Household Items by Numbers of Syllables in Their Names	Do some traveling with syllables. Grab a few bags, collect different items around your house, and pretend to pack for a trip. You can have your child tell you the syllables they hear in each item (for example, *brace – let, um – bre – lla*) so you know which bag to pack it in (a bag for one-syllable words, a bag for two-syllable words, and a bag for three-syllable words).	A B C

What to Do	How to Do It	Age(s)
Play Syllable Identification and Deletion Games with Snacks	Have your child lay out a Cheerio (or other snack) for each syllable he or she hears in a word, such as *pumpkin* (*pump – kin*). Then when you ask, "What is pumpkin without *pump–*?" your child can eat the first Cheerio and tell you what is left over. Your child can also look for ideas for words to use by looking through foods and beverages you might have at your house (for example, *al – monds, cinn – a – mon, le – mo – nade*).	ABC

TABLE 2-9. ONSET-RIME AWARENESS

What to Do	How to Do It	Age(s)
Play Onset–Rime Awareness Games	Use a puppet and speak in silly, choppy language. Invite your child to ask questions to which you can respond in onsets and rimes. Ask your child to tell you what the puppet is saying. If your child asks the puppet what it wants for breakfast, you could respond with *t – oast*. Once he has acquired the ability to perceive onsets and rimes, your child should be able to tell you that the puppet wants *toast*.	ABC
Use Your Child's Name in a Rhyming Song	Use popular rhyming songs, especially any that can use the child's name to provide entertainment, and build your child's capacity to separate onsets and rimes. The Name Game is one example that works well: "Sofia, Sofia, bo bia, banana, fana, fo fia, me, my, mo mia, Sofia!"	ABC

continues

TABLE 2-9. CONTINUED

What to Do	How to Do It	Age(s)
Replace Initial Phonemes of Words in Children's Songs	Manipulate the words of most children's songs to create numerous opportunities for your child to be entertained with rhyming. For example, instead of singing the traditional "Mary Had a Little Lamb," you can replace the initial phoneme of each word with with /r/ to get "Rary rad a rittle ramb, rittle ramb, rittle ramb, rits reece ras right ras row…"	ABC
Play Onset-Rime Guessing Games While Running Errands	Play general guessing games while driving or running errands. For instance, say, "I'm a word that starts with /b/ and ends with –at. What am I?" Your child should be able to determine that you are a *bat*.	ABC
Play Guessing Games with Toys	Play guessing games using toys you have around the house. For example, while playing with toy farm animals, show your child the sheep and the dog, and ask her to give you the *sh – eep*.	ABC
Play Onset-Rime Bingo	Play onset–rime bingo. Use rhyming bingo boards, but instead of giving clues via rhyming words (for example, the picture is a *mouse*, and your clue is *house*), you can give the clues using the onset and rime (for example, if the picture is a mouse, the clue is m – ouse).	ABC

TABLE 2-10. PHONEME AWARENESS

What to Do	How to Do It	Age(s)
Sound Search	When at the grocery store, ask your child to search for items that start or end with the same sound. For example, in the produce section, ask your child to find the fruits and vegetables that begin with the "b" sound (*banana, beets, broccoli, beans*). Telling your child to search for items in a particular row or section should help to ensure he stays close to you while playing.	
Read Alliterative Books	Read books (for example, *Berenstains' B Book*[113]) with alliteration, and draw your child's attention to how many words sound the same at the beginning.	
Sing Songs	Play with sounds while singing songs. For example, while singing the popular "Apples and Bananas" song, you might sing about eeples and baneenees, ayples and banaynays, and so forth.	
Sort Pictures by Their Initial Sounds	Play Sound Basketball, or sort pictures by their salient sounds in another way if your child does not enjoy basketball. Gather two baskets (or other containers, like pots, tupperwares, or small garbage cans), a ball, two letter tiles (for example, one for the letter B and one for the letter D), and printed picture cards of words that begin with the sounds represented by the letter tiles (for example, pictures of *bed, boat, bat, dart, dance,* and *dog*). Place each letter tile by one of the containers, and then have your child select a picture card and identify which sound is at the beginning by shooting the ball at the corresponding "basketball hoop." If your child has trouble recognizing the picture on the card, you can prompt her by saying, "That's a picture of a *dart*. Should we throw the ball toward the basket for /b/ or for /d/?"	

continues

TABLE 2-10. CONTINUED

What to Do	How to Do It	Age(s)
Use a Mirror to Look at How Your Mouth Moves When Saying Different Words	Look in the mirror with your child and say different silly words together. Point out how your mouths look either the same or different when different sounds are made. For instance, when we say "mouse" and "milk," our mouths start with our lips closed for a while. When we say "fox," our mouths are open a little, and our top teeth touch our bottom lips.	(ABC blocks)

Concepts of Print

What Are Concepts of Print?

Though children's basic understanding of print may begin very early on in life through their exposure to books and other written materials in their environment, children must develop knowledge of numerous *concepts of print*.[46] These concepts include an understanding that print—the written words on the page—carries a message and that it is organized and read in a particular way. For example, to become able to independently read a book, children need to develop an understanding that print moves from left to right and top to bottom on a page, and they must learn how to hold a book upright and move the pages from front to back.[47] Children must also understand that print carries a meaningful message and can be used to serve a variety of useful functions (e.g., telling a story, listing items to get at the grocery store, labeling items).[48] Additionally, children must come to recognize that although pictures in books are meaningful, what we read are the printed words on the pages, and further, that this text represents spoken words that are written

CONCEPTS OF PRINT
An understanding of the general conventions of text (for example, print carries meaning, is generally written from left-to-right, words are composed of letters).

down.[49] Children must also learn that words are made up of letters, that words are separated by spaces, and that punctuation marks play a role in what we read. Concepts such as book cover, title, and author fall into this category as well.

Why Are Concepts of Print Important for Future Reading Development?

When a child wants or is asked to read a story, she must know where to turn to in the book, where to start reading, how to follow along in the text, that the little letters by each other with space on both sides represent a word to be read, and that this printed word represents a word we speak. Given that these are just some of the concepts of print that a child must understand to even begin to read a story, it is not surprising that children who have well-developed concepts of print are more likely to have success with reading in early elementary school.[50] In contrast, children who are not fluent in concepts of print are likely to have greater confusion when learning to read.

How Do Children's Concepts of Print Develop Over Time?

The period of development prior to elementary school provides rich windows of opportunity for parents to cultivate children's skills in this area. From about two-and-a-half to four-and-a-half years of age, children are still learning how to arrange their writing units in a line and will often write their letters or letter-like forms all over the page, indicating that print conventions are still developing for children in this age range.[51] By the time children are four and five years old, their writing is often characterized by markings that go in a line from left to right, especially for the older children.[52] It appears that children's knowledge of print directionality improves during this developmental period, as we will demonstrate when we talk about emergent writing in chapter 3.

Children's understanding that print, rather than pictures, provides us with the words included in stories emerges during this period as well. When young children listen to and watch adults read, they are generally unaware of what it is the adults are reading. Three-year-olds are likely to indicate that images that do not include print, such as pictures or squiggles, are good for reading.[53] Similarly, when shown books and asked to point to what we read, three-year-olds typically point to the pictures.[54] Around five years of age, children are more likely to recognize that we cannot read pictures or other non-alphabetic displays, but some confusion often still remains.[55] Additionally, children's awareness that printed words are made up of strings of letters rather than a single letter develops during this time period.[56] With ample exposure to and interaction with print, many children will likely develop an understanding of a range of print concepts by the time they enter elementary school, and they will refine this understanding throughout the early elementary school years, especially with the support of their parents.

What Is the Role of Parents in Fostering Concepts of Print?

When young children are given numerous opportunities to engage in a wide variety of literacy and language activities with their parents, they are more likely to have greater knowledge of concepts of print.[57] That is, your child's knowledge of concepts of print is likely to be stronger if you start reading to your child at an early age, if you read with your child as often as possible, and if your child's encounters with books and the library are abundant.[58] Using a broad range of activities can produce positive effects that are likely to be maintained over time.[59]

Research also suggests that parents can foster their children's understanding of concepts of print by engaging them in activities that specifically draw their attention to features of print. For example, parent–child shared storybook reading experiences can improve children's concepts of print.[60] Moreover, shared reading is most effective in helping children develop concepts of print when parents engage in **print referencing,** or drawing children's attention to the printed text on the page. Research has shown that preschool-age children typically do

PRINT REFERENCING
Drawing children's attention to the printed text on the page.

not look at print during shared reading when adults do not point to the print or draw attention to the print in some way.[61] This finding makes sense in light of the fact that young children are generally unaware that it is the print that adults are reading.[62] Children of this age may still not distinguish between print and pictures and may focus their attention only on the colorful pictures that illustrate the story. Fortunately, by frequently reading and rereading storybooks and focusing on the print using verbal and nonverbal cues, your child is likely to develop a greater understanding of how print works.[63]

Developing Concepts of Print: How Can I Support the Individual Needs of My Child?

To support the development of concepts of print, it is once again imperative to maintain your child's interest in print. That is, between the ages of three and four years, children who show high interest in literacy, such that they amuse themselves with books almost daily, are less likely to have later reading struggles than same-age peers who are interested in looking at books only two or three times per week.[64] Therefore, finding an array of books that are exciting and interesting for your child to engage with on their own is another important aspect of ensuring many positive interactions with print. As with efforts to develop phonological awareness, when you use any of the activities and strategies that will be discussed shortly, it is important that you respond to your child's interests and developmental needs in order to ensure your child's success, as well as his interest in literacy and sense of competence.

What Activities and Strategies Can I Use to Support Concepts of Print?

Let us now consider activities and strategies that will help support your child's development of concepts of prints. These strategies and activities include developing print-rich environments and engaging in shared storybook reading and print referencing.

Print-rich environments. As suggested above, you can help your child develop her knowledge of concepts of print by exposing her to an environment that is full of print. For example, children respond to seeing printed labels for items in their environments.[65] Using index cards, markers, and some tape to post labels on items such as your desk, refrigerator, bed, bookcase, toy box, and mirror helps children develop an understanding that print can represent the words we use in our spoken language. Making such labels can become a fun game if you allow children to pick which objects to label, and to write or decorate the labels themselves. Additionally, when you give children good props to help them play out scenarios such as being at a post office, library, office, restaurant, or grocery store, they are likely to independently embed literacy-rich activities into their play.[66] Exposing children to literacy-focused materials does not have to be expensive, as you can construct a play area using common household items such as cardboard boxes, pads of paper, markers, and scissors. For example, when Anne was supporting her son Michael's development of concepts of print, she would often help Michael create a "diner." Together they would create a sign and pretend menus for the restaurant, gather pads of paper and crayons for taking orders and giving receipts, leave newspapers out for customers to read, create a box to represent the cash register, and so forth. Through this experience, Michael was able to see numerous functions of print, recognize that print carries a message, and see that people read print on menus and newspapers. If you play this game with your child, he could became the server, and practice "writing" from left to right (if this was an appropriate developmental expectation depending on the age of your child), and if your child became the cook, he could practice "writing" a grocery list for necessary ingredients or "reading" a recipe. Similarly, by simply inviting your child to play out common household tasks, such as cooking and grocery shopping, with you on a regular basis, he will be exposed to many more authentic opportunities to engage with print and will be more likely to develop concepts of print.

Shared storybook reading and print referencing. Although shared reading experiences can help your child develop so many skills, including language and self-esteem, as described throughout the rest of this book, they also provide many opportunities for parents focus on emergent literacy development. As we mentioned previously, children are more likely to develop knowledge of print concepts when adults point to or otherwise draw attention to the print in books. Verbal cues that can increase your child's focus on print and thus improve print concepts include questions (for example, "Do you remember who the author of this book is?" or "Where should we look to find the author's name?"), comments (for example, "Wow, look at this word, it's a long one. It says *caterpillar*."), and requests about print (for example, "Can you show me where I should start reading on this page?").[67]

In addition to verbal cues, nonverbal print referencing while reading storybooks with your child significantly increases how much your child will pay attention to the print in books.[68] Nonverbal print referencing entails pointing to the words or tracking the print with your finger (that is, running your finger under the print from left to right). Essentially, such nonverbal cues help children look less at the pictures and more at the print and thus give children more opportunities to develop knowledge of print concepts and conventions. Pointing to and tracking print are simple strategies that are not likely to interrupt the flow of your shared reading experiences, and your child can benefit even if she is not ready or in the mood to answer many questions about the print.[69] Nonetheless, since some of your shared reading experiences will be focused elsewhere, such as on story comprehension, consider using those books that your child likes you to read over and over again as an opportunity to reference the print itself.

Parents can further cultivate their child's development of print concepts by selecting *print-salient* storybooks to guide their shared reading experiences.[70] Print-salient storybooks have prominent print features, such as text bubbles, print embedded in pictures, or emphasis on certain words in the text (for example, *POW!*, *ZZZZ*, or *STOP*).[71] A list of examples of additional print-salient books can be found in Box 2-1.

The Monster at the End of this Book[72] is an excellent example of a print-salient storybook, with prominent print features on each and every page. If a parent is reading this book with his child, he might introduce

---

BOX 2-1. EXAMPLES OF PRINT-SALIENT BOOKS

- Eastman, P. D. (1973). *Big Dog . . . Little Dog*. New York: Random House.
- Hill, E. (1980). *Where is Spot?* New York: G. P. Putnam Sons.
- Seuss, D. (1963). *Hop on Pop*. New York: Random House.
- Sierra, J. (2004). *Wild about Books*. New York: Alfred A. Knopf.
- Stone, J. (1971). *The Monster at the End of This Book*. New York: Golden Books.
- Willems, M. (2003). *Don't Let the Pigeon Drive the Bus!* New York: Hyperion Books for Children.
- Willems, M. (2004). *The Pigeon Finds a Hot Dog!* New York: Hyperion Books for Children.
- Willems, M. (2007). *Knuffle Bunny Too: A Case of Mistaken Identity*. New York: Hyperion Books for Children.
- Wilson, K. (2003). *A Frog in the Bog*. New York: Scholastic.

---

it by commenting, "The name, or title, of this book is *The Monster at the End of this Book*" while tracking his finger under the title. To highlight other important aspects of the book, like who it is going to be about, he might also say, "There's Grover on the cover." Then, he might further draw his child's attention to print by saying, "Look at this street sign. It says *Sesame Street*. That must be where Grover lives." He then may comment about how he holds the book and ask his child if he should turn to the end of the book to start reading. His child may find this silly and will hopefully respond that we start reading at the beginning of books. Subsequently, the father may request that his child turn the front page or cover. On the first page, the father might comment, "Look at what Grover is saying here, *Oh, I am so scared of monsters!*" while pointing to each word. "See how the words tell us what he

> **ALPHABETIC KNOWLEDGE**
> Children's ability to recognize letters of the alphabet and their knowledge of letter–sound relationships.

said?" Then after reading the next page and tracking the print, he might ask his child to guess which word says *monster,* as it is in a different color print than the rest of the words. On subsequent pages, he may request that his child point to some of the fun words sprinkled throughout the book (for example, *SHHH, BING, KLONK*) with him. Overall, parents should use a mixture of verbal and nonverbal print referencing cues— like those suggested in Table 2-11—to cultivate their child's knowledge of concepts of print while reading together.

TABLE 2-11. CONCEPTS OF PRINT: STRATEGIES FOR PARENTS

What to Do	How to Do It	Age(s)
Expose your child to a Print-Rich Environment	Post labels on items throughout the house such as your desk, refrigerator, bed, bookcase, toy box, and mirror. Encourage your child to pick out objects to label and to write or decorate the labels himself.	
Reference the Print in Books	Ask your child questions that focus on elements of print in the book. For example, "Where should we look to find the author's name?" or "Can you show me where I should start reading on this page?" Another way to highlight print is to comment on word length. As you read together, point to the words on the page, and occasionally make comments such as, "Wow, look at this word, it's a long one. It says, *caterpillar.*"	
Pretend Read	Have your child pretend to read a story to you or a favorite stuffed animal. This type of practice can foster confidence, interest in reading, and opportunities to practice print conventions and concepts.	

continues

TABLE 2-11. CONTINUED

What to Do	How to Do It	Age(s)
Make a Book Together	Make a book together. Your child can use familiar photographs, paint, or draw pictures on the pages and you can help write labels or words on the page as your child dictates the story. Then you can read the words together while you or your child point to them while you read. Writing down a story that your child tells is a great activity any time your child is interested in doing so.	
Write in Front of Your Child	In front of your child, engage in various writing activities yourself. Examples include making grocery and to-do lists, writing checks, doing crossword puzzles, and writing postcards while on vacation. When your child observes you writing, say the words aloud to help develop her understanding that print represents spoken language. You can also "think aloud" and explain how you are writing (for example, from left to right, in a straight line).	
Read in Front of Your Child	Read a variety of print in front of your child. Examples include reading books, magazines, emails, street and store signs, recipes, coupons and advertisements, and labels at the grocery store. You can even read your grocery list aloud and have your child try to "read" the corresponding words on the items you are buying. By allowing your child to see you reading different things, he is more likely to learn that people read print for a variety of reasons.	

What to Do	How to Do It	Age(s)
Practice Reading at a Restaurant	When you are at a restaurant, show your child the menu and how you read the words, pointing to them while you do so. When the server arrives to take the order, your child can show the server what she wants by pointing to the appropriate words on the menu.	
Write a Card Together	When you give a gift to someone, have your child help make a card with a message in it. Show your child how you write the name of the gift recipient on the envelope or tag.	
Re-write the Words to Songs	Sing songs that help your child remember certain concepts of print. For example, the following verses of a song can be sung to the tune of "The Farmer in the Dell":"The author writes the book, the author writes the book, Hi ho librario, the author writes the book. The illustrator draws, the illustrator draws, Hi ho librario, the illustrator draws."	

Alphabetic Knowledge

When parents think about helping their children get ready for school, promoting alphabetic knowledge may be one of the first things that comes to mind. In fact, alphabetic knowledge may have been what you initially thought this chapter on emergent literacy was going to be all about. *Alphabetic knowledge,* one of the significant "roots" of reading, includes children's ability to recognize letters of the alphabet and their knowledge of the relationship between sounds and the letters that represent them. You can probably see now, though, that alphabetic knowledge is just one of the many important roots of reading and that all of these roots work together to help children become readers.

Why Is Alphabetic Knowledge Important for Future Reading Development?

Research suggests that alphabetic knowledge is one of the strongest factors in reading acquisition and achievement.[73] Children with greater alphabetic knowledge are much more likely to learn to read quickly and experience reading success than those with less developed alphabetic knowledge. For example, when a child is first learning to read the word *bat*, she will need to quickly remember that the first letter is a *B* and symbolizes the sound /b/ before she can even attempt to put the sounds together and recognize the word on her own. Research indicates that knowledge of both letter names and letter sounds is predictive of later reading,[74] suggesting that parents need to help their children develop both phoneme awareness and alphabetic knowledge in order to begin decoding texts.

> **Research indicates that knowledge of both letter names and letter sounds is predictive of later reading, suggesting that it is important that parents' early efforts support the development of both aspects of alphabetic knowledge.**

How Does Children's Alphabetic Knowledge Develop Over Time?

You may wonder which letters children are likely to learn first. Should you start with the beginning of the alphabet? What about the letters in their name? Are uppercase or lowercase letters easier for children to learn? Researchers have actually spent countless hours investigating these questions, and we have outlined some of their general findings to help give you a sense of how children's alphabetic knowledge typically develops and how you might use this knowledge to support their growth by following their natural interests and tendencies. Box 2-2 gives even more information.

BOX 2-2. LETTER LEARNING TIPS

1. Pick a letter that gives a clue to what sound it makes (like "dee" for *Dog* instead of "double-u" for *Whale*) and ask your child to guess the letter sound.
2. Letters that make more than one sound (such as *G* in *goat* and *giraffe*) will be trickier for your child.
3. Your child's name is exciting for him! Consider starting to teach about letter names and sounds with your child's name.
4. Your child will probably be more interested in and better at learning uppercase letters first.

Uppercase versus lowercase letters. When learning the names of letters, young children tend to prefer uppercase letters, despite the fact that they see more lowercase letters in books.[75] Perhaps because of this preference, children are most commonly able to name uppercase letters prior to lowercase letters.[76] Then, when they begin to learn lowercase letters, they most quickly learn names of those letters they already know in the uppercase.[77] Children are also more likely to easily learn the names of lowercase letters that are similar in form to their uppercase counterpart (for example, *Z* is very similar to *z*, but *D* is not very similar to *d*).[78]

Children's names. Although one might expect that the order in which children learn their letters would follow the order of the alphabet, moving from *A* to *Z*, young children are not quite as methodical as that. Although children are slightly more likely to learn letters that appear earlier in the "ABC" song, they are far more likely to learn the letters in their own names.[79] This may be due to how much more often children typically see their own names in print (for example, on their backpack, in their room, on a clothing label) relative to other words, or it is possible that children are actually more excited and motivated to know letters from their own names.[80] Although familiarity with uppercase letters appears to have the strongest effect on children's acquisition of lowercase letter-name knowledge, children also learn lowercase letter names at a faster rate for those letters found in their own names.[81]

Letter–sound knowledge. While children are learning the names of letters, the development of letter–sound knowledge is being helped along as well. That is, children appear to use their knowledge of letter names to learn letter–sound correspondences.[82] For example, imagine a young child whose mother is reading *Brown Bear, Brown Bear, What Do You See?*[83] to him. She points to the letter *B* and asks, "What sound do you think this letter makes?" The child is able to use the letter name, "bee" as a clue that the sound it represents is /b/, demonstrating how the child's knowledge of the letter name makes it is easier for him to learn this letter–sound correspondence as well.[84]

Children have an easier time learning the sounds for letters when the letter name provides a "clue" to the sound. For example, learning the sounds for *B* or *F,* letters that contain the sounds they make in their names, is easier than for *W* or *H,* letters that do not contain the sounds they make in their names. Furthermore, children have an even easier time learning the sounds of letters if the clue in the letter name is at the beginning of the letter name rather than the end.[85] For example, learning that the letter *B* ("bee") makes the sound /b/ is easier than learning that *F* ("eff") makes /f/. Children also have more difficulty acquiring letter–sound knowledge for letters that represent more than one sound.[86] For instance, it is not uncommon for children to become confused by the letter *C* ("see") which can make the /s/ ("sss") sound as in *circus* or the /k/ sound as in *car.* This is just one example of how the English language does not have a one-to-one correspondence between letters and sounds.

In fact, as alluded to earlier in this chapter, the writing system of the English language is quite complex and poses many more challenges for children than the writing systems of all other alphabetic languages. As we mentioned before, some sounds can be represented by more than one letter (for example, *ck* in *chick* represents only one sound /k/), and some sounds can be spelled with a variety of letter patterns (for example, the long *i* sound can be represented by –*i_e* as in *mice* or *–igh* as in *light*, among other possibilities). Of course, most of what children learn about alphabetic knowledge before they head to kindergarten is centered mostly on those letters and letter sounds that do not have complex relationships. Nonetheless, because the writing system of the English language is the most complex of all alphabetic languages, learning to read in English is much more difficult and will take more time than learning to read other alphabetic languages.[87] Despite these challenges, with appropriate support at home and school, most children learn to decode, or sound out, words in English during their early elementary school years. A beginning reader's development is dependent upon their understanding of the **alphabetic principle**—

the idea that letters and letter patterns represent the sounds of spoken language and can be applied to letter sequences to read words fluently. In an alphabetic system such as English, acquiring the alphabetic principle is a major milestone.

> **ALPHABETIC PRINCIPLE**
> The idea that letters and letter patterns represent the sounds of spoken language and can be applied to letter sequences to read words fluently.

To help children make progress toward this significant accomplishment, it can be helpful for parents to know what would be considered "typical" development of alphabetic knowledge. It should be noted, however, that it is normal for children to develop foundational literacy skills at different rates, and therefore the milestones detailed in Table 2-12 are meant to offer guidance rather than be prescriptive.

What Is the Role of Parents in Fostering Alphabetic Knowledge?

You probably engage your child in both informal and formal literacy experiences at home. Through some activities, like more traditional storybook reading, parents are providing children with *informal* interactions with print. That is, when parents read children bedtime stories, shared attention is probably on the meaning of the story rather than the features of

TABLE 2-12. ALPHABETIC KNOWLEDGE MILESTONES

Age	Milestones
Age 4	Approximately half of all children can: • recognize the first letter of their name • identify the names of some printed letters
Age 5	Many children can: • recognize their own name and other familiar words (for example, a friend's name) in print • identify the names of more than half of uppercase and lowercase letters in print • begin to understand letter–sound correspondences
End of Kindergarten	Children should be able to: • identify most uppercase and lowercase letters quickly and effortlessly • be relatively proficient in basic letter–sound correspondences
Early Elementary School	• Children develop knowledge of more complex correspondences between letter and sound patterns

print on the pages. In these types of interactions, parents are still exposing children to printed material, but the exposure is informal.[88] In contrast, *formal* literacy activities are when parents and children focus on print, and parents choose to use reading time as a teaching opportunity by talking about letters or providing the name or sound of specific letters.[89] Research suggests that although traditional parent–child shared story reading and parent teaching of print are both important for later literacy development, they affect children's skills through different pathways.

In one study, Monique Sénéchal and her colleagues[90] looked at how often parents engaged their children in informal interactions with print, such as traditional shared read-alouds, and how often they involved children in activities that included more formal interactions with print, such as more explicit teaching about letter names. The study found that informal literacy experiences were related to the development of children's oral language skills (such as vocabulary and listening comprehension), whereas more formal parent teaching experiences were related to children's emergent literacy skills, such as alphabetic knowledge. A follow-up study found that these early experiences continued to affect children's reading skills through first and third grade, suggesting that both formal and informal literacy experiences are valuable in building some of the foundational skills needed for later reading success.[91]

One of the other important findings from this study was that parents' tendencies to engage their children in informal literacy activities weren't necessarily related to their tendencies to engage in formal literacy activities. That is, parents who frequently read books with their children did not necessarily also engage in a lot of teaching about letters and print.[92] This finding has been supported in other research as well.[93] In the study described above, researchers looked at "high-teach/low-read" parents (parents who engaged in frequent teaching of alphabetic knowledge skills, but infrequent book reading) and "low-teach/high-read" parents (parents who did not frequently teach alphabetic knowledge skills, but frequently engaged in book reading).[94] They found that the children of these two groups of parents showed different trajectories of reading skill development in elementary school. The children in the high-teach/low-read group performed better on achievement tests in first grade. However, by the time children were in third grade, this advantage disappeared, and the children in the low-teach/high-read group were now outperforming their peers. This may be reflective of the fact that when children initially learn to read, skills such as alphabet knowledge are more important as children are learning the mechanics of reading. However, once children begin to read more difficult texts, their oral language skills (for example, vocabulary knowledge) become more important in determining their success as a reader. It is important to note that in the study described above, a third group of children, whose parents were described as high-teach/high-read outperformed all other groups by grade three, highlighting the importance of engaging in multiple types of early literacy activities with your child.[95] Given the apparent benefits of having high-teach/high-read experiences, even parents who read with their children frequently should try to foster alphabetic knowledge in their children using myriad early literacy activities, including additional strategies that will be discussed shortly.

Developing Alphabetic Knowledge: How Can I Support My Child's Individual Needs?

Beyond the benefits of using a host of strategies to help your child develop her alphabetic knowledge, research also suggests that it is best to adjust your activities to engage your child in a way that maintains individual interest and excitement about print. Moreover, because children develop alphabetic knowledge at different rates, it will be best for parents to use their awareness of how it develops to pick the strategies and prompts they use. We discuss some general guidelines here. Start with concentrating on uppercase letters while engaging in any activities.[96] Once you have incorporated a focus on lowercase letter development into activities, your child will have more success if you start with letters your child already knows in uppercase form.[97] Moreover, when focusing on letter–sound correspondences with a child who is just beginning to pair letters and sounds, it will be best to strategically select letters for which the letter name gives a clue to the sound it represents and the clue is at the beginning of the letter name (for example, *B* rather than *F*).[98] In contrast, for a more advanced child, focusing on a range of letter–sound correspondences, including those sounds for which clues are not provided by the letter name (for example, *W* or *Y*) may be appropriate. For all children, using their names—or any words of great interest—may help engage them with print and promote the development of alphabetic knowledge.[99]

What Activities and Strategies Can I Use to Support Alphabetic Knowledge?

We will now look at activities and strategies to support your child's development of alphabetic knowledge. As you can see, the strategies are becoming very familiar! They include creating print-rich environments, engaging in shared reading and print referencing, and participating in shared writing activities. We hope you are beginning to grasp how these activities can be used to encourage the development of many different skills. Even though these are skills that require practice, these suggestions highlight ways to make that practice playful and enjoyable for your child. Even more examples are included in Table 2-13 and appendix B, so be sure to look those activities over too.

Print-rich environments. Just as print-rich environments can support the development of phonological awareness and concepts of print, providing a multitude of experiences with printed texts can augment the development of alphabetic knowledge as well. For example, incorporating print into play can be useful for promoting alphabet knowledge.[100] When you create a "grocery store" with your child, you can make labels with all uppercase letters when she is younger or has less well developed alphabetic knowledge skills, and you can incorporate lowercase letters as her skill develops over time. Your use of common household materials can also support alphabetic knowledge. For example, you might save old cereal and snack boxes to put in the "grocery store." You can ask your child to find certain letters on the labels you created or on a given cereal box. Children who practice this at home will feel increasingly confident when you ask them to locate the box of cereal that starts with the letters *CH* when you go the real grocery store.

Shared reading and print referencing. Parents who frequently engage in shared reading experiences and frequently teach about alphabetic knowledge have children with the most reading success after a few years of elementary school. Therefore, we hope it is clear that reading books and teaching about alphabetic knowledge are not mutually exclusive experiences. Indeed, adult–child shared reading is an excellent time to cultivate your child's acquisition of alphabetic knowledge because books provide many opportunities for you to support your child's learning of letter names and sounds. That is, by drawing your child's attention to the print in books, rather than solely the pictures, you provide your child with additional opportunities to learn the letters of the alphabet and their corresponding sounds as you point them out. In turn, your child is more likely to develop alphabetic knowledge skills as needed for future reading success in elementary school.[101] To maximize your support of alphabetic knowledge, you can use books that are, by design, more likely to draw your child's attention to the print, such as alphabet books (for example, *Chicka Chicka Boom Boom*[102]; *Click, Clack, Quackity-Quack*[103]; *Dr. Seuss' ABC Book*[104]) or other print-salient storybooks. A list of print-salient storybooks can be found in the previous section on concepts of print.[105]

Nonetheless, verbally referencing print can potentially support letter–name and letter–sound learning wherever print is available, be it new or favorite storybooks, alphabet books, signs on the road, items in the pantry, or labels at the grocery store. Verbal cues can include comments, requests, or questions about print and can be focused on alphabetic knowledge.[106] For example, while reading *Wild About Books*,[107] a parent might say, "That's the letter *B*. It says /b/, like in *book*," "Help me find the *O*," "Let's see how the *O* is made. Watch how I trace the *O* with my finger. Now you try," or "What letter is this? Do you know what sound it makes?" Although all these forms of print referencing can be beneficial, asking questions (for example, "Which letter on this page makes a /t/ sound?") is significantly more likely to produce responses from your child than making comments (for example, "This is the letter *K*.").[108] Furthermore, children are actually more likely to learn letter–sound correspondences if strategies focus on promoting the acquisition of letter names and sounds jointly, rather than focusing on letter–sound instruction alone.[109] Thus, when engaging in activities with your child, you can use comments, requests, and questions that encourage children to think about both letter names and the sounds that are represented by those letters.

Shared writing activities. Beyond the value of shared reading experiences, shared writing activities and games can help your child acquire alphabetic knowledge as well.[110] There are a number of enjoyable ways to have your child share in the writing process with you, a topic we will talk about much more in the next chapter. Because it is both familiar and exciting, teaching children to recognize their own name

TABLE 2-13. ALPHABETIC KNOWLEDGE: STRATEGIES FOR PARENTS

What to Do	How to Do It	Age(s)
Create a Print Rich Environment	Incorporate print into play by creating a "grocery store" with your child. When her alphabetic knowledge skills aren't fully developed, make labels with all uppercase letters; incorporate lowercase letters as your child's skill develops. Also, use common household materials to support alphabetic knowledge. For example, you might save old cereal and snack boxes to put in the grocery store.	
Draw Attention to Letters in Books	Read books such as *Chicka Chicka Boom Boom*; *Click, Clack, Quackity-Quack*; and *Dr. Seuss' ABC Book* or other print-salient storybooks designed to draw your child's attention to print. Also, verbally refer to print. When reading *Wild About Books,* say, "That's the letter *B*. It says /b/, like in *book*," "Help me find the *O*," "Let's see how the *O* is made. Watch how I trace the *O* with my finger. Now you try," or "What letter is this? Do you know what sound it makes?"	
Write with Your Child	Encourage your child to write his name using refrigerator letter magnets, stickers, or newspaper cutouts. Writing favorite letters or words in finger paint, sand, shaving cream, bath water, and even the air is another fun way to practice.	
Make Letter Drawings	Draw pictures of items that look like the letter. For example, draw an *f* for a flower stem. This is especially great for budding artists who get excited to express themselves in this way.	
Play Letter Bingo	Play Letter Bingo. You can make your own boards by drawing the squares and picking the letters (or have your child pick the letters you write). You can call out letter names or sounds when having your child search for a letter on the bingo board.	

continues

TABLE 2-13. CONTINUED

What to Do	How to Do It	Age(s)
Create Writing Centers at Home and Writing Kits for When You Are on the Move	Have a "writing center" in a play area of your house, and bring a mobile "writing kit" with you while you are running errands. Provide crayons, pencils, markers, stickers, newspaper, and writing paper. Not only can you include conventional writing tools, you can try using novel materials such as sidewalk chalk, sand, shaving cream, or honey.	A B C
Have Letters for Breakfast	Make pancakes into letters. You can either pour the batter into letter shapes or make traditional pancakes and cut them accordingly. Your child will love having a pancake message for breakfast.	A B C
Use Your Back as a Chalk Board	Play a guessing game by writing out letters or whole words, using your finger on your child's arm or back. Have him try and guess what you have written and then switch roles, so you need to guess.	A B C
Make Dough Letters	Construct letters out of play dough or cookie dough. You can either roll out the dough and construct the letters yourself or use cookie cutters.	A B C
Make Alphabet Soup	Eat alphabet soup and discuss the letters and sounds they make.	A B C
Play Letter Games in the Bath	Provide sticky letters for bath time. Make up a variety of games using these.	A B C
Play I Spy...	Play I Spy. You can look for letters in books, around the room, while driving, or at the grocery store. You can search for uppercase or lowercase letters, letters by names or the sounds they make, or for letters by describing their features (for example, it has a tall leg and a line across it that looks like arms, for the letter *T*).	A B C

and providing them meaningful opportunities to write their name (for example, having them sign in at preschool with your help) can be valuable. Children may also respond well to recognizing and writing any words or names that they find particularly interesting (for example, the name of a parent or pet). Further, your child may be more engaged in shared writing experiences if you offer a variety of materials and methods. For example, your child may enjoy looking for the letters in his name using refrigerator letter magnets, writing his name using stickers or newspaper cutouts, or writing favorite letters or words in finger paint, sand, shaving cream, bath water, and even the air. Since writing is developmental and actually begins with scribbles, a young child's active engagement in shared writing is more important than needing to write "correct" letters with a pencil and paper. Having a young child taking a first stab at narrating his own story by including scribbles at the bottom of the page is an emergent writing activity. Even though those scribbles are not comprehensible to others, he will likely be able to "read" his story back to you if you ask him. Over time, he will be able to represent the story using more accurate letter and word representations, beginning by approximating word length with the length of each scribble (for example, drawing a short scribble for *the* and a longer scribble for the word *elephant*). Although an older child will have had formal instruction in how to correctly write letters, he will still likely enjoy writing with a variety of materials. There is much more to come on this topic in the next chapter!

Conclusion

Children develop many varied skills that, during their early years, lay the groundwork for learning to read. Although phonological awareness is not yet commonly known as an important early literacy skill, the focus on it in this chapter has hopefully helped you becoming familiar with what it is, why it is so immensely significant for your child, and how to help develop it. Whereas a small number of children are already quite strong in phonological awareness and can do things such as speak Pig

Latin on their own, the overwhelming majority of children need and benefit from explicit strategies that help them become consciously aware of the structure of our spoken language. You can play a pivotal role in preventing reading difficulties by providing an enriching environment and activities that incorporate such strategies. Similarly, you can help your child understand a broad range of concepts of print, which will facilitate future interactions with printed texts in elementary school and future success with reading acquisition and achievement. Before you read this chapter, alphabetic knowledge was likely the skill you considered most when thinking about skills that lay the groundwork for reading development. Now that you know how this skill is reciprocally related to the others we discussed in this chapter, we hope you have come to understand the greater intricacies of this skill and additional means by which you can foster its development in order to increase your child's ability to benefit from literacy instruction in the early years of formal schooling.

Although phonological awareness, concepts of print, and alphabetic knowledge were generally discussed separately in this chapter, they in fact develop at the same time and in relation to one another.[111] Indeed, each of these roots of reading support each other and work together to generate a stem that can break through the soil and eventually flower into skilled reading. Therefore, by providing support in all three areas during the early years of your child's life, you will be able to maximize his or her emergent literacy development and in turn ensure your child's capacity to blossom into a delightfully skilled and lifelong reader.[112] By providing a strong language- and literacy-rich environment in your home, which includes shared reading and writing activities, as well as opportunities to play numerous games and activities that target phonological awareness, concepts of print, and alphabetic knowledge, your child will be more fully prepared for reading instruction and able to take advantage of what each grade has to offer. In addition, picking activities that your child is developmentally ready for and enthusiastic about makes it more likely that your emerging reader will become a confident and voracious reader years down the line.

TABLE 2-14. TECH TIPS FOR PARENTS: EMERGENT LITERACY

Tech Tips: Emergent Literacy

Technology tools can allow your child to practice skills that are learned through a great deal of exposure, like many phonemic awareness and phonics skills. But they cannot replace the experience of sitting down and reading with a parent: technology tools cannot help a child how to handle a book, or develop many concepts of print. For those of us who love the smell or a new book or paging through the worn pages of a book we've loved for years, the idea of reading electronically can lack some magic. Use the activities in this table sparingly, to build specific skills your child may need more practice to master.

What to Do	How to Do It	Age(s)
Listen to Audiobooks While Looking at The Print Version, or Read an E-book	Your child can build word recognition skills by following along with an audiobook while tracking the words in the printed version of the book. Reading along with an electronic version of the book can facilitate these skills even more, because many ebooks provide visual tracking devices and break down sentences into chunks that should be read together before taking a pause (a strategy called phrase-cued reading). This type of visual tracking device can also help your child develop concepts of print.	

continues

TABLE 2-14. CONTINUED

What to Do	How to Do It	Age(s)
Seek Out Television Programs and Computer Applications That Focus on Specific Emergent Literacy Skills	There are so many ways that you can foster emergent literacy skills at home with your child, but you also have many other things to keep you busy! There may come a time when you feel like your child needs more direct practice playing with sounds, identifying letters, and putting these two skill sets together. Because practicing these skills can be tedious, the programs and games below can help make the process fun. To build a variety of emergent literacy skills, children can watch PBS's *Super WHY!* program. There is also an associated application called *Super WHY! ABC Adventures: Alphabet* for smartphones and tablets that helps children learn to recognize letters and letter sounds. To build phonemic awareness and letter–sound correspondence, children can play electronic games (for instances, those that help them distinguish between sounds like *B* and *P* or ask them to identify the letter that represents a sound voiced by the technology took). To build letter–name knowledge, playing *LetterSchool* on an iPad is a wonderful way to learn upper and lower case letters. It allows children to trace the letters and numbers. To build and practice sight word recognition, find "beat the clock" games that make this activity exciting for children.	

TABLE 2-15. ENGLISH LANGUAGE LEARNER TIPS FOR PARENTS: EMERGENT LITERACY

English Language Learner Tips: Emergent Literacy

Emergent literacy refers to the very first stages of literacy development, and includes the development of phonological awareness, concepts of print, and alphabetic knowledge. Being raised bilingually will support your child's development of emergent literacy as he is exposed to songs, poetry, and stories to build phonological awareness and vocabulary in both languages, and a wider variety of literacy materials that can be compared and contrasted to highlight similarities and differences in books across languages. Moreover, it is well known that knowledge of letter names and sounds among preschoolers is one of the best predictors of reading and spelling acquisition later, in school. This finding holds true in English, French, Dutch, Brazilian Portuguese, and Hebrew. At the same time, your child might face unique challenges in the development of emergent literacy due to exposure to different alphabets or principles of print. As your child develops an understanding of L1, he may have difficulty when exposed to books in L2 if he tries to generalize emergent literacy skills across both. For example, a child who has learned to read from right-to-left in Hebrew may attempt to read a book printed in English from right-to-left. By using just a few simple strategies, you can make a significant difference in helping your child become an avid, successful reader. In this table we have included a wide range of strategies that can have far reaching, positive impacts on your child's emergent literacy learning.

What to Do	How to Do It	Age(s)
Play with Words in Your Home Language	Nursery rhymes, children's songs, and poems can help build children's sensitivity to the sound structure of spoken language. Sing songs, rhymes, chants, or tongue twisters in your home language. Children's books in L1 that use rhyme, substitution, alliteration (that is, words that begin with the same sound help your child focus on different aspects of language). As children attend to and manipulate sounds in their home language, help them transfer phonological awareness skills to English by switching back and forth between the two languages to help your child perceive or hear the sounds.	

continues

TABLE 2-15. CONTINUED

What to Do	How to Do It	Age(s)
Make Labels of Objects in Both Languages	All children can benefit from being exposed to an environment rich in print, with labels for objects throughout the house. Labels and signs can have both pictures and words in L1 and L2. You could use different colored paper or ink to display each language.	
Sing the Alphabet Song in Both Languages	Sing the alphabet song in L1 as well as in English. Knowing the alphabet song in an orthography helps a child to learn the letter names.	
Use Letter Tiles When Sounding Out Words	Children who have learned to read in L1 have a distinct advantage because they are able to learn this concept with familiar sounds and words. However children who have not learned to read in L1 may struggle to put together the sound/symbol correspondence concept, new words, and new sounds all at once because they don't have a firm base in L2. Use letter tiles to scaffold the sounding out of words in both languages.	
Make a Connection between Sounding Out Words in L1 ad L2	For children with strong L1 literacy skills, help them understand that the process of sounding out words is the same across languages. Explain some letters may make the same or similar sounds in both languages. Knowing this can help Spanish-dominant children, for example, as they learn to decode words in English.	

Notes

1. Sulzby, E., & Teale, W. H. (1991). Emergent literacy. In R. Barr, M. L. Kamil, P. B. Mosenthal, & P. D. Pearson (Eds.) *Handbook of Reading Research, vol. 2* (pp. 727–758). Mahwah, NJ: Lawrence Erlbaum; Whitehurst, G. J., & Lonigan, C. J. (1998). Child development and emergent literacy. *Child Development, 69,* 848–872.

2. National Early Literacy Panel (NELP). (2008). *Developing Early Literacy: Report of the National Early Literacy Panel.* Washington, DC: National Institute for Literacy.

3. Ibid.

4. Ibid.

5. Ibid.

6. Anthony, J. L., & Francis, D. J. (2005). Development of phonological aware-ness. *Current Directions in Psychological Science, 14*(5), 255–259.

7. Blachman, B. A. (2000). Phonological awareness. In M. L. Kamil, P. B. Mosenthal, P. D. Pearson, & R. Barr (Eds.), *Handbook of ReadingRresearch, vol. 3* (pp. 483–502). Mahwah, NJ: Lawrence Erlbaum; Bradley, L., & Bryant, P. E. (1983). Categorizing sounds and learning to read: A causal connection. *Nature, 301*(5899), 419–421; Byrne, B., & Fielding-Barnsley, R. (1993). Evaluation of a program to teach phonemic awareness to young children: A 1-year follow-up. *Journal of Educational Psychology, 85*(1), 104–111; Cunningham, A. E. (1990). Explicit versus implicit instruction in phonemic awareness. *Journal of Experimental Child Psychology, 50,* 429–444.; Ehri, L. C., Nunes, S. R., Willows, D. M., Schuster, B. V., Yaghoub-Zadeh, Z., & Shanahan, T. (2001), Phonemic awareness instruc-tion helps children learn to read: Evidence from the national reading panel's meta-analysis. *Reading Research Quarterly, 36*(3), 250–287; Hatcher, P. J., Hulme, C., & Ellis, A. W. (1994). Ameliorating early reading failure by integrating the teaching of reading and phonological skills: The phonological linkage hypothesis. *Child Development, 65*(1), 41–57.; Kjeldsen, A.-C, Niemi, P., & Olofsson, A. (2003). Training phonological awareness in kindergarten level children: Consistency is more important than quantity. *Learning and Instruction, 13*(4), 349–365; Lundberg, I. (1988). Effects of an extensive program for stimulating phonologi-cal awareness in preschool children, *Reading Research Quarterly, 23*(3), 263–284; National Institute of Child Health and Human Development. (2000). *Report of the National Reading Panel. teaching children to read: An evidence-based assessment of the scientific research literature on reading and its implications for reading instruc-tion.* NIH Publication No. 00-4769. Washington, DC: U.S. Government Printing Office; Stanovich, K. E. (1986). Developmental changes in the cognitive corre-lates of reading ability and the developmental lag hypothesis. *Reading Research Quarterly, 21*(3), 267–283.

8. Share, D. L., & Stanovich, K. E. (1995). Cognitive processes in early reading development: A model of acquisition and individual differences. *Issues in Education: Contributions from Educational Psychology*, *1*, 1–57.

9. Ibid.

10. Blachman, (2000); National Early Literacy Panel (2008); NICHD (2000).

11. Stanovich, K. E. (1986). Matthew effects in reading: Some consequences of individual differences in the acquisition of literacy. *Reading Research Quarterly*, *21*, 360–407.

12. Stanovich, K. E. (2000). *Progress in Understanding Reading: Scientific Foundations and New Frontiers*. New York: Guilford.

13. Ibid; NELP (2008); National Reading Panel (NRP; 2000).

14. NRP (2000).

15. Lonigan, C. J., Burgess, S. R., & Anthony, J. L. (2000). Development of emergent literacy and early reading skills in preschool children: Evidence from a latent-variable longitudinal study. *Developmental Psychology*, *36*, 596–613.

16. Blachman (2000); NELP (2008); NRP (2000).

17. Anthony, J. L., Lonigan, C. J., Driscoll, K., Phillips, B. M., & Burgess, S. R. (2003). Preschool phonological sensitivity: A quasi-parallel progression of word structure units and cognitive operations. *Reading Research Quarterly*, *38*, 470–487.

18. NELP (2008).

19. Ibid.

20. Phillips, B. M., Clancy-Menchetti, J., & Lonigan, C. J. (2008). Successful phonological awareness instruction with preschool children: Lessons from the classroom. *Topics in Early Childhood Special Education*, *28*, 3–17.

21. Ibid.

22. Ibid.

23. Anthony, J. L., Lonigan, C. J., Burgess, S. R., Driscoll, K., Phillips, B. M., & Cantor, B. G. (2002). Structure of preschool phonological sensitivity: Overlapping sensitivity to rhyme, words, syllables, and phonemes. *Journal of Experimental Child Psychology*, *82*, 65–92.

24. NELP (2008); NRP (2000).

25. Bus, A. G., & van IJzendoorn, M. H. (1999). Phonological awareness and early reading: A meta-analysis of experimental training studies. *Journal of Educational Psychology*, *91*, 403–414; Byrne, B., & Fielding-Barnsley, R. (1991). Evaluation of a program to teach phonemic awareness to young children. *Journal of Educational Psychology*, *83*, 451–455; NRP (2000); Schneider, W., Roth, E., & Ennemoser, M. (2000). Training phonological skills and letter knowledge in

children at risk for dyslexia: A comparison of three kindergarten intervention programs. *Journal of Educational Psychology, 92*, 284–295.

26. Hogan, T. P., Catts, H. W., & Little, T. D. (2005). The relationship between phonological awareness and reading: Implications for the assessment of phonological awareness. *Language, Speech, and Hearing Services in Schools, 36*, 285–293; Perfetti, C. A., Beck, I., Bell, L., & Hughes, C. (1987). Phonemic knowledge and learning to read are reciprocal: A longitudinal study of first grade children. *Merrill-Palmer Quarterly, 33*, 283–319.

27. Sénéchal, M., LeFevre, J., Thomas, E. M., & Daley, K. E. (1998). Differential effects of home literacy experiences on the development of oral and written language. *Reading Research Quarterly, 33*, 96–116.

28. Stephen Burgess (1997). The role of shared reading in the development of phonological awareness: A longitudinal study of middle to upper class children, *Early Child Development and Care, 127*(1), 191–199.

29. Ibid.

30. Foy, J. G., & Mann, V. A. (2003) Home literacy environment and phonological awareness in preschool children: differential effects for rhyme and phoneme awareness. *Applied Psycholinguistics, 24*, 59–88.

31. Phillips et al. (2008).

32. Cooper, D. H., Roth, F. P., Speece, D. L., & Schatschneider, C. (2002). The contribution of oral language skills to the development of phonological awareness. *Applied Psycholinguistics, 23*, 399–416; De Cara, B., & Goswami, U. (2003). Phonological neighbourhood density: Effects in a rhyme awareness task in five-year-old children. *Journal of Child Language, 30*, 695–710; Metsala, J. L., & Walley, A. C. (1998). Spoken vocabulary growth and the segmental restructuring of lexical representations: Precursors to phonemic awareness and early reading ability. In J. L. Metsala, & L. C. Ehri (Eds.), *Word Recognition in Beginning Literacy.* (pp. 89–120). Mahwah, NJ: Lawrence Erlbaum.

33. Zemach, M. (1976). *Hush, Little Baby.* New York: E. P. Dutton.

34. Galdone, P. (1968). *Henny Penny.* New York: Scholastic.

35. Wood, D., & Wood, A. (1984). *The Napping House.* Orlando, FL: Harcourt Brace.

36. Carle, E. (1993). *Today Is Monday.* New York: PaperStar.

37. Brown, M. W. (1949). *The Important Book.* New York: HarperCollins.

38. Martin, B., & Carle, E., (1992). *Brown Bear, Brown Bear, What Do You See?* New York: H. Holt.

39. Brown, M. W. (1942). *The Runaway Bunny.* New York: HarperCollins.

40. Wood, J. (1991). *Moo, Moo, Brown Cow.* London: All Books for Children.

41. Numeroff, L. (1984). *If You Give A Mouse A Cookie*. New York: HarperCollins.

42. Guarino, D. (1989). *Is Your Mama A Llama?* New York: Scholastic.

43. Langstaff, J. (1957). *Over in The Meadow*. Orlando, FL: Harcourt Brace.

44. Roberts, B. (1992). The evolution of the young child's concept of word as a unit of spoken and written language. *Reading Research Quarterly, 27*, 125–137.

45. Aram, D., & Brion, S. (2004). Joint storybook reading and joint writing interventions among low SES preschoolers: Differential contributions to early literacy. *Early Childhood Research Quarterly, 19*, 588–610.

46. Clay, M. M. (2000). *Concepts About Print: What Have Children Learned About the Way We Print Language?* Portsmouth, NH: Heinemann; NELP (2008).

47. Clay, M. M. (2002). *An Observation Survey of Early Literacy Achievement,* 2nd. ed. Portsmouth, NH: Heinemann.

48. Purcell-Gates, V. (1996). Stories, coupons, and the *TV Guide*: Relationships between home literacy experience and emergent literacy knowledge. *Reading Research Quarterly, 31*, 406–428.

49. Purcell-Gates, V., & Dahl. K. L. (1991). Low-SES children's success and failure at early literacy learning in skills-based classrooms. *Journal of Reading Behavior, 23*, 1–34.

50. NELP (2008).

51. Levin, I., & Bus, A. G. (2003). How is emergent writing based on drawing? Analyses of children's products and their sorting by children and mothers. *Developmental Psychology, 39*, 891–905.

52. Brenneman, K., Massey, C., Machado, S. F., & Gelman, R. (1996). Young children's plans differ for writing and drawing. *Cognitive Development, 11*, 397–419.

53. Bialystok, E. (1995). Making concepts of print symbolic: Understanding how writing represents language, *First Language, 15*, 317–338.

54. Hiebert, E. H. (1981). Knowing about reading before reading: Preschool children's concepts of reading. *Reading Psychology, 4*, 253–260.

55. Bialystok (1995); Hiebert (1981).

56. DeGoes, C., & Martlew, M. (1983). Beginning to read and write: An exploratory study of young children's understanding of metalinguistic terms and graphic conventions. *First Language, 4*, 121–130.

57. Bracken, S. S., & Fischel, J. E. (2008). Family reading behavior and early literacy skills in preschool children from low-income backgrounds. *Early Education and Development, 19*, 45–67; Levy, B. A., Gong, Z., Hessels, S., Evans, M. A., & Jared, D. (2006). Understanding print: Early reading development and the contributions of home literacy experiences. *Journal of Experimental Child Psychology,*

93, 63–93; Weigel, D. J., Martin, S. S., & Bennett, K. K. (2006). Contributions of the home literacy environment to preschool-aged children's emerging literacy and language skills. *Early Child Development and Care, 176*, 357–378.

58. Bracken & Fischel (2008).

59. Ibid.

60. Justice, L. M., & Ezell, H. K. (2002). Use of storybook reading to increase print awareness in at-risk children. *American Journal of Speech-Language Pathology, 11*, 17–29.

61. Evans, M. A., Williamson, K., & Pursoo, T. (2008). Preschoolers' attention to print during shared book reading. *Scientific Studies of Reading, 12*, 106–129; Justice, L.M., Pullen, P.C., & Pence, K. (2008). Influence of verbal and nonverbal references to print on preschoolers' visual attention to print during storybook reading. *Developmental Psychology, 44*, 855–866.

62. Hiebert (1981).

63. Justice & Ezell (2002).

64. Scarborough, H. S., Dobrich, W., & Hager, M. (1991). Preschool literacy experience and later reading achievement. *Journal of Learning Disabilities, 24*, 508–511.

65. Neuman, S. B., & Roskos, K. (1990). The influence of literacy-enriched play settings on preschoolers' engagement with written language. *National Reading Conference Yearbook, 39*, 179–187; Neuman, S. B., & Roskos, K. (1990). Play, print, and purpose: enriching play environments for literacy development. *Reading Teacher, 44*, 214–221.

66. Ibid.

67. Justice et al. (2002); Justice et al. (2008).

68. Evans, M. A., Williamson, K., & Pursoo, T. (2008). Preschoolers' attention to print during shared book reading. *Scientific Studies of Reading, 12*, 106–129; Justice et al. (2008).

69. Lovelace, S., & Stewart, S. R. (2007). Increasing print awareness in preschoolers with language impairment using non-evocative print referencing. *Language, Speech, and Hearing Services in Schools, 28*, 16–30.

70. Justice & Ezell (2004).

71. Smolkin, L. B., & Yaden, D. B. (1992). The effects of genre, visual design choices, and discourse structure on preschoolers' responses to picture books during parent-child read-alouds. *National Reading Conference Yearbook, 41*, 291–301.

72. Stone, J. (1971). *The Monster at the End of This Book*. New York: Golden Books.

73. Lonigan, C. J., Burgess, S. R., & Anthony, J. L. (2000). Development of emergent literacy and early reading skills in preschool children: Evidence from

a latent-variable longitudinal study. *Developmental Psychology, 36*(5), 596–613; NELP (2008); Storch, S. A., & Whitehurst, G. J. (2002). Oral language and code-related precursors to reading: Evidence from a longitudinal structural model. *Developmental Psychology, 38*, 934–947.

74. McBride-Chang, C. (1999) The ABCs of the ABCs: The development of letter-name and letter-sound knowledge. *Merrill-Palmer Quarterly, 45*, 285–308.

75. Treiman, R., Cohen, J., Mulqueeny, K., Kessler, B., & Schechtman, S. (2007). Young children's knowledge about printed names. *Child Development, 78*, 1458–1471.

76. Worden, P. E., & Boettcher, W. (1990). Young children's acquisition of alphabet knowledge. *Journal of Reading Behavior, 22*, 277–295.

77. Turnbull, K. L. P., Bowles, R. P., Skibbe, L. E., Justice, L. M., & Wiggins, A. K. (2010). Theoretical explanations for preschoolers' lowercase alphabet knowledge. *Journal of Speech, Language, and Hearing Research, 53*, 1757–1768.

78. Ibid.

79. Justice, L. M., Pence, K., Bowles, R. B., & Wiggins, A. (2006). An investigation of four hypotheses concerning the order by which 4-year-old children learn the alphabet letters. *Early Childhood Research Quarterly, 21*, 374–389; Treiman, R., & Broderick, V. (1998). What's in a name: Children's knowledge about the letters in their own name. *Journal of Experimental Child Psychology, 70*, 97–116.

80. Nuttin, J. M. (1987). Affective consequences of mere ownership: The name letter effect in twelve European languages, *European Journal of Social Psychology, 17*, 381–402.

81. Turnbull et al. (2010).

82. McBride-Chang (1999); Share, D. L. (2004). Knowing letter names and learning letter sounds: A causal connection. *Journal of Experimental Child Psychology, 88*, 213–233; Treiman, R., Tincoff, R., Rodriguez, K., Mouzaki, A., & Francis, D. J. (1998). The foundations of literacy: Learning the sounds of letters. *Child Development, 69*, 1524–1540.

83. Martin, B., & Carle, E., (1992). *Brown Bear, Brown Bear, What Do You See?* New York: H. Holt.

84. Piasta, S. B., & Wagner, R. K. (2010). Learning letter names and sounds: Effects of instruction, letter type, and phonological processing skill. *Journal of Experimental Child Psychology, 105*, 324–344; Share (2004); Treiman et al. (1998).

85. Treiman, R., Tincoff, R., Rodriguez, K., Mouzaki, A., & Francis, D. J. (1998). The foundations of literacy: Learning the sounds of letters. *Child Development, 69*, 1524–1540.

86. Ibid.

87. Seymour, P. H. K. (2005). Early reading development in European orthographies. In M.J. Snowling & C. Hulme (Eds.), *The Science of Reading: A Handbook*. Oxford: Blackwell.

88. Sénéchal, M., & LeFevre, J. (2002). Parental involvement in the development of children's reading skill: A 5-year longitudinal study. *Child Development*, 73, 445–460.

89. Smolkin, L. B., & Yalden, D. B. (1992). "O" is for "Mouse": First encounters with the alphabet book. *Language Arts, 69*, 432–441.

90. Sénéchal, M., LeFevre, J., Thomas, E. M., & Daley, K. E. (1998). Differential effects of home literacy experiences on the development of oral and written language. *Reading Research Quarterly, 33*, 96–116.

91. Sénéchal, M., & LeFevre, J. (2002). Parental involvement in the development of children's reading skill: A five-year longitudinal study. *Child Development*, 73(2), 445–460.

92. Sénéchal, LeFevre, Thomas, & Daley (1998).

93. Sénéchal, & LeFevre (2002); Evans, M. A., Shaw, D., & Bell, M. (2000). Home literacy activities and their influence on early literacy skills. *Canadian Journal of Experimental Psychology, 54*, 65–75.

94. Sénéchal, M., & LeFevre, J. (2001). Storybook reading and parent teaching: Links to language and literacy development. In P. R. Britto & J. Brooks Gunn (Eds.), *New Directions in Child Development: No. 92. The Role of Family Literacy Environments in Promoting Young Children's Emerging Literacy Skills* (pp. 39–52). San Francisco: JosseyBass.

95. Ibid.

96. Treiman et al. (2007); Worden & Boettcher (1990).

97. Turnbull et al. (2010).

98. Piasta & Wagner (2010); Share (2004); Treiman et al. (1998).

99. Aram & Brion (2004); Justice et al. (2006); Nuttin (1987); Treiman & Broderick (1998).

100. Neuman & Roskos (1990).

101. Justice, L. M., & Ezell, H. K. (2000). Enhancing children's print and word awareness through home-based parent intervention. *American Journal of Speech-Language Pathology, 9*, 257–269; Sénéchal & LeFevre (2002).

102. Martin, B., Archambault, J., & Ehlert, L. (1989). *Chicka Chicka Boom Boom*. New York: Simon & Schuster.

103. Cronin, D. (2005). *Click, Clack, Quackity-Quack: An Alphabetical Adventure*. New York: Simon & Schuster.

104. Seuss, Dr. (1963). *Dr. Seuss' ABC*. New York: Beginner Books.

105. Smolkin, L. B., & Yaden, D. B. (1992). The effects of genre, visual design choices, and discourse structure on preschoolers' responses to picture books during parent-child read-alouds. *National Reading Conference Yearbook, 41*, 291–301.

106. Justice & Ezell (2000).

107. Sierra, J. (2004). *Wild about Books*.New York: Alfred A. Knopf.

108. Justice, L. M., Weber, S. E., Ezell, H. K., & Bakeman, R. (2002) A sequential analysis of children's responsiveness to parental print references during shared book-reading interactions. *American Journal of Speech-Language Pathology, 11*, 30–40.

109. Piasta, S. B., Purpura, D. J., & Wagner, R. K. (2010). Fostering alphabet knowledge development: A comparison of two instructional approaches. *Reading and Writing, 23*, 607–626.

110. Aram & Brion (2004).

111. Dickinson, D. K., McCabe, A., Anastasopoulos, L., Peisner-Feinberg, E. S., & Poe, M. D. (2003). The comprehensive language approach to early literacy: The interrelationships among vocabulary, phonological sensitivity, and print knowledge among preschool-aged children. *Journal of Educational Psychology, 95*, 465–481; Lonigan, C. J., Burgess, S. R., & Anthony, J. L. (2000). Development of emergent literacy and early reading skills in preschool children: Evidence from a latent-variable longitudinal study. *Developmental Psychology, 36*, 596–613.

112. Ibid.

113. Berenstain, S., & Berenstain, J. (1971). *The Berenstains' B Book.* New York: Random House, 1971.

Chapter 3

Learning to Write

How Writing Makes Your Child a Better Reader and Thinker

In schools, reading and writing are often referred to together as the *Language Arts*. This phrase may sound quaint and old-fashioned, but it is a nice reminder that these two skills are closely interconnected and that both focus on the art of using language to convey meaning. For this reason, the oral language skills that we discussed in chapter 1 continue to be important throughout each chapter in this book—language development is the foundation on which reading and writing development rests. Young children, of course, need to learn the mechanics of reading—how to recognize letters (including the *alphabetic knowledge* skills we talked about in chapter 2), sound out words, and read fluently—before they are able to focus on the meaning of a written text. Similarly, they need to learn the mechanics of writing—how to form written letters, spell out words, and write fluently—before they are able to describe their feelings, write stories, and make persuasive arguments in writing in ways that other people can understand easily. Yet, just as toddlers who are not able to read independently can begin to develop story comprehension skills through dialogic reading, even children who are not able to write independently can begin to thoughtfully express themselves on paper with the help of their parents or caregivers. Some of the writing skills we talk about in this chapter may sound advanced, but the roots of writing development also form early, and it may take months or years to see the blossoming evidence that your focus on writing is paying off.

Although adults often do not recognize young children's output as "writing," even three- and four-year-olds demonstrate that they have the intention to write by putting marks on paper and then orally sharing a story that the marks represent, or by brainstorming about what they want to say in a card or about a picture. Throughout this chapter, you will see examples of children's early writing that demonstrate how adept young children are at expressing their feelings and ideas through words and pictures. Our hope is that this chapter will help you recognize the importance of encouraging young children to think like writers, and how being a skilled writer supports reading development. As you will see throughout the chapter, becoming a writer allows your child to think like an author, whose job it is to focus on various qualities of written work, build many language skills, identify different genres of writing, and recognize why texts are organized in particular ways.

> **COMPOSING**
> The act of writing, or selecting the appropriate written language to use when expressing oneself, as well as planning and executing a piece of writing carefully.

As children become writers, they are developing multiple sets of skills. The first set of skills involves **composing** writing, or selecting the appropriate written language to use when expressing oneself, and then planning and executing a piece of writing carefully. Later in this chapter, we will discuss the different genres of writing that children become familiar with, as well as the qualities to look for in any composition. Creating a written composition involves higher-level thinking skills like taking the perspective of the reader, organizational skills like structuring an essay or story, and the language skills we talked about earlier, like word choice and syntax. These composition skills are not skills that you either have or do not have, but instead they are skills that gradually develop over time, beginning when children are still toddlers. Writing with fluency and accuracy also requires being able to match up speech sounds with their corresponding written symbols, or to spell what one wants to say, using the alphabetic knowledge skills we discussed in chapter 2. Finally, the act of writing is also dependent on a child's motor development, and young children's writing becomes more and more recognizable to adults as their motor skills develop and their ability to represent sounds with written letters grows.

As you can see, the act of writing is a developmental process. It requires the maturation of several systems in the brain, including the motor and cognitive systems. Children develop their written language before entering school and through the school years, and move from writing brief and sometimes cryptic statements to becoming writers who plan and carefully select words that convey their intentions and meaning with precision. Children go through different stages while practicing the act of writing, from making repetitive squiggles, to random strings of "letters," to conventionally spelled words. Understanding the development of the writing process will allow you to support your child's growth as a writer, and to uncover the meaning that even those first brief statements and repetitive scribbles hold.

These rudimentary attempts at writing indicate that children are paying attention to the world around them and have realized that the printed word holds meaning. When Jamie was a young child, she—like many other little girls—often tried to behave just like her mother in an attempt to be grown-up. On her fourth birthday, she received a pocketbook as a gift. Eager to begin using it, she immediately filled it with paper clips and coins, and wrote out a bunch of scribbles on a long, thin sheet of paper. Jamie explained to the adults at her party that she was off to the grocery store with her shopping list and that she had put that jumble of objects into her purse so that it looked just like her mother's purse (which then prompted her mother to clean out her own pocketbook). Many children begin to display **emergent writing** because they are mimicking the adults around them,

> **EMERGENT WRITING**
> Children's earliest attempts to explain their ideas in print, ranging from random squiggles to partial representations of words.

> **SPELLING DEVELOPMENT**
> Children's movement through a series of developmental stages, in which they progressively encode more of the sounds they hear into print using appropriate letter representations.

and because they recognize that putting information on paper is a way to both remember it and convey that information to others.

In this chapter, we will focus on the importance of these early acts of writing, as well as the different components and genres of written compositions, and explain how they can assist in the development of key reading skills. We will also talk about **spelling development** and how learning to spell accurately helps children learn to read accurately. Finally, we will provide you with strategies for expanding your child's writing and making written expression a part of everyday life. Helping your child become a writer is important because writing is a vehicle for both developing basic skills, like translating speech into print by using the written representations of letter sounds, and for higher-level skills like developing background knowledge about particular topics.[1]

Writing Development

Although we often think of writing as the act of putting down on paper what we already know, writing is actually an act of reflection and active learning. When we decide to write a letter to someone or an essay for class, we need to consider what the reader already knows and what information we need to provide (and we will talk more about this skill, perspective-taking, in chapter 6). We need to determine the best way to present that information. Sometimes, we need to refer to a dictionary, an encyclopedia, or research found in the library or online in order to make a specific point. For those reasons, writing provides us with an opportunity to organize our thoughts, to engage in planning, and to assess our own knowledge of a particular topic. Even young children display these skills when they write—perhaps by asking their parents questions about a word they want to use or by drawing a picture before titling it as a way to think more deeply about the topic at hand. In many ways, writing is a tool for accessing your own mind in ways that daily life does not always provide.

What Is Writing?

We have already said that writing involves the act of composing, or generating ideas and putting them down on paper. But beyond that broad definition, it is difficult to provide a simple explanation of what constitutes writing, because children's writing abilities change dramatically over time in many ways. As fine motor control increases, scribbles become letters and writing becomes neater, and therefore more of a child's attention can be allocated to thinking about sophisticated writing skills. As a child learns new words, it becomes easier for him to write a story that vividly describes a situation or provides important facts about an event. But children's emergent writing is not yet legible, and often conveys just a small bit of information, which others may or may not be able to comprehend. The multiple skills that **conventional writing** requires generally develop in tandem as children proceed through six stages of writing development.[2]

We will focus on the first stage in depth, because it spans from preschool through first grade, and then briefly discuss the later stages, so that you know what to expect as your child grows and develops.

> **CONVENTIONAL WRITING**
> Legible writing that follows standard rules of grammar, syntax, spelling, and language.

It is especially important for us to discuss all of these stages, because your child won't just move cleanly from one stage to the next. These stages blend into one another, and your child may exhibit some characteristics of one stage and some characteristics of another. As you start to analyze your child's writing more closely, do not use one example alone to make a decision about which writing stage he is in,

TABLE 3-1. STAGES OF WRITING DEVELOPMENT

Stage of Writing Development	Age*	Description	
Imitation	Preschool – First Grade	Children express themselves in writing by mimicking, as best they can, the writing of adults. Children write using squiggles until they realize that letters are meaningful, and then begin to use letters to approximate the spellings of words, often using their own invented spellings.	Emergent Writing Development
Graphic Presentation	First Grade – Second Grade	Children's primary focus is learning to present their writing more clearly, by focusing on writing legibly and beginning to use written conventions (like capitalization and punctuation).	Conventional Writing Development
Progressive Incorporation	Second Grade – Fourth Grade	Children begin to incorporate many qualities of good writing into their work—focusing on both the presentation of the words themselves and issues like word choice and organization.	
Automatization	Fourth Grade – Seventh Grade	Children dedicate attention to planning and revising work because less sophisticated skills like writing legibly and spelling correctly have become automatic	
Elaboration	Seventh Grade – Eighth Grade	Adolescents' written language becomes more sophisticated than their speech, and is used to elaborate upon what they read and know.	
Personalization and Diversification	High School and Beyond	As adolescents develop a voice, writing becomes more personalized. Additionally, writing becomes more diverse in that older students and adults use writing for a wide variety of purposes.	

* Age ranges are approximate

and do not be surprised if all of his writing does not seem to be of the same quality. Some words will be easier for your child to spell accurately than others, and some ideas will be easier to express clearly. Although these stages (defined in Table 3-1) can help you identify general trends in your child's writing development, it is more appropriate to think of about your child's writing being a good illustration of a particular stage, rather than thinking about your child as falling into that stage.

Stage 1: Imitation. The first stage is called *imitation* because young children, who are just beginning to develop control over their fine motor skills, begin to imitate what the adults around them do. This stage, characterized by emergent writing development, lasts roughly from preschool until first grade. In Figure 3-1, three-year-old Theo shows his mother that he can write letters. Notice how he's discovered that writing involves connecting straight lines with circles.

These children pretend to write, making their own writing look as much like their parents' writing as possible. Initially, their writing may

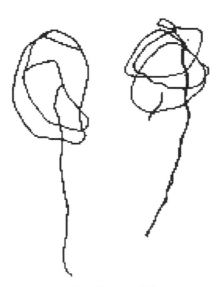

Figure 3-1 Theo (age 3 years, 0 months): "Here is "P.""

be entirely scribbles, but as they realize that letters are meaningful, children—with varying degrees of success—begin to copy them down and try to arrange them in a sequence or on a line, sometimes leaving breaks between groups of letters. As children become familiar with the letters of the alphabet, they begin using these letters to approximate the spellings of words, often using their own invented spellings. Many adults may be familiar with the experience of being handed a page full of scribbles made by a three-year-old who then demands that the adult "read it!" Indeed, at the beginning of this stage, you might not even recognize much of the writing produced by children as such; instead, you might be thinking that the marks are merely shapes or scribbles. However, children recognize that there is special meaning behind the scribbles and shapes their parents draw on paper, and therefore assume that the scribbles and shapes on their own paper must also have special meaning, even if the meaning is not initially tied to particular letters. But by the end of this stage, you will generally get the gist of what a child was trying to convey, even if deciphering his print requires some detective work. Here, we give you some examples of how emergent writing gets more sophisticated over time.

In Figure 3-2, notice that Sophie understands that print goes across the page; that strokes repeat themselves, that writing often consists of

Figure 3-2 Sophie (age 3 years, 7 months): "Dinosaurs are far away."

i ʤn ɡoeʔ ɢ ⁺o ɑ ɧeʍ ɘcy l

Figure 3-3 Clara (age 4 years, 10 months): "I am going to a new school."

lines and circles, as well as angles and curves. She also understands that print represents meaning, as the title she dictates to her teacher shows.

Clara is a year older than Sophie. Figure 3-3 shows how she clearly demonstrates the understanding that pictures and print differ, that words are bound by spaces, and that letters represent sounds. Like Sophie, Clara understands that print carries meaning.

The eldest in our sample, Alden, also understands that each word conveys a separate idea, though he adds dashes in addition to the spaces between them (see Figure 3-4). Like both Sophie and Clara, Alden understands that print carries meaning. Alden also understands, as does Clara, that print represents sound. In addition, however, Alden uses both uppercase and lowercase letters. While he isn't yet aware of how to use them correctly, he does know that letters can be represented both ways, as we can see with his use of both *B* and *b*.

Earlier, we said that deciphering your young child's emergent writing required some detective work, and here, we want to give you some clues so that you can better understand the strategies that your child is using when she tries to produce written work. Written work is different

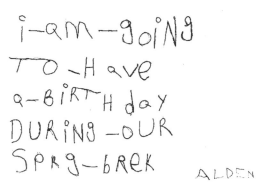

Figure 3-4 Alden (age 5 years, 0 months) shows his awareness of upper and lowercase letters.

than the pictures that children draw in many ways. Drawings are meant to visually represent actual people, objects, or places—the sketch that a child makes (however imperfect) is supposed to look like something that he has seen before. Writing, in contrast, is an abstract description of that person, object, or place that relies upon using arbitrary symbols (that is, letters) to capture the spoken words that the child might say about that thing.[3]

These arbitrary symbols, which adults form with ease, are difficult for young children to begin to use for reasons related to both motor and cognitive development. Fine motor skills, which are required to grip a pen or pencil and make the straight lines and curves that depict written language, develop over the course of many years. And the same principles that govern children's growing understanding that phonemes and letters are related, discussed in more depth in chapter 2, also take several years to fully develop. Before children recognize the significance of each individual letter, they notice that all letters are formed by making straight lines and curves. For that reason, children's earliest attempts at writing focus primarily on using these shapes in ways that mimic what they see adults doing as they write. Attempts at early writing display a number of graphic principles that embody children's rudimentary attempts to replicate written language.[4] You can use these principles to recognize your child's early writing attempts.

These principles include the *recurring principle,* meaning that the same shapes recur over and over again in young children's writing. Very early attempts at writing may include a series of repeating curves or waves, or a series of lines. Slightly more sophisticated attempts will include both curves and lines, like those that we saw in Sophie's writing in Figure 3-2. This ability to vary the marks made on the page—to include both curves and lines in different combinations—is referred to as the *generative principle.* Even before a child is able to convey meaning through his writing, this ability to form different types of marks and multiple letters will make his writing look more like the written language we are used to seeing, just like Theo's approximations of the letter *P* (Figure 3-1).

As children begin to pair the sounds in words with the arbitrary symbols that represent those sounds, they may discover that there are a limited number of shapes that they can use to depict these symbols. The tools at their disposal include:

| – / ∩ ∪ ⊃ ⊂ O .

Using these same shapes in different combinations produces different letters. For example, pairing a line with a curve can form a lowercase *b, d, p,* or *q.*

| + ⊃ gives us a *b*
| + ⊃ gives us a *p*
⊂ + | gives us a *d*
⊂ + | gives us a *q*

When you look at letter formation from a child's eyes, it becomes easier to understand why certain letters can be easily confused. If a child has not yet developed the alphabetic principle, or the ability to match sounds with the letters that represent them, and subsequently incorrectly paired the sound /b/ in bed with the letter *d* instead of the letter *b,* then the particular pairing of the line and the curve may not seem as meaningful as just using those two shapes. In other words, to him, the sound /b/ should be represented by a straight line and a curved line—but the order in which those two shapes appear and their orientation on the page do not seem particularly important to him.

This idea that the particular pairing of a letter's component parts is meaningful becomes even more confusing if you consider the fact that, for the objects we see and draw, flipping or rotating a shape does not change the meaning of the shape. The example that reading researchers often give to explain this idea is that of a chair.[5] Take a look at any chair in the room you are sitting in right now or glance at Figure 3-5. If that chair was turned upside down, would you still recognize it as a chair? If the chair were rotated to face the wall instead of the table, would you still know what it was? Of course. Yet, if we take the letter *b* and do the same thing, it takes on a different meaning.

This idea—that the direction something is facing matters—is fairly unique to writing. A child needs to experiment extensively with writing in order for this notion to gel in his mind, and for him to begin to differentiate a *b* from a *d,* he will need time and practice. These types of letter transpositions and reversals are to be expected in the writing of young children—with great frequency when children first begin forming letters (when they are four to six years old) and then with decreasing

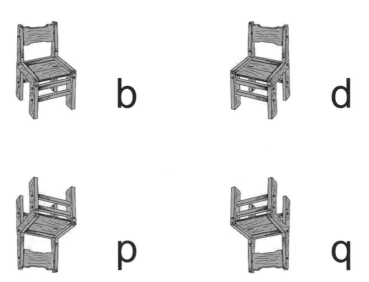

Figure 3-5 Flipping or rotating a shape does not change the meaning of that shape.

frequency as these letters become more familiar (when they are six to eight years old).

The way that children arrange their words on a page also develops over time. Young children often write where it is most convenient—in the space left after they complete a drawing, or the part of the page that is easiest for them to access, without regard for whether the paper is parallel with their desk or on a diagonal. Writing from left to right on each line, and top to bottom on each page, is another arbitrary convention. In fact, this convention is not consistent across languages. Jamie works with a number of children who read both in English and in Hebrew. These children need to remember to read from left to right in English but from right to left in Hebrew! Just as children begin to recognize print conventions in the books they read through exposure, they need time and practice to apply these conventions to their own writing. As we will see in the next stage of writing development, issues of letter formation and page arrangement start to get sorted out when children receive formal instruction in reading and writing.

Stage 2: Graphic Presentation. As children continue through first grade and into second grade, they enter stage 2, *graphic presentation,* which begins the process of conventional writing development. The stage is aptly named, because children's primary focus at this point in time is learning how to present their writing more clearly, by focusing on writing legibly and beginning to use written conventions like capitalization and punctuation. Children continue to use invented spellings and may become more self-conscious about how their work looks. Some children, in particular the kids whose ability to form letters clearly and spell with some accuracy develops slightly later, may be unhappy when classroom writing is displayed publicly.

Stage 3: Progressive Incorporation. In the later part of second grade and through much of fourth grade, children now begin to incorporate many aspects of the writing process into their work—focusing on both the presentation of the words themselves and issues like word choice and organization. Children in this stage are increasingly able to format their writing appropriately, by indenting paragraphs or adding a salutation to a letter. In classrooms, teachers should begin to focus much more on the rewriting and revision process at this point in time.

Stage 4: Automatization. Through the end of elementary school and much of middle school, children are in the phase of *automatization*. The lower-level writing processes become much more automatic for them, and more attention can be dedicated to the planning and revising processes. A graphic organizer, or a very simple visual representation of the main points to be discussed in a written piece, can help a child plan for writing or revising a piece of writing. In the next section of this chapter, we will provide some examples of graphic organizers that can help children think about how to structure a story so that it includes a clear beginning, middle, and end or how to structure an essay to make all the points they wanted to make. It is in the later elementary school years that children begin to recognize that the writing process begins even before they have a pen or pencil in hand, and requires reflection and planning. The stories and essays written in school unfold over the course of days or weeks as children learn to move from conveying ideas using brief notes to writing a detailed outline and then creating a rough draft. Children learn that the first draft they write is nowhere near complete and spend time revising and proofreading their own work. Helping your child, from an early age, view writing as a process that unfolds over time will help prepare her for this stage of writing development.

In school, during this time period, children begin to develop their expository skills and learn how to use library resources to conduct research. Their primary goal when writing is to convey information to others, perhaps restating the main point made in a book they read. The written language of fourth through seventh graders often approximates their speech, in terms of style and sophistication, although many fourth graders are well aware that they must present information in an organized, well-articulated, and engaging fashion. The example here is from a report prepared by Nathan, a fourth grader in real transition as a writer, who is beginning to recognize how to organize information into paragraphs.

> Hernando Cortez needed to conquer land, but in order to do that he needed every single Aztec to think he was powerful. Cortez went to the Aztec king named Montezuma. Cortez's plan was to make the king believe he was a god, then the Aztecs would do what he said. He could kill the Aztecs, and take over their land.
>
> The battle began. The Spanish army took the Aztec's horses and land. Cortez and his army tricked the Aztecs into thinking they had a disease that could only be cured by gold, so the Aztecs mined gold for Cortez and his army. The Aztec weapons were flint knives, javelins, and clubs made of wood, but the weapons were useless in the battle against Cortez's guns, horses, swords, and dogs.

Stage 5: Elaboration. In the *elaboration* stage, a student's written language is more sophisticated than her speech. Adolescents of this age can use writing for the purpose of problem-solving and clarifying their own ideas, and also to influence others. They no longer just summarize the writing of others, but also elaborate upon what they read and know.

Stage 6: Personalization and Diversification. Finally, throughout high school and beyond, young adults enter the phase of *personalization and diversitification*, where writing becomes more personalized, in that competent writers develop their own styles. Additionally, writing becomes more diverse as older students and adults begin to use writing for a wide variety of purposes. For students who achieve this level of skill, writing becomes a tool that can be utilized by the writer to remember information previously learned, synthesize new information, solve problems and express emotions, and persuade others. Writing can become a joyful way to keep in touch with friends and family, a powerful mechanism for seeking admission to college or applying for a new job, and a way to organize one's thoughts before an important meeting.

However, developing these more sophisticated writing skills over time requires a child to stay motivated and engaged for many years.

Because writing can sometimes feel like (or be taught like) an arduous and tedious task, we need to help children maintain their early enthusiasm for writing and recognize its importance in the development of other literacy skills.

Why Is Writing Important for Future Reading Development?

Children generally make their first attempts to write before they make their first attempts to read independently.[6] That means that they attempt to **encode** spoken language (spell out words while writing) into print before they try to **decode** written language (sound out words from print) and speak the words they see on the page. Encoding and decoding are really aspects of the same process, although we often do not realize how closely connected they are.

ENCODING
Using written language to represent speech sounds in writing.

DECODING
Using spoken language to crack the code of written language and sound out text.

Beginning to write helps children recognize that printed words contain meaning because, by encoding, they are working to get their own meanings meaning down on paper. In contrast, when children are decoding, they need to figure out what another person meant. This underlying understanding that print conveys meaning helps motivate children to engage in the decoding process. Through writing, children develop concepts of print, or understanding the general rules that texts follow, and knowledge of the alphabetic principle, or the ability to pair letters and sounds. We will discuss these issues more in the second half of this chapter on spelling development.

Engaging in writing activities also allows children to reflect upon the varied goals and structures of different types of writing, and therefore identify these aspects of what they read more easily as well.[7] For example, later in this chapter you will see examples demonstrating that even young children attempt to write persuasively. Doing so helps them understand, from the inside-out, that writing can be used to change people's minds—or not! Additionally, there are specific words and phrases, such as "on the other hand" or "once upon a time," that writers use when expressing or introducing different types of ideas. Being familiar with these text features helps children explain their ideas more clearly and better understand what other writers are trying to accomplish when they use these words and phrases. For example, saying "on the other hand" indicates that the writer is comparing and contrasting two different ideas. If a child who is familiar with this type of text feature notices this phrase, she will be ready to identify the points of view that are being compared. You can help familiarize your child with these types of **clue words** by creating refrigerator magnets that your child can use to make stories or use these words in a playful way.

> **CLUE WORDS**
> Words or phrases that indicate some sort of relationship between events, like *because, so that, next, before,* and *after.*

With younger children, you might tell a story aloud with your child by trading off the role of storyteller. After your child says, "John had a good day," you can add, "And he liked dinner, too. But then..." Your child will then need to add a next sentence that changes the tone of the story, and explain what happened to make John's evening worse than his day. If adults first model how to use these transitional phases verbally, and then help children incorporate them into written language, these clue words will show up more frequently in children's writing and speech.

Even acts of writing that may seem very inconsequential can have powerful effects upon reading and cognitive development. Taking notes on what one reads is a good example because annotating helps build broader knowledge about what one is reading. Children learn more about the books they read when they are given activities to complete that require reflection, even if these activities are as simple as drawing a picture about the story or writing down one question that the story raised. You can select an activity that seems most appropriate for your child's age, interest level, and reading skills. For example, a four-year-old

INVENTIVE SPELLING
Young children's natural tendency to experiment with letters and sounds, using a rudimentary understanding of the alphabetic principle to represent words in print.

may be able to independently draw a picture about the story he just heard, whereas a five-year-old may be able to draw a picture and, with prompting, give it a title (using **inventive spelling** techniques). By the time he turns six, he may be able to write down a sentence about the story or a question it raised (still using inventive spelling techniques). As your child grows older and more confident in his writing abilities, your prompts can require him to do more writing and more reflecting.

For example, your four- or five-year-old might write a note to grandparents who are coming to visit, excitedly saying *I C U SUWN* or asking *HW R U?* Often, when a child uses inventive spelling, letter names that sound like full words (*B* for BE, *C* for SEE, *R* for ARE) are used to represent those words.

How Does Writing Develop Over Time?

We have already shared the six stages of writing development and highlighted the changes that children go through as they move from being emergent writers to conventional writers with increasingly more sophisticated ways of explaining themselves. As children become more adept at explaining themselves, they also begin to use writing for many different purposes and to write in different styles or genres. Through exposure to books, children begin to recognize the many ways that written language can be used and to write in varied styles, as the examples in this section will show. The different types of writing children become proficient at using include *narrative writing, descriptive writing, expository writing, persuasive writing,* and *annotating*. Children as young as four and five years old can create written output that falls into these categories. Moreover, by writing in these styles, children also become attuned to the details included by other authors who write in these styles, and begin to develop stronger reading comprehension skills.

Narrative writing. When we think about reading books with children, we most often think about *narrative writing*, or the type of language that is used to tell a story. A written narrative includes a starting point, events that typically lead up to a climax, and then a resolution. In other words,

> **NARRATIVE WRITING**
> The type of written language that is used to tell a story, narrative text includes a starting point, events that typically lead up to a climax, and then a resolution.

written stories have a structure. In addition, the audience isn't present to ask for more details or clarification and must be imagined, thus the writer must be the sole monitor of the story's effectiveness.

These aspects of written stories make them very different in structure and tone than stories told orally. When we tell stories orally, many people have a tendency to jump around a lot, add tangential facts, and get sidetracked. For instance, if you were about to tell the story of running into an old friend in the mall, you might start off by saying, "You'll never guess who I ran into the other day! I saw Becky from college. She looks great—she wasn't even limping. I remember back in college..." Your conversation would be filled with interesting snippets about your encounter and things that happened in the past, but it might not follow a linear structure. You might also rely on the person you were talking with to demonstrate interest, share her own knowledge, and provide feedback that affected the next piece of information you chose to share. In other words, this conversation is a story exchanged between two speakers, where both speaker and listener can monitor the exchange: the burden of understanding is shared.

In contrast, the above personal narrative in writing would probably sound something like,

> A long time ago, I had a friend named Becky. We met at the beginning of college. Becky was so funny and smart. She was also an incredible athlete, and ran track at school. But she got hurt during a meet, and had to have surgery on her knee. For the rest of college, it was really hard for her to walk around campus and do all of things she wanted to do.

I worried that her injury would make life really hard for her. Becky and I lost touch after college, but I kept wondering if she was okay. Just the other day, I ran into Becky, and she looked great. She said that she had to go to physical therapy for a long time after getting hurt, but she had fully recovered, and she was on her way to go jogging! The doctors had figured out how to help her, and now she is doing great.

To turn these separate facts into a written narrative requires the writer to have a developed understanding of story structure and monitor the story's effectiveness by making sure that readers understand its meaning.

The predominant way that children begin to gain such an understanding is through hearing storybooks read aloud, but dictating stories to be written down or beginning to write independently also allows them to try out this understanding and construct their own narratives that include beginnings, middles, and ends. You can see what we're talking about by reading this short, dictated story composed by Julie, a kindergartener. Based on her own knowledge of a story that she had heard many times, through book reading and television, she drew the pictures to illustrate a story called *Frosty the Snowman*.[8] Her dictated story read:

There was once a snowman. His name was Frosty. He made a friend. They melted! Mrs. and Mr. Santa knew they melted. They both danced around and loved each other. The end.

Although this narrative includes a clear beginning, middle, and ending, there are many gaps to be filled in. Julie does not explain why the snowmen melted, or what made the Clauses feel better and begin to dance. Over time, children's narratives become more sophisticated—the set-up for the story grows more complex, several events rather than just one event occur at the mid-point of the story, and the ending shifts from "the end" to include a more nuanced resolution. Rather than assuming that readers understand what is happening "between the lines"—like perhaps that Santa and Mrs. Claus danced because they knew Frosty would come back again some day—the writer explicitly explains these ideas. By third grade, Julie was writing out her own stories, some of which spanned several chapters. But, as this initial attempt shows, even young children engage in narrative storytelling, and we will continue to illustrate their capacity to do so throughout this chapter.

Descriptive writing. The story that we told about running into Becky after so many years probably did not strike you as a very engaging story. In part, that is because this story lacked the details and descriptions that draw readers into any particular tale. *Descriptive writing* is just what it sounds like— it uses words to paint a picture in the reader's mind. Writers describe how people, objects, and places look and make them feel. In more sophisticated narratives, authors do not merely present the facts, but set a scene. In *The Polar Express,* Chris Van Allsburg uses descriptive writing to make our mouths water when talking about the food the children were served on their journey to the North Pole. He doesn't merely say that everyone on board got to eat candy and drink hot chocolate, but that they "ate candies with nougat centers as white as snow. We drank hot cocoa as thick and rich as melted chocolate bars."[9] The beautiful language that he uses to describe these treats, and to describe other events throughout this magical story, is what makes the book so enchanting to young and old readers. The narrative alone is not enough to be compelling—it is *how* the story is told that gets us hooked.

> **DESCRIPTIVE WRITING**
> The type of written language that is used to make a story come to life; descriptive text includes vivid imagery, as well as similes and metaphors, to explain how people feel and act.

Young children can begin to develop these descriptive skills by creating Mother's Day and Father's Day cards or by being asked to write thank you notes after a birthday or holiday. Often a picture will carry a great deal of the meaning, and including picture details allows children who are on their way to understanding descriptive writing to express themselves without many words. In the Father's Day card shown in Figure 3-6, five-year-old Saul lets his grandpa know that he loves swimming with him. Notice the details that let the reader know Saul is in a swimming

Figure 3-6 Saul (5 years old) makes a Father's Day card.

pool, not the ocean or a lake. And, given the facial details, is there any mistaking how Saul feels or how he thinks his grandpa feels?

Just two years later, in November of his second-grade year, Saul was asked by his teacher to describe an eventful day. From his many encounters with description through drawing, Saul had become used to "describing." Now, Saul was being asked to write. Here's an excerpt from Saul's descriptive piece, with his misspellings and punctuation errors included:

> I HAD A CAVITY
>
>   I had just gotten out of school. It was a hot day. Mom and Theo were with me. I went to the dentist,s office. I was scared.... (The office is a room with lots of equiptment.) Dr. Levi put the lotion on my gum. Then she gave me the shot.... Then she put the drill in my mouth. Then they put a filling in my tooth. Then I went home. My gum felt numb.... Then I went to bed. In the morning it felt better.

This narrative outlines the events that occurred very clearly and includes descriptive details that evoke a particular feeling and mood. Saul doesn't just tell us about going to the dentist; he lets us know it was a hot day, and he was scared. We can picture this young boy, nervous in the stuffy car on his way to the appointment. His description enriches the story. Similarly, Julie, who dictated that brief story about Frosty in kindergarten, was able to share many more details about events just a few years later. In March of second grade, after taking a trip to a bed and breakfast with her family, Julie wrote about her vacation. Here's an excerpt:

MIKE AT THE BED AND BREAKFAST

Mike is 27 years old. He is a man. He works in a bed and breakfast. He is a great cook and baker. He makes great pancakes and oatmeal. Mike is a very, very nice person. One time he made banana bread. It had nuts in it. My sister does not like nuts. The next day he made brownies. Jamie asked if they had nuts. Mike said, "Oh! I like nuts but I remembered you don't so I made it without nuts." That is very nice.

As they got older, both Saul and Julie were able to express their feelings and experiences through writing. Saul's story is evocative of anyone's uncomfortable trip to the dentist's office, and Julie's interpretation helps us understand how much of an impact one person's kindness can have on others. By engaging children in purposeful tasks, we help them recognize that there are many different ways of communicating and sending a message about their own lives and thoughts. This process does not just occur during the school day, but can be scaffolded by parents in many ways.

Expository writing. *Expository writing* provides a thorough explanation of an idea. When a child's parents go away for the weekend and they provide the babysitter a four-page list of instructions for how to complete tasks around the house, they are engaging in this type of exposition.

> **EXPOSITORY WRITING**
> The type of written language that is used to provide a detailed explanation of an idea, like a recipe, a set of instructions, or a how-to guide.

Through exposure to examples of expository writing, such as recipes, rules that accompany board games, or factual information about objects or people, children learn that writing can be instructive.

We want to demonstrate that children engage in expository writing, too. When asked to describe how to ride a bike, second grader Lois wrote: "All you have to do is petel the bike and the wheels will turn around and around."[10] If Saul's teacher had asked her students to explain a procedure, we can see that Saul would be able to describe what typically happens when a person gets a filling. After writing her story about the bed and breakfast, Julie would be able to tell us what people do to prepare for a vacation. It may seem as if this type of writing is too advanced to expect of young children, but in fact, the Common Core Standards that many states use to develop school curricula include the fact that kindergarteners should be able to "use a combination of drawing, dictating, and writing to compose informative/explanatory texts in which they name what they are writing about and supply some information about the topic."[11] If we know that kindergarteners are expected to display this skill at school, it stands to reason that it is a skill we want to preview at home—just as the dialogic reading you do with your child enriches storytime at school. Activities such as creating simple "how-to" books, dictating or writing out favorite recipes, and writing down biographical information can help children develop their expository skills.

Persuasive writing. *Persuasive writing* is intended to express one's ideas in a way that will change other people's minds, instead of just describing a situation or providing facts about how to complete a task. To write persuasively requires an understanding of the issue at hand and the point of view of the reader. Children and adolescents can practice this type of writing by putting their requests—for a puppy, a higher allowance, or a later curfew—in writing. Crafting this type of argument makes it necessary for children to research issues (perhaps determining how expensive it is to have a dog), take a position ("I want one!"), and offer an argument that supports

> **PERSUASIVE WRITING**
> The type of written language that is used to make a point, take a side in a debate, and convince others of the validity of that viewpoint.

that position (maybe offering to put aside half of one's allowance to pay for pet-related issues). Learning how to write in this way also helps children recognize and critique the persuasive writing of others when they see it, rather than thinking that anything that is written is a fact. Being able to state an opinion or preference in writing, an important precursor to persuasive writing, is another expectation schools hold for kindergarten students, indicating that persuasive writing skills are also important to develop at home.

Annotating. *Annotation* refers to the notes that people make when they are reading. These notes allow them to reflect on the text they are reading in the moment, by marking down other information they need to look up or by summarizing the main point of a paragraph, making it easier for them to revisit these ideas

> **ANNOTATION**
> The act of writing on a text one is reading, for the purpose of remembering key points (underlining or highlighting, for example) or jotting down questions to be addressed in the future.

when looking over the text at a later date. For example, when reading the *Little House on the Prairie* series with her mother, eight-year-old Hannah kept a reading journal and asked questions like, "How will they stay warm during the hard winter? Can you still make your own butter when it snows?" Sometimes, annotating can simply mean underlining or highlighting key points in a story, so that these main ideas jump out at the reader. When young children get into the habit of annotating, they again build higher-level skills, because they begin to think about writing as a mental activity that helps them keep track of what they are reading. Annotating allows a reader to interact with the book in his hands. The conversations you have with your child during dialogic reading time (when you ask your child many questions while reading together) can act as a precursor to annotating because you are modeling the acts of question-asking and information-seeking for your child. When you ask those questions aloud, it will prompt your child to do so as well. If you then take the time to say, "Let's not find out the answer right now. Let's write it down. After we finish this chapter, we'll go look it up," you begin to model why writing down our spoken words can be a helpful device for remembering and organizing our ideas. Many children do not begin to annotate until teachers require them to do so in high school or college, but forming the habit much earlier in life helps children recognize how reading, writing, and thinking are connected processes. Some children may be reluctant to write in their books, and we certainly don't want them to write in books that they borrowed from friends or the library. You can address this important issue when annotating together by deciding whether it makes most sense to write in the book itself, on a sticky note, or in a journal (like Hannah did).

It is important to keep these different types of writing in mind as you read the rest of this chapter, so that you don't forget how big a task it is for a child to become a writer and how much background knowledge is required to write in these different styles. Without vocabulary skills and exposure to books, children have few opportunities to express themselves in writing in ways that others can easily follow. Early stages of writing development may begin before these vocabulary skills are intact and much reading has occurred at home, but continued skill growth requires children to build the skills discussed in chapters 1 and 2.

IMPORTANT QUALITIES OF WRITING
Traits that strong writing should possess, including a focus on
- Ideas and content
- Organization
- Word choice
- Sentence fluency
- Voice
- Conventions
- Presentation

What Are the Important Qualities of Writing?

Researchers have identified six qualities that all writing should possess,[12] and we can think of ways that these six big ideas can be used to help children build their own writing abilities. These six traits include *ideas and* content, organization, voice, word choice, sentence fluency, and conventions. Some models also include a seventh quality, presentation. Remember, we said earlier that composition skills are not skills that one just has or does not have, but instead skills that develop gradually over time. Similarly, each of these writing traits unfolds and is strengthened over time. Focusing on these traits as you read and write with your child will help her focus on them, too, in her own writing and the writing of others.

Ideas and content. The essence of the story or essay that a child is writing or sharing with you orally is conveyed through the *ideas and content*. Both before any child—of any age—begins writing, and as she keeps working, she needs to think about what ideas she wants to convey. What important details need to be shared with the reader? Good writers convey meaning, speak with authority, and help the reader develop an understanding of the topic when communicating these ideas and content.[13] As a parent, you can help your child develop these skills by asking questions about the details of a story or whether the reader is going to learn something new, which will support your child in expanding upon his work.

Organization. A writer's capacity to present information in a particular format develops as she learns *organization* skills. Well-organized writing always depends on advance planning and revision. This capacity, of course, grows over time. A first grader who is asked to complete a report on insects may write down all of the information he learns from an encyclopedia, Internet searches, and books from the local library, but then include this information in one large paragraph and in no particular order. Of course, when a first grader does this type of writing during the school day, his teacher will provide instruction to help him organize this information. The third draft of his report will look very different than the first draft of the report. Children hone these skills through practice, and the first step is just getting ideas down on paper. The writing that you see your preschool or early elementary age child do at home will probably lack this organization, and that is okay—you can think of the information that he writes down as a lump of modeling clay that you can help him shape over time.

In contrast to this first grader who works hard just to write down these ideas, a student in late elementary school might independently develop a multi-paragraph essay, focusing on one insect in each paragraph. Finally, by middle school, a student may organize that same essay by talking about the features that are common to many insects, as well as the features that are unique to particular insects. Tools like **graphic organizers**, which visually present the important points of a story, can help with the organization of ideas. These graphic organizers serve as guides that help writers recognize the important points that need to be addressed in their writing and can help children learn how to be writers who think ahead and structure their writing before putting pen to paper. Most adults no longer use graphic organizers when writing a short letter because we have internalized the skills we learned from these types of guides. But when writing a long speech or a multi-page document for work, adults will still write an outline because we know that we still need some sort of guide to help us keep our writing focused. Modeling the outlining process or working with young children to use graphic organizers pays off because it helps them get into the habit of being thoughtful and organized writers. Also, learning how to organize a text can facilitate reading comprehension through helping children more easily recognize the structure of other texts, too.[14]

> **GRAPHIC ORGANIZERS**
> Visual representations of information to be learned or expressed, presented in a simple format that aids organization.

Some graphic organizers can be very simple, and are just intended to provide young writers with a visual way to keep track of and sort what is going to happen in their narrative. A basic graphic organizer might look like this:

Beginning	Middle	End

Graphic organizers for expository or persuasive writing may be lengthier, and used to help writers think about the best way to structure an essay, as well as to ensure they remember to include all of the important points they want to make. These more detailed organizers might include information like:

- Thesis: _____
- Topic Sentence: _____
- Point #1, Summary:_____
  - Supporting Detail #1: _____
  - Supporting Detail #2: _____
  - Supporting Detail #3: _____
  This same structure would then repeat itself for however many points (usually three) the author wanted to make.
- Concluding Point:_____

If you want to help your child plan out a story before writing, creating an informal graphic organizer can be a very helpful tool. You can find many pre-designed graphic organizers online or by asking your child's teacher for some templates, but making your own notes and outlines on scrap paper or a whiteboard can be just as helpful. By writing down notes informally as you brainstorm together, you can model for your child that organization is always a part of the writing process.

Word choice. A child's ability to write original text and select appropriate and descriptive words stems from their *word choice*. Children who do not have adequate vocabularies often have difficulty putting information that they have read into their own words when writing about this information later. Revising text based on word choice can help children make good stories great, and brainstorming synonyms for words can be a playful activity. For example, if you and your child were writing together about going trick or treating, you might want to begin by thinking of words like *spooky, frightening,* and *startling,* so that he could use other words besides *scary* to describe all the various sights he might see. All of the vocabulary development activities we discussed in chapter 1 remain as important for writing development, because it is easier for children to express themselves when they have a wide range of words at their disposal.

Sentence fluency. As children begin to readily use more words, *sentence fluency* develops. Children demonstrate this quality in their writing and talking when they become familiar with the many different ways that sentences can be structured and syntax can be used. Beginning writers, perhaps in the first grade, often write simple sentences like, "John was tired. He ate dinner. Then he had dessert. At ten o'clock, he went to bed." In later elementary school, children can begin to combine those sentences, perhaps saying, "John was tired, but ate dinner and dessert. At ten o'clock, he went to bed." Even older children may further elaborate upon the information provided, saying something like, "Even though John was tired in the early evening, he ate dinner and dessert. Then, at ten o'clock, he finally went to bed." In this final version of the sentences, both fluency and word choice help make these sentences more interesting. And this child could keep on embellishing from here by substituting the words "by dusk" for "in the early evening." Punctuation and connector words like *since* and *although* are components of sentence fluency.

Voice. The style that an author uses when writing—the length of his sentences, the words he chooses, his tone—is called his *voice*. Unlike word choice and sentence fluency, which are separate qualities, voice is displayed through the author's use of word choice and sentence structure. We can't separate authors' voices from the other qualities of their writing, indicating that writers with highly developed vocabularies and sentence fluency can more skillfully change their voice. But, even young children are aware of the different authorial tones of other writers and can imitate the style of writers like Dr. Seuss and Laura Numeroff (the author of *If You Give a Mouse a Cookie*[15]). When writing fiction, children can create a voice for their narrator that may be dissimilar from their own voice and that allows readers to understand the world that they have created in their story. Patricia MacLachlan's book *The Fact and Fictions of Minna Pratt*[16] begins:

> Melinda Pratt rides city bus number twelve to her cello lesson, wearing her mother's jean jacket and only one sock. Hallo, world, says Minna. Minna often addresses the world, sometimes silently, sometimes out loud.

From these very first lines, the way that MacLachlan writes about Minna sets a tone for the book. Through the voice she uses, we quickly learn about how Minna thinks and feels. Stories that have a strong voice make it easy for readers to remember the characters and to get a good sense of the subtle cues that the author is conveying about the emotional content of the story, rather than just the facts. In *Fancy Nancy,*[17] by Jane O'Connor, Nancy laments:

> Nobody in my family is fancy at all.
> They never even ask for sprinkles.
> There's a lot they don't understand...
> Lace-trimmed socks *do* help me play soccer better.
> Sandwiches definitely *do* taste better when you stick in frilly toothpicks.

When you read this passage, you can almost hear Nancy's real voice and how she would say these words, pouting cutely and whining just a bit. Similar to word choice and sentence fluency, the quality of voice is developed through practice—the more opportunities children have to write, the more they can play with words and phrases and develop their own individual style.

Conventions. All of the basic aspects of writing that help convey meaning clearly, like proper spelling, punctuation, and indentation, are the *conventions* of writing. When children have not yet mastered these mechanics or conventions of writing, it can be difficult for others to make sense of their writing. Meanwhile, children who need to spend much of their time correcting these mechanical issues have less time for planning and revising what they write. Later in this chapter, we will talk more about how spelling skills develop over time, and how to encourage young children to begin writing even before they can spell with accuracy. But it is important to recognize that for young children, getting ideas down on paper in any form leads to stronger reading skills over time.[18] So, even though it is important for children to make sense of these conventions, we want to encourage young children not to focus on making corrections or revisions when they first write a story, but just excitedly getting those ideas down on paper. Dictating stories to parents, or writing a story using invented spellings, allows children to develop many of the other important qualities of writing, even before learning writing conventions.

Presentation. Finally, an aspect of written language that we do not focus on until children are able to write conventionally is *presentation*, or how writing looks, and whether the text is written neatly. As a parent who is encouraging your young child to begin to express herself in writing, we cannot stress enough that presentation begins to matter only *after* a child has already developed many emergent writing skills— which is why we have discussed writing to learn before learning to write legibly and spell accurately. Of course, you can focus on neatness from a broader perspective, perhaps by encouraging your child to color on a card slowly rather than scribbling quickly, or to first make a picture in pencil and then color it in. This early focus on presentation can help your child recognize that putting ideas down on paper takes time and concentration. But, our expectations always need to be aligned with children's abilities. In the same way that providing frequent corrections while a child reads aloud can discourage him from attempting to sound out unfamiliar words, focusing on issues like letter formation, spacing between words, and writing within the lines on a page too soon or too often can undermine your goal. The same rules of scaffolding that we have discussed throughout other chapters in this book apply here as well—it may be appropriate to pick one aspect of your child's work to focus on and attempt to improve, but do not try to do too much at once! First, praise your child's attempts at writing, being very specific about the skill or behavior you are praising, saying something like, "Wow! You did such a nice job taking your time and not rushing when you wrote that sentence," so that your child knows exactly what he did well. Then, find a fun and constructive way to draw his attention to a presentation skill that can be improved. We'll give you some strategies later in this chapter.

These presentation skills become more important as children progress through elementary school. Although handwriting is not focused on in classroom instruction with the same intensity that it used to be, particularly as we do more and more of our writing on the computer, it remains important for children to be able to present their ideas neatly and write without difficulty. In elementary schools, almost all writing continues to be done by hand, and students need to hand-write essays for many important exams. When children struggle with letter formation, writing can become a frustrating process for them,[19] and their work can be more difficult for someone else to interpret. For these reasons, presentation matters. However, before focusing on issues of presentation, there are many other ways you can foster writing development.

What Is the Role of Parents in Supporting Writing Development?

Parents of elementary school students often begin to assist with writing development when children are completing homework, and they ask for help spelling a word, figuring out how to punctuate a sentence, responding to a short answer question, or developing their own essay. But we often do not think about how we can foster the writing development of pre-writers, and we would like to help you start supporting writing development when your child is still in diapers. Building these pre-writing skills early on can be so important and powerful, both because of how such skills spur reading development and because once writing becomes a habit, children will continue to develop these abilities as they get older. The more one writes, the better of a writer he will become. One of the most important ways that parents can help support writing development is by starting young and encouraging preschoolers to express themselves in writing.

Focusing on the fine motor skills that aid in writing development when your child is a preschooler will make his transition into elementary school easier. You can help him build these fine motor skills by using safety scissors, peeling stickers off a sheet, or using modeling clay to strengthen his fingers. Children need time and practice to begin holding writing implements properly, and some children may have more trouble than others developing an appropriate grip. However, it is also important not to push your child to hold a pencil like an adult might before he is ready to do so. Even though writing is a fine motor skill, it depends on gross motor developments like the growth of arm and shoulder muscles. Your three-year-old will likely be able to grasp fat crayons or thick pencils with a fisted grip that slowly begins to open up as he uses more of his palm to hold the pencil, and he begins to stick his elbow out to the side. At around four years old, he will then begin to use all five fingers to hold a writing implement. By the age of five or six, he will move on to using the three finger grip that we use as adults, although perfecting this more advanced grip may take some time. Rather than correcting your child's grip too often or too early, focus on building his muscles so that he can grasp writing tools more easily. Fun activities like picking up objects with tongs or tweezers, sliding coins into a piggy bank, or playing at a water or sand table can be helpful. Some children find it helpful to use adaptive pencil grips (geometric pieces of plastic that fit over the bottom of a pencil), which shape the way they hold pencils and can be particularly helpful when they move on to using thinner pens and pencils.

There are many other ways you can support writing development. Just as many of the early strategies for reading can be fun, interactive, and not even involve printed books, many of the ways we suggest fostering early writing skills are playful and do not require that your child toil away with a pen or pencil. One of the most important things you can do is to demonstrate to your child that you are a writer. This doesn't need to mean that you are a professional writer. When Jamie was little, the reason she wanted to carry a grocery list around in her purse was because that is what her mother did. So, modeling writing behavior for your child, and demonstrating that writing is a part of everyday life, can be very powerful. This means not only writing, but explaining why you are writing. For example, when making a to-do list, you can say, "I am writing down all of the things that I need to do today so that I can remember them. Sometimes, when we have a lot to do, it can be hard to keep track of them without writing them down." After receiving a set of photos in the mail from your mother, you can tell your child that you are about to write an email to Grandma to let her know how happy they made you. If your child ends up saying, "I want to make a list, too!" or "I want to tell Grandma that I liked them also!" your child is a writer, too. The more opportunities you give a child to see how writing can be useful, the more likely you are to spur on interest in writing. Take a few minutes to think about how you use writing in your daily life and how you could include your child in these writing activities.

Once that interest is sparked, you can then take a more active role in helping your child write. Three- and four-year-olds can "write" stories by drawing pictures and narrating the plot to you while you transcribe their ideas. Often, they may want to first write the story themselves by approximating writing and including their own scribbles at the bottom of the page. As they begin to recognize letters and become familiar with letter sounds, kindergarten-age children may begin to write these stories with their own invented spellings. You should encourage them to do so, as well as help them sound out words that they are unfamiliar with and provide them with the spelling of unfamiliar words if they get stuck or frustrated. A parent's goal should be making writing feel fun and relevant, rather than perfecting a story.

Developing Writing Skills: How Can I Support My Child's Individual Needs?

Writing should always feel fun and relevant. Because the act of writing helps your child build feelings of competence, it is important to have a good sense of your child's current skills, in terms of her ability to form letters and words that others can easily recognize and to express herself using language and a structure that draws people in. By allowing her to build these specific skills, and providing encouragement as she works towards slightly more advanced skills, you will be able to scaffold her writing. Of course, making some corrections and providing guidance is helpful. But for a parent, it can be tough to figure out the right balance between providing corrective feedback and making sure that writing does not start to feel like a chore.

First, make sure to praise your child's efforts and be specific about what you liked. You can say something like, "I really love that story. You did such a nice job of describing what the old man looked like—I can really picture his beard!" Then, if you think it is appropriate, you can pick just one new skill to teach your child—like leaving spaces between words, adding periods at the end of sentences, or brainstorming synonyms for a word that is used multiple times. But again, your goal should be to get your child writing, however you can. So if giving feedback makes him less likely to write, just focus on the positives for now. The act of writing is the best way to become a better writer!

In fact, several research studies have shown that if children engage in writing regularly—even if they only spend 15 minutes each day writing—their writing and reading skills increase as a result.[20] An excellent way to improve children's reading comprehension skills is to have them write about the stories they read or have heard read to them. When writing about a story, we focus on both major plot points and small details and try to understand how characters are thinking and feeling. An excellent way to expand upon the dialogic reading sessions you have with your child could be to then spend time drawing and writing together about the book that you read. In chapter 1, we gave you suggestions for questions you might ask while reading three books with your child. Table 3-2 includes examples of writing and drawing activities you might suggest after reading these same three books.

What Activities and Strategies Can I Use to Support Writing Development?

John Irving, author of 14 novels (including *The World According to Garp*), once said that to be a great writer, "You have to get obsessed and stay obsessed." What he meant was that becoming a good writer takes a lot of time. For that reason, having children write on a regular basis, even when

TABLE 3-2. SAMPLE DRAWING AND WRITING PROMPTS

Book	Drawing Prompt	Writing Prompt
Caps for Sale: A Tale of a Peddler, Some Monkeys and Their Monkey Business, by Esphyr Slobodkina	"What do you think the monkeys are doing while they hide behind the tree? Let's draw a picture of them."	"We said the monkeys were being sneaky. Let's write down two reasons why they might be acting this way. Why do you think they want the peddler's hat?" (Providing this introduction can help your child begin his sentence by saying *The monkeys were sneaky because* . . . or *The monkeys wanted the peddler's hat because* . . .)
There's a Nightmare in My Closet, by Mercer Mayer	"What would the nightmare who lived in your closet look like? Draw that monster for me!"	"The little boy in this story decided to get rid of his monster for once and for all. I want you to come up with your own plan for getting rid of nightmares. What would you do? Write down your plan."
Ladybug Girl and Bumblebee Boy, by David Soman and Jacky Davis	"Ladybug Girl and her friends had a lot of fun on the playground, using their imaginations. Draw a picture of another game they could have played together at the playground."	"Ladybug Girl and Bumblebee Boy had to compromise in order to have fun together. Write a story about a time that you compromised with one of your friends."

their writing is entirely or largely symbolic (just pictures and scribbles) helps them think like writers. The act of writing helps us think about how to share information in a way that will make sense to an audience, and to synthesize what we know so that we can make a coherent point. These skills do not just make us better writers, or even better readers, but also better scholars and students.

Scaffold skill development. Throughout this book, we have often said that it is helpful to focus on helping your child reach the very next step in any particular process, but not pushing him to do something that he does not yet understand. For example, if your child is writing stories by using strategies of imitation, or stage 1, he is not ready for you to start spelling out words for him as he writes. However, if his writing resembles one long scribble that takes up an entire line, you might begin to suggest that he write out one scribble for each word in his story. Beginning to represent each word independently will help him understand the connection between the printed and spoken word. Gradually, as this idea begins to make sense to him, he will start to represent not just the individual words, but also the sounds in them. At this point, you will again be able to help him reach the next step in the process and focus on helping him hear and represent the sounds in those words, as we will discuss more in the section on spelling development. You can also scaffold skills like vocabulary development by brainstorming synonyms with him or help build sentence fluency by suggesting transition words. As always, pick just one area of focus at a time, and first and foremost, try to keep your writing activities fun.

Incorporate writing into play. Many of the imagination games that you play with your child probably already include writing. When she was young, Jamie loved playing restaurant, and she created many written materials to be used in this game. Her restaurant had a sign that hung out front, with the store hours and name. She wrote up separate breakfast, lunch, and dinner menus for all of her patrons. And when people placed their orders, she wrote them down on a small note pad. At the end of the meal, she provided a bill. As we described in chapter 2, Anne used to play "diner" with her son Michael. Every child, no matter what the skill level, will benefit from these kinds of activities.

The most important concept that children must acquire about written language is that print conveys meaning. You don't have to sit down to write novels with your child. Instead, find ways to infuse the games you already play with your child with writing. In a restaurant, you write out menus, price lists, and ingredients. At the post office, write letters and address envelopes. Even when playing "cops and robbers," the police officer can write up a citation or take notes about a crime. As your child's writing skills become more sophisticated, the writing you include in your games can become more sophisticated as well. For instance, playing "newspaper" can evolve from scribbling headlines to writing articles about current events or recent trips. Playing "hotel" can involve writing up a welcome packet that includes a history of the city and brochures of interesting sights in the area. These activities are much more complex than merely writing up a bill or menu.

Model writing in daily life. Lists are not the only forms of writing that parents can model for their children, although helping children create written schedules and homework reminders can certainly kill two birds with one stone! Parents can also model expository writing, through writing directions to a restaurant, jotting down a recipe for a friend, or typing up instructions for a houseguest about how to use the DVD player. Descriptive writing can be modeled through writing thank you notes or letters about a recent holiday celebration. Examples of persuasive writing include letters to the editor and emails about why everyone should go see one movie over another movie the following weekend.

Once children are presented with these models, it becomes more likely that they will think to engage in these types of writing independently, and it is possible that you can focus on one activity to generate all of these different sorts of writing. For example, children can be encouraged to help write out the guest list for their own birthday parties. If your child knows what snacks she would like served at the party, she can write out recipes for those treats and provide instructions for how the room should be decorated. If there is a particular gift she would like, she can write a persuasive letter to you explaining why it would be such a good purchase. Once you begin thinking creatively about how to get your child writing, the options are truly endless.

Use writing as form of reminiscing. It is much more fun for a child to write about something that happened recently and something that feels relevant to his life than to write about an abstract topic. Remember that what is most relevant, exciting, or funny to your child might not be the topic you are most excited to write about together. However, the focus of your writing activities should be exactly those topics that he wants to spend more time discussing with you. Even before your child is able to engage in the activities described here and in Table 3-3 independently, he can dictate his ideas to you and draw a picture to accompany your writing. The key is for you to demonstrate that writing can be used to remember good times and fun information.

Keeping a family trip diary that everyone writes in is an excellent way to both model writing for your children and keep them engaged in documenting the memorable things that happen on a vacation. Picking different topics each day and letting different family members choose— like the best meal of the day, the weirdest thing that happened all day, the best place we visited this week—is a fun way to keep the diary from becoming a chore. Similarly, writing can be a nice way to keep track of family stories and lore. Children can interview older relatives to find out interesting facts about their lives and create biographies. Through these types of activities, children will learn that writing is a way to remember information and share it with others. Parents must model these skills and behaviors and do so with enthusiasm. The benefit of the activity, and the motivation to keep doing it, comes from the satisfaction of sharing memories together.

There are many different ways to use writing as a form of recollection, so we urge you to be creative and come up with ideas that you think will work well for you and your family. Making a family joke book or a recipe book with stories about the events for which each dish was first made might be something that your kids are interested in. Whatever they would find worth writing about is what you should be writing about, even if the topic doesn't seem particularly interesting to you. The pay-off will come when you see them blossom into independent and creative writers.

Discover the power of pen pals. Having someone to whom they write regularly can also be very beneficial for children. Knowing that they will

TABLE 3-3. WRITING DEVELOPMENT: STRATEGIES FOR PARENTS

What to Do	How to Do It	Age(s)
Scaffold Skill Development by Building On Your Child's Current Writing Abilities	First, identify your child's current writing level by taking a look at the strategies he uses when expressing himself in writing. If your child's writing resembles one long scribble, you might begin to suggest that he write out one scribble for each word. This will help him mimic the segmentation of real writing and recognize that sentences are made up of several words. If your child has begun to write words independently, you can scaffold vocabulary development by brainstorming synonyms with him or suggesting transition words to help build sentence fluency.	
Model Writing in Daily Life	Include your child in everyday activities that involve writing, such as writing directions to a restaurant or jotting down recipes. Once writing can be done independently, have your child help out with tasks like writing a guest list for a birthday party which rides to go on at an amusement park. Remember, activities that take advantage of topics and activities your child finds intrinsically motivating will be more appealing!	
Use Writing as a Form of Reminiscing	Keeping a family trip diary is a fun way to model writing for your child and to encourage her to reflect back on things that happen on vacation. Another fun strategy is for your child to interview family members to find out interesting facts about their lives to create biographies.	
Discover the Power of Pen Pals	Having a pen pal will encourage your child to think like a writer, to develop a voice, and to focus on relevant ideas that should be included in letters. For the younger child, dictating letters and drawing pictures to accompany stories they tell is a fun way to work on this skill.	

What to Do	How to Do It	Age(s)
Help Children Be Planful Writers	Ask your child questions to help her think about how to organize her ideas. For example, if your child does have a pen pal, ask her to remember three exciting events from the beginning, middle, and end of a recent vacation. Then, sit down together and talk about the events to be shared before she composes the letter. Such preparation will help create a mental outline to follow.	
Use Play Time to Practice Writing	Incorporate writing into playtime, through games like restaurant (for which you need to make menus and take orders), post office (for which you need to address letters), and beauty parlor (for which you need to create a list of services). Find a way to fit writing into whatever your child is interested in!	
Build Complex Sentences Together Using Connector Words	Have your child build complex sentences through using connector words like *and, then, because, so,* and *but.* You can take turns building these sentences verbally by saying, "Dad went to the store and..." and then leaving a pause for you child to say "bought everything we need for dinner, but..." As your child becomes more comfortable using these words appropriately, you can begin to play this game in writing, instead.	
Start a Journal	Encourage journal writing, whether your child is keeping a private diary, writing in a family trip journal, or both. Take time from your own day to write in a journal or to write a letter to a friend or a relative, so that your child sees an example of this behavior.	

What to Do	How to Do It	Age(s)
Play Word Games	Play *Mad Libs* to help your child think about issues of sentence structure and word choice. Create your own *Mad Libs* by taking passages from familiar stories and whiting out select words.	
Create Outlines	Help your child create outlines for his writing and develop paragraphs with topic sentences and concluding sentences.	

need to describe an event to someone else later helps children think like writers, develop a voice, and focus on the ideas that should be contained in a letter. Just as we—as advanced readers and writers—review essays and underline their main points so that we can summarize them later, novice writers can begin by mentally reviewing events that occurred and remembering the most important details to share with a pen pal later. Younger children begin to develop these skills by writing letters through dictation and by drawing pictures to accompany the stories they tell. Older relatives who live far away or the children of your friends may make good pen pals. If your child would rather have an email buddy than a pen pal, communicating electronically (as long as the proper safeguards are in place) can yield many of the same benefits. However, you will want to make sure that your child takes the time to write thoughtfully and to review what he or she has written before sending the letter or email. Writing electronically, although it has many benefits, does not allow children the same opportunity to work on written presentation and other important writing traits, which writing by hand does.

Help children become planful writers. As we mentioned earlier, an important skill that writers acquire over time is the ability to plan what they are going to write, rather than only beginning to think about their topic once they have a pen in hand. Planful writers brainstorm about topics before they get started, write outlines and drafts, and read through resource materials with ideas in mind because they already know what information they need to get from those resources. Although parents of younger children might not think this applies to them yet, even preschoolers and early elementary school students can become planful writers—they will just require more of your assistance. A second grader may need help thinking through the planning process but be able to write independently, whereas a preschooler might need help planning and also need to dictate the story to you. But through scaffolding, you can help children of all ages recognize that writing is a process.

To help young children become planful writers, you can ask questions to help them think about how to organize their ideas. For instance, if your child does have a pen pal and will be writing to him about your apple-picking trip, you might ask your child to think about three details from the beginning of the trip, the middle of the trip, and the end of the trip that he thinks his pen pal will be interested in. You can jot these ideas down for or with your child during the trip or even collect objects together that will remind him about those things—like a pamphlet from the farm, a picture from a smartphone of the cat that lives in the orchard, and a leaf from a tree. Then, when your child is ready to write that letter or dictate it to you, you can talk together about the things he wanted to share with his pen pal. By doing so, you've created a mental outline for the letter and primed him to include important details.

As your child advances through elementary school and begins to write longer expository pieces, usually in second or third grade, you can use additional tools to help him write in a planful way. When your child works on assignments for school, you can help him organize a paper by verbally or visually creating graphic organizers or semantic webs (both tools for visually representing important ideas that are related to one another). It may be helpful, even for your kindergartener or first grader, to put up a blackboard or easel in your kitchen, near your dinner table, or in whichever room your child does homework, that you can use to jot down ideas and develop these semantic webs. As your child works on his story, you may need to help him search out new vocabulary words or think about how to structure his narrative. Writing together, and taking notes in this way, is another great way to model writing. You can also encourage your child to annotate whatever he is reading—for example, to write down questions he wants to ask you or the teacher, or to write down or underline key points he wants to remember.

For example, when Anne's son Michael was in first grade, he was asked to write a story for homework about one of his favorite activities. An enthusiastic athlete, Michael started playing tennis at the age of four and was eager to talk about his experiences on the court. Shortly before he got this assignment, his coach had made all of the students complete several running drills, and Michael chose to write about that experience. When Anne looked at his story, the word *ran* appeared in each sentence, sometimes more than once. After he read his story out loud to Anne, she said, "You did such a nice job of describing what your lessons are like! Is there another word you could use instead of *ran*?" Michael looked at her as if she was making no sense and said, "No. That's what I did. I ran all day!" To help Michael think of synonyms for *ran*, Anne pulled over the easel that they always kept by their kitchen table and Michael was able to fill his story with vivid descriptions of how fast he had to go that day. Anne wrote the word *ran* in big block letters in the center. She drew circles all around the easel, each connected to that first word, and filled one in with the word *jogged*. She filled in another with the word *dashed*, and then Michael chimed in with the word *sprinted*. In the next few minutes, they had filled the whole board. Their semantic web looked something like that shown in Figure 3-7.

This is just one of the strategies that Anne could have used to help Michael flesh out this story. We don't want you to feel like you need to engage in all of these activities at the same time. It would probably be overwhelming for your child (and for you!) to create a semantic web like

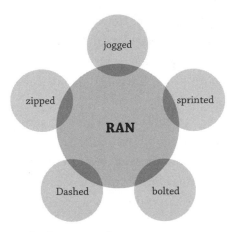

Figure 3-7 A semantic web of synonyms for *ran*.

the one Anne and Michael created and, at the same time, to draft a graphic organizer focusing on the structure of Michael's story. Remember to pick just one aspect of your child's writing to work on, and to praise all of his efforts. As you will see from the additional examples in Table 3-3, writing activities can be playful and brief.

Spelling Development

The skills that we discussed earlier in this chapter—planning, revising, developing ideas and sentence fluency, building one's vocabulary—are all of the skills that a child needs in order to write to learn. But many of the skills related to that seventh trait of writing that some teachers talk about, presentation. We talked earlier in this chapter about the important gross and fine motor skills that help a child write legibly. Writing neatly is an important component of presentation, as is spelling accurately. Although handwriting is a very important skill, we are going to focus the rest of this chapter on issues related to spelling because spelling development is such a crucial element of reading development. If your child is having difficulty with handwriting, ask his teacher for suggestions about activities that might be helpful at home, or look into a program like Handwriting Without Tears (www.hwtears.com).

What Is Spelling?

Spelling is the act of putting the alphabetic principle into practice. In other words, a great deal of early phonics instruction focuses on the idea that written letters represent

> **SPELLING**
> The act of putting the alphabetic principle into action and encoding speech sounds into print.

spoken sounds. When young children begin reading, they need to decipher the words on the page and pair written letters with their associated sounds. Spelling, on the other hand, gives children a chance to use what they know about spoken sounds and written letters to put their own thoughts and spoken language into this written code. By learning to spell, children can express themselves in writing (encode speech into print) rather than focusing on understanding the written expressions of others (decode print into speech), as they do when reading.

Why Is Learning to Spell Important for Future Reading Development?

We have emphasized the relationship between encoding and decoding throughout this chapter, since it is precisely because of this close relationship that spelling is important for future reading development. Trying to spell gives children practice with letter patterns, and with pairing sounds and letters. Being able to represent a word in writing makes it very likely that a child will also be able to recognize that word when he comes across it in a book—in other words, good spelling predicts good reading, but good reading is not as likely to ensure good spelling.[21] Correct spelling requires a sophisticated and complete understanding of letter–sound correspondence, whereas children can sometimes read words accurately even when this understanding is incomplete. For example, when reading the sentence, "We went swimming down by the bay," a child can determine that the word is *bay* and not *boy* through a partial representation of the word and the context of the sentence, whereas correctly spelling the word would require recognition of the middle sound as well.

TABLE 3-4. THE MANY SOUNDS OF THE LETTER *S*

Animal	Phonetic Representation	Conventional Spelling
	c a t **s**	cats
	f r o g **z**	frogs
	h o r s e **i z**	horses

To make matters even more confusing, sometimes the ability to pair sounds and letters actually makes spelling accurately more difficult for children. As fluent writers and readers, we become accustomed to the idea that the plural forms of all words are spelled with an *s* at the end. But, if you were to read a book about animals with your child and say each of the animal names aloud, you would start to realize that the letter *s* actually represents a few different sounds. Table 3-4 provides a few examples.

In all of these cases, we use the letter *s* to indicate that we are talking about more than one cat, frog, and horse, because using that same letter all the time helps us preserve meaning. These small parts of speech and language—like -*s* and -*ed*—convey a great deal of information when they are used, but recognizing that they are always used in the same way is a process for children, who go through these developmental stages in sequence. A child will spell *rocked* with a "t" as its final sound and *printed* with "id" as its final sound before adopting the conventional spelling and ending both words with "ed." Learning to spell with accuracy is an incremental process, so it is important to praise and celebrate your child's phonetic spellings. Once your child is able to represent these words easily and uses the same word endings regularly, you can begin to give feedback that will help him convert these phonetic spellings to common English spellings by teaching just a few specific rules.

Because being able to spell a word requires recognition of all of the letters in the word, it also increases a child's capacity to recognize words[22] and builds understanding of word meaning when children learn to distinguish between **homophones** like *here* and *hear*. Spelling accuracy also bolsters both reading fluency and comprehension.[23] So you can see that, although spelling may be perceived as a less essential skill for children to learn in a world with spellcheckers on all word processing programs and text messaging programs, it still serves an important purpose. Children learn to spell and to read in tandem, and each skill strengthens the other.

Fluent spelling is also what allows children to focus on expressing themselves in writing at a con

> **HOMOPHONES**
> Words that sound the same when spoken aloud, but differ (1) in meaning despite being spelled the same way (referred to as homonyms or homographs) or (2) in meaning and spelling (referred to as heterographs).
>
> An example of (1) is *rose*, which can be both a flower and a description of someone standing or ascending.
>
> An example of (2) is *carrot*, *caret*, or *karet*, which can refer to a vegetable, the weight of a diamond, or the purity of gold, respectively.

tent level, rather than getting bogged down by mechanics. Kids who can spell well write more words and express themselves in more sophisticated ways than children who struggle to spell the words that they want to use.[24] Again, very similar issues are at hand in reading and spelling development. For children who need to laboriously consider the relationship between each letter and sound, whether encoding or decoding, reading and writing fluently becomes an impossibility. By spending so much time focusing on each individual letter and word, these children have no time to consider the broader meaning of the whole sentence or passage when reading or writing. For nonfluent readers, this means that children do not have the chance to learn new vocabulary words or truly comprehend the passage. Nonfluent children will use simple, easy-to-spell words to express themselves, write short sentences, and not have the time or energy to engage in planful writing. You can probably see how this becomes a vicious cycle—poor readers are able to decode fewer new words and therefore have fewer words at their disposal when spelling, and children who use the same limited words over and over again when they write never build the skills to identify new and unfamiliar words.

Moreover, difficulties in either of these areas can—understandably—lead to frustration with the reading or writing process, and resistance to trying these sorts of activities. That is why it is so important for parents to strike the right balance and encourage children to develop these skills without pushing too hard or correcting too often. Remember, all of these skills develop on a continuum, so it is absolutely appropriate to pick activities at your child's current skill level and then build from there.

How Do Children's Spelling Skills Develop Over Time?

Children go through five stages of spelling development, beginning with period when they have no ability to pair sounds and letters and culminating in the stage where they can very reliably pair sounds and letters.[25] Understanding these stages will help you identify the progress that your child is making. Because all people at all ages misspell words sometimes, and children's strategies can vary depending on the difficulty of the words that they are attempting to spell, these stages are not entirely distinct from one another. In other words, your child may spell words in more than one of the ways described in Table 3-5. You can think of him as being in the stage that best describes the majority of his spelling behaviors, but it is more important to focus on the process than on the stage.

Your toddler or preschooler is likely in the *precommunicative stage* of spelling development. The marks that he makes on paper may convey meaning to him, but other people are not able to interpret them because he is not yet able to pair letters and sounds at all. The marks that he makes on the page may be entirely invented symbols or may include some real letters, but in no particular order. Look back at Sophie's depiction of the phrase "dinosaurs are far away" on page 154 for a good example of precommunicative writing.

Then, your child—often by the end of preschool or the beginning of kindergarten—will enter the *semiphonetic stage* of spelling development. She will begin to connect letters with their sounds, usually

TABLE 3-5. STAGES OF SPELLING DEVELOPMENT

Stage of Spelling Development	Age	Description	Example—How To Spell the Word "little"
Precommunicative	Preschool	Children become enthusiastic about writing, but the marks they make on paper are not yet meaningful to other people because they are not yet able to pair letters or sounds at all.	
Semiphonetic	End of Preschool – First Grade	Children begin to connect sounds with letters, representing a word by writing out its most salient sounds and focusing on consonants, rather than vowels.	LDL
Phonetic	First Grade – Second Grade	Children begin to represent all of the sounds with letters, representing a word by writing out all of its sounds (but representing some sounds in unconventional ways).	LIDEL
Transitional	Second Grade – Fourth Grade	Children continue to represent all of the sounds with letters, and begin to follow conventional spelling rules with more frequency.	LITTLE
Conventional	Late Elementary School and Beyond	Children spell most words accurately or conventionally.	LITTLE

* Age ranges are approximate and children may display characteristics of more than one stage at the same time

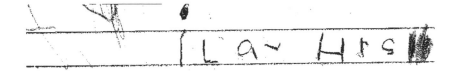

Figure 3-8 Asher (Kindergarten): "I love hearts."

by using the consonants in a word to represent it. For example, she may spell the word *house* as *HS*. Often, a child will not attempt to use vowels at all in this stage, and if she does, she will have a great deal of difficulty determining which vowel to use. You can see that in Figure 3-8, Asher is at this stage of development, and is making good progress toward becoming a phonetic writer who represents all of the sounds in words.

From here, your child will move into the *phonetic stage*, meaning that he will represent all of the sounds in words with letters. However, he may rely upon letter names to represent some of those sounds. For example, a child may represent the word *boat* as "bot" because he is relying on that middle letter to make the long "o" sound. He may represent the "be" in the word *because* with the letter "b" because he is relying on that first letter to be pronounced just like its name. Jamie's nephew Max, at the end of kindergarten, wrote out a list of snakes that he liked, including "Kng Cbr" (King Cobra) and "Pfon" (Python). You can see that Max is transitioning between the semiphonetic and phonetic stages here, as he sometimes represents the vowels in words and sometimes does not.

In order to make sense of children's writing at this stage, adults often need to think like beginning readers themselves. Most consonants make the sound associated with their name, and vowel names are equivalent to long vowel sounds. Figuring out a child's logic may not be too hard in most instances, once you begin thinking this way. However, it becomes harder to decipher children's emerging spellings when they are trying to represent sounds that cannot be represented simply by using a letter's name. For example, the letter name for "W" ("double U") does not help a child spell *whine*. So when a child is searching his memory to figure out which letter makes the /w/ sound, he may stumble across "Y" ("why") and use this letter name to represent the sound he needed, spelling the word as "Yn." Over time, children become more familiar with the sounds that are made by letters that do not provide clues to the sounds they make—letters like *G, H, K, W,* and *Y*. However, you may be likely to see many inventive spellings of words that contain these sounds, even as children begin to spell other words conventionally. Here's an example by Saul, at six years, three months:

> bug.
> By Saul.
> Deap awtin space a butterfly was fling. It was the multi colored and He got sucd in a black hoel He had aspecl spot on it had spesl pours He uwsd the paurs to get out.
>
> (Deep out in space a butterfly was flying. It was the multi-colored, and he got sucked in a black hole. He had a special spot on it and special powers. He used the powers to get out.)

Sometime in second or third grade, children move into the *transitional stage* of spelling development. At this time, children have discovered many spelling rules and attempt to use them, although they often use them imperfectly. Vowels are used in each syllable of a word, and children begin to use vowel digraphs (when two vowels are paired together to make one sound), perhaps representing *take* as *taik*. Similarly, children may begin to use the correct letters to represent a word, but use them in the wrong sequence (such as representing *boat* as *baot*). We see an example of this in Saul's writing: for example, in the word *deap*, which is meant to be *deep*. It is also interesting to see how Saul experiments with the right way to spell *special*, representing its second syllable as *cl* and *sl*. He uses phonetic strategies here, despite the fact that most of his writing is emblematic of the transitional phase. Soon, he will likely add a vowel to that final

syllable, spelling it as *cil* or *sil*. Spelling this word is particularly difficult because it its second syllable is irregular, meaning that the way
it is spelled (*cial*) is not how you would expect from sounding out the
word. But, as he continues through this transitional phase, Saul will
begin to use common letter sequences (like the *oat* in *boat*) with more
and more frequency, and have a better recall for the ways that some
irregular words are spelled.

By late elementary school, children enter the *conventional stage*,
where they begin to spell words conventionally rather than in inventive ways. Table 3-6 provides another example of how children's writing and spelling develops over time. You can see that conventional
spellers spell the majority of words that they use automatically,
although writers of all ages revert to strategies used in earlier developmental stages when spelling unfamiliar and sophisticated words.
Certainly, the process of becoming a conventional speller takes years
to unfold, just as becoming a fluent reader does not happen overnight. But American adults, including many American teachers, rely
on technology tools to help them with spelling and the use of memorization when teaching or recalling spelling rules. Our language system often seems mystifying even to those of us who have already
mastered it. We often cannot explain why a word is spelled a particular way, but we know when a word looks right and when it looks
wrong. Because there are some words that do not follow conventional
spelling rules and need to be learned through memorization, many
people have come to think that spelling is best learned through rote
memorization. It is easy to understand how this misconception has
emerged, but it is misguided. Just about 50 percent of the words
in the English language have perfect sound-symbol correspondence,
37 percent can be learned through instruction of letter patterns, and
13 percent are truly irregular.[26] So, children can learn nearly 90 percent of the words they will need through applying the patterns of
the English language and becoming aware of the common ways that
words are spelled.

TABLE 3.6. STAGES OF WRITING AND SPELLING DEVELOPMENT

3 years → 10 years

pre-communicative

- draws symbols to communicate
- copies or invents random strings of letters
- understands that speech can be written as text

semi-phonetic

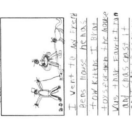

- "invented spelling"
  I want to read and want to take gym and take Sundae (hamster) horse.
- recognition of sounds of letters, primarily consonants at the beginning or end of words
- letter formation is more recognizable

phonetic

- represents all major sounds with letters
- word segmentation and spacing more evident

transitional

- spells common words without error
- uses visual memory to write words
- creates more complex words using morphemes (smallest units of meaning)

conventional

- mastery of sound/symbol principles
- spells and writes common and complex words
- atypical spelling patterns are still challenging

This book is about a dog named Squirrel and her adventures as a stray. She loses her brother when she's about one year old. She fights through losses and is brave no matter what. She meets a dog named Moon who is friendly. One day Moon is run over by a car and Squirrel is lonely after that. She travels through the woods and goes through towns. Squirrel lives with kind and mean people. She has rough years and fights through bad ones.

What Is the Role of Parents in Supporting Spelling Development?

Helping your child learn to spell may sound a lot less fun than helping your child learn to read. We do not mean to imply that you should be giving your child a list of spelling words to memorize each week or that you should be correcting each and every misspelled word that she uses. Part of the reason that we devoted so much attention earlier in this chapter to helping kids stay motivated was for this exact reason—we want to discourage you from taking that sort of approach! There are many ways that you can encourage spelling development without a red pen in hand.

Strong phonemic awareness, which allows children to perceive and manipulate the sounds in words, is a necessary prerequisite for decoding and encoding skills, so using the strategies in chapter 2 of the book is the first step in supporting your emerging speller. While you work on these linguistic skills, you should be encouraging your child to write and praising the use of invented spellings. We want you to celebrate precommunicative writing because it is a child's first attempt to use symbols to make meaning. Then, of course, you must continue to support this growing ability as more of those symbols become recognizable letters.

WORD STUDY
The practice of exploring the patterns of letter use in words, including a focus on spelling patterns that help explain, among other things, which words use a letter's hard vs. soft sound (e.g., *call* vs. *cell*).

Another way to help your child is to engage in playful **word study** based on sound patterns, visual similarities, and word meaning.[27] Word study is just what it sounds like—studying words to understand the patterns of letters they contain and what sounds those letters make. By selecting words to spell that are part of the same word family (for example, *lack, rack,* and *tack*), children become familiar with when the letters "ack" are used together and what sounds these letters represent. This familiarity will make it easier for them to spell less familiar words like *attack* and *black*. Similarly, sorting a list of words that start with the letters "b" and "d" into two separate columns will help them focus on the differences between words like *bill* and *dill* or *bin* and *din*. When children recognize that there are rules that govern spelling, it becomes easier for them to generalize what they learned about one word to other similar words. For this reason, if your child misspells a word and you want to correct him, think back to this idea of word study. Then, instead of just telling him the right way to spell the word, share examples of other words that are spelled using the same rule so that he has the opportunity to study and analyze this spelling rule. Examples of activities that promote word study are included in appendix B.

It is also important to help children recognize that they cannot depend on electronic spellcheckers to correct all spelling errors.[28] One problem with using such programs is that, when writing longhand, children will end up using simpler words that they do know how to spell, rather than the more descriptive synonyms of those words. This becomes especially important when older children are required to write in longhand for tests and other school work and inventive spelling is discouraged. Their writing will lack sophistication and they will not have a rich vocabulary to draw upon when writing. Think about the difference between the sentence *The disgruntled man scanned the room furiously* and *The mad man looked around the room and seemed mad*. The first sentence engages the reader with rich description, whereas the second sentence is awkward and difficult to understand due to the repetition of the word *mad*, which has multiple definitions. When a child does not know how to fluently spell a word, he—wisely—selects a word that he can spell and moves on to the next part of the sentence (or becomes frustrated and gives up, an even worse outcome). Thus, without the ability to spell fluently, your child would not be able to craft the former and more eloquent sentence.

Another problem with electronic spellcheckers is that they will not pick up on the type of errors a child might make when sounding out a word (and are more effective for correcting two letters that are written in the wrong order or identifying errors due to hastiness). For example, if a semiphonetic speller represents the word *large* as "lrj," the first word that Microsoft Word's Spelling and Grammar program will suggest is *lark*. Similarly, if a transitional speller represents *phrase* as "fraze," the first option that pops up is *froze*. In both of those cases, the program does not suggest the word that the child was searching for at all. Even on the computer, this child would need to resort to simpler language to get his point across. Making spelling an important focus of reading and writing together will help your child become willing and able to sound out new words independently.

Developing Spelling Skills: How Can I Support My Child's Individual Needs?

As you think more about how to help your child become a strong speller, it may be helpful to think about how spelling skills are related to the skills that we have already talked about in earlier chapters, as well as the skills we talked about earlier in this chapter. As you can see from Table 3-7, strengthening spelling skills—at all points in this developmental process—helps free children to write in ways that are increasingly more recognizable to others around them, and of course, to become more proficient encoders and decoders. For that reason, figuring out exactly what hints and tips your child needs to progress to the next stage of spelling development also supports writing and reading development.

As we've mentioned, spelling errors can indicate a lack of phonemic awareness, so correcting spellings with explanations about what letter sounds are actually in a word can help build both skills. For example, a child might spell the word *dress* as "jres." With support, she will eventually come to recognize that her mouth and tongue are in a different position when making the /d/ sound than then /j/ sound. Modeling the difference between these two sounds may help her understand why she needs to spell the word differently. Additionally, she will probably need some direct instruction to realize that the *S* at the end of the word needs to be doubled, the rule for which we explain below. Working through these issues together and scaffolding her knowledge rather than just telling her the correct spelling will prepare her to spell similar words (e.g., *drama* or *less*) accurately in the future.

TABLE 3-7. COMPARISON OF STAGES: WRITING AND SPELLING DEVELOPMENT

Age*	Stage of Writing Development	Stage of Spelling Development	
Preschool – First Grade	Imitation	Precommunicative	Semiphonetic
As children learn to express themselves on paper, they mimic what they see adults do and gradually begin to include some recognizable consonants in the written work.			
First Grade – Second Grade	Graphic Presentation	Phonetic	
As children begin to pair letters and sounds, they focus on writing in a way that can be interpreted by others			
Second Grade – Fourth Grade	Progressive Incorporation	Transitional	
As familiarity with many aspects of the writing process grows, children apply their knowledge of qualities of good writing and spelling accuracy in their work.			
Fourth Grade – Seventh Grade	Automatization	Conventional	
As students learn to spell conventionally, the act of writing becomes an automatic process.			

* Age ranges are approximate

You can also help your child by knowing the basic rules of spelling and teaching or reinforcing these rules, when the time is right. We are not suggesting that you teach these rules out of the blue. But, when your child is struggling to spell a word, providing a clear explanation of why it should be spelled a particular way will help more than just giving him the correct answer. It may be difficult for you to articulate these rules yourself, because you have internalized them a long time ago. If that is the case, doing detective work together to find out more about spelling rules can be a helpful activity that allows you to model curiosity about

TABLE 3-8. COMMON SPELLING RULES

Silent *e* Rule	When words follow the pattern of consonant, vowel, consonant, and final *e* at the end (as in *rate*, *cute*, or *bide*), the first vowel "says it name" or uses the long vowel sound and the *e* is silent.
Suffix Rule, also Known as *E* Drop Rule	When a word ends with the letter *e*, drop the final letter before adding a suffix that starts with a vowel (for example, change *rate* to *rating*). But if the word includes a short vowel sound followed by a consonant (like in *mad*), then double the final letter before adding a suffix that starts with a vowel (changing it to *madder*). If the suffix starts with a consonant, do not double the final letter (leaving the word as *madly*).
Doubling Rule	When words are one syllable long and the letters *f, l, s,* and sometimes *z* follow a vowel at the end of the word (like in *stuff, sill, dress, miss,* and *fizz*), the last letter needs to be doubled.
Plural Rules	Most words become plural by simply adding an *s* (like *dogs, cats,* and *legs*), but words ending in *s, x, z, ch,* and *sh* add *es* (like *misses, fizzes, boxes, bunches, crashes*). And it doesn't end there. Words that end with the letter *y* (like *sky*) drop their final letter and add *ies* (becoming *skies*), except if the letter *y* comes after a vowel (like *toy*, which becomes *toys*), and words that end with *f* or *fe* (like *self* or *life*) changes to *ves* (becoming *selves* or *lives*).

language and literacy for your child. To give you a quick refresher, these simple rules are summarized in Table 3-8.[29]

Earlier in this chapter, we suggested praising your child for her accomplishments and then, if appropriate, selecting one aspect of her writing to improve upon or correct. The same is true when focusing on your child's spelling development. Drawing attention to her successes is important, because it lets her know that spelling is important. If your child is in first or second grade, and spells *mess* as "mes," you might say, "Wow! I am impressed with how you spelled that word. You know that *mess* starts with the /m/ sound." If she seemed engaged enough in the task to receive other feedback, you might also say, "Words like this, that have a short vowel sound and then a /s/ sound at the end, actually have two letter *s*'s at the end. Look, we also spell *less* this way." We wouldn't expect every child in kindergarten, or even early in first grade, to be familiar with the difference between long and short vowel sounds, so this type of feedback would only be appropriate if you knew that your child already had prior knowledge that would help her follow the rule. By being responsive to your child's individual spelling strengths and weaknesses, you can make corrections that will help her become a more proficient speller.

What Activities and Strategies Can I Use to Support Spelling Development?

Because spelling skills emerge in a developmental sequence, just as reading skills do, it is important for parents to become comfortable with their children's inventive spellings and encourage children in preschool and early elementary school to explore the relationships between letters and sounds, rather than exclusively focusing on spelling words correctly. It is helpful to keep your child's zone of proximal development in mind when you contemplate how to provide feedback about spelling errors and what strategies will work best for your child. If your daughter is a semiphonetic speller, she is ready to get tips about how to spell a word more phonetically—for example, if she spelled the word *rope* as "rp," you could sound the word out slowly and ask her what sound comes in between the /r/ and /p/ sounds, and help her realize that she needed to add the "o" there. However, talking about the "silent *e*" rule with her would be too advanced for her current developmental stage. All of the activities we describe in this section can be used with children of any age, but the specific feedback you give will change as your child progresses in her reading and spelling development.

Print-rich environments. As we have discussed in earlier sections of the book, being surrounded by print is a primary way for children to build many language and literacy skills. Focusing on words in print during shared reading time will help familiarize your child with the way words are represented in print. Asking your child to point out a word that begins or ends with a particular letter on the page you are reading together will help him begin to develop rudimentary spelling skills, and searching through a storybook together to find rhyming words and examine them in print will help him begin to recognize the similarities between the way *make* and *take* are spelled. You can create print-rich environments outside of the home, too, by focusing on the signs and advertisements around you wherever you go. A trip to the grocery store provides endless opportunities for spelling development if you ask your child to look for one item in each aisle that starts with the letter "m." The goal of activities like these is to focus your child's attention on written words, and allow him to analyze the way our spoken language is represented in print.

Build spelling skills during shared writing. Earlier in this chapter, we suggested several activities that you might use to get your child writing, or to write together as a family. Inevitably, when writing together, your child will turn to you and ask, "How do you spell...?" Regardless of whether your child is three or ten years old, this question provides you with a great opportunity to give some developmentally appropriate spelling support. Resist the urge to spell the word for your child immediately and instead turn spelling the word together into an activity. For example, let's say your daughter asked how to spell the word *heart,* which has an irregular spelling. You might say, "Hmmm...heart. Hhh—rr—ttt. What letter do you think *heart* starts with?" As you worked your way through the word together, you could ask questions like "What sound do you hear next?" or "What letter does *heart* end with?" After answering these questions, your child would have spelled the word to the best of her ability—perhaps it would be spelled "hrt" (semiphonetically), 'haret' (phonetically), "hart" (transitionally), or "heart" (conventionally). Based on your daughter's stage of spelling development, you could then decide at what point to say "Great job!" and leave the word as it was, and at what point to give her a tip. If your daughter were a semiphonetic speller, you might help her add some representation of the vowel sound into the word, and not worry at all about what letters she used to represent that sound. If your child spelled the word phonetically, you might help her find a simpler and shorter way to represent the sounds in "are." And if your child spelled the word transitionally, you might at this point share the rule for this irregular word, and say, "*Heart* follows its own special rule. It is spelled h-e-a-r-t." Words spelled with the letters *ear* are ones that your child will need more practice to learn to spell accurately, because the pronunciation of words with that letter pattern is not consistent. For instance, think about the words *bear* and *early*, which also do not conform to the expected pronunciation (in contrast to *ear*, *near*, and *fear*).

The example above may seem challenging, and it is meant to be! We want you to feel confident helping your child puzzle out the spelling of even these words that defy our expectations. Remember, 50 percent of words in the English language are spelled regularly and do conform to our expectations. The majority of other words can be learned by paying attention to letter patterns (like *what*), and only 13 percent of words are truly irregular (like *once*). Even those words that are irregular are not irregular throughout, but tend to have just a few letters that cannot be sounded out using our knowledge of spelling rules—so memorization alone is not the best way to learn to encode these words (although you can refer to appendixes C and D for examples of commonly used irregular words and some strategies for identifying them by sight). There are many strategies you can use for helping your child spell new and unfamiliar words, whether they are regular or irregular. These strategies include:

- Sounding out the word, as described in the example focused on spelling *heart*.
- Thinking of other words that sound the same, and using them to help spell this new word. For example, if your child knows how to spell *car*, he can use his knowledge to help him tackle a new word like *cart* or *scar*.
- Breaking a word into syllables and tackling each part separately. For example, if your child has to spell *cartographer*, his knowledge of the words *car* and *graph* can help him work through this longer word.

- Using the "cover-copy-compare" strategy of looking at the word in print and examining it, then covering it up and trying to spell the word independently, and finally comparing one's own spelling to the original version.
- Brainstorming about word families by generating lists of words with common parts. For example, your child may ask you how to spell *light*. Once you and your child together establish how to spell this word, you can make a list together of other words that are spelled the same way like *fight, light, might, night, right, sight,* and *tight*. Once your child notices *right* on that list, it will help him spell words like *bright* and *fright* as well. As you can see, learning to spell one new word unlocks the key to many other words as well through learning by analogy.
- Teaching your child about the small percentage of irregular words in the English language and helping him become familiar with these exceptions to spelling rules through frequent exposure.
- Playing word games that allow your child to use hands-on materials to spell words (like Scrabble Junior) and recognize words (like Boggle Junior). Similar games can also be found online or on handheld tablets, although they don't allow your child the same opportunity to actually manipulate the tiles and blocks.

Approaching spelling in a playful and inquisitive way will help your child see this process as an interesting puzzle to be solved, rather than a series of rules to be memorized. The reason we talk about learning to read as decoding and learning to spell as encoding is because both skills require breaking a code, an activity which children find interesting and exciting. If we can model enthusiasm in the process for them, through conversation and games that encourage spelling, this aspect of literacy development can become very rewarding. Many of the strategies discussed in the "Alphabetic Knowledge" section of the prior chapter are helpful here as well as those listed in Table 3-9, so be sure to look back at those ideas once you are ready to work on these skills.

TABLE 3-9. SPELLING DEVELOPMENT: STRATEGIES FOR PARENTS

What to Do	How to Do It	Age(s)
Immerse Your Child in a Print-rich Environment	Focus on written language during shared reading time by asking your child to point out words that start or end with specific letters. Do the same thing outside of the home using signs or items in the grocery store. Print is everywhere!	
Build Spelling Skills During Shared Writing	When your child asks you how to spell a word, resist the urge to just do it yourself. Instead, sound out the word and have your child tell you what letters to use.	
Play Hangman Together	Use a paper and pencil or play *Hangman* electronically, alternating turns as the speller and the guesser.	
Play Ghost Together	*Ghost* is a game in which a group of people spells a word collaboratively, and the first person to spell a full word loses the round. For example, if you went around the room spelling *R-O-U-T-E*, the person who said the *E* would lose. If that person instead said *I*, to help spell *routine*, the game would keep going until a full word was spelled.	

continues

TABLE 3-9. CONTINUED

What to Do	How to Do It	Age(s)
Do Wordsearches	Complete wordsearches that have children search for specific letter patterns, but not ones that include words written upside down or backwards, as these may be confusing to beginning readers and spellers.	
Do Crossword Puzzles	Complete crossword puzzles that have children look for specific letter patterns.	
Be Writers	Write stories or poems together that use words from the same word family, mimicking the style of Dr. Seuss or other writers you enjoy.	

Conclusion: Enjoying Encoding

The ability to put our ideas down on paper is one of the most amazing skills humans possess. The ability to speak is what allows us to communicate with one another, but it is the fact that we can write down what we say that keeps us from having to repeat the same information over and over again to each individual person. When you think about writing as a tool that keeps us from having to repeat ourselves endlessly and as a way to store human knowledge, it becomes clear that learning to write is an incredible feat, one that has led to a more civilized world.

The goal of engaging with children in playful activities that support writing and spelling development is to introduce them to the idea that writing helps us remember information as well as take pleasure in communicating with others. Writing is about meaning-making, not just about forming correct sentences, and all attempts at meaning-making should be encouraged. Similarly, spelling is about learning to pair letters and sounds, and all attempts to do that—especially highly creative attempts—should be praised. Do not rely on memorization as the only spelling strategy you teach your child, and instead figure out the nuances of the English language together. In sum, our motto for this chapter might be, "Don't correct. Help your child reflect!"

TABLE 3-10. TECH TIPS FOR PARENTS: LEARNING TO WRITE

Tech Tips: Learning to Write

Technology tools have facilitated writing for a long time, from the advent of typewriters to computers to smartphones. However, the kinesthetic act of actually writing letters, rather than identifying them on a keyboard, can be beneficial when initially learning letters and eventually when spelling words. Although some applications will allow your child to trace letters, many do not provide this option—so be on the lookout. And, as we discuss in the chapter, spellcheckers on computers and smartphones can actually impede spelling development, so be sure to use these tools judiciously. The suggestions in this table should help you get started.

What to Do	How to Do It	Age(s)
Record Your Child's Stories, and Use Technology to Animate Them	Being able to tell stories is an important skill for any emergent writer. Throughout this chapter, we have mentioned several times that children who are learning to tell stories may want to dictate these stories to you, for you to write down. We know that you don't always have time to do that, at least right away, which is why tools like the voice memo function on a smartphone can come in handy—your child can dictate stories anytime you are stuck in the car or waiting in line. Moreover, applications like *Puppet Pals* (available through iTunes) allows your child to select characters and settings, and then record a story and dialogue that the characters will act out electronically. By bringing narration and illustration together, tools like these will allow your young child to understand the role that written language plays in media other than books.	

What to Do	How to Do It	Age(s)
Use Technology Tools for All Stages in the Writing Process	Children can use applications like *Notes* or *Ideas* on tablets to write and scribble when you are on the go. Application like *StoryBuilder* and *Toontastic* help children map out a story from beginning to end. Many applications, like *Popplet*, allow children to create graphic organizers electronically.	
Create a "Real" Book	Many companies provide the technology for children to print and bind their own storybooks. Allowing your child to turn a final draft of a story she wrote into a "real" book (perhaps to give as a gift to another family member on a special occasion) might motivate her to work on the story even harder.	
Explore Multiple Genres and Learn From Professionals	Scholastic's *Writing with Writers* webpage (http://teacher.scholastic.com/writewit/) provides elementary school students with opportunities to learn from published authors and write in a variety of genres. This is a great example of one way that the Internet can serve as an incredible resource—children can receive information and advice from people whom they may never come into contact with personally.	

continues

TABLE 3-10. CONTINUED

What to Do	How to Do It	Age(s)
Make Spelling Practice Fun	Although we highly encourage spelling development through everyday exposure to new words and rules, there may come a time when you feel like your child needs more direct practice understanding sound patterns in words or memorizing the spelling of particular irregular words. Because practicing this skill can be one of the drier ones, applications like those listed on Reading Rockets top ten list (www.readingrockets.org/pdfs/Top-10-Spelling-Apps.pdf) can help children in kindergarten and up playfully engage in spelling activities. Games like *Words with Friends for Kids* can also be a playful way to make sense of letter patterns. You can also seek out other games that allow children to build words using electronic letter tiles. These applications often will not allow a letter to stay where it is placed if it does not build a word, and thus can provide children with some feedback about their choices.	

TABLE 3-11. ENGLISH LANGUAGE LEARNER TIPS FOR PARENTS: LEARNING TO WRITE

English Language Learner Tips: Learning to Write

Emergent writing refers to children's early attempts to translate the spoken word into print, beginning with scribbles and progressing to include pseudo-letters and eventually real print. Research suggests that developing a proficiency in writing in L1 will help support your child's development of writing in L2, because these children already understand what it means to put spoken words into print and have the dexterity required to write. Practicing writing in both L1 and L2 can support your child's developing proficiency in both languages. However, your child may experience frustration when the rules of the written word differ between languages. It is not uncommon for a child to combine the rules for writing L1 and L2 before she has mastered the distinction between the two. For example, a child who is learning both Spanish and English may use punctuation that is found in Spanish, but not English, texts. Although it may be tempting to correct your child when she writes a story in L2 and uses some words from L1 to describe particular ideas or phrases, it is important to recognize that this type of code switching is developmentally appropriate in the early years of writing development. With practice and through exposure to print, your child will be able to master writing in both languages. This table includes some tips that will encourage your child to practice writing with activities that can be experienced in either L1 or L2.

What to Do	How to Do It	Age(s)
Draw and Label	As your child begins to learn about words in his home language as well as in English, he can draw pictures in a little book made of pages you have stapled together. After his picture is complete, ask him what he has drawn and label the items in the drawing (L1 or L2, or in both languages). By writing the words next to his drawing, the connection of print and meaning can be powerful.	

continues

TABLE 3-11. CONTINUED

What to Do	How to Do It	Age(s)
Label Objects in Your Home	Using sticky notes or index cards, have your child write the names of common items in L1 or L2, or in both languages, to help him practice forming the letters in a variety of words. He may also want to make a small drawing on each card to help him to remember the word.	
Have Your Child Dictate a Story	Encourage your child to talk about a pet, a book, a trip, etc. As your child speaks, write down his words exactly as he says them. After each sentence, read the words back to him, pointing to each word. Invite your child to read along with you on a second reading together. Finally, whisper read the words to help support your child's attempt to read the words by himself.	
Suggest Purposeful Writing	Your child can be encouraged to practice writing through correspondences with relatives and friends in near and faraway places by cards, letters, postcards, or emails.	
Keep a Shared Journal	You can use the "secret messaging" system with your child. In a small spiral notebook, encourage your child to draw or write a message to you in L2. The notebook can then be placed in a special location where you can respond to your child's message in a unique way by asking a question or by making a comment about what he shared. The next day, your child can "read" and "respond" to your message. Your correspondences will accumulate over time and can create a wonderful keepsake.	

What to Do	How to Do It	Age(s)
Model the Writing Process	While you are writing down your child's dictated stories, verbalize your thinking as you write. For example, "I'm going to put a period at the end of my sentence to show that I'm finished with my thought." Or, "I need to start my sentence with an upper case letter like this." This will help to clarify the differences of punctuation in various languages and demonstrate the writing process.	
Create Word Banks	Spelling in English is challenging for all students, but especially for students who are just acquiring English. Provide your child with a small notebook for "My Book of Words" so that he can access frequently used words in writing.	

Notes

1. Shanahan, T. (2006). Relations among oral language, reading, and writing development (pp. 171–183). In C. A. Macrthur, S. Graham, & J. Fitzgerald (Eds.), *The Handbook of Writing Research*. New York: Guilford.

2. Levine, M. (1998). *Developmental Variations and Learning Disorders*, 2nd ed. Cambridge, MA: Educators Publishing Service.

3. Temple, C., Nathan, R., & Temple, D. (2013). *The Beginnings of Writing*, 4th ed. Boston: Allyn and Bacon.

4. Clay, M. (1976). *What Did I Write?* Portsmouth, NH: Heinemann.

5. Bruner, J. as cited in Temple, C., Nathan, R., Temple, F., & Burris, N. A. (1993). *The Beginnings of Writing*, 3rd ed. Boston: Allyn and Bacon.

6. Shanahan (2006).

7. Ibid.

8. Nelson, S., & Rollins, J. (2003). *Frosty the Snowman*. New York: Grosset & Dunlap

9. Van Allsburg, C. (1985). *The Polar Express*. Boston: Houghton Mifflin.

10. Temple et al. (2013).

11. For more information about the Common Core Standards, see www.corestandards.org/assets/CCSSI_ELA%20Standards.pdf

12. Pritchard, R. J., & Honeycutt, R. L. (2007). Best practices in implementing a process approach to teaching writing (pp. 28–49). In S. Graham, C. A. Macrthur, & J. Fitzgerald (Eds.), *Best Practices in Writing Instruction*. New York: Guilford.

13. Murray, D. M. (1980). Writing as process: How writing finds its own meaning. In T. R. Donavan & B. W. McLelland (Eds.), *Eight Approaches to Teaching Composition* (pp. 3–20). Urbana, IL: NCTE.

14. Graham, S., & Hebert, M. A. (2010). Writing to read: Evidence for how writing can improve reading. Carnegie Corporation Time to Act Report. Washington, DC: Alliance for Excellent Education.

15. Numeroff, L. (1985). *If You Give a Mouse a Cookie*. New York: HarperCollins.

16. MacLachlan, P. (1988). *The Facts and Fictions of Minna Pratt*. New York: Harper & Row.

17. O'Connor, J. (2005). *Fancy Nancy*. New York: HarperCollins.

18. Temple et al. (1993).

19. Coker, D. (2007). Writing instruction for young children: Methods targeting the multiple demands that writers face (pp. 101–118). In S. Graham, C. A. MacArthur, & J. Fitzgerald (Eds.), *Best Practices in Writing Instruction*. New York: Guilford; Graham, S., Harris, K. R., & Fink, B. (2000). Is handwriting causally related to learning to write? Treatment of handwriting problems in beginning writers. *Journal of Educational Psychology*, *92*(4), 620–633.

20. Graham, S., & Hebert, M. A. (2010). *Writing to Read: Evidence for How Writing Can Improve Reading. A Carnegie Corporation Time to Act Report*. Washington, DC: Alliance for Excellent Education.

21. Foorman, B. (1997). Why direct spelling instruction is important. *Scholastic Spelling: Research Paper, Vol. 2*. New York: Scholastic.

22. Shanahan (2006). Ibid.

23. Ehri, L. C. (1998). Grapheme-phoneme knowledge is essential for learning to read words in English (pp. 3–40). In J. L. Metsala & L. C. Ehri (Eds.), *Word Recognition in Beginning Literacy*,. Mahwah, NJ: Lawrence Erlbaum; Ehri, L. C. (2000). Learning to read and learning to spell: Two sides of a coin. *Topics in Language Disorders*, *20*, 19–49; Graham& Hebert (2010).

24. Ehri, L. C. (1997). Learning to read and learning to spell are one and the same, almost (pp. 237–269). In C. A. Perfetti, L. Rieben, & M. Fayol (Eds.), *Learning to Spell: Research, Theory, and Practice across Languages*. Mahwah, NJ: Lawrence Erlbaum; Moats, L. C. (2005-6). How spelling supports reading: And why it is

more regular and predictable than you may think. *American Educator, 29*(4), 12–22, 42–43.

25. Gentry, J. R. (1982). An analysis of developmental spelling in GNYS at WRK. *The Reading Teacher, 36,* 192–200; Gentry, J. R. (2006). *Breaking the Code: The New Science of Beginning Reading and Writing.* Portsmouth, NH: Heinemann.

26. Foorman (1997).

27. Honig, B., Diamond, L., & Gutlohn, L. (2008). *Teaching Reading Sourcebook,* 2nd ed. Berkeley, CA: Consortium on Reading Excellence.

28. Joshi, R. M., Treiman, R., Carreker, S., & Moats, L. C. (2008). How words cast their spell: Spelling is an integral part of learning the language, not a matter of memorization. *American Educator,32*(4), 6–16, 42–43.

29. Henry, M. K. (2003). *Unlocking literacy: Effective decoding and spelling instruction.* Baltimore: Paul H. Brookes.

Chapter 4

Story Comprehension

"Once upon a time..." Young children recognize these words as a signal that story time is beginning. Upon hearing these words, children settle down and anticipate the adventure to come—whether it be a trip to The Hundred Acre Wood where a stuffed bear and his friends roam; to the little town of Whoville, located within a speck of dust on a clover flower; or to the great green room in *Good Night Moon,* where there is a telephone, a red balloon, and a picture of a cow jumping over the moon. Reading can transport us anywhere and everywhere; the magic of the journey comes from more than just deciphering the words on the page. The process of decoding and identifying words is critical to successful reading, but the true art transcends these mechanics. Comprehension is about lifting the text from the page and incorporating it into our own world of knowledge and experience.

What Is Comprehension?

The focus of this chapter is on comprehension, or the process of deriving meaning from written language, whether the child is listening to a storybook or reading on his own. This is the ultimate goal of the reading experience, whether a child is reading poetry, a scientific text, a to-do list, or a storybook. Although we begin with a broad definition of **comprehension,** we will focus in on **listening comprehension** and **reading comprehension,** both of which contribute to **story comprehension** (see Figure 4-1). In general, when people

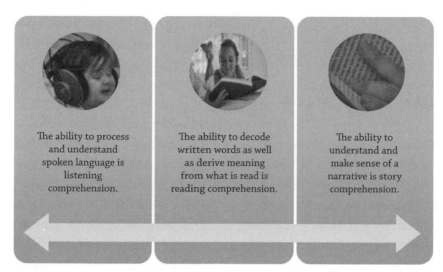

Figure 4-1 Types of comprehension.

comprehend something, it means that they understand the meaning and intent of what is said or read. They are able to follow the general message, sense its design and developments—beginning,

> **COMPREHENSION**
>
> The ability to understand the meaning of what is said, or read, as well as its intent.

middle, and end—and, for the most part, understand how it relates and connects to a larger context.

This capacity to understand how events relate to one another is especially important for understanding stories. In order to understand the story as a whole, the reader must make multiple connections and develop multiple story comprehension skills. These skills include placing events in logical time sequences, recognizing cause and effect associations, understanding the relationships between characters, and perceiving the motivations behind their actions. Once a child begins to possess these skills, reading becomes a way to learn about how people feel and behave, a means to explore new worlds, and a chance to lose oneself in the magic of a good story. Lifelong readers become hooked on books because they provide these types of experiences and, as we have discussed in earlier chapters, a child does not need to be ready to read independently

> **LISTENING COMPREHENSION**
> The ability to process and understand spoken language.

in order to develop these skills. Children begin to understand stories well before they start to read on their own.

Listening and reading comprehension. Reading researchers like Philip Gough and his colleagues have put forth a "simple view" of reading comprehension, which states that a person's reading comprehension develops to the level of their listening comprehension, but does not surpass it.[1] As discussed in the chapter on oral language, listening comprehension, or receptive language, starts to develop when children are very young and continues well into adulthood. These early language skills are critical to the foundations for later reading success.

Reading comprehension involves the joint processes of being able to decode text (sounding out and identifying words) and derive meaning from what is actually being read. If a word is not in a child's vocabulary, or

> **READING COMPREHENSION**
> The ability to decode written words as well as derive meaning from what is read.

if she can't understand something when she hears it, it is unlikely that she will be able to understand it when the same information is in printed form. As a result, reading comprehension skills often lag behind listening comprehension

skills when the child is still developing the ability to actually decode text. When a child can understand language equally well in verbal or written form, the distinction between listening and reading comprehension ceases to be important. However, research suggests that most children don't reach this point until seventh or eighth grade.[2]

Given that many researchers believe that listening comprehension forms the "ceiling" of what children can understand when reading, meaning that their reading comprehension skills will not surpass their listening comprehension skills, it is vital to keep developing their listening comprehension skills, even after they have learned to read. This means it is important to keep reading to your child—even after he has learned to read independently. By using the shared reading techniques discussed in chapter 1, parents can stimulate children's higher-level thinking, understanding of cause and effect, and understanding of abstract and academic language. Parents can also support comprehension skills beyond shared reading through complex and information-rich narratives in everyday conversation.[3] Using open-ended questions as frequently as possible will support children's higher-level thinking, which will be discussed in greater detail later in this chapter.[4] These interactions help build children's abilities to comprehend spoken language. In turn, the ability to comprehend spoken language then provides the foundation for—and is highly predictive of—their later ability to comprehend text when reading independently.[5]

Despite the close association between listening and reading comprehension, there are some important differences to note between spoken and written language, making children's listening comprehension during shared reading an important bridge between understanding everyday spoken language and comprehending texts. First, the way people write differs from the way they talk in quite profound ways, including the fact that written sentences tend to be more complex and formal. In order to understand texts, children must master the structures, conventions, and complexities of written language. For many children, this adjustment from everyday conversation to academic discourse is challenging. Reading aloud to young children provides the early exposure to text structure and written language that facilitates this transition and sets the stage for successful comprehension of text. Second, when engaging in spoken conversation, speakers will often check for understanding. They might periodically ask questions like, "You know what I mean?" and will try to clarify accordingly. In contrast, when reading, the burden of monitoring comprehension is solely on the reader. Similarly, in chapter 3, we talked about the fact that writers need to independently determine whether their readers will have all of the necessary information to understand the story they have written. Whereas spoken language allows two people to share the responsibility for comprehension, written language requires one person to shoulder this responsibility alone.

To help your child develop the ability to monitor comprehension independently, you can turn reading back into a spoken language activity by reading together. As with the dialogic reading approach explained in chapter 1, you can simply ask questions during reading, like "Why do you think he did that?" or "Do you know what that word means?" This approach allows you to clarify meaning or help your child gain information when you sense that something in the text doesn't make sense to her.

Why focus on story comprehension? Both listening comprehension and reading comprehension contribute to *story comprehension*, the ability to understand and make sense of a narrative. Some psychologists say that stories have a "privileged status" in our minds—that there is something inherently appealing about stories with which the human mind connects.[6] Research suggests that compared with other types of writing, people generally find **narrative texts,** or writing that tells a story, more interesting, easier to understand, and easier to remember.[7] Most of the printed materials you read to your child are likely narrative texts and, in fact, approximately 90 percent of the texts children are exposed to in elementary school are also narrative texts.[8]

> **NARRATIVE TEXT**
> Writing that describes a story or an experience rather than describing facts or attempting to persuade the reader.

Research suggests that children who enter kindergarten with more developed narrative skills tend to perform better on later measures of reading achievement than their peers with lower narrative competence.[9] But there are other benefits to building a child's story comprehension skills. Developing the ability to comprehend narratives can also facilitate children's understanding of other types of texts as well. The same processes children use to connect elements of a story can be used to draw connections between concepts in a scientific text, connect the logical arguments in a persuasive essay, or understand the unfolding of events in a historical account.

   Although definitions of what a "story" is might vary, we use "The Four Cs" to help define the elements of a story:

Causality: Events in stories are related to each other through causal pathways. In *Corduroy,*[10] Corduroy, the teddy bear, longs to be taken home by a child. However, he discovers that he is missing a button (making a mother pass him over), leading him to search the store for his button at night.

Conflict: In every story, characters have goals and challenges they face in trying to meet their goals. Corduroy is unfamiliar with the store he is in and ends up in unfamiliar territory during his search. He mistakes the button on a mattress for his own button and tries to take it.

Complications: If a story merely proceeded through a series of episodes in which characters work toward achieving their goals, it would be boring, which is why most stories introduce new problems and twists. In *Corduroy,* a night watchman hears the bear trying to get the button, prematurely ending his search.

Character: In order to keep readers engaged in these conflicts and complications, stories need main players drive the plot forward. *Corduroy* features the bear, the little girl who wants to bring him home, her mother who discourages her purchase, and the night watchman. Readers are invested in the outcome of stories when they care about what will happen to the people and creatures they read about, and *Cordoruy*'s fans are thrilled when the bear and the little girl are reunited.

When we say we comprehend a story, we mean that we are able to follow cause and effect relationships, understand the main problem and resolution, appreciate the effects of complications, and follow its characters' motives, actions, and subsequent reactions. A further goal of story comprehension is to identify themes implicit in the writing—that is, a classic idea such as friendship, adventure, a person battling against the elements, and so on. We begin to recognize these themes because they are familiar, and we focus on situations we have experienced or read about previously. For instance, when reading *Cordoruy,* we understand how and why the story began, how it evolved, and how it ended because we already have an understanding of how an adventure story unfolds.

What Skills Support Story Comprehension?

Research has identified several skills that support the process of story comprehension. These include having knowledge of *story schema, causal reasoning,* and *inferential thinking* (see Figure 4-2).[11]

Story schema refers to an understanding of the general framework of stories, including an understanding of the parts of a story, including its setting, characters, main problem, climax, and resolution to the problem. *Causal reasoning* is the ability to understand what made certain events happen and predict future consequences, whereas *inferential thinking* refers to reasoning that goes beyond the text or pictures to deduce or infer what the author is discussing. These aspects of comprehension will be explored in depth throughout this chapter. Strategies to support the development of these skills and your child's overall comprehension

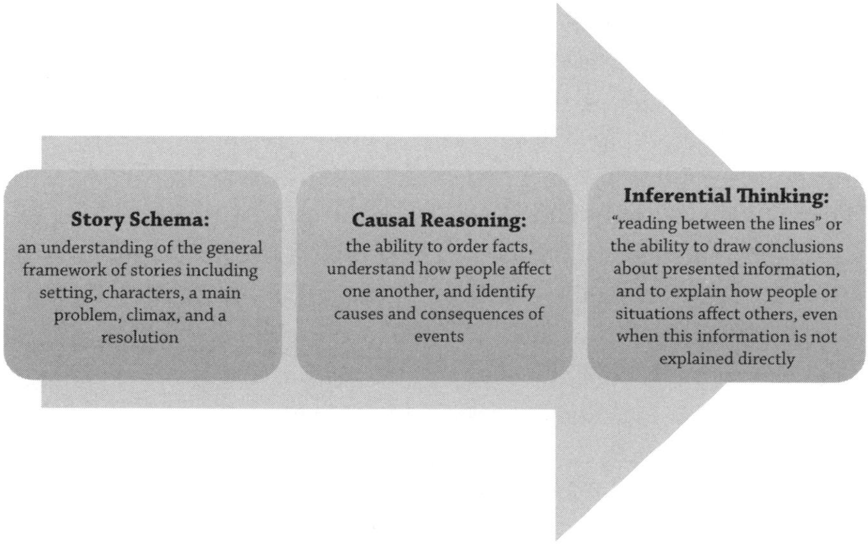

Story Schema: an understanding of the general framework of stories including setting, characters, a main problem, climax, and a resolution

Causal Reasoning: the ability to order facts, understand how people affect one another, and identify causes and consequences of events

Inferential Thinking: "reading between the lines" or the ability to draw conclusions about presented information, and to explain how people or situations affect others, even when this information is not explained directly

Figure 4-2 Skills that support story comprehension.

development during shared reading and everyday interactions will also be discussed.

Story Schema

In order to comprehend a narrative, it is helpful for children to have a mental picture or template in which to organize and store information. Experts call this organizing framework a **story schema.**[12] Like the border pieces of a jigsaw puzzle, the story schema acts as a framework that makes it easier to understand, organize, and store information in a meaningful context. You might have a schema for a birthday party, in which guests arrive, cake is eaten, and presents are opened.

> **STORY SCHEMA**
> An understanding of the general framework of a story including its setting, characters, main problem, climax, and resolution.

Even though details of specific birthday parties may differ, the general schema of a birthday party helps you know what to expect and how to interpret the events that unfold.

When children know what to expect in a story, it becomes easier for them to make sense of what is happening. As an example of how having expectations can aid in comprehension, try to make sense of the story in Box 4-1, which a group of researchers asked participants to read in order to demonstrate the importance of *schemas* in helping people make sense of and retain new information.[13]

Does it make sense to you? Could you tell a friend how to complete the procedure as described? What if we tell you the "procedure" is *doing laundry*? Does this make following the story easier for you? Would it be easier for you to relay this information to your friend with this piece of knowledge? While the text may have originally seemed very confusing, this one piece of information makes it click into place—because it now conforms with our expectations.

When this passage was read in the research study, some of the participants read it with no surrounding context and remembered very few

BOX 4-1. A STORY WITHOUT A SCHEMA

The procedure is actually quite simple. First you arrange things into different groups. Of course, one pile may be sufficient depending on how much there is to do. If you have to go somewhere else due to lack of facilities that is the next step, otherwise you are pretty well set. It is important not to overdo things. That is, it is better to do too few things at once than too many. In the short run this may not seem important but complications can easily arise. A mistake can be expensive as well. At first the whole procedure will seem complicated. Soon, however, it will become just another facet of life. It is difficult to foresee any end to the necessity for this task in the immediate future, but then one never can tell. After the procedure is completed one arranges the materials into different groups again. Then they can be put into their appropriate places. Eventually they will be used once more and the whole cycle will then have to be repeated. However, that is part of life.

details about it later. Other participants were told beforehand that they were going to read a paragraph about *doing laundry*. This group of participants had a much higher rate of recall. Similarly, when children have a picture in their mind of how stories are structured and can use a schema to make sense of the story, they have an easier time organizing information into this template and can better remember and comprehend what happens in a text.

Just as you have developed schemas for birthday parties and about the process of doing laundry through a great deal of exposure and experience, over time children develop story schemas that allow them to connect individual pieces of information into a coherent whole. As children are exposed to more narratives, they begin to construct a cohesive story schema, recognizing that most narratives have common building blocks: stories begin by establishing a setting, introducing main characters, and proposing a problem. You can help your child see these common building blocks, always keeping in mind that it isn't necessary for

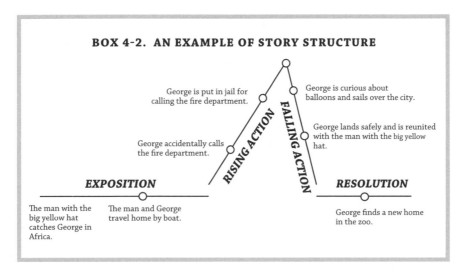

BOX 4-2. AN EXAMPLE OF STORY STRUCTURE

George is put in jail for calling the fire department.

George is curious about balloons and sails over the city.

George accidentally calls the fire department.

George lands safely and is reunited with the man with the big yellow hat.

RISING ACTION

FALLING ACTION

EXPOSITION

RESOLUTION

The man with the big yellow hat catches George in Africa.

The man and George travel home by boat.

George finds a new home in the zoo.

your child to understand every part of a story schema on the first reading of a narrative.

After many sessions of shared story time, your child will start anticipating common narrative patterns, like the one depicted in Box 4-2. To facilitate your understanding of how teachers view narrative patterns (and teach these patterns to children), it may be helpful to look at story structure as it is presented in late elementary classrooms, by focusing on a story's characters, rising action, episodes, and climax. The rising action of a story is made up of multiple episodes in which characters attempt to achieve goals. The story builds to a climax, followed by the falling action; the story ends when the problem is successfully resolved. You certainly don't need to insist that your child can recite each story element while reading for pleasure. However, if you find that your child is receptive to comparing similar stories, you can occasionally use the same terms (e.g., episodes, climax, and characters) that teachers are likely to introduce as children gain familiarity with stories.

Why Is Story Schema Knowledge Important for Future Reading Development?

A child who has a well-developed sense of story schema will be better equipped to develop comprehension skills through identifying and interpreting important information within a story.[14] An awareness of how stories are generally structured frees a child's cognitive resources to focus on the content of the particular story she is reading or hearing at that time.

Conversely, a poor understanding of story structure has been linked to difficulties in reading comprehension. For example, psychologists Kate Cain and Jane Oakhill[15] looked at reading comprehension scores for a group of seven- and eight-year-old children and divided them into two groups: skilled comprehenders and less skilled comprehenders. They asked the children to tell stories prompted by a title such as "Pirates." Children who had lower comprehension scores tended to tell stories that were poorly structured, with missing, unexplained, or nonsequential elements. One child who had poorer comprehension skills wrote the following:

> The pirates were on the boat for a long time. They wanted to find the treasure so they sailed around. They all got lots of gold and they were happy.

In contrast, a child who had higher comprehension abilities told this story:

> Once there was a group of pirates who found a treasure map. While they were searching for the treasure, a big storm came and shipwrecked them on an island. Luckily, this was the island on the map and they found a giant cave with lots of gold and treasure. They decided to quit being pirates and lived on the island forever.

The results of this study show that children with stronger knowledge of story schema are better prepared to comprehend new stories that they read because they know how to look for relevant details and place them in a narrative arc.

How Does Children's Story Schema Knowledge Develop Over Time?

Children's knowledge and use of story schema develops dramatically between ages three and five. As indicated by the examples in Box 4-3, three-year-olds tend simply to name and describe events and objects

BOX 4-3. HOW CHILDREN OF DIFFERENT
AGES NARRATE A STORY

In a series of investigations, children of a range of ages from a variety of linguistic and cultural backgrounds, were asked to narrate, one picture at a time, a wordless picture story entitled *Frog, Where Are You?* by Mercer Mayer. In this picture story, a young boy first loses, then searches for, and finally finds his pet frog. Below are examples of children of various ages narrating the first 7 (of 24) pictures, with quotes taken directly from the research study.[a]

3-year-old child's narration: "There's a frog there. He's in there dusty. Here's a moon. Those are boots. Dog is going to fall over. He cry and it fall down. He hold dog. He see them fall down. Dog fall down. They outside."

5-year-old child's narration: "There was a boy. He had a dog and a frog. When he always goes to sleep the dog goes to sleep on his bed with him. And when they're asleep the frog sneaks out. And then they both wake up and then the frog is gone. So he gets dressed and the dog gets dressed and then he put his boot on his head and then he put the other boot on his foot. And after he went out calling for the frog."

9-year-old child's narration: "Well there was a boy and he had a frog and a dog. He loved his frog very much and maybe his dog did too. One night when he was asleep the frog climbed out of his jar. The boy woke up. The next morning the frog was gone. The dog looked concerned. The boy quickly got dressed and the dog put his head in a jar. He got stuck there but the boy did not pull it off. Instead he opened the window and yelled for his frog. The boy and the dog went looking for the frog. They yelled for the frog."

As is apparent in these examples, there is a pattern of developmental progression in the use of story schema. The three-year-old's account of the story is a simply a list, naming and describing isolated objects and events. In contrast, in the five-year-old's version, we see a story structure begin to take shape: the child introduces characters and describes a cohesive episode including character's goals and attempts to achieve those goals. The nine-year-old goes even further by elaborating on actions and purposes and by adding character's reactions to events (for example, "The dog looked concerned").

---

[a]Trabasso & Stein (1997).

and cannot yet connect events in a sequential manner. However, by age five, children usually include information about main events, characters, settings, and problems. Five-year-olds are also beginning to think and talk about the order of events in stories and the relationship between cause and effect.[16] By age nine, children structure stories in a similar way to adults, including information on characters' goals, attempts to reach those goals, and the outcomes of their actions. By this age children have neared adult-like competence, but their knowledge of story schema becomes increasingly sophisticated and refined into adolescence.[17]

What Is the Role of Parents in Fostering Story Schema Knowledge?

Multiple studies have shown that one way children learn about story schema is through conversations with their parents.[18] In fact, the way in which parents relate stories about past events to their children is related to the children's abilities to tell a cohesive personal story about a past event, recall fictional narratives, and produce well-structured stories. For example, one study asked parents to reminisce about past shared events with their four- to nine-year-old children and then asked the children to come up with a story based on a wordless picture book.[19] The researchers found that children created well-structured stories if their parents had provided more information about how and why things happened and if they drew children's attention to the sequence of events (e.g., "At the beginning of our trip...Next...").

These results imply that children use their parents as models when learning how stories are structured, and this modeling has a significant impact on their learning. Thus by sharing your own experiences with your child, you can help her develop her own narrative skills. When sharing what happened in your day, you can highlight story structure by using signal words like *first, then,* and *after.* When talking about shared experiences with your child, whether it is a family camping trip or a visit to the doctor's office, you can use these opportunities to model for your child how all stories are structured (they have a beginning, middle, and end) and talk about how and why things happen. The more time that you spend talking about the reasons why an event happened—what a person was thinking and how she felt—the more likely it is that your child will discuss these issues as well.

Developing Story Schema Knowledge: How Can I Support My Child's Individual Needs?

To enhance parent-child conversations, both in day to-day activities and within shared reading experiences, parents can tailor their questions and responses in ways that address their child's unique developmental needs. One way to get a sense of a child's knowledge of story schema is to ask him to retell a story. By seeing how he reconstructs a narrative, you will get a sense of the way he organizes the information in the story. One group of researchers asked children to retell a story about their past and then categorized their narratives into one of the following categories: **classic, ending-at-the-high-point, chronological, leapfrogging,** or **impoverished**.[20] All children begin retelling stories using an "impoverished" (or limited) style. Over the course of the preschool and early elementary years, children begin to demonstrate more complex story structure in their retellings, with classic retellings emerging last. Table 4-1 includes a description of each narrative pattern and an example of what that might look like if a child were retelling the story of *Harry the Dirty Dog,*[21] in which a dog who hates baths buries his scrub brush in the yard and runs away. Over the course of his adventures he becomes quite dirty, and the little white

TABLE 4-1. NARRATIVE PATTERNS IN RETELLING A STORY

Narrative Structure	Description	Example	Parent Prompts
Classic	• Follows a linear sequence of events • Builds, then dwells on a highpoint • Ends with a resolution	"Harry hated baths, so he ran away from home. Then he got real dirty playing and when he came home, his family didn't know who he was even though he did his tricks for them. But he got in the bathtub and then he was clean and they knew who he was and his family was happy. Then he went to bed."	*You remembered what happened at the beginning, middle, and end of the story! It was a problem when Harry's family didn't recognize him, but he helped solve it by taking a bath, and everyone was happy!*
Ending-at-the-Highpoint	• Contains elements of a classic narrative • Cuts off at the highpoint or crisis in the story without resolution	"The doggie didn't want to take a bath and he hid his scrub brush then he went and played in the mud. He came home and they thought he was a different dog so he took a bath."	*That was the exciting part of the story, wasn't it? And how did Harry feel after his family realized who he was?*
Chronological	• Describes successive events • May sound like a laundry list • Lacks coherent organization and does not recognize cause and effect	"Harry ran away with his brush. Then he played by the train. He did his tricks and played dead. Harry took a bath and they were happy. Then the doggie took a nap."	*What happened on this page when he was playing in the street and by the train? . . . Yeah, he got so dirty and looked very different to his family. What did he do to show them who he was?*

Narrative Structure	Description	Example	Parent Prompts
Leapfrogging	• Jumps from one event to next • Difficult to follow	"The dog was really dirty and he jumped in a puddle and he didn't like his brush and he was yucky and they gave him a bath. He played with the other dogs and they didn't know who he was and then he went to sleep."	*Harry did run away and got very dirty while he was playing. What did his family think when they saw him?*
Impoverished	• Too few events are described structurally • Confusing or contradictory for the listener to understand	"The dog wanted to play and his family didn't like him."	*You're remembering that Harry didn't like to take baths and just wanted to play and play. What happened to him while he was playing in the mud?*

Source: Adapted from Peterson, C., & McCabe, A. (1983). *Developmental Psycholinguistics: Three Ways of Looking at a Child's Narrative.* New York: Plenum.

dog with black spots becomes a little black dog with white spots. His family doesn't recognize him, and in a desperate attempt, he unearths his scrub brush and begs for a bath. Once he is clean, they realize that he is in fact their dog, and he contentedly goes to sleep with the scrub brush tucked under his pillow.

Using story schema to make sense of a narrative is a bit like following a recipe to make a cake. The children who have well-developed story schema have a complete recipe, with all the ingredients they need and a detailed plan for getting from start to finish. Just as following a complete recipe will result in a well-made cake, following a story schema results in a classic structured narrative. Children who have not reached this stage in development seem to have gaps in their recipe, with an incomplete list of ingredients or missing steps in the procedure. A child who ends at the highpoint may follow the recipe perfectly but miss the crucial last step of putting the cake in the oven. Likewise, a child who takes a leapfrogging approach may haphazardly combine ingredients and perform the steps in a random order, resulting in a half-baked cake with the frosting ingredients baked right into it instead of beautifully decorating the top. A story schema helps children combine the key ingredients of a story (setting, characters, events, actions, and outcomes), organize them in a logical sequence, and understand the story as a cohesive whole. However, it is important to note that although your child may tell the story (using expressive language) in a truncated or haphazard way, it does not necessarily mean that he did not "understand" the story (relying on receptive language) when it was read to him or when he read it on his own.

Being attuned to your child's zone of proximal development can help you know how best to support her understanding of story schema by recognizing where she currently is and the next steps you need to take to scaffold her development. As described in Table 4-1, if you notice that your child ends many of her stories at the highpoint, she may benefit from additional prompting and encouragement. Meanwhile, if your child often engages in leapfrogging, you might insert yourself more frequently in her narratives, making connections, and asking guiding questions, and labeling parts of the story for your child, such as "In the *beginning* of the story...The *problem* was..." When children are in the beginning stages of understanding story schema, you may want to focus only on a few main story components, such as the main characters, the beginning, middle, and end. As children become more sophisticated in their understanding of stories, they will become more adept at identifying more complex elements, such as the main problem of the story, the resolution, and smaller events that happen throughout the story. Remember, no matter what style your child uses when retelling a story, you don't want to discount the effort he puts into retelling it. Instead, you should acknowledge his attempts and use specific feedback to let him know that you appreciate the information he shared. Then, you can give a prompt or ask another question; once he responds, follow up by expanding on what he said, again praising his efforts, and moving on to talk about something else. You don't need to force a classic retelling right away. It will take more than one reading session to turn your leapfrogging storyteller into a classic storyteller, but by slowly strengthening his skills rather than trying to cram it all into one session, you make it more likely that he will become and remain an engaged reader.

What Activities and Strategies Can I Use to Support Story Schema Knowledge?

There are many strategies parents can use to support their child's development of story schema knowledge. We will discuss using wordless picture books, modeling story schema during shared reading, using narrative retellings, and providing additional strategies in Table 4-2. However, any activity that will allow you to help your child recognize the formal structure of a book or story, whether that involves formally discussing a book's narrative structure or informally discussing the plotline of a television show or movie, will support your child's development of this important knowledge.[22]

Wordless picture books. Much of the research we have discussed in this section examined children's narrative comprehension through the use of wordless picture books. This format can help children develop

TABLE 4-2. STORY SCHEMA DEVELOPMENT: STRATEGIES FOR PARENTS

What to Do	How to Do It	Age(s)
Use Wordless Picture Books	Tell your child that you are going to read a book without words. Ask your child to narrate the story as you turn the pages together. This activity will promote your child's growing sense of story and schema and allow you to learn what he understands about the story.	
Model Story Schema During Shared Reading	During shared reading, explicitly point out the elements of the story (like its characters, main problem, climax, and resolution) in the order in which they occur. Or, provide your child with a framework in advance by talking about story structure. This will help your child to make sense of what will be read.	
Narrative Retellings	After reading a story with your child, suggest that she retell it to another family member. You can be creative by turning the activity into a fun, interactive game in which you take turns retelling the story one line at a time. If no family members are present, the story could be retold to a favorite toy!	
Make a Photo Album	Take pictures during family vacations or outings. Have older children help you make a photo album, putting the pictures in order. Look through your album together, providing framing words such as, "At the *beginning* of our trip, we got on an airplane..."	
Write a Book Together	Encourage your child to tell stories and write down what he says. You can have him illustrate his story and turn it into a book. There are many simple ways you can bind this book, from stapling the pages together to using a hole punch and ribbons to keep the pages together.	

What to Do	How to Do It	Age(s)
Retell a Favorite Story	Ask your child to read a favorite storybook to you, either reading the words on the page or reciting the story from memory and picture prompts. Provide gentle prompts if she forgets an important part of the story.	
Act Out Favorite Stories	Re-enact favorite stories during play time with toys available around the house. For example, for *Goldilocks and the Three Bears,* you might get three different sized bowls and blankets.	

a well-structured story schema and help refine their causal reasoning skills by encouraging them to create their own narrative based on the "clues" provided by the pictures. Books that are best for this kind of activity reveal a clear storyline without depending on text, and present an obvious sequence of events that contains key story elements (i.e., setting, characters, problems, resolutions).[23]

EXAMPLES OF WORDLESS PICTURE BOOKS

The Lion and the Mouse (2009) by Jerry Pinkney

Flotsam (2006) by David Wiesner

You Can't Take a Balloon into the Metropolitan Museum (2011) by Jacqueline Preiss Weitzman

A Ball for Daisy (2011) by Chris Raschka

Home (2004) *by Jeannie Baker*

The Boy, the Bear, the Baron, the Bard (2004) by Gregory Rogers

The Yellow Balloon (2003) by Charlotte Dematons

The Red Book (2004) by Barbara Lehman

Sea of Dreams (2011) by Dennis Nolan

Wave (2008) by Suzy Lee

The Surprise (2007) by Sylvia van Ommen

Peep! (2003) by Kevin Luthardt

Oops! (2006) by Arthur Geisert

continues

> *Ice* (2011) by Arthur Geisert
> *The Treasure Bath* (2009) by Dan Andreasen
> *Bow-Wow Bugs a Bug* (2007) by Megan Montague Cash
> *Chicken and Cat* (2006) by Sara Varon

Modeling story schema during shared reading. Another way you can help your child develop a story schema is to explicitly point out the elements of a story and the order in which they occur. For example, after reading *The Giant Jam Sandwich*,[24] you could describe the story to your child:

> Let's see if we can remember what happened in the story of *The Giant Jam Sandwich*. In the beginning of the story, we met the people who live in the town of Itching Down and learn that they have a problem: millions of wasps have come to their town. To solve the problem, they have a town meeting to think of ideas. Bap the Baker comes up with the idea to make a giant jam sandwich to trap the wasps. The townspeople work together to make the dough, bake the bread, and spread the jam on the giant sandwich. The most exciting part of the story is when the wasps come and get stuck in the jam and the people in the flying machines drop another slice of bread and trap the wasps. The townspeople have a party to celebrate that the wasps are gone. At the end of the story, the giant sandwich is carried off by birds so that they can eat it.

You can also directly talk about story structure before reading a book to model how to make sense of the story and to provide children with a framework in advance. You might keep your narrative briefer here, to ensure that your child would still be excited to hear the story itself. For example, before reading *Curious George*,[25] you might say:

> In this story you're going to meet a very curious monkey named George. George wants to find out about everything, but this sometimes gets him into trouble. At one point he even gets put in jail! Let's find out about George's adventures, why he gets put in jail, and how he gets out.

Narrative retellings. Research suggests that children's comprehension is facilitated by their active reconstruction of stories, and the effect is particularly pronounced if the child engages in frequent retellings.[26] After sharing a story with your child, suggest that she retell the story to her sister or a favorite doll who has never heard it before. If your child is uncertain about beginning the story, you can turn the activity into a game where you take turns telling one line of the story. Suggest that she starts with "Once upon a time" or "Once there was." You can fill in the next sentence, then encourage her to continue the story by asking "What comes next?" or "Then what happened?" If your child needs further prompting, ask questions that are relevant to her stopping point such as "How did she try to solve her problem? What did she do first?"[27] Many studies have shown that comprehension skills transfer across different media,[28] so you can engage in the same type of retelling activity by asking your child to relate the plot of a television narrative or a short movie.

Causal Reasoning

In addition to being able to view events in relation to one another as part of a story schema, it is also important for children to understand the specific connections between events. Although events can be connected in many ways, perhaps the

> **CAUSAL REASONING**
> The ability to think logically; to order facts, understand how people affect one another, and identify causes and consequences of events.

most important type of connection is causal.[29] The 18th-century philosopher David Hume referred to causality as the "cement of the universe,"[30] implying that causal connections bind together isolated events in a cohesive way that helps us make sense of our world.

Why Is Causal Reasoning Important for Future Reading Development?

Understanding causality helps us understand what made certain events happen, anticipate future consequences, and weave together a cohesive picture of a series of events.[31] Research suggests that events that are causally connected are much more likely to be remembered than are isolated events, or even events that are temporally related but not necessarily causally connected.[32] If someone told you she gave her friend a straw, a mirror, a glass of milk, a napkin, and a cookie, you'd probably forget at least one of these items if asked about it later. But if you were given explanations of causality, as Laura Numeroff gives readers in *If You Give A Mouse A Cookie*,[33] such as the mouse was hungry so your friend gave him a cookie, which made him thirsty so your friend gave him some milk, but the glass was too tall so he needed a straw, but the milk gave him a mustache, so he needed a napkin, which made him want to look in the mirror to make sure he got every last spot, you would have a significantly easier time recalling all these items. Your memory of the information shared would be better because the events became a unified chain instead of isolated fragments. Just as Hume surmised, causality is the "cement" that connects these discrete facts together into a unified narrative.

To illustrate the importance of **causal reasoning**, we want to tell you about a seminal study in which a group of researchers presented four- and six-year-old children with a set of four picture stories, each consisting of 15 to 18 pictures without text.[34] Each child saw two stories with pictures presented in their normal order and two stories with the pictures in a scrambled order, and they were asked to describe each picture in the story. After seeing all of the pictures, they were then asked to tell the story back to the researchers, but without the pictures. Children tended to describe pictures in greater detail, use more narrative conventions, and more accurately recall information about the pictures when the pictures were presented in the normal order as compared to when the pictures had been scrambled.

In other words, when the pictures were in a normal sequence, children were able to construct a coherent representation of events. However, when pictures were scrambled, causal and other cohesive ties between the pictures had been broken. The series of pictures ceased to be a coherent whole and was instead regarded as a group of isolated fragments. You can imagine that for a child who lacks basic causal reasoning skills, it may seem like *all* stories are in a scrambled order because he is unable to see the causal associations that link together a sequence of events. Without the ability to identify cause and effect relationships between events, it is difficult to organize information into a story schema and to retain the information in a text.

How Does Children's Causal Reasoning Develop Over Time?

The scrambled pictures study provides clues about children's development of causal reasoning skills. In general, the six-year-olds told more cohesive stories than did the four-year-olds. Interestingly, even when the pictures were scrambled and there were no apparent relationships in the pictures, the six-year-olds tried to impose causal relationships between events in the pictures. As children get older, they start spontaneously looking for meaningful causal links between events, even if they are not immediately apparent.

Causal reasoning skills generally tend to emerge around age four and continue to grow increasingly advanced until around age nine when development begins to plateau.[35] As is evident in the scrambled pictures study, although four-year-olds can engage in basic causal reasoning, they often need explicit supports in order to do so.[36] Anne remembers reading *The Tree,* a book about the trees and animals in a rainforest that is in danger of being destroyed, with her son Michael when he was around four years old. Anne stopped on a page that showed a group of animals fleeing from the forest, a field of felled trees and stumps behind them. When Anne asked, "Why do you think all the animals are running?" Michael replied, "They're chasing each other. See? The wolf says, 'I'm gonna get you, deer.'" Anne recognized that Michael was relying heavily on the pictures in the book, and prompted Michael to consider the causality from the text by reading the book and saying, "Hmm, let's see what the page before said—Oh! It says, *But now I hear bulldozers coming.* I wonder if the bulldozers knocked down all of these trees." With this prompt, Michael replied "Yeah! Maybe the animals are scared of the bulldozers and are mad because they don't have any more trees to play in, so they're running away."

As this example illustrates, although young children often have difficulty engaging in causal reasoning spontaneously, they can correctly identify causes and consequences with a bit of scaffolding. Indeed, research suggests that four-year-olds are more likely to cite appropriate reasons for characters' actions when adults use the types of dialogic reading questions and prompts described in the oral language chapter, just as Anne did with her son Michael. Young children are also more likely to identify cause and effect relationships when information is explicitly presented in an illustration.[37] If a bulldozer had actually been present in the picture of the animals fleeing from the forest, this relationship may have been more apparent to Michael. Just as you might help your child get a stepstool to reach something off a shelf until he is tall enough to reach it on his own, when you provide your child a little additional support while engaging in causal reasoning, you are helping him grow and develop these skills so that he will eventually be able to use these strategies independently.

What Is the Role of Parents in Fostering Causal Reasoning?

As Anne and Michael's discussion of *The Tree* illustrates, parents can have a powerful impact on their children's development of causal reasoning skills. Studies have found that parents who use more explanations when they talk to their children and discuss causality more often when their children are two and a half years old have children who talk more about causality when they are five years old.[38] Furthermore, researchers have realized that the timing of parents' talk about causality predicts when a child first spontaneously talks about causality without adult prompting.[39] Parents of very young children talk about causal relationships very rarely. However, at a certain point, parents recognize that their child is ready to connect events in this way, and their explanations and expressions of causality suddenly spike. Over the course of the next five to six months, children gradually start responding to parental prompts and answering their questions about causality, and eventually make causal connections independently.[40] Fairly consistently, children then begin to spontaneously bring up causality on their own five to six months after this spike in parental talk of causality.[41]

Although the pattern of child–parent talk of causality developing about a half-year after parental talk of causality is common in many households, researchers have found a wide degree of variability in the age at which parents first begin to focus on causal links. Some parents invite their children to engage in causal thinking and talk when their children are as young as two, while others do not engage in this sort of discussion until their children are almost five. Given the fact that children begin to talk about causality about six months after their parents introduced causal talk into their conversation, this means that children may begin to independently make causal links anywhere between age two and a half and age five and a half.[42] Children who are exposed to early and frequent parental talk about causality may experience an advantage in their development of reading comprehension. In addition, engaging your child in talk about why things happen or why someone feels a certain way also helps develop their social cognition skills like perspective-taking and empathy, skills we will talk about more in chapter 6 when we discuss social and emotional development. Thus, research highlights the importance of using explanations and causal reasoning with your child as early as possible.

Developing Causal Reasoning: How Can I Support My Child's Individual Needs?

Young children sometimes appear not to understand cause and effect. For example, when asked "Why do clouds move across the sky?" a child may respond, "Because they want to." However, studies have shown that children as young as three can distinguish between cause and effect and explain basic physical phenomena if they have the background knowledge to do so.[43] Upon learning about wind, the same child may be able to answer the question by saying "wind pushes the clouds." To help your child make sense of complicated cause and effect relationships in a storybook, you can help your child develop causal reasoning skills by asking *why* questions and providing relevant background information. While reading *The Snowy Day*,[44] you might say, "Peter just looked in his pocket for the snowball he made, but his pocket is empty. Why do you think the snowball is gone?" If your child has never seen snow, you may have to let her know that snow melts when it gets warm.

The further events are separated in a text, the more difficult it is for children to notice the causal relationships between them.[45] Therefore, it's especially helpful to call your child's attention to clues or preceding events that do not happen right before the resulting cause in the text. You might say, "Remember before Peter took a bath, he put the snowball in his pocket and then the book said he went into his *warm* house: Well, now his snowball is gone because it was too warm in the house for snow, and it melted." Providing these explicit links between cause and effect when your child is younger or less able to do so will help her make the connection independently in the future.

What Activities and Strategies Can I Use to Support Causal Reasoning?

There are numerous activities that can foster the learning of cause and effect and are fun to do with your child. For example, when cooking with your child, each action within the cooking process will cause a change and provides an opportunity to discuss cause and effect after each step in the process. Posing the question "What will happen if we add salt?" offers the opportunity to see and discuss the fact that the taste is changed as a result of adding this ingredient. A few of those activities that promote the understanding of cause and effect are discussed here and in Table 4-3.

Dramatic play. Dramatic play is related to the development of narrative comprehension.[46] You can help your child develop comprehension skills by engaging in dramatic play in which you and your child take on roles and act out parts that tell a story. For example, you and your child may be

TABLE 4-3. CAUSAL REASONING DEVELOPMENT: STRATEGIES FOR PARENTS

What to Do	How to Do It	Age(s)
Engage in Dramatic Play	Through dramatic play, you can support your child's development of causal reasoning by helping narrate the experience and making causal connections explicit. While playing house, you could say "Oh no! Baby spilled her bottle! What should we do?"	
Prompts and Questions During Shared Reading	During read-alouds, ask open-ended questions that have to do with causes and consequences in the story, characters' goals, and that require predictions about future cause and effect relationships. For example, ask things like "What made her do that?" or "What do you think will happen because he did that?"	
Employ Graphic Organizers	Scaffold your child's understanding of a sequence of relationships by using a graphic organizer, consisting of squares and circles drawn on a piece of paper or whiteboard, to represent the different aspects of a situation. Then, work together to fill them in. Encourage your child to come up with his own causes or outcomes relevant to the situation you're discussing.	

continues

TABLE 4-3. CONTINUED

What to Do	How to Do It	Age(s)
Demonstrate Causal Statements	Make explicit causal statements throughout the day. For example, when you play simple board or card games with your child, say "Because I drew the card with the 'x' on it, I lose my next turn" or "You landed on the square with the ladder on it, so you get to go all the way up here. When you land on a ladder, you get to move lots of squares."	
Point Out Causal Relationships	Help your child develop his social reasoning skills by pointing out causal relationships. For example, "You shared your snack with her sister, so she smiled and gave you a big hug."	
Give Examples of If...Then Relationships	Use "if...then" statements such as, "If you don't pick up your toys after you're done playing, then I'll put them on the shelf until tomorrow" or, "If you help me set the table, then we'll have time to read a book before dinner."	

What to Do	How to Do It	Age(s)
Use Causal Statements Frequently	Model using causal reasoning in your own relationships by saying, "Grandma sounded so happy when we called her today. It makes people happy when they know that other people are thinking about them." Hearing frequent statements about causal reasoning will familiarize your child with thinking in this way.	
Conduct Science Experiments	Do simple science activities with your child and talk about cause and effect. For example, make a ramp and roll cars down it, changing the slope of the ramp by adding or subtracting blocks. Talk about how changing the angle of the ramp can make cars go faster or slower or measure the distance the cars move off the ramp with masking tape.	

pretending you are auto mechanics. During this play, you can help your child narrate the experience and make causal connections explicit with comments such as, "Oh, someone just called from down the street with a flat tire. What happened? Do you think the car would work with only three tires? What can we do to help him fix his car?" Dramatic retelling of stories, such as fairy tales or frequently read books, can also help children develop their story schema and understand cause and effect relationships between actions.

Prompts and questions during shared reading. Questioning during read-alouds is an effective strategy for promoting your child's later reading comprehension ability, particularly because it helps children understand the causal links in stories. By asking open-ended questions, you can help your child identify causes and consequences in the story (for example, "Why did this happen?"), characters' goals (for example, "What made her do that?"), and make predictions about future cause and effect relationships (for example, "What do you think will happen because he did that?"). You can also show children how to use clue words (remember, words or phrases that indicate some sort of relationship between events) in the story such as *because, so that, next, before,* and *after.* Wordless picture books, like those discussed in the previous section, also help children to practice identifying and articulating causal relationships. Ultimately, the aim is for children to transfer these strategies of generating and answering questions and using clues in the text to their own repertoire of reading behaviors.

Graphic organizers. Helping your child to visualize cause-and-effect relationships via a graphic organizer can also be very helpful. Drawing a series of boxes or circles on a piece of paper or a white board to represent the different aspects of a situation will scaffold your child's understanding of a sequence of relationships. For example, as displayed in Figure 4-3, parent and child can work together to fill in the potential causes for the causes and effects of losing a library book. First, write a sentence such as "Toby lost her library books. As a result, she has to pay a fine." Then ask your child to say the cause (losing library books) and the effect (paying a fine). You can fill in the boxes with these answers, just like we did in the figure. A good exercise is to then ask your child to make up his own causes about why Toby lost her library books, or to think of other outcomes that might have happened too.

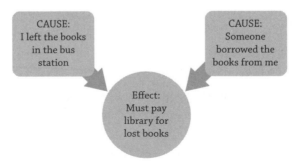

Figure 4-3 A graphic organizer for cause and effect.

INFERENTIAL THINKING

The art of comprehending a text is like a detective work—we are given certain clues within the text, but in order to solve the whole puzzle, we must fill in gaps and do some cognitive legworks to connect the dots. The clues with which we are provided are the **literal elements** of the text, or the ideas that are "right there" and immediately accessible within the text and illustrations. To fill in the gaps and understand the entire, coherent picture, we must engage in **inferential thinking,** going beyond the text or pictures to deduce or infer what the author is discussing.

> **LITERAL ELEMENTS**
> Ideas that are "right there, on the page" and immediately accessible within the text and illustrations.

> **INFERENTIAL THINKING**
> Going beyond the text or pictures to deduce or infer what the author is discussing.

Why Is Inferential Thinking Important for Future Reading Development?

Helping children develop the "detective" skills necessary to effectively make inferences is important because they will be expected to employ these strategies independently as they read to learn new information. Successful readers use the literal language of texts to make inferences on a number of different levels.[47] Children may use clues in a story to infer the meaning of an unfamiliar or nonliteral word or phrase.

Imagine you were reading *Sylvester and the Magic Pebble*[48] with your child and came across the following passage: "To his great surprise, the rain stopped. It didn't stop gradually as rains usually do. It CEASED." Although your child may have never heard the word *ceased* before, there are clues in the text that indicate that this word means *to stop suddenly*. Children use inferential thinking to follow the meanings of sentences, relying on clues in the text and their background knowledge to correctly interpret ambiguous sets of sentences like "*Jane watched Patty fall down the stairs. She ran for a doctor.*" to understand that it was Jane and not Patty who ran for a doctor.[49]

As inferential thinking skills become more sophisticated, children are able to make more complex inferences, such as predicting how a character might feel in a certain situation or what might happen next in the story. Indeed, inferential thinking is a particularly important skill for academic success because the reading materials children are exposed to during elementary school become increasingly abstract. Children who are less-skilled comprehenders are often unable to make appropriate inferences when they read; instead they tend to interpret text literally.[50] Research suggests that children do not generally interpret stories literally because of a lack of relevant knowledge, but rather because they are unsure of when to use relevant knowledge to make appropriate inferences.[51]

How Does Children's Inferential Thinking Develop Over Time?

A critical part of making inferences is being able to go beyond what is explicitly stated in the text. Taking this step is often challenging for young children, who tend to focus on the literal elements of a story. When listening to a story, they tend to concentrate on the information that is easily accessible in the book, such as the pictures or the *literal language* used in the text. However, in order to successfully fill in the gaps that are not explicit in the text, children must learn to use *inferential language,* which goes beyond the "here and now" and requires that children think abstractly and mentally represent abstract events that are more distant from the written text on the page.

Children's abilities to make inferences follow a developmental progression. Using their budding causal reasoning skills, children are first able to make inferences about relationships between physical events. After reading "Molly dropped a banana peel on the floor. Jack fell on his back," your child may assume that Jack slipped *because* Molly dropped the banana peel, even though this information is not explicitly stated in the text.[52] Causal reasoning can be thought of as a prerequisite for inferential thinking. However, inferential thinking involves not only inferring the cause or consequence of an event, but also, at its more sophisticated levels, using relevant knowledge to attribute motivations and feelings to characters, to discover authors' intentions, and to make connections within and across texts. In our example of Jack and Molly, your child will need to use inferential thinking to deduce whether or not Molly dropped the banana peel on purpose, if she is mean or nice, and how Jack will most likely interpret Molly's behavior. This type of inferential reasoning is challenging for young children.

Not all inferences are equally difficult for young children to make; events that occur closer together in time are easier for children to link inferentially than are distant events. In a study examining children's abilities to make inferences based on picture sequences, researchers found that after seeing three pictures that told a story in order, five-year-olds could easily identify what the fourth (next) picture in the series would be, but had a more difficult time correctly inferring what the sixth picture in the series would be.[53] However, six- and seven-year-olds were more successful at identifying the sixth picture.

As children get older, their capacity to make inferences regarding physical relationships grows, and they also develop the ability to make inferences about internal states, such as characters' feelings, goals, and desires.[54] Eventually, children are able to make inferences that translate the events of a story into some sort of moral or theme. A very young child may enjoy listening to *The Sneetches*[55] by Dr. Seuss with her focus primarily on the whimsical illustrations and almost musical language. However, as that child gets older, she may begin to appreciate the allegorical nature of the story, which centers around discrimination and prejudice. She may also make connections between this book and books with similar themes of feeling left out or different, such as *Chrysanthemum*,[56] *The Story of Ferdinand*,[57] or *Amazing Grace*.[58] When children begin to move beyond the confines of the mere content of a story, they are able to build important bridges between different books and make connections to their own real-world experiences. Through focusing on the emotional content of stories, and the important messages they convey, children are exposed to a whole new world of ideas and develop the capacity to make inferences about events that they themselves may not have experienced.

What Is the Role of Parents in Fostering Inferential Thinking?

Adults can help foster children's inference-making skills well before they are required to use these strategies as independent readers. After your child begins to read on his own, it will be important for him to continue working on these advanced skills. During shared book reading, you can use a wide variety of strategies to engage your child in the experience. Some comments or questions will be examples of *literal language,* such as labeling, locating, and counting objects in pictures and comments like "What is this?" or "Find the ball." You can then ask your child questions that require going beyond the literal level and encourage him to engage with inferential language, including asking him to make inferences, judgments, predictions, or explanations. A number of studies have endeavored to figure out what kind of talk is most beneficial for children's development.[59] As it turns out, children benefit when adults use a mixture of literal language, which requires children to comprehend a statement at face value, and inferential language, which requires children to "read between the lines" in order to comprehend meaning. Using literal language can help children develop basic vocabulary skills. It can also give children a feeling of mastery and success when they can correctly answer a question posed to them. However, challenging a child to answer a more difficult question can help her develop to think beyond the page and make inferences about the events occurring in a story.

It is important to remember that as your child develops, his level of mastery is constantly increasing. What was once a challenging question for him is now something he can easily answer. Thus, you will have to constantly shift and adapt the level of demand you place on your child. When your child is younger, you may focus mainly on literal language with some inferential language. As your child gets older, you can gradually "up the ante" and focus increasingly on inferential language while using less and less literal language.

Developing Inferential Thinking: How Can I Support My Child's Individual Needs?

Preschool children are capable of interacting with text beyond a literal level, but many only do so when prompted or questioned. Further, although younger children can most easily make inferences about physical events (for example, "It looks like Goldilocks is about to sit on a chair that's a little too small for her. What do you think will happen?"), it is important to give children the opportunity to practice making higher level inferences as well. With additional clues and prompts, children can begin to make inferences about characters' emotions and the message of a story. You might say, "The bears are coming back from their walk. They don't know Goldilocks is sleeping inside their house. How do you think the bears will feel when they find someone they don't know asleep in their house?" You can also model making more complicated inferences, such as connecting events to a story theme: "A lot happened in this story. Goldilocks ate all of Little Bear's porridge, she broke his chair, and she scared him and his family when they found her in Little Bear's bed. Something I learned from this story is that it would be better to wait and ask someone before you

In one study, children who were proficient in using literal language but whose inferential language skills were still developing made the greatest gains when their parents made comments during reading that mostly focused on literal language but also involved a substantial portion of inferential language. This finding is consistent with experts' recommendations that 70 percent of discourse should be at levels that the child has mastered and will clearly be able to successfully understand while the remaining 30 percent should be at higher levels, presenting a challenge to the child. So, if you make ten comments during a book reading session, you should try to make sure that seven of those comments are pretty easy for your child to interpret and that three of those comments should require some more thought or reflection.

use their things or before you go into where they live. How do you think you would feel if your little sister came into your room without asking and used some of your things?" These strategies help your child develop inferential thinking, much as recounting a story's beginning, middle, and end can help a child develop story schema. By focusing on this aspect of the story, you will help your child recognize the importance of trying to understand a story's overall message or how characters in the story feel.

As young children develop inferential thinking skills, they often make faulty inferences, resulting in a misunderstanding of a text. Two common mistakes that children make as they develop inferential thinking are focusing on the pictures of a book instead of the text, and interpreting the text literally. By understanding the sources of their confusion, we are better able to ask questions that guide their inferential thinking and engage them in conversations that ultimately support the development of their comprehension skills. Here, we provide some examples of these types of faulty inferences.

As we have discussed earlier in this section, young children also tend to focus on the "here and now," especially what is perceptually salient and tangible (for example, vivid illustrations in a book). Children are accustomed to accessing information in the world around them using their physical senses. Therefore, it makes sense that they are more likely to focus on information in the pictures than information in the text of the book. Although illustrations in children's books are often helpful clues in constructing meaning from text, sometimes the salient nature of pictures can detract from a child's understanding of a story. Let's pretend Rachel is reading a book called *Socrates*[60] with her son, Henry. The cover of the book depicts a dog wearing a pair of large, red glasses. The first pages of the book explain that Socrates' parents were captured by the dog catcher and Socrates is now alone on the streets without any friends and with no one to care for him. "How do you think Socrates feels right now?" Rachel asks. Henry replies, "Sad because he needs glasses." Although Henry may have correctly predicted Socrates' emotional state, he was distracted by the information presented in the illustration and missed out on the content of the text, causing him to construct a very different conception of the central problem the character faces.

Another mistake that is common for very young children or children who have difficulty comprehending is interpreting the text literally. Let's take the case of a young mother, Elise, who is reading *Tammy and the Gigantic Fish*[61] with her two children, Lucy, age three and a half, and Owen, age six. The story is about a young girl who has a disappointing day fishing with her family. After not catching any fish all day, Tammy catches a gigantic fish, but it looks at her with big, sad eyes. Tammy's family praises her for having the catch of the day and tells her it's time to load up the fish in the truck. However, Tammy decides to put it back in the water. "I just remembered," says Tammy, "I don't like to eat fish." After reading the book, Elise asks Jack and Lucy, "Why do you think Tammy decided not to bring the fish home?" Lucy replies, "Because she doesn't like fish. She thinks it's yucky." "No," Owen chimes in, "It's because she felt sad for the fish and didn't want to take it away from its home." A younger child, like Lucy, might take the text at its face value, but a slightly older child, like Owen, may have learned to read between the lines and make inferences about characters' actions and their underlying motivations.

Developing the type of reasoning skills necessary to infer characters' feelings and motivations is related to children's social-emotional development. In our daily lives, we are constantly making inferences about the world around us—Susan may infer that she got a poor grade on a test because the teacher dislikes her, while Jill may attribute the poor grade to the fact that she had a cold that day. Kevin assumes that Jesse deliberately pushed him in the lunch line, whereas Dave supposes Jesse must have accidentally tripped over his shoelace. Children often acquire information through stories that help them understand real-world situations. Helping your child develop more sophisticated inferential thinking skills may allow her to generate many alternative hypotheses for attributions she may make in the real world. Beginning to connect thoughts, feelings, and behaviors in this way prepares children to take the perspective of others and respond empathetically when others are in distress.

What Activities and Strategies Can I Use to Support Inferential Thinking?

While inferential thinking is often one of the most challenging tasks for young readers, there are many activities and strategies that you can engage in with your child to scaffold his development in this important skill. These strategies involve sharing with your child how *you* think about a problem or situation in order to model it for him. While these strategies often employ books as a tool to foster inferential thinking, other types of opportunities to promote this type of thinking in your child abound in everyday life.

Model "think-alouds" during shared reading. Skilled readers go beyond the literal elements of the text and draw inferences about what is implied but not stated. However, doing so is not easy for young children, as they often rely on pictures and the text's literal meaning to support their understanding. As described previously in this chapter, you can help your child develop good reading habits from an early age by modeling inferential thinking and identifying opportunities to practice this skill. For example, in *Curious George,* the curious little monkey observes the man with the big yellow hat using the telephone, and, intrigued, George picks up the phone and reaches the fire department. Trouble ensues when the fire department realizes it was a false alarm and George is carted off to jail. You might take this opportunity to ask about what is not explicitly stated in the text: "Why do you think that George called the fire department? Do you think he knew who he was calling?"

You can also model inferential thinking by engaging in "think-alouds," which can help your child identify opportunities when thinking aloud on her own would be useful, as well as demonstrate what an internal monologue of a reader might look like. You might say, "I wonder why the firemen were so angry at George for calling them. Maybe they were afraid that if someone else had an actual emergency they wouldn't be able to help them because they were at George's house where there wasn't a real emergency. I wonder if they knew he called them by accident or if they thought he was trying to play a joke on them."

Make and confirm predictions. Making and confirming (or disconfirming) predictions is an important problem-solving strategy used by skilled readers. You can help your child develop hypotheses about what they are reading by explaining that a prediction is your best guess about what might happen and asking them to make a prediction about a book you are reading. You might ask, "What do you think will happen next? Why do you think so?" You can also ask hypothetical questions that may never be answered in the book, "What do you think would have happened if George hadn't escaped from jail? . . . How do you think the man in the big yellow hat would feel if he knew George was in jail?"

Another important skill you can model is following up on one's predictions. You might think aloud,

> The title of this book is *Alexander and the Terrible, Horrible, No Good, Very Bad Day.*[62] Hmmm . . . looking at the cover, there is a little boy lying in bed who looks cranky. I think this must be Alexander and I wonder if he feels sick and that's why he is in bed and looks so unhappy. I predict that's why he's having such a terrible, horrible, no good, very bad day.

After reading a few pages, you can revisit your prediction and revise as necessary:

> Remember the prediction I made at the beginning of the story? I thought that Alexander was having a bad day because he felt sick. I was thinking that when I feel sick sometimes it seems like not such a good day. Well, it seems like Alexander is having a bad day for different reasons, like waking up with gum in his hair. Maybe that's why he looked so cranky in the picture on the cover!

As is illustrated in this example, don't be afraid that your prediction might be wrong! Watching you make an inaccurate prediction teaches children that our initial hunches may not always be correct, and we can revise our predictions as we get more information. By explaining your predictions early on in the story, you demonstrate that it is okay to make a guess about what will happen next based on the current information and provide examples of logical conclusions to draw.

Going on a picture walk. Another way to help support your child's inferential thinking is to go on a "picture walk" through books you have not yet read or through wordless picture books.[63] This strategy is especially helpful for younger children for whom it may be easier to engage in the complex process of inferential thinking if there are visual aids. Look through the story together and ask your child to narrate what he is thinking as he looks at the pictures. Ask guided questions that will encourage your child to integrate information and make inferences ("Why do you think the family got the robot?" or "What do you think he would be saying here?") and predictions ("This is the last picture in the story. What do you think happens next? Why do you think so?"). Once you prompt your child to consider questions like these when reading, he will be more likely to do so—independently—in the future. More suggestions for supporting inferential thinking are included in Table 4-4.

TABLE 4-4. INFERENTIAL THINKING DEVELOPMENT: STRATEGIES FOR PARENTS

What to Do	How to Do It	Age(s)
Model "Think-Alouds" During Shared Reading	Model inferential thinking during shared reading by asking about what isn't explicitly stated in the text. For example, while reading Curious George, who has just called a false alarm into the fire department, you might think aloud to yourself, "Hmm...Why would George called the fire department? I wonder if he knew who he was calling? I think he made a mistake."	

What to Do	How to Do It	Age(s)
Make and Confirm Predictions	Ask your child to make predictions about books you are reading by asking questions such as, "What do you think will happen next?" Or ask hypothetical questions that will never be answered in the book. An important point to remember is that, even though predictions may be wrong, it is still important to make them as they can always be revised once new information is learned.	
Going on a Picture Walk	Tell him to narrate what he thinks is happening based on the pictures and ask guided questions that will encourage the integration of information to make inferences ("What do you think he would be saying here?") and predictions ("This is the last picture in the story. What do you think will happen next?").	
Watch a Silent Movie	Watch a few minutes of a television show or movie without the sound. Ask your child if she can guess what was happening or how a character was feeling based on clues that she saw, for example facial expressions.	
Play Charades with the Family	Play charades with your family, acting out various physical and emotional states such as *tired*, *shy*, and *excited*. Process with your child what clues he used to guess the answers.	

What to Do	How to Do It	Age(s)
Play Guessing Games	Play guessing games by giving your child clues, for example, "I am a fruit...I am yellow...Monkeys like to eat me...I have a peel you take off before you eat me." Potential categories for guessing games include food, people in your family, household objects, body parts, and items of clothing.	
Be a Scientist	Help your child develop her scientific thinking skills by encouraging her to *observe, predict,* and *check.* For example, before cutting open a bell pepper, encourage your child to carefully look at, feel, and smell the pepper, describing what she observes (for example, "It's red and smooth and hard"). Ask your child to predict what the inside of the pepper will be like (for example, "Wet and juicy and red"). Check the prediction by cutting open the pepper and talking about what was predicted and what was actually observed.	

Conclusion

The roots of reading comprehension begin to develop far before a child can actually read independently. Acquiring a strong knowledge of story schema, causal reasoning, and inferential thinking skills early on helps set the stage for employing these strategies once your child learns to read independently. As research suggests, parents can help children develop the foundational skills necessary for them to bolster their reading comprehension. By using complex and information-rich narratives in conversations and labeling parts of stories (for example, *beginning, characters, problem, solution*), you can help your child develop knowledge of story schema so that she will have a strong framework through which to understand narratives. You can also use *Wh* questions in a variety of ways to support your child's development, such as by asking *who* or *where* questions to help children identify important characters and settings in stories and by asking *how, why,* and *what if* questions to help children build their higher-order skills such as causal reasoning and inferential thinking. Finally, parents can model comprehension strategies by engaging in "think-alouds." By witnessing your modeling and practicing these good reading behaviors themselves, children will eventually begin to internalize these strategies and will be able to use them to support comprehension once they begin reading independently.

TABLE 4-5. TECH TIPS FOR PARENTS: READING COMPREHENSION

Tech Tips: Reading Comprehension

Although technology tools can be very helpful for building basic reading comprehension skills, more sophisticated skills like causal reasoning and inferential thinking tend not to be addressed by simple applications and fun programs. These higher-level comprehension skills really require individualized, thoughtful feedback that only another person can provide. The activities suggested here can support other comprehension skills and get your child ready for engaging in more sophisticated activities with you.

What to Do	How to Do It	Age(s)
Use All of an E-book's Functions to Improve Comprehension	Technology tools can assist children's reading comprehension by allowing them to initially listen to a story as it is read aloud to them (by an application like Scholastic's *Storia* program). The text itself is generally highlighted as it is read aloud, which facilitates comprehension. When reading an unknown word, many e-books allow children to touch it for a definition or quickly search a dictionary for the meaning to facilitate ongoing comprehension. Similarly, many e-readers allow for annotation, so questions and notes regarding the content of the story can be written down electronically for the reader to later discuss or clarify.	

continues

TABLE 4-5. CONTINUED

What to Do	How to Do It	Age(s)
Get Background Information Quickly	When your child comes across an unfamiliar idea, time period, or place while reading, she does not need to go to the library and do extensive research before continuing to read. Information is at her fingertips electronically, although you will need to help vet the sources.	
Seek Out Programs and Applications That Focus on Comprehension and Scaffold Learning	Shows or applications that ask meaning-making questions, pause, and then give a clue about the answer (like *Dora the Explorer*) help children think about cause and effect and making inferences. Programs and applications like these may keep your child engaged even when you are not watching or playing as well, but your child will be more likely to truly understand what is happening on the screen if you also give clues and provide clarification.	

TABLE 4-6. ENGLISH LANUGAGE LEARNER TIPS FOR PARENTS: READING COMPREHENSION

English Language Learner Tips: Reading Comprehension

To successfully comprehend a story, children must be capable of causal reasoning and inferential thinking. An understanding of story schema is also important. And as we discussed in the Preface, a cross-language transfer of reading comprehension occurs when bilingual children read in one language or the other.[65] Therefore, these skills may be developed in both languages by providing your child with ample opportunities to read and discuss the meaning of texts in both L1 and L2. But remember it's important to be aware of your child's ability level, using the concept of the zone of proximal development to provide scaffolding when necessary. Using the strategies listed below during shared reading will aid reading comprehension development in both languages.

What to Do	How to Do It	Age(s)
Help Your Child Learn New Words	Shared reading provides a rich opportunity for building vocabulary. Select a few words from the book before reading together to help you prepare. You can translate certain words to your child's L1 or use a familiar synonym in English to communicate meaning. Other words require more explanation and discussion. Use information from a book's pictures to support understanding. A simple gesture can be effective for illustrating the meaning of *gasp*, *frown*, and *clamber*. Try to connect the new word to your child's own experience (for example, "Remember the small *dormer* windows on Grandma's roof?"). Say the new word aloud clearly and have your child repeat it to help secure a phonological imprint.	

What to Do	How to Do It	Age(s)
Provide Background Information for Your Child	Before reading a story together, ask your child what she already knows about the subject to assess her background knowledge. If she is unfamiliar with the topic or demonstrates misconceptions, support her understanding by providing relevant background information. For example, when reading the book *How Many Days to America? A Thanksgiving Story,* you could ask: "What is Thanksgiving?" If she is unfamiliar with Thanksgiving, use the story to help you explain the holiday and its significance.	
Point Out Words Shared in Both Languages	English shares many commonalities with other languages, so you may encounter English words similar to your child's L1. For example, English and Spanish share many Latin root words or cognates (e.g., *study/estudiar; curious/ curioso*). When a word in English is similar to one in your child's L1, point out the similarities, as well as the differences. Using this "metacognitive" strategy is also effective in exploring other differences between languages, such as grammar or syntax. Bilingual books, with adjacent print translations, can be useful in making such comparisons.	

continues

TABLE 4-6. CONTINUED

What to Do	How to Do It	Age(s)
Simplify Complex Sentences	When your child has difficulty in understanding the meaning of a long or complex sentence, you can help her break it down into shorter phrases. For example: "After John finished jogging, he went home and took a shower" may be broken down into: "John finished jogging," "John went home," and "John took a shower." Once your child shows she can understand these three short sentences, ask her to read the original one again.	
Check Sentence- Level Comprehension	During shared reading, check in with your child by occasionally asking "What does this sentence mean?" Not understanding a few key words can interfere with comprehension. If she's not sure about meaning, provide two or more meanings for her to choose from. For example, after your child reads or listens to the sentence "I do not agree with you anymore," you can ask her, "Does agreeing mean that you have the same opinion as someone else or that you have a different opinion?" Her answer will let you assess her current sentence-level comprehension.	
Review New Words Frequently	Write down target words and translations in your child's L1 in a small notebook or in a digital media format. Look at the growing list with your child and try to use a new word in conversations during the day.	

continues

What to Do	How to Do It	Age(s)
Ask Questions in English about Books Your Child Is Reading in L1	When reading books in L1, make a plan to ask and answer questions in English. Questions can explore such story elements as characters, settings, actions, and themes. For older children, strengthen the ability to "infer" by asking questions that go beyond the information presented directly in the text.	

Notes

1. Hoover, W. A., & Gough, P. B. (1990). The simple view of reading. *Reading and Writing: An Interdisciplinary Journal, 2,* 127–160.

2. Ibid.

3. Fivush, R. (1991). The social construction of personal narratives. *Merrill-Palmer Quarterly: Journal of Developmental Psychology, 37*(1), 59–81.

4. Peterson, C., & McCabe, A. (2004). Echoing our parents: Parental influences on children's narration. In M. W. Pratt, & B. H. Fiese (Eds.), *Family Stories and the Life Course: Across Time and Generations* (pp. 27–54). Mahwah, NJ: Lawrence Erlbaum; Zevenbergen, A. A., Whitehurst, G. J., & Zevenbergen, J. A. (2003). Effects of a shared-reading intervention on the inclusion of evaluative devices in narratives of children from low-income families. *Journal of Applied Developmental Psychology, 24*(1), 1–15. doi:10.1016/S0193-3973(03)00021-2

5. Perfetti, C. A., Landi, N., & Oakhill, J. (2005). The acquisition of reading comprehension skill. In M. J. Snowling & C. Hulme (Eds.), *The Science of Reading: A Handbook* (pp. 227–247). Oxford: Blackwell.

6. Willingham, D. T. (2004). Ask the cognitive scientist: The privileged status of story. *American Educator, 28*(4), 43–45, 51–53.

7. Ibid.

8. Trabasso, T. Lehr, F., & Osborn, J. (Eds.) (1994) The power of the narrative. *Reading, Language, and Literacy: Instruction for the Twenty-First Century* (pp. 187–200). Hillsdale, NJ: Lawrence Erlbaum.

9. Roth, F. P., Speece, D. L., & Cooper, D. H. (2002). A longitudinal analysis of the connection between oral language and early reading. *Journal of Educational Research*, *95*(5), 259–272. doi:10.1080/00220670209596600; Snow, C. E., Tabors, P. O., Nicholson, P. A., & Kurland, B. F. (1995). SHELL: Oral language and early literacy skills in kindergarten and first-grade children. *Journal of Research in Childhood Education*, *10*(1), 37–48.

10. Freeman, D. (2008). *Corduroy*. New York: Penguin Group.

11. Poulsen, D., Kintsch, E., Kintsch, W., & Premack, D. (1979). Children's comprehension and memory for stories. *Journal of Experimental Child Psychology*, *28*, 379–403.

12. Ibid.

13. Bransford, J. D., & Johnson, M. K. (1972). Contextual prerequisites for understanding: Some investigations of comprehension and recall. *Journal of Verbal Learning and Verbal Behavior*, *11*(6), 717–726.

14. Anderson, R. C., & Peason, P. D. (1984). A schema-theoretic view of basic processes in reading comprehension. In P. D. Pearson, R. Barr, M. L. Kamil, P. Mosenthal, & R. Dykstra (Eds.), *Handbook of Reading Research* (pp. 255–291). New York: Longman.

15. Cain, K., & Oakhill, J. (1996). The nature of the relationship between comprehension skill and the ability to tell a story. *British Journal of Developmental Psychology*, *14*, 187–201.

16. Trabasso, T., & Stein, N. L. (1997). Narrating, representing, and remembering event sequences. In P. W. van den Broek, P. J. Bauer, & T. Bourg (Eds.), *Developmental Spans in Event Comprehension and Representation* (pp. 237–270). Mahwah, NJ: Lawrence Erlbaum; Mandler, J., & Johnson, N. (1977). Remembrance of things parsed: Story structure and recall. *Cognitive Psychology*, *9*, 111–151.

17. Trabasso & Stein (1997).

18. Fivush, R., Reese, E., & Haden, C. A. (2006). Elaborating on elaborations: Role of maternal reminiscing style in cognitive and socioemotional development. *Child Development*, *77*(6), 1568–1588. doi:10.1111/j.1467-8624.2006.00960.x; Lange, G., & Carroll, D. E. (2003). Mother-child conversation styles and children's laboratory memory for narrative and nonnarrative materials. *Journal of Cognition and Development*, *4*(4), 435–457. doi:10.1207/S15327647JCD0404_03; Wenner, J. A., Burch, M. M., Lynch, J. S., & Bauer, P. J. (2008). Becoming a teller of tales: Associations between children's fictional narratives and parent-child reminiscence narratives. *Journal of Experimental Child Psychology*, *101*(1), 1–19. doi:10.1016/j.jecp.2007.10.006

19. Ibid.

20. Peterson, C., & McCabe, A. (1983). *Developmental Psycholinguistics: Three Ways of Looking at a Child's Narrative*. New York: Plenum.

21. Zion, G. (1956). *Harry the Dirty Dog*. New York: HarperCollins.

22. Duke, N. K., & Pearson, P. D. (2008). Effective practices for developing reading comprehension. *Journal of Education, 189*(1), 107–122.

23. Paris, A. H., & Paris, S. G (2003). Assessing narrative comprehension in young children. *Reading Research Quarterly, 38*, 36–76.

24. Lord, J. V. (1987). *The Giant Jam Sandwich*. New York: Houghton Mifflin.

25. Rey, H. A. (1941). *Curious George*. New York: Houghton Mifflin.

26. Morrow, L. M. (1985). Retelling stories: A strategy for improving young children's comprehension, concept of story, and oral language complexity. *The Elementary School Journal, 85*(5), 647–661.

27. Ibid.

28. See, for example, Kendeou, P., Lynch, J. S., van den Broek, P., Espin, C. A., White, M. J., & Kremer, K. E. (2005). Developing successful readers: Building on early comprehension skills through television viewing and listening. *Early Childhood Education Journal, 33*, 91–98. doi:10.1007/s10643-005-0030-6.

29. van den Broek, P. (1997). Discovering the Cement of the Universe: The Development of Event Comprehension from Childhood to Adulthood. In P.W. van den Broek, P.J. Bauer, & T. Bourg (Eds.), *Developmental Spans in Event Comprehension and Representation* (pp. 321–342). Mahwah, NJ: Lawrence Erlbaum.

30. Hume, D. (1748/1955). *An Inquiry Concerning Human Understanding*.Indi anapolis: Bobbs-Merrill.

31. van den Broek (1997).

32. Trabasso & Stein (1997).

33. Numeroff, L. J. (1984). *If You Give a Mouse a Cookie*. New York: HarperCollins.

34. Poulsen, D., Kintsch, E., Kintsch, W., & Premack, D. (1979). Children's comprehension and memory for stories. *Journal of Experimental Child Psychology, 28*, 379–403.

35. Brown, D. D. (2008). The use of causal connections by young children: Implications for school readiness. *NHSA Dialog, 11*(1), 44–53.

36. Hirsch Jr, E. D. (2003). Reading comprehension requires knowledge—of words and the world. *American Educator, 27*(1), 10-13, 16-22, 28-29.

37. Trabasso, T., Stein, N. L., Rodkin, P. C., Munger, M. P., & Baughn, C. R. (1992). Knowledge of goals and plans in on-line narration of events. *Cognitive Development, 7*, 133–170.

38. Fivush, R. (1991). The social construction of personal narratives. *Merrill-Palmer Quarterly, 37*, 59–81; Haden, C. A., Haine, R. A., & Fivush, R. (1997). Developing narrative structure in parent-child reminiscing across the preschool years. *Developmental Psychology, 33*, 295–307.

39. McCabe, A., & Peterson, C. (1997). Meaningful "mistakes": The systematicity of children's connectives in narrative discourse and the social origins of this usage about the past. In M. Favol, & J. Costermans (Eds.), *Processing Interclausal Relationships in the Production and Comprehension of Text.* (pp. 139–154). Mahwah, NJ: Lawrence Eribaum.

40. Ibid.

41. Ibid.

42. Ibid.

43. Alder, B., Abraham, C., van Teijlingen, E. & Porter, M. (Eds) (2009). *Psychology and Sociology Applied to Medicine,* 3rd ed. Edinburgh: Elsevier.

44. Keats, E. J. (1996). *The Snowy Day.* New York: Viking.

45. van den Broek, P., Kendeou, P. Kremer, K. Lynch, J. S., Butler, J., White, M. J., & Lorch, E. P. (2005). Assessment of comprehension abilities in young children. In S. Paris & S. Stahl (Eds.), *New Directions in Assessment of Reading Comprehension* (pp. 107–130). Mahwah, NJ: Lawrence Erlbaum.

46. Pellegrini, A., & Galda, L. The effects of thematic fantasy play training on the development of children's story comprehension. *American Educational Research Journal, 19,* 443–452; Saltz, E., Dixon, D., & Johnson, J. (1977). Training disadvantaged preschoolers on various fantasy activities: Effects on cognitive functioning and impulse control. *Child Development, 48*(2), 367–380. doi:10.2307/1128629

47. Van Dijk, T. A., & Kintsch, W. (1983). *Strategies of discourse comprehension.* New York: Academic Press.

48. Steig, W. (1969). *Sylvester and the Magic Pebble.*New York: Simon & Schuster.

49. Kintsch, W. & Rawson, K. A. (2005). Comprehension. In M. J. Snowling & C. Hulme (Eds.), *The Science of Reading: A Handbook.* Malden, MA: Blackwell.

50. Oakhill, J. (1993). Children's difficulties in reading comprehension. *Educational Psychology Review, 5*(3), 223–237.; Garnham, A., & Oakhill, J. (1988). "Anaphoric islands" revisited. *Quarterly Journal of Experimental Psychology.A.Human Experimental Psychology, 40*(4), 719–735; Oakhill, J., & Yuill, N. (1986). Pronoun resolution in skilled and less-skilled comprehenders: Effects of memory load and inferential complexity. *Language and Speech, 29*(1), 25–37; Yuill, N., & Oakhill, J. (1988). Effects of inference awareness training on poor reading comprehension. *Applied Cognitive Psychology, 2*(1), 33–45; Yuill, N., & Oakhill, J. (1991). *Children's Problems in Text Comprehension: An Experimental Investigation.* Cambridge: Cambridge University Press.

51. Perfetti, C. A., Landi, N., & Oakill, J. (2005). The acquisition of reading comprehension. In M. J. Snowling & C. Hulme (Eds.), *The Science of Reading: A Handbook* (pp. 227–247). Oxford: Blackwell.

52. van den Broek et al. (2005).

53. Schmidt, C. R., Paris, S. G., & Stober, S. (1979). Inferential distance and children's memory for pictorial sequences. *Developmental Psychology*, *15*(4), 396–406.

54. van den Broek et al. (2005).

55. Dr. Seuss. (1961). *The Sneetches*. New York: Random House

56. Henkes, K. (1996). *Chrysanthemum*. New York: HarperCollins.

57. Leaf, M. (1977). *The Story of Ferdinand*. New York: Perfection Learning

58. Wolfe, D., & Good, N. (2008). *Amazing Grace*. New York: North Atlantic Books

59. Blank, M., Rose, S. A., & Berlin, L. J. (1978). *The Language of Learning: The Preschool Years*. New York: Grune & Stratton; DeLoache, J. S., & DeMendoza, O. A. (1987). Joint picturebook interactions of mothers and 1-year-old children. *British Journal of Developmental Psychology*, *5*(2), 111–123; van Kleeck, A., Gillam, R. B., Hamilton, L., & McGrath, C. (1997). The relationship between middle-class parents' book-sharing discussion and their preschoolers' abstract language development. *Journal of Speech and Hearing Research*, *40*(6), 1261–1271.

60. Rascal, G. B. (1995). *Socrates*. New York: Chronicle Books.

61. Gary, C., & Gary, J. (1983). *Tammy and the Gigantic Fish*. New York: Harper & Row.

62. Viorst, J. (2012). *Alexander and the Terrible, Horrible, No Good, Very Bad Day*. New York: Simon & Schuster.

63. Paris, A. H., & Paris, S. G (2003). Assessing narrative comprehension in young children. *Reading Research Quarterly*, *38*, 36–76.

64. August, D., & Shanahan, T. (Eds.). (2006). Developing literacy in second-language learners: Report of the National Literacy Panel on Language Minority Children and Youth; Jiménez, R. T., García, G. E., & Pearson, P. D. (1996). The reading strategies of bilingual Latina/o students who are successful English readers: Opportunities and obstacles. *Reading Research Quarterly*, *31*(1), 90–112.

Chapter 5

The Effects of Reading Volume

Vocabulary and Knowledge Growth

If you walk into the public library in Louisville, Colorado, you'll see a young girl carrying a tall stack of books, her knees bent under the weight and her chin perched precariously atop the tower of books as she tries to balance her way to the checkout counter. Though she struggles with her heavy load, you can tell she is happy to carry the mountain of books. This depiction of a decidedly avid reader is a life-size bronze sculpture entitled *Check It Out* and was inspired by the artist's daughter, Kelly. Kelly is characteristic of the avid reader. Taken to the library frequently early on in her life, she developed a love of books and reading. *Check It Out* is a testament to the quandary that many avid readers find themselves in when at the library or bookstore: choosing among the endless possibilities, and so many books that seem exciting, is almost impossible. Kelly's parents' rule that she could take home as many books as she could carry solved the dilemma but also resulted in the comical scene of the young girl balancing as many books as she could hold without toppling the stack.

Kelly's arms surely became stronger from carrying these countless piles of books, but many researchers and educators would also argue that the sheer number of books she read over the years promoted growth in other important ways too. Indeed, research suggests that the amount and frequency with which one reads, or one's **reading volume,** has profound implications for the development of a wide variety of cognitive capabilities, including verbal ability and general knowledge. Those who

> **READING VOLUME**
> The cumulative amount of reading a person does over time.

read more are likely to score higher on tests of verbal intelligence. And this is not just because people with higher cognitive abilities to begin with may be predisposed to read more. Research suggests that the relationship is in fact reciprocal, and that *regardless* of initial cognitive abilities, the act of reading itself serves to develop abilities.[1] In other words, it's not just the case that "smart" people read more, but rather reading more can make people smarter! The people you might immediately think of as avid readers are often the same people who are aces at Scrabble and highly sought after as team members on trivia nights.

As a parent, you may have many different questions about the importance of reading volume. You may have heard that some children are just born readers and some are just nonreaders; so, does it really matter how much your child reads? What can you do to help your child

> ... it's not just the case that "smart" people read more, but rather reading can make people smarter!

develop a love for reading and learning that will last long after he is curled up on your lap as you share a story together? This chapter will explore the fascinating and significant consequences of reading volume over the course of a child's life and will give you ideas about how to support your child's interest in and motivation to read, thus starting her on a trajectory of reading and learning that that might well last a lifetime.

On Becoming a Reader: Two Roads Diverged . . .

Have you ever read one of the dire stories in the newspaper or a magazine about the educational crisis in this country and wondered how children of the same age can vary so drastically in their abilities and achievement? Experts believe that children's reading volume, or how much they read and have been read to, may help explain some of the vast differences we see in children's achievement by mid-elementary school. For example, imagine two young children, Pablo and Megan, who are the same age. Pablo's parents read to him frequently and greatly value the shared experience of exploring books together. As a result, Pablo has many positive associations with the experience of reading. Because his parents have capitalized on the many teaching opportunities present during shared reading, he has a good grasp on many of the important emergent literacy skills discussed in chapter two of this book. Consequently, Pablo learns to "break the code" relatively easily and is eager to use his reading skills. Pablo loves to try to read anything and as he practices more, the process becomes more automatized; he is able to recognize more and more words. Pablo enjoys the feelings of success and competence that come with reading and his ability to explore the worlds of books independently. Because he reads whenever he can, Pablo is exposed to a great number of vocabulary words, and the word knowledge he acquires builds his word recognition and comprehension. As part of this cycle, he is gaining new background knowledge that will help him understand more complicated texts he will encounter in the future.[2] In short, Pablo has entered into a *positive feedback loop* in which experiencing a high reading volume improves his reading abilities, which results in greater reading volume, and so on. He is set on a path toward reading and academic success.

In contrast, Megan is not exposed to many shared reading experiences at home or in school. Although her kindergarten class was excellent in other ways, shared reading time was not a priority. The same was true at home—although Megan's loving parents spent plenty of time playing with her, indoors and outdoors, they thought she was too young to spend much time looking at books. In part because her parents weren't able to take advantage of the many teaching opportunities that arise during shared reading, Megan has a difficult time "breaking the code." When she finally reaches first grade and formal reading instruction begins, she feels inexperienced and sometimes lost compared to her peers. In some schools, formal reading instruction begins even earlier, but many children whose parents do not spend time on literacy activities still have experiences similar to Megan's: as a result of her slow and laborious decoding of words, she dreads reading instruction at school, which is both frustrating and embarrassing for her. Because she avoids practicing reading, Megan's fluency remains relatively low, and she is unable to recognize many words. For Megan, reading is a laborious process and because much of her cognitive energy is spent trying to decode individual words, Megan frequently has no idea what she has read at the end of a sentence. To comprehend, Megan needs to look back over each sentence multiple times, so that by the time she has gotten to the end of a paragraph or page, it is hard for her to remember what the first sentence was about in the first place. Reading is an exhausting and joyless task for Megan, so it is no wonder she does not want to engage in it. But Megan's avoidance of books means that, compared to Pablo and some of her other peers, she has had fewer opportunities to develop her vocabulary and store of background knowledge. For Megan, as she moves through elementary school and beyond, the task demands of reading shift from sounding out words to comprehending more complex texts. The vocabulary is more challenging and the text requires more background knowledge to understand it. Because of the limitations in her reading and language ability early on, and in turn the limited opportunities to increase her vocabulary and general knowledge, Megan falls further and further behind once the demands of her class work require that she *read to learn*. As you can imagine, if she cannot comprehend what she reads, Megan is likely to face numerous academic challenges, whether she is struggling to solve math word problems or understand why the Pilgrims made the long journey to the United States.

This phenomenon, in which skills build upon each other in a snowballing fashion, likely contributes to the widening achievement disparities between the educational "haves" and "have-nots." The trend that

> **MATTHEW EFFECT**
> The idea that the "rich get richer and the poor get poorer"—children who start out with stronger initial reading skills will build their skills at a faster rate, while those with weaker skills will fall further and further behind.

begins as a small gap between children who have a slight advantage in early literacy skills over their peers that grows wider over time is often referred to as the **Matthew Effect.** The Matthew Effect comes from a biblical passage that describes a situation in which the rich get richer and the poor get poorer.[3]

As the stories of Pablo and Megan illustrate, a child's reading volume, beginning with shared reading experiences, has reciprocal and exponential effects on his or her overall reading ability. As you can see from this example and Figure 5-1, there is an ongoing relationship between a child's reading skills, her attitude toward reading, and her propensity to engage in reading, which in turn builds reading skills.

The remainder of this chapter will explore the relationship between reading volume and its specific effects on the development of vocabulary and general knowledge. We will discuss how these reciprocal processes develop over time and we will also describe strategies you can use to help your child become an avid reader, such as how to cultivate an interested and motivated reader.

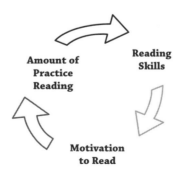

Amount of Practice Reading

Reading Skills

Motivation to Read

Figure 5-1. The reciprocal effects of reading volume.

The Relationship between Reading Volume and Vocabulary

As was discussed earlier in this book, possessing adequate vocabulary knowledge is an essential part of being a successful reader. In many ways, the relationship between vocabulary and skilled reading is readily apparent: if a reader does not know the meaning of key words within a text, it will be difficult to derive meaning from what one is reading. For example, if a reader is unfamiliar with the meanings of the words "fabricating" and "whereabouts," it will be difficult to understand the reason a character receives a detention for "fabricating a story about the whereabouts of his homework."

In addition to this more direct association, vocabulary knowledge also facilitates children's **word recognition** skills. If a reader encounters an irregular word (that is, a word that does not follow the typical letter–sound correspondence rules and therefore cannot be "sounded out"), knowledge of vocabulary can help her decipher

> **WORD RECOGNITION**
> The ability to recognize written words correctly and with little effort.

what the word might be. For example, if a reader encountered the irregular word *laughter* in the sentence, "I could hear the joyful sound of their laughter," knowing the meaning of the word *joyful* may help the reader to generate a "mental list" of word options that represent happy or joyful sounds and use that list to take an educated guess about how the word should be pronounced. In contrast, if a reader has a limited vocabulary, it may be more difficult for her to generate word options or benefit from other contextual clues, thus decreasing the chances that she will be able to successfully identify these irregular words.[4]

Overall, because of the direct and indirect effects of vocabulary knowledge on reading, a child with limited vocabulary is at a double disadvantage when he is trying to understand what he is reading. First, he cannot understand what he is reading. Second, because the text he reads does not make sense to him, the child with a poor vocabulary will often avoid further reading. In contrast, when a child has well developed vocabulary skills, reading is much easier and more appealing, which then increases the likelihood that the child will want to read more. Reading more, in turn, results in many more benefits for a child's reading and cognitive development. Ensuring that you can help your child reap these benefits is what this chapter is all about.

How Does Reading Volume Foster Vocabulary Development?

Given the important role of vocabulary knowledge in reading success, you may wonder how vocabulary learning takes place. Is it enough to expose your child to rich and stimulating conversation, as we suggested in chapter 1? Should you invest in sets of flashcards? Research suggests that although some vocabulary growth occurs as a result of structured language experiences, such as explicitly teaching new vocabulary words,[5] the majority of vocabulary encounters with new words are within the context of children's daily experiences, such as while reading.[6] In fact, many researchers believe that it is *reading volume* that explains most of the differences over time in children's vocabulary knowledge.[7]

Perhaps one of the most amazing accomplishments of human development is the acquisition and growth of language over time. As a parent, you have undoubtedly marveled at your child's journey from a newborn with no words to a babbling baby to a child that utters her celebrated first word. And after that milestone, so many other words likely followed quickly, turning into phrases, then sentences, and the ability to have an almost adult-like conversation. But how does this process of language learning happen?

It is estimated that an 18-month-old child learns an average of five new words a day in order to develop a receptive vocabulary of around 8,000 words by the time the child is six years old.[8] At the time of high school graduation, it is estimated that the average student knows approximately 40,000 words.[9] In order for a child to increase his vocabulary from 8,000 to 40,000 words in roughly twelve years, he needs to learn approximately 32,000 words between first grade and twelfth grade (i.e., 7 words a day, every day of the year for 12 years). And although a vocabulary of 40,000 words may be average for a twelfth-grade student, analyses of texts suggest that an even larger vocabulary is needed to allow a reader unassisted comprehension of a newspaper and many high school–level novels![10] Thus, students who excel academically are likely mastering an average of almost 100 words a week for twelve years. When we consider that the average school program of direct vocabulary instruction covers only a few hundred words and word parts per year, it seems evident that the type of vocabulary development that is necessary for skilled reading is beyond the scope of even the most intensive programs of vocabulary instruction. Therefore, in addition to direct instruction, children's word knowledge must also be developed indirectly through authentic experiences with language, such as shared or independent reading experiences.

The power of print. Some interesting studies done in the field of linguistics suggest that written language, including language found in children's books, is far more sophisticated and complex than is spoken language, even that of college educated adults. This finding is probably surprising to you. But, in a seminal paper, Hayes and Ahrens compared the frequency of "rare" words in forms of spoken language to those found in written language.[11] They looked at forms of spoken language such as casual conversations between college-educated adults, expert witness testimony, and dialogue from a variety of different television programs and compared the overall rarity of words used during these instances to the overall rarity of words used in forms of written language, including children's books, adult books, magazines, newspapers, and abstracts of scientific articles.

Overall, the words used in print are much more complex than those used in spoken language, leading experts to conclude that speech is "lexically impoverished" when compared to written language. For example, in this same study, Hayes and Ahrens found that children's books had more rare words than any form of spoken language, including expert witness testimony. Children's books contained 50 percent more rare words than did adult primetime television and the conversation of college educated adults! Moreover, basic adult reading materials (for example, books, popular magazines, and newspapers) contained words that were two to three times rarer than those heard on television. As one might imagine, the prevalence of unique words found in printed materials, including books written for children, has direct implications for vocabulary development. Compared to other language experiences, such as watching television or even engaging in conversation with well-educated adults, book reading provides the greatest opportunity to be exposed to new and complex words. What's more, the more one reads, the larger and richer one's vocabulary store becomes, making reading easier and more enjoyable. Thus, increasing one's interest in reading usually results in an increase in the number of opportunities to expand one's vocabulary.

Although one might expect that books written for children contain only simple and basic vocabulary words, it is surprising to discover just how rich and sophisticated words in children's books can be. For example, you can see the benefit of a young reader hearing sentences from classic texts, like Aesop's *The Hare and the Tortoise:* "There was a hare who was rudely poking fun at a Tortoise for being so slow, and at the same time bragging about his won speed in running,"[12] which includes words and phrases the child would be unlikely to encounter in conversation. Box 5-1 includes a few more examples of the rich vocabulary found in popular children's books. Many of these words are rarely used in spoken language, or are likely to be replaced with simpler terms, such as using *sad* instead of *miserable* or *climbed* instead of *clambered.* Although these terms might not be as urbane as those we typically associate with "vocabulary words," when we consider how relatively limited a young child's general exposure to language has been (just given his years on earth), it is easy to see how shared book reading could provide him with his first exposure to a wide variety of rich and descriptive words.

You can use Figure 5-2 to compare the number of rare words found in different types of print and television programming. Perhaps the most important thing this graph sheds light on is the fact that children's books and comic books introduce more rare words than any sort of television programming or conversation, because we use less sophisticated language when we talk than when we write. Thus, if you want your child to build his vocabulary, reading books is the most efficient and effective way to familiarize him with less common words.

BOX 5-1. VOCABULARY IN CHILDREN'S BOOKS

Cloudy with a Chance of Meatballs[a]

- abandon
- drizzle
- sanitation
- stale
- temporary

Stellaluna[4b]

- babble
- clambered
- murmured
- peculiar
- sultry

Sylvester and the Magic Pebble[c]

- ceased
- fetlock
- insisted
- miserable
- remarkable

---

[a] Barrett, J. (1978). *Cloudy with a Chance of Meatballs*. New York: Atheneum.
[b] Cannon, J. (1993). *Stellaluna*. San Diego, CA: Harcourt Brace Jovanovich.
46. Steig, W. (1969). *Sylvester and the Magic Pebble*. New York: Simon & Schuster.

How differences in reading volume add up. Given that books are a rich source of vocabulary learning, it would follow that if some children read a lot (high reading volume) while others read only a little (low reading volume), these groups of children should have different levels of vocabulary skills. In order to investigate the degree to which differences in reading volume might affect children's opportunities for vocabulary learning, a group of researchers asked fifth-grade students to fill out diaries over a period of several months, documenting how long they spent engaging in

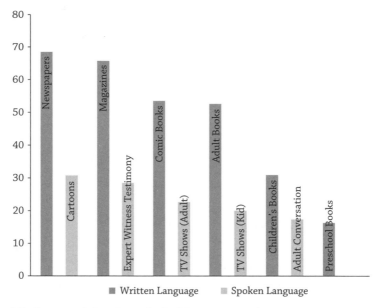

Figure 5-2. Rare words in print and television programming.

various activities each day, including reading outside of school.[13] As you
can see from looking at Figure 5-3, a child whose volume of independent reading placed her in the 50th percentile read approximately 4.6
minutes a day, or about a half an hour per week, which is over six times
as much as the child in the 20th percentile in reading time, who only
read for less than a minute daily. In contrast, a child in the 80th percentile in amount of reading time read for approximately 14.2 minutes
per day, which is over *twenty times* as much as the child at the 20th
percentile.

Although the difference between the child in the 50th percentile and
80th percentile may seem trivial when considered in terms of minutes per
day, the cumulative differences add up quickly over time. The authors of the
study used estimates of children's reading rates and the amount of time
they read per day to estimate the number of words read per year. This figure
illustrates the striking differences in word exposure generated by children's
differential proclivities toward reading. For example, that child at the
50th percentile (who is reading just ten minutes per day less than the child
at the 80th percentile) ends up reading about one-fifth of the words that

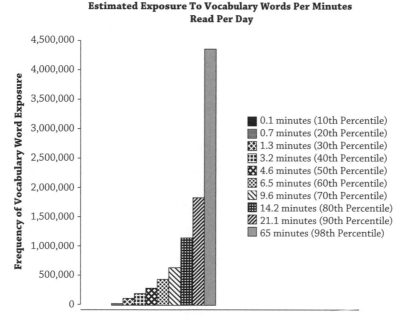

Estimated Exposure To Vocabulary Words Per Minutes Read Per Day

Figure 5-3. Variability in reading engagement among third- to eighth-grade students. SOURCE: Adapted from Anderson, R. C., Wilson, P. T., & Fielding, L. G. (1988). Growth in reading and how children spend their time outside of school. *Reading Research Quarterly*, 23(3), 285–303.

the child in the 80th percentile will read. Similarly, children at the 90th percentile read nearly 2 million words per year outside of school, which is more than 200 times more words than the child at the 10th percentile, who reads just 8,000 words outside of school during a year. To put it another way, the entire year's out-of-school reading for the child at the 10th percentile amounts to just two days reading for the child at the 90th percentile! Of course, not all of these words will be unique words that will increase a child's vocabulary, but the fact that an avid reader is exposed to so many more words greatly improves the odds that she will encounter new words that she will incorporate into her lexicon.

In these past few pages, we have highlighted the fact that print provides many meaningful opportunities to be exposed to rich, descriptive words, as well as the fact that there are dramatic differences in the number of words to which children are exposed based on their desire to engage in independent reading. All of this research indicates that reading volume is indeed a strong contributor to children's growth in verbal skills. A series of studies done with students from third grade through college examined the connection between reading volume and several areas of knowledge, including vocabulary and word knowledge.[14] These studies found that even after accounting for factors such as general intelligence and reading ability, reading volume significantly contributed to verbal skills. That is, children who read more, regardless of their initial nonverbal IQ or incoming level of reading ability, have larger and better-developed vocabularies than children who do not read as much. Thus we can conclude that the activity of reading promotes knowledge and really does make you smarter. And it bears repeating that for children with increasingly well developed verbal knowledge, reading will come easier and will therefore be more fun and exciting, which will generally lead to increases in reading volume.

The Relationship between Reading Volume and General Knowledge

In addition to vocabulary, general knowledge is a meaningful piece of the reading development puzzle. General knowledge refers to all kinds of knowledge about the world, such as knowing what branch of the national government makes laws, or knowing the term for a piece of land completely surrounded by water, and so on. As one might imagine, in order to understand any text, it is necessary that the reader possess some relevant background knowledge. You might remember the passage we shared in chapter 1 about a cricket game, which referred to "men in slips and covers" and reported scores in a way that was probably not familiar to you. Similarly, if someone were not familiar with football, terms like "end zone" and "running back" would not hold much meaning for him. As you can see, having knowledge about a topic is essential to understanding the true meaning of the text. In particular, background knowledge becomes increasingly important as children transition from "learning to read" to "reading to learn."[15]

In order to integrate new information into their existing knowledge base, readers must rely on their prior knowledge as a foundation and point of reference. For example, when reading a passage in a biology textbook about monotremes (egg-laying mammals), a reader would have to have a general understanding of the concept of *mammal* (that is, animals that are warm-blooded, have hair, and generally give birth to live young) to understand what is so special about this class of animals that includes the platypus. Students who lack sufficient background knowledge or are unable to appropriately activate this knowledge often have difficulty accessing the curriculum in school across subjects. Indeed, research indicates that prior knowledge has a strong influence on reading comprehension, explaining up to 81 percent of the variance in test scores.[16]

How Does Reading Volume Foster General Knowledge?

Have you ever wondered, "Where does this prior knowledge come from? How do we learn that Rome is the capital of Italy; that potatoes grow underground; that in Britain, an elevator is called a *lift* and a cookie is called a *biscuit*?" Researchers have also wondered where the roots of knowledge lie, and they have found that it is largely reading volume that contributes to this type of general knowledge. For example, children who read more than their peers demonstrate a better recall of basic facts and knowledge of history and science, regardless of their general intellectual abilities. As you can see, the relationship between reading volume and general knowledge is another cyclical one—reading frequently helps build general knowledge, which in turn supports reading comprehension. Readers who comprehend text easily can quickly process what they read and generally enjoy reading, making it more likely that they will have high reading volume.

In the series of studies mentioned earlier in this chapter, Anne and her mentor, Keith Stanovich,[17] investigated the effects of reading volume on several types of knowledge. In their first study,[18] they found that among fourth through sixth graders, reading volume was significantly related to students' general knowledge, vocabulary, verbal fluency (that is, the ability to generate and name objects quickly), and spelling. A skeptic might point out that it is entirely possible (and even likely) that this relationship between reading volume and general knowledge might be due to a shared relationship with a third variable such as IQ or reading ability (in other words, children who are smarter and/or better readers might read more and children who are smarter and/or better readers might also have a greater amount of knowledge). In order to account for this possibility, the researchers used statistical techniques to control for the effects of general intelligence and basic reading skills. The study found that reading volume significantly contributed to students' language abilities and general knowledge above and beyond IQ and reading ability. Follow-up studies with even more rigorous ways of making sure that reading volume was making a unique contribution to students' knowledge (for example, controlling for reading comprehension) found similar results with younger children (third and fourth graders)[19] and with college students.[20] As you might expect, in the study done with college students, the researchers found that students who read more scored better on tests of general knowledge, whereas students who watched more television performed worse on tests of general knowledge.

In sum, these studies have demonstrated that the relationship between reading volume and general knowledge persists from elementary school through college, with students who read more consistently scoring better on tests of knowledge.[21] This relationship is similar to the reciprocal relationship between reading volume and vocabulary knowledge, whereby reading more promotes greater vocabulary knowledge, which makes reading easier and more appealing, thus increasing the likelihood that one will read more. Similarly, the relationship between reading and the growth of background knowledge is not a one-way street but, rather, a cyclical process that builds over time and continues to accrue over the course of one's entire lifetime.

What Types of Readers Do Children Develop into Over Time?

Given the immense benefits of vast reading experiences throughout the life span, you are probably wondering what experiences will affect your child's reading volume and the type of reader he will become. Many experts have speculated about the same thing. Dr. Kylene Beers, a former teacher and now a reading researcher, notes that despite living in a time when more children's and young adult books are being published, more is known about how children learn to read and how to help them, and more funds being spent on reading programs, many children choose not to read outside of the classroom, where it is required. These observations led Dr. Beers to wonder, "Why would a child who can read choose not to read?"[22] In order to explore this thought-provoking question, she interviewed many middle school students and their parents about their reading habits and attitudes.

When reading through the transcripts of her extensive interviews, Dr. Beers began to notice patterns emerging and was able to categorize most of the middle school students into one of five categories. Although Dr. Beers did not interview younger children, these descriptions (summarized in Table 5-1) could easily also be applied to readers of any age:

- **The avid reader:** identifies as a reader, enjoys reading, makes time to read, and sees reading as a "way of life."
- **The dormant reader:** in many ways similar to the avid reader, but doesn't have or make time to read.
- **The uncommitted reader:** does not identify as a reader (though doesn't judge those who do) and views reading as a functional skill rather than an enjoyable activity.
- **The unmotivated reader:** thinks reading is boring and tends to think of those who do read as "weird" or "nerds." These children have difficulty visualizing what is happening while reading and struggle to connect emotionally to text.
- **The unskilled reader:** lacks the skills necessary to engage in reading.

Characteristics of different types of readers. Dr. Beers points out that avid readers set themselves apart from their peers in three important dimensions: time spent reading voluntarily, identification of self as a reader, and feelings about others who enjoy reading. First, in contrast to all other groups of readers, *avid readers* put such high value on reading

TABLE 5-1. CHARACTERISTICS OF DIFFERENT TYPES OF READERS

	Avid	Dormant	Uncommitted	Unmotivated	Unskilled
Enjoys reading?	✓	✓	⊗	⊗	?
Makes time to read?	✓	⊗	⊗	⊗	?
Identifies as a reader?	✓	✓	⊗	⊗	⊗
Feels positive about other readers?	✓	✓	✓	⊗	?
Calls reading…	a "way of life"	a "neat experience"	"knowing words"	"saying words"	"figuring out words"
See the purpose of reading as…	entertainment	entertainment	functional	functional	functional

Source: Adapted from Beers, K. (1998). Choosing not to read: Understanding why some middle schoolers just say no. In K. Beers (Eds.), *Into Focus: Understanding and Creating Middle School Readers* (pp. 37–64). Norwood, MA: Christopher-Gordon.

that they make time to read no matter what their other commitments. These are the children who would rather sneak a book and a flashlight under the covers than sleep, the children who keep a book in the car at all times to make the most of even a five-minute drive and who attempt to do chores like vacuuming or walking the dog with one hand holding a book in front of them. Imagine the opening scenes of the Disney classic *Beauty and the Beast* in which the heroine, Belle, navigates the busy village streets, runs her daily errands, blocks water falling from a gutter with her hand and walks through a game of jump rope without missing a beat, all without ever lifting her eyes from the pages of her book.[23]

Second, avid readers self-identify as readers and take pride in their love of reading. One student whom Dr. Beers interviewed said, "I'm a reader, an avid reader, like some people are avid sports fans. It's what I do. I'll always do it. I don't care if anybody else thinks it's nerdy or anything." Avid readers place great value on reading and therefore also value their identity as readers. For many avid readers, it's likely that reading is such an integral part of who they are that they are often unaware that they are doing it. Have you ever caught yourself intently reading the cereal box while eating breakfast or noticed that you have read every single ad on the bus or subway including the fine print? In many ways, for avid readers, reading is as natural as breathing. *Dormant readers* also tend to label themselves as readers and take pride in this aspect of their identity despite the fact that they lack the time to engage in reading. In contrast, *uncommitted* and *unmotivated readers* do not see themselves as readers, and Dr. Beers noted that unmotivated readers were often offended when she asked them if they were readers.

Finally, different types of readers tend to have different reactions to others who like to read. Avid readers (and dormant readers) typically have positive reactions to other people who identify themselves as "readers." Dr. Beers reported that uncommitted readers also had favorable things to say about other students who enjoyed reading. They acknowledged that although they did not personally enjoy reading, that didn't mean that others shouldn't. These students were also very willing to engage with students who identified as readers (for example, working on a project with them). In contrast, unmotivated readers were far less willing to associate with readers and reported that they tried to avoid sitting near, working with, or listening to students who were readers. Unmotivated readers tended to surround themselves with other nonreaders and had very negative attitudes toward readers, referring to them as "really weird," "nerds," or "strange ones." Recall again the Disney heroine, Belle, walking down the street, absorbed in a book as the townspeople sing, "Look there she goes, that girl is so peculiar.... With a dreamy far-off look, and her nose stuck in a book. What a puzzle to the rest of us is Belle." Although it's likely that these citizens of a small village in 18th-century France are *unskilled*, rather than unmotivated readers, their attitudes toward the "strange" girl are characteristic of those who do not place high value on reading. Belle's character likely appeals to many modern-day girls who love to read and who are reminded of some of their classmates' disinterest in reading and readers.

What Is the Role of Parents in Fostering Reading Volume?

We hope that it is clear that children who read more experience many advantages, including greater vocabulary and background knowledge (which in turn, makes them better readers and smarter). Further, after learning about the different types of readers children can develop into, you are likely hoping that your child will become an avid reader. But you might wonder, "What can I do as a parent to help my child develop a love for reading and books? How do I inspire my child to become an avid reader?" Therefore, this section will focus on describing what the parents of avid readers do, so that you can, in fact, motivate your child to become this type of reader and reap the many benefits that ensue.

Shared reading experiences. After listening to the many middle school students she interviewed for her study, Dr. Beers noticed that avid (and dormant) readers tended to have many memories of early shared reading and story time experiences. These students talked about being read to almost every day "for as long as I can remember" and "every day that I was little" and "all the time—everywhere we went." In order to confirm these memories and further explore the roots of avid reading,

Dr. Beers also talked to the parents of the students. Most parents of avid and dormant readers reported that they did indeed read to their children at least four times week, if not every day, and what's more, did so from birth until their child was seven or eight years old. They also read for long periods, reporting that by the time their child was four or five, they might read for 30 minutes at a time and up to an hour over the whole day. Parents of avid and dormant readers also read to their children at different times of day, not just at bedtime, and kept books throughout the house and in their cars, making sure that story time could happen anytime and anywhere. Furthermore, these parents also made sure that even when they weren't around, their children would still be read to. If they enrolled their child in preschool or child care, they made sure that reading was a priority—if the child care center had a bigger video library than book library, they left.

> **Parents of avid and dormant readers read to their children at different times of day, not just at bedtime, and keep books throughout the house and in the car, making sure that story time can happen anytime and anywhere.**

In contrast, when Dr. Beers interviewed parents of uncommitted and unmotivated readers, she found very different patterns of shared reading experiences. Whereas parents of avid and dormant readers read to their children starting at birth and continuing until age seven or eight, parents of uncommitted and unmotivated readers generally did not start reading to their child until around age two and usually stopped when their child reached about age four. Furthermore, when these parents did read with their children, it was generally not often, with some parents estimating two to four times a week, while others recalled reading only on weekends or perhaps one weekday night. When asked how long they read during each story time session, these parents' answers ranged from "as long as it took to read one picture book" to "about 15 minutes" to "I really can't remember, but probably not very long." Last, parents of uncommitted and unmotivated readers generally reported only reading to their children at bedtime. Interestingly, some uncommitted and unmotivated readers said that this practice actually *decreased* their motivation to read as they interpreted their parents' message to be that reading is boring. Said one unmotivated reader, "[I]t was an activity meant to keep me quiet and make me go to sleep."

From both the examples of children who learned that books can fill any free moment with adventure and the children who learned that books were only good for calming down at bedtime, it is clear that parents can convey powerful messages (like those displayed in Table 5-2) that shape their children's motivation and attitudes toward reading. Furthermore, it is clear from this research that even before your child begins to read independently, the type of shared reading experiences you provide your child can help set her on a trajectory toward the benefits of high reading volume. By frequently engaging in shared read alouds with your child, you are helping her in a number of ways.

First, by reading frequently with your child, you are providing the benefits of high reading volume, including exposing your child to unfamiliar and rich vocabulary words. By discussing and defining these words with your child, you are helping her expand her vocabulary, making the recognition and comprehension of those words easier for your child when

TABLE 5-2. PARENTAL READING BEHAVIORS

Parents of Avid/Dormant Readers	Parents of Uncommitted/ Unmotivated Readers
Read aloud to their children from birth to age 7 or 8	Read aloud to their children from about age 2 to age 4
Read aloud at least 4 days a week, if not every day	Read aloud 2 to 4 times a week or perhaps only on the weekends
Read aloud for extended periods of time (e.g., 30 minute sittings for 4- to 5-year-olds), multiple times per day	Read for shorter periods of time (e.g., time it takes to finish a picture book; 15 minutes a day)
Read at different times of the day	Read only at bedtime

Source: Adapted from Beers, K. (1998). Choosing not to read: Understanding why some middle schoolers just say no. In K. Beers (Eds.), *Into Focus: Understanding and Creating Middle School Readers* (pp. 37–64). Norwood, MA: Christopher-Gordon.

she encounters them later while reading independently. Second, you are exposing your child to a wide variety of valuable information, building her background knowledge in a way that will further support her ability to make sense of what she reads for years to come. Third, as detailed in other chapters of this book, you are supporting other emergent literacy skills that will help your child learn to read on her own. As we've mentioned earlier in these pages, research shows that children who master decoding earlier tend to be more avid readers, thus reaping the benefits of being exposed to a higher print volume.[24] Last and perhaps most important, if you make reading together an enjoyable, pleasurable experience, your child is more likely to have positive associations with and attitudes toward reading, thus increasing the odds that she will become an avid reader.

The benefits of reading aloud with your child can continue even after he has started learning to read independently. Continued shared reading may be particularly important during the beginning stages of reading acquisition, when your child may primarily be reading "easy readers" or beginning primers. Books written to help children learn to sound out words typically consist of simple stories that contain mainly easily decodable words and contain high-frequency words for them to memorize. But because the goal of these type of "learning to read" books (filled with text like *The rat sat. The cat sat.*) is primarily to make decoding simple, they often lack the rich, unique vocabulary words and information found in other genres of children's books. Therefore, as children transition into becoming independent readers, it may be especially important to continue shared read alouds that will provide ongoing access to more enriching verbal and general knowledge.

Parents' reading habits and attitudes. It is important to note that parents' realm of influence on their children's motivation and attitude toward reading extends beyond their direct interactions reading with their children. For example, Dr. Beers found that aside from some occasional newspaper reading, the parents of uncommitted and unmotivated readers rarely did any personal reading in front of their children. These results are very similar to those found in another study conducted by Leslie Morrow,[25] which demonstrated that parents' own reading habits and attitudes toward reading can have a powerful influence on their children's preference for reading. In this study, kindergarten children who were rated as having a high interest in reading were compared to peers who were rated as having a low interest in reading, and Morrow found that children who frequently engaged in self-initiated literacy activities and showed great interest in reading came from families that placed a high value on literacy. These children also watched less television and had books in multiple rooms of their home, including the kitchen and their bedroom. Even though parents of high- and low-interest readers spent about the same amount of time reading the newspaper and technical materials related to work, parents of high-interest readers were significantly more likely to engage in reading for pleasure or as a leisure-time activity. By showing your child that you value reading and by modeling positive reading habits, you can help shape your child's attitudes toward and motivation to engage in reading—both crucial factors in determining your child's reading volume.

Developing Vocabulary and General Knowledge in an Avid Reader: How Can I Support My Child's Individual Needs?

Given the importance of increasing reading volume, and the connections between reading volume, vocabulary, and general knowledge, you may be wondering what to do if your child is struggling in one or more of these areas. It is helpful to remember our core practices for encouraging reading development: working in the zone of proximal development, scaffolding, and giving specific praise. You will first want to figure out where your child is and target an area right in his zone of proximal development. It is obvious that you would not expect your toddler to pick up a copy of *Moby Dick* tomorrow; this tome is way beyond his zone. Similarly, you should not expect your child to pick up the same books your friends' and neighbors' children are reading simply because they are close in age to your child. The materials they are capable of comprehending are based on their experiences and their personal reading histories. So we urge you to put aside any comparisons between your child and other children you may know. You will know you have chosen appropriate material when your child is familiar with most of the words and ideas, but needs a little bit of guidance to understand some new words or ideas. This "sweet spot" may be different for each child, and finding the right difficulty level depends on considering not only his or her reading ability and motivation level, but also other attributes like attention span and persistence. Once you choose the right book, you want to scaffold your child's developing skills while providing specific feedback and praise.

Vocabulary. As your child develops a more sophisticated vocabulary, remember to take time to define words and check for comprehension while reading together. If you come upon a new word, ask your child to come up with his own definition based on his understanding of the text and pictures. Help him refine this definition by asking questions. If needed, consult a dictionary. Remember to praise his work in figuring out the definition by highlighting the process he used to figure out the answer.

Before children develop rich semantic webs, they can easily forget the definition of a word that they encountered in the past. Similarly, it can be difficult for a child to understand a word that is used in multiple ways, depending on the situation. For example, if a child learned the definition of *enough* in the context of asking, "will there be enough?," he may have a hard time understanding the meaning of the same word in the phrase, "I've had enough!" This can be confusing for parents who feel that they've gone over the same material many times. Remain patient with your child and continue to guide him to use context clues, his general knowledge, and resources like the dictionary to come up with an answer on his own before you supply it for him.

General knowledge. Building general knowledge and accessing general knowledge during reading interactions are two different things and should be addressed in different ways. If you find that your child does not have the familiarity with a subject to allow for better comprehending of a new book, you may want to help her search for more information about that subject.[26] As mentioned in chapter 4, your child may struggle to understand Peter's experience in *The Snowy Day*. The text never explains why the snowball Peter put in his pocket disappeared after he'd been in his warm house. Children who live in areas that don't see snow frequently may be confused about this experience. If this is the case, you can help your child develop her general knowledge by providing background information about snow (for example, snow is made of little ice crystals and ice is water that has frozen when it is very cold), and then asking her to think about this new knowledge about snow when reading the book together and making predictions. An older child may be shown how to look up information about a new topic using reputable online sites.

If your child is familiar with snow, but does not seem to use this knowledge base while reading books with you, you will want to try another strategy for helping her comprehend the book. Remember that activating prior knowledge is a learned skill that young readers may not engage in readily. First, choose books that are related to experiences with which you know your child is familiar. For example, if she has recently attended a birthday party, you may choose a book about a birthday party. Before reading the book with your child, have her look at the book and listen to the title. Ask her what she thinks will be in the book. Next, you can go on a "picture walk" of the book by looking at the pictures in the book and discussing what she thinks will happen in the story. Help her create a connection between the pictures and her experience by highlighting salient objects, such as a birthday cake and balloons. After you have laid the groundwork for activating your child's previous knowledge, you can start to read the story together. When you come to a part where your child's story from the picture walk and the story in the book align, congratulate her for using her power of prediction to figure out what would be in the story. Check for comprehension regularly during the book by asking questions about what just happened and what your child thinks will happen next. Finally, reread the same book several times over the course of a week or a month so your child can become familiar with the story. After a while, she will feel pride as she is able to answer all of your questions about the book, and possibly read the book to you.

Avid reading. What should you do when your child has the ability to read and comprehend books, but simply doesn't want to pick up a book? First and foremost, be aware of any negative talk or attitudes about reading to which your child is exposed. If he has a friend or family member who insinuates that avid readers are nerds, he may internalize this message. This message can be very powerful and may discourage him from reading, even if he enjoys the activity himself. At the same time, be careful of treating reading as a chore that your child must complete before he can engage in "real fun," like watching TV or playing outside. As we discussed in Dr. Beers's study, children who pick up a message from their parents that reading is not enjoyable are less likely to be motivated to engage in independent reading.

You can increase your child's motivation to read by using several different strategies while engaging in shared reading. As he becomes an independent reader, you can take turns reading each page of a book. This way, he can enjoy the story without becoming frustrated by the burden of decoding an entire book. You can also introduce books that come in a series. While many series are chapter books, like the *Harry Potter* collection, there are several picture books series that may be appropriate for younger readers, including the *Madeline* books. Establishing and completing the goal of reading all the books in a series can encourage the development of mastery motivation, something that will be discussed more in chapter 6, and which may increase a child's desire to engage in independent reading.

Another strategy is to choose books that are two years ahead of your child's current reading level. When choosing a book that is ahead of your child's level, you will want to read the bulk of the book to him. However, children often enjoy more advanced literature for several reasons. First, many kids like to feel "grown up," and reading an advanced book shows your child that you think he is ready for this grown up material. Second, as books become more advanced, they often become more enjoyable as they introduce new ideas and use more advanced vocabulary. Reading such books allows you to support your child's vocabulary and general knowledge development, which can then empower your child to read books independently.[27]

Finally, it is possible to increase your child's motivation to read by creating a reward system for independent reading. Carefully consider what rewards would be motivating for your child. Sometimes simply receiving accolades for reading can be enough to motivate a child, particularly very young readers. Other times, your child may be motivated to read a book if he then gets to retell the story during dinner time. Sometimes kids are motivated by external rewards like stickers or small toys. You will know your child best and what will motivate him. If you do use this strategy for increasing your child's independent reading, it is very important to plan to fade the external reinforcer over time, so that your child becomes intrinsically motivated to read. After you have established that your child will read so many pages or for so many minutes to get the reward, slowly increase the amount of independent reading required to get the reward or decrease the extravagance of the reward itself. Always pair any external reward with specific praise, so that your child will associate the reward with his hard work.

What Activities and Strategies Can I Use to Help My Child Become an Avid Reader?

You may be wondering, "But what if my child just isn't into reading?" Some children, despite their parents' efforts, may not be voluntarily drawn to books for a variety of reasons. Perhaps they have an older sibling who has defined his role as "the reader" in the family and the younger sibling wants to seek a different path. Perhaps due to difficulties with phonological processing (being able to notice and manipulate the sounds of language; refer back to chapter 2 for more information), learning to read is a frustrating and slow process. Or perhaps these children prefer a lot of social interaction over the quiet moments required by independent reading. Even if your child seems less inclined to engage in reading activities, there are still many ways to encourage her motivation to read and cultivate positive attitudes toward reading.

Choose books with the appropriate level of difficulty. Books that are too challenging for your child may discourage him from reading altogether. On the other hand, sticking to books that are relatively easy for him to finish might not encourage him to learn new skills. While you should never discourage your child's reading, even if he picks out an easy book or a book he's read a million times already, you can encourage him to tackle more difficult reading material by paying attention to his zone of proximal development—that is, choosing books that are difficult, but not too difficult. When selecting books that best meet your child's reading needs, there are several characteristics that will help you understand which "level" of book is suitable for your child. The readability of the text can be determined using many components, including vocabulary, sentence length and complexity, length of the book, structure of the book, and the book's content.

Vocabulary. Books that have many unfamiliar words will pose greater difficulty and, at times, frustration for your child. Some books may include many unfamiliar and sophisticated words that he neither understands nor is able to decode. However, when books primarily use vocabulary your child is familiar with, he can use context clues to determine the meaning of new words, and does not need to exercise his developing decoding skills. To strike the right balance between these two extremes, you want to find books in which only about one out of ten words is challenging for your child. Use caution when selecting books with complex vocabulary to make sure your child can access meaning, and if you notice him struggling with more than one out of ten words, suggest that you two read that book aloud together and help him select a more appropriate book to read independently. It is much easier to know what words are giving your child difficulty if you ask him to read aloud, which provides yet another great reason to keep shared reading time alive even as your child gets older.

Sentence Length and Complexity. Sentence complexity has to do with syntax or the way words are put together. Shorter sentences with single subjects and predicates, such as *The dog ran down the street* are usually easier to comprehend. Meanwhile, longer sentences with compound subjects and/or predicates, clauses, and phrases can help to determine the complexity of a book or story. *While running down the street, the dog noticed he no longer recognized his surroundings and began to wonder how he would get home* is much more difficult to break down and understand. When your child is still focused on decoding individual words, sticking with books that have mainly short sentences with single subjects will be helpful. As your child begins to read more fluently and be able to hold additional information in mind, usually at around eight or nine years old, moving on to books with longer sentences will be appropriate.

Length. As a rule, the longer the text, the more demanding the book may be. Longer stories require the reader to attend to meaning for longer periods of time, which can be fatiguing. Be aware of how many pages are in the book and how many words are on the page. You certainly don't need to read a book in just one session, but you should select books that will allow your child to get involved in the meat of the story in just ten or twenty minutes of reading time.

Structure. Structure of text is the way the story or information is presented and organized. As we've discussed, predictable books that rely on a repetitive structure can facilitate your child's ability to tackle reading independently. Look through the book you are considering for your child and notice how the author supports meaning for the reader with time sequencing, illustrations, or graphics, as these will facilitate understanding. For children younger than eight or nine, stories that begin each page with the same phrase or repeat the same information multiple times can be fun and encourage independent reading.

Content knowledge. Your child's background knowledge strongly connects to his ability to understand the world around him as well as to the books he reads. When choosing reading material for your child, consider his interests and experiences and try to match them with books that will stimulate and support his learning.[28]

Promote choice through a limited selection. Research suggests that although reluctant readers express a desire to choose their own reading material, they often feel overwhelmed by total freedom.[29] In Dr. Beers's study, she found that uncommitted and unmotivated readers reported that when they did find themselves in a library, they often wandered aimlessly up and down the aisles, feeling uncomfortable in a place that was "too big," with "too many books" and that they "wouldn't know where any of the good [books] were." In one experiment, researchers placed about thirty books in a box labeled "Good Books," and found that students who identified as "nonreaders" felt much more comfortable choosing a book when their selection had been narrowed. This finding suggests that for some children, it may be beneficial to present them with limited options, while still allowing them to maintain their freedom and autonomy in making choices about what they read.

Explore different genres of books. Another strategy is to explore different types of books with your child, trying to find out what most sparks his interest. Some children prefer narrative storybooks whereas others prefer nonfiction or information-based books. For many children, you can encourage a love of reading by providing a variety of books that center around a topic of interest, such as dinosaurs, cooking, construction vehicles, or insects. For example, if your child is interested in penguins, you might read *Tacky the Penguin* by Helen Lester[30] and *See How They Grow: Penguin* by DK Publishing.[31] The first is a classic about a boisterous penguin, and the second is a factual book about how penguins grow. Exploring books that speak to one of your child's interests is also a terrific way to engage her in vocabulary learning. For instance, for a child who loves penguins, you might introduce the terms *blubber, glacier,* and *aquatic.* Although these words may seem complicated at first glance, they are all important in the world of penguins and can be easily described and illustrated.

Many children also find other forms of text more engaging and accessible than books. Magazines such as *Cricket* provide exposure not only rich and varied vocabulary but also to vivid graphs and pictures that promote background knowledge and draw the reader into the story or article, and children may find it exciting to receive magazines in the mail or check online to see when new information is posted. Even children who are reluctant readers often enjoy graphic novels and comic books. Although adults often view these types of reading material as frivolous or limited in their educational value, they actually provide exposure to rich and varied vocabulary. With the growing popularity of tablets and ebooks, children can easily and immediately choose the genre of text they enjoy and prefer.

Help your child visualize stories. For many avid readers, reading is like watching a movie that they have complete control over—they design the set, cast the actors, and can replay exciting scenes or fast forward at their will. When Dr. Beers asked what kind of books they liked best, many avid readers responded that they preferred books without illustrations, as pictures "ruin" what they have created in their mind's eye. In contrast, some children have great difficulty visualizing what is happening in a book, which may lead them to feel disengaged from reading. These children often report enjoying the process of reading far more when there are some illustrations to accompany the text. If, even after your child has learned to read unillustrated texts, like chapter books, he still shows a marked preference for books with pictures, you can use illustrated books to help kindle his interest in reading while using unillustrated books during shared reading time to encourage him to form pictures in his head (for example, asking him to describe or draw a picture of what he thinks a particular character or scene looked like).

Continue shared reading. As we have discussed before, although research suggests that children who master the spelling-to-sound code earlier are more likely to become avid readers,[32] there are some children for whom learning to read is a frustrating and slow process, perhaps because of difficulty perceiving the sounds in words. Furthermore, like Megan, the girl at the beginning of this chapter, some children may find reading unrewarding and be unmotivated to practice, leaving them further behind their peers. In such cases, a parent's role in helping his child become an avid reader is even more important. If your child struggles to learn how to read, it is especially important to provide opportunities to maintain interest in reading. One way to do so is to continue reading books aloud with your child, particularly books about topics your child finds very interesting. Many parents transition from reading picture books at bedtime to reading a chapter or two a night from a chapter book with their child before bed. Given that bedtime reading is not always well received by the most reluctant readers, it may be helpful to also share chapter books at other times of the day, such as after school over cookies and milk, or first thing in the morning before making pancakes on the weekend. Continuing shared reading, even after your child learns to read independently, ensures that she is consistently exposed to rich and unfamiliar vocabulary and can help sustain an interest in the magical world of books, and provides continued motivation for children to master the art of reading.

Provide opportunities for interactive book reading. There is some emerging evidence that a child's inclination towards avid reading is, at least in part, determined by individual characteristics such as personality.[33] In a way, independent reading requires, at least temporarily, introverted qualities. That is, for a set period, we stop interacting and talking with others, and we must remain quiet and focused so that we can process and understand what we are reading. Therefore, if your child is more gregarious, active, talkative, and energetic, he may have less of a desire to engage in reading because of a preference for social interaction and external stimulation. If this is the case, you can consider ways to help your child get his needs met with book reading experiences that involve such social interaction. For example, extroverted children might get more excited by reading if they are given additional opportunities for ongoing shared and interactive storybook reading. Additionally, if your child is extroverted, she might benefit from participating in a book club or story hours at local libraries or bookstores. You could even have a parent-child "book club" between the two of you that meets in your own house or maybe even at a coffee shop. Together, while drinking your drinks of choice, you can discuss the latest things your favorite (and least favorite) characters have been doing in the book you are each reading. You can also have "Family Read-Ins" when the whole family crowds onto the couch, a bed, or another cozy location. A close friend of Jamie's fondly remembers her own family's weekend tradition from when she was a child, which entailed her and her siblings all piling into her parents' bed and coloring in their coloring books while her father read aloud to them. There are so many different ways to create a family reading ritual and to personalize it so that it is most fun for you and your children, picking the books, snacks, and location that work best for you. Family members can take turns reading aloud, or as children grow older, everyone can engage in their own pleasure reading of choice. Even more suggestions for encouraging avid reading are included in Table 5-3.

TABLE 5-3. RAISING AN AVID READER: STRATEGIES FOR PARENTS

What to Do	How to Do It	Age(s)
Choose Books with the Appropriate Level of Difficulty	Select books that best meet your child's level of reading by checking their readability. These characteristics will help you in your decision: 1. **Vocabulary:** find books in which only about one out of ten words is challenging for your child; 2. **Sentence length complexity:** move to books with longer sentences when your child begins to read more fluently and is able to hold additional information in mind, usually around ages eight or nine; 3. **Length of the book:** as a rule, the longer text, the more demanding the book; 4. **Structure of the book:** For children younger than eight or nine, stories that begin each page with the same phrase or repeat the same information multiple times can be fun and encourage independent reading; 5. **Content:** consider your child's interests and experiences and try to match them with books that will stimulate and support his learning.	
Explore Different Areas of Interest through Books	Provide a variety of books that center around a topic of interest, such as dinosaurs, cooking, construction vehicles, or insects. For example, if your child is interested in penguins, you might read *Tacky the Penguin* by Helen Lester and *See How They Grow: Penguin* by DK Publishing. Allow your child to read other forms of text that might be more engaging and accessible such as magazines, graphic novels and comic books.	

What to Do	How to Do It	Age(s)
Help Your Child Visualize Stories	After reading a book without illustrations, ask your child to describe or draw a picture of what he thinks a particular character or scene looked like. Although illustrated books help your child kindle his interest in reading, unillustrated books encourage your child to form pictures in his head.	
Continue Shared Reading with Your Child as She Gets Older	Continuing shared reading, even after your child learns to read independently, ensures that she is consistently exposed to rich and unfamiliar vocabulary and can help sustain an interest in the magical world of books, and provides continued motivation for children to master the art of reading. Continue reading books aloud with your child, particularly those that are about topics your child finds very interesting.	
Provide Opportunities for Reading with Others	Provide social interaction through book clubs or story hours at local libraries or bookstores. Create a family reading ritual each week and personalize it by encouraging your children to pick the books, snacks, and location. Family members can take turns reading aloud, or as children grow older, everyone can engage in their own pleasure reading of choice.	

continues

TABLE 5-3. CONTINUED

What to Do	How to Do It	Age(s)
Take Turns Reading to Your Child at Bedtime	A great way to involve both parents (or any skilled readers in the house) in reading with your child is to rotate who reads at bedtime (or any other special time!). Some families will have one parent read a book, then switch readers for the next book. This can give family members some wonderful one-on-one bonding time. When children are old enough to enjoy chapter books, the caretakers could switch reading chapters every other night.	
Keep Track of the Family's Reading	Set family reading goals and try to meet or beat them. For instance, everyone in the family can keep track of the amount of time that he or she reads for a week or a month. It can be fun to visually track this information by moving a toy car around a track or adding up the minutes on a thermometer. When you reach your goal, everyone in the family can earn a reward...perhaps buying a new book!	
Question Your Child about the Books You Read Together	Ask your child what he did and didn't like about books you read together. You'll learn about his particular interests and encourage him to engage in reflection about books and reading.	

What to Do	How to Do It	Age(s)
Model Reading Often	Model one of the key traits of avid readers—taking advantage of any moment you can to enjoy a good book. "Sneak" time in for reading on mass transit, while you're waiting at the dentist's office, or while your child is eating her breakfast!	

What Activities and Strategies Can I Use to Support the Development of Vocabulary and General Knowledge Through Reading Experiences?

Because reading provides such a unique and valuable opportunity to develop general knowledge about the world and exposure to unique and rare words, finding many opportunities to support this activity is essential. As a parent, it can feel daunting to generate many of the activities that motivate children. Yet, the reality is that there are numerous opportunities to support vocabulary and general knowledge development with your child that are not only pleasurable and fun, but also offer yet another chance to learn more about your child and his or her interests.

Building bridges while reading. In order for children to acquire new knowledge (in any context), there must be some sort of a bridge connecting new ideas to what they already know. Shared reading experiences often present ideal opportunities for parents to help their child develop conceptual and world knowledge by constructing bridges between their child's existing understanding of the world and new information. During shared reading experiences, parents can model learning strategies such as "activating prior knowledge" (prompting children to think about what they already know about a topic) and making connections between information in a book and past experiences in the child's own life.[34]

One study found that children with higher emergent literacy skills tended to have parents who were more likely to "contextualize" information while reading by relating it to their child's own experiences.[35] For example, imagine a mother and her five-year-old daughter, Alana, reading *Rumpelstiltskin,*[36] the fairy tale in which a mysterious little man spins flax into gold. When Alana asks, "Mama, what's flax?" her mother responds, "Well, it's a kind of plant that grows—it's a grain, like wheat. You can eat it, like that cereal Daddy likes has flax, but you can also make it into fabric. First you have to turn it into thread—remember when we went to that farm and they showed us how they made yarn out of sheep's wool with a spinning wheel? Then once you spin thread out of the flax, you weave the thread into a material called linen. You know our best tablecloth? The one with the blue flowers? That's linen. But in this story, Rumpelstiltskin isn't making a tablecloth—he's spinning the flax into gold!"

By using specific examples such as the cereal Alana's father eats, the spinning wheel seen on their visit to a farm, and the tablecloth with white and blue flowers as familiar landmarks, Alana's mother helped Alana construct and navigate the landscape of an unfamiliar concept. Furthermore, Alana's mother demonstrated to her daughter that books can be a source of new information and that these learning opportunities can be interpreted within the context of one's own experiences. In contrast, consider another pair, James, age five, and his father, reading *Rumpelstiltskin*. When James asks, "What's flax?" his father replies, "Flax? Flax is something that grows and people pick it to make things out of. Like clothes or cloth."

Even though both children were given information about the same topic, we would predict that Alana might have a deeper, richer understanding of *flax* and related concepts, such as *spinning,* and *linen*. Her mother provided Alana with many clear links to her own experience, increasing the likelihood that she was able to integrate these new ideas into her understanding of the world and likely come away with a better understanding of the story as well. Similar to the examples presented in chapters 1 and 2 on oral language and emergent writing, respectively, Alana's semantic web might look something like Figure 5-4.

Alana's mother gave her many "points of entry" to understand this new concept, many directly related to her own experiences, making these links stronger and more salient. In comparison, James's father provided fewer materials with which James could construct bridges from his existing knowledge to these new ideas. It is likely that James has a less-developed understanding of *flax*, perhaps interpreting his father's explanation to mean that all cloth is made of flax.[37] James's semantic web might look like Figure 5-5.

Helping your child make links between what he already knows and the new information presented in books is a powerful way to help him

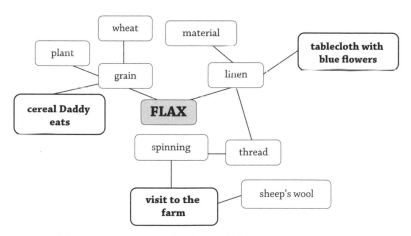

Figure 5-4. Elaborate semantic web for the word *flax*.

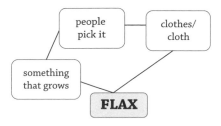

Figure 5-5. Rudimentary semantic web for the word *flax*.

construct knowledge of the world around him and to help him build his
reading comprehension skills.

Book selection. Although exposing your child to any books will
help build verbal and general knowledge and understanding about the
world, you can also strive to provide your child with both breadth and
depth of reading experiences. For example, you can introduce your
child to a variety of book types and genres, including narrative stories
and informational texts, across a host of topics, providing your child
a multitude of learning opportunities and chances to discover new
interests. When your child does express an interest in a certain topic
(for example, trains, plants, ballet, art, shadows, the moon), you might
encourage her to select multiple books at the library about the same
topic, thus providing her with opportunities to make connections
between texts, learn about different aspects of the same topic, and gain
a depth of background knowledge about that topic. If, say, a child were
interested in outer space, you might check out *The Magic School Bus Lost
in the Solar System*,[38] *Stargazers*,[39] *A Book About Planets and Stars*,[40] and
Papa, Please Get the Moon for Me.[41] By selecting a number of books with
similar themes, you will have many more opportunities to build bridges
about new words and information (such as those related to astronomy in
this example) while reading.[42]

Modeling intellectual curiosity about words. Another way you can
help your child gain the greatest benefit from what he reads is to model
personal interest in and excitement about learning new words. When
encountering novel vocabulary, you can help your child develop increased
word consciousness, or the awareness of and interest in words and
their meanings,[43] and you can model word learning strategies that he will
be able to utilize as he learns to read on his own. For example, you might
model through a "think aloud" how children might act as detectives to use
context clues to approximate the meaning of an unknown word. While
reading *The Way I Feel,* by Janan Cain,[44] you might wonder aloud, "It says
she's frustrated. I wonder what *frustrated* means. It looks like she's trying
to tie her shoe, but she's having a hard time. It says, *I'm frustrated because*

I can't do it. It's hard and I want to cry. I think frustrated might mean that you're unhappy that you can't do something. Have you ever felt frustrated about something?"

> **WORD CONSCIOUSNESS**
> The awareness of and interest in words and their meanings.

Helping your child become aware of when he doesn't know a word and to think critically about the meanings of unknown words will enhance his abilities to benefit from frequent reading.

Model using books as a source of information. You can also model intellectual curiosity about general knowledge found within books. There are many ways in which you can demonstrate for your child that books can be read not only for enjoyment and pleasure, but can also be used as resources and places to look when you need an answer. If you see an interesting type of butterfly on a walk, you might say, "I wonder what kind of butterfly that was. Let's see if we can find a picture with its name in that book of insects we have when we get home." As your child gets older, you can also model how to use a table of contents or an index to locate information. For instance, "I've been wanting to make lasagna like Grandma always makes when we go to her house. Let's see if we can find the recipe in this cookbook. We have to go to the back part of the book here where they list all of the recipes. What letter do you think *lasagna* starts with? . . . That's right, it starts with *L*. Let's look under the L section here for *lasagna*." Another way to help your child harness the informational power of books is to visit the library together and model how to find information and ask for assistance when trying to learn more about a specific topic.

You can also model for your child other ways of finding out the meaning of unknown words, such as how to properly use a dictionary. Before looking up the definition of a word, encourage your child to take a guess using the contextual clues available (or you can model hypothesizing about the word meaning using a think aloud). Explain that many words have more than one meaning and that you might have to "try on" a few different meanings to see if they make sense in order to find the correct definition. Encourage your child to become familiar with both print and online versions of dictionaries.

Use the "K-W-L" strategy. Once you and your child decide to explore a topic within books, it can be helpful to utilize the **"K-W-L" strategy** developed by Donna Ogle.[45] Because you most likely have a pretty good idea of what your child's specific areas of interest are, you probably also have an idea of how much knowledge your child has about certain areas.

> **"K-W-L" STRATEGY**
> A technique for helping your child activate and expand his or her knowledge while reading. Ask your child to reflect on these questions:
> • What do I *know*?
> • What do I *want* to find out?
> • What did I *learn*?

As we've discussed, when children are able to "activate" their current knowledge about a topic before reading new information, they are better able to integrate and process what they are reading.[46] You can use the "K-W-L" strategy to help your child activate and expand her knowledge. This strategy helps children think about "What do I *know*?" "What do I *want* to find out?" and after reading, "What did I *learn*?" If your child is reading a book about whales, you might ask him what he already knows about whales. Depending on how much exposure he has had to information about whales, a child might know many facts about whales, or he might only know a few. He may even have some misconceptions ("Whales are fish"). Before you read, you can help your child generate a few questions he would like to find out about whales ("What do whales eat? How big is the biggest whale?"). After reading, you can ask your child what he thought was the most interesting or important thing he learned; you can revisit his previous knowledge ("We learned that even though whales live in the ocean, they're not really fish. They're mammals!") and determine whether your child's questions were answered ("We learned that some whales eat plankton, but the book didn't tell us how big the biggest whale is. Maybe we can look that up on the Internet..."). By going through this process with your child when he is young, you are modeling important strategies that he can use as he starts reading independently. Tables 5-4 and 5-5 include some other strategies that you can use as well.

TABLE 5-4. VOCABULARY DEVELOPMENT: STRATEGIES FOR PARENTS

What to Do	How to Do It	Age(s)
Build Bridges While Reading	Make links between what your child knows and the new information presented in a book. For example, when reading the story *Rumpelstiltskin*, a child might ask his Mom, "What is flax?" A bridging response would be, "Well, it's a kind of plant that grows—it's a grain, like wheat. You can eat it, like that cereal Daddy likes has flax, but you can also make it into fabric."	
Choose Similarly Themed Books	Select four to five books with similar themes. If your child is interested in outer space, check out *The Magic School Bus Lost in the Solar System*, *Stargazers*, *A Book About Planets and Stars*, and *Papa, Please Get the Moon for Me*. Discuss the overlap in words related to astronomy in the books.	
Model Curiosity about Word Meanings	While reading a book model thinking about word meaning by using a think aloud technique. You might wonder aloud, "It says she's frustrated. I wonder what *frustrated* means?" As you then explain that many words have more than one meaning, "try on" a few different meanings to see if they make sense in order to find the correct definition.	
Model Using Books as a Source of Information	Model intellectual curiosity about information found within books. If you see an interesting type of butterfly on a walk, you might say, "I wonder what kind of butterfly that was. Let's see if we can find a picture with its name in that book of insects we have when we get home."	

continues

TABLE 5-4. CONTINUED

What to Do	How to Do It	Age(s)
Use the "K-W-L" Strategy	Once you and your child decides to explore a topic within books, utilize the **"K-W-L"** technique for helping her activate and expand her knowledge while reading. Ask your child to think about: **What do I *know*?** **What do I *want* to find out?** **What did I *learn*?** For example, if you and your child read a book about whales, ask your child what she already knows about whales. Before reading, generate a few questions she would like to find out about whales ("What do whales eat? How big is the biggest whale?"). After reading, ask your child what was the most interesting or important thing he learned. Revisit your child's previous knowledge (e.g., "We learned that even though whales live in the ocean, they're not really fish. They're mammals!")	
Practice Using Descriptive Words	Encourage your child to use descriptive words to talk about taste, smell, sight, sound, and tactile experiences. "How would you describe the taste of that sparerib? Was it salty? Bitter? Smoky?" "What did it feel like when you pet the snake at the zoo? Did her skin feel rough like sand or smooth like glass?"	

What to Do	How to Do It	Age(s)
Use the "SEER" Technique (Say, Explain, Exemplify, Repeat!)	When introducing your child to new words, use the "SEER" technique : **S** - Say the word in context ○ "Stellaluna quickly *clambered* out of the nest..." **E** - Explain the word in child-friendly terms ○ "*Clamber* means to climb using your hands and feet." **E** - Exemplify using examples of the child's experience ○ "Remember when we went on that hike and you and your sister climbed all over that big rock? Daddy said you were *clambering* around like mountain goats!" **R** - Repeat the word and have the child say it after you. ○ "That's a fun word to say— *clamber*. Try it!"	
Use New Words Repeatedly	Repeat and reinforce new words by using them in different contexts throughout the day. For example, you can say, "Look at the cat! She's very curious about the bag we brought home. That means she's very interested in it and wants to find out more. Just like Curious George was very curious about finding out how telephones work." A few minutes later, you might add, "I'm very curious about how your day at school was. I want to know more about it."	

TABLE 5-5. GENERAL KNOWLEDGE DEVELOPMENT: STRATEGIES FOR PARENTS

What to Do	How to Do It	AGE(S)
Read Books That Repeat New Vocabulary Words	First chapter books, such as the Magic Tree House series (including *Night of the Ninjas* and *Dinosaurs Before Dark*), engage children in world history with the adventures of Jack and Annie, a brother and sister. Key vocabulary words are repeated and connected in each story. (You can learn more at www.magictreehouse.com.)	
Talk about the Experiences You and Your Child Share	Experiences with new places can broaden your child's world. Having conversations about houses or plants on a walk around your neighborhood, visiting a bakery, a science or art museum, or taking a short ride on a train all contribute information to your child's long-term knowledge about the larger world. Activities such as cooking, gardening, or making art are also valuable experiences. Remember, vocabulary development is about making meaning of new words, which comes through multiple associations with your child's real-life experience.	
Read Books about How Things Work	Children are interested in understanding more about their world—books that use pictures and words to explain the science of how things work can be enjoyed by all ages! Paging through Richard Scarry's delightful picture books with your child helps her learn key vocabulary and early concepts related to a town or transportation. As they grow, children can build more complex knowledge from specialized books.	

What to Do	How to Do It	AGE(S)
Read Informational Books with Your Child	Read books with informational text with your child. A good source for baby books through childhood years, with brilliant photos and clear writing, is Dorling-Kindersley Press (see www.dk.com). Subjects include oceans, pets, firefighters, ancient Rome, the solar system, and cooking.	
Take Advantage of Opportunities to Develop Knowledge	Use special events in your family (a vacation, a new pet, a trip to a museum or zoo) as opportunities to develop rich knowledge about a new subject. For example, if your child wants to get a dog, encourage everyone in the family to read books about dogs in order to decide what kind of dog to get, where to get it, and how you will take care of it. If you're visiting a new city, you and your child can read up on the city's history and current attractions. This way, you and your child will build and begin to use a shared vocabulary that is relevant to your life.	
Use Your Child's Interests to Guide Learning Experiences	If your child loves a particular movie, you can use this interest as a springboard to delve more deeply into learning about where or when it takes place. For example, if your child watches *The Lion King* over and over again, you can help him learn more about the continent of Africa. Visit your local library and ask the children's librarian for recommendations. For older children, check out the *Rookie Reader-About Geography* series (www.scholastic.com).	

Conclusion

As Dr. Seuss wrote, "The more that you read, the more things you will know. The more you learn, the more places you'll go."[47] More practically, the dean of admissions at the prestigious Williams College once offered this advice to parents: "The best SAT preparation course in the world is to read to your children in bed when they're little. Eventually, if that's a wonderful experience for them, they'll start to read themselves."[48] Although there are many ways in which we gather and absorb information, it seems that one of the richest and most robust ways to gain knowledge is by reading. Indeed, compared to other sources of information, such as conversation with others and watching television, written text offers much more complex language and greater opportunities for knowledge building. Research has unequivocally shown that children who read more have greater vocabularies and stores of knowledge, which makes reading easier and more pleasurable, which in turn, makes children more prolific readers.

As a parent, there are many things you can do to help your child become an avid reader and lover of books. Every time you open a book with your child, you are helping to clear the path.

TABLE 5-6. TECH TIPS FOR PARENTS: READING VOLUME

Tech Tips: Reading Volume

Although technology allows us near constant access to information, being able to do everything on the go is not always beneficial. Reading online, by virtue of its format and the environment in which reading can take place (for example, in the car or while waiting in line) encourages reading in small doses and may undermine aspects of the reading experience that require time and reflection. As we said earlier, using technology to supplement home reading activities can be wonderful. But be sure that quick reading sessions while on the move do not end up replacing other shared reading time. The suggestions below should point you in the right direction.

What to Do	How to Do It	Age(s)
Access Books and Other Text Online	Technology affords the opportunity to download new books immediately. There are many ways in which families can do this, including using websites like *Spreadsong* that allow free downloads, reserving e-books from the local library, or paying to purchase an e-book from commercial sites. Children can also—with your support—look at comic books online, educational websites, or blogs about areas of interest for them. Reading online also allows access to many different genres of writing, from narrative to informational text. Even when you are unprepared for reading time, being able to download a book or read something on a phone or tablet means that text is always accessible. Additionally, if your child is able to read what she wants when she wants it (rather than waiting until you can go to the library and pick it up), she may be more excited to read, so access feeds into motivation.	,

continues

TABLE 5-6. CONTINUED

What to Do	How to Do It	Age(s)
Chronicle Reading Activities Online	Create a family reading web page with book reviews, lists of favorite books and characters, and other information that your child suggests including. Creating this type of site will allow your child to maintain connections to favorite authors, characters, and books, and see you model enthusiasm for reading. Sites like www.goodreads.com, which allow you to keep track of the books you read and receive recommendations from friends, provide social reinforcement for reading, especially for children who are more motivated to read when reading is connected to social interactions.	
Use Technology to Motivate Reluctant Readers	Many children who are reluctant to read print books are more enthusiastic about reading on tablets or the computer. If your child expresses enthusiasm for reading online, build this activity into your reading routine. Again, it is important to make sure that technology usage does not end up replacing time already spent reading, but electronic reading can be a great way to supplement a meager reading diet.	,

TABLE 5-7. ENGLISH LANGUAGE LEARNER TIPS FOR PARENTS: READING VOLUME

English Language Learner Tips: Reading Volume

The advantages of reading volume, meaning the amount of print children are exposed to, are well examined in this book. For English language learners, reading volume is an especially essential component for the development of literacy. Increasing reading volume for bilingual children is important in both languages in order to build understanding both orally and in print. However, you may find there are periods during which your child may demonstrate a preference for books in one language over the other. As your child is making the transition to independent reading in his first language, you can continue to provide shared reading opportunities in the second. Seek out books in both languages as you read frequently with your child. You could decide as a family to have one parent be in charge of one language, and another parent in charge of the second language; this method may help the child feel at ease if he has progressed further in one than the other. Over time you can guide your child to choose a wide variety of books in both languages. Use the tips below to promote your child's increased reading volume.

What to Do	How to Do It	Age(s)
Discuss and Define New Words	In either L1 or L2, help your child discover new words during shared reading. If you have a good grasp of L2, you can discuss and define unfamiliar vocabulary, including sophisticated words and academic vocabulary not often used in conversations. Each time you read, try to find three new words.	

continues

TABLE 5-7. CONTINUED

What to Do	How to Do It	Age(s)
Build Background Knowledge	While you help your child increase her reading volume, provide a wider variety of valuable information sources in both languages. Using supplemental non-fiction and informational books or online resources can help her to build background knowledge and enhance comprehension. Try to find subjects that interest your child, and ask her to share her new knowledge with you in both languages.	
Encourage Positive Associations for Reading	Show your child that shared reading is a valued and enjoyable experience. Find a book or story that was one of your favorites in your childhood and read it together in your first language. Or if the target is L2, there are many children's books that have been translated and can be shared in either or both languages. Positive associations with all types of reading in multiple languages can make it more likely that your child will become an avid reader. As children transition to independent reading, shared reading can continue to enrich their verbal and general knowledge.	
Encourage Your Child to Choose Books in the Second Language	As with the first language, offering a variety of books in the second language can keep your child interested without becoming overwhelmed. Some strategies include providing choices within a limited selection, or exploring some fun new genres together. Partner with your child in choosing books that they will enjoy as well as broadening their interest areas.	

What to Do	How to Do It	Age(s)
Use Technology to Increase Reading Volume	There are a wide variety of tools and software available to English language learners that encourage interactive learning. These include games and activities that allow children to read and listen to stories and songs in both languages.	
Wisely Use a Reward System	Sometimes, your child may be reluctant to read in L2 because reading it is much harder than reading in L1. You can create a reward system for your child in order to increase his reading volume in L2. For example, you can give your child a sticker book, and tell him that if he finishes in reading a book written in hL1, he will receive a sticker. However, if he finishes in reading a book written in L2, you will give him two stickers. After he collects a certain amount of stickers, he can redeem them for a thing he wants. When he redeems his stickers, you may want to mention that he is not only gaining the thing he wants, but also developing his reading skills, increasing his vocabulary, and improving his understanding about the world.	

Notes

1. Cunningham, A. E., & Stanovich, K. (1998). What reading does for the mind. *American Educator, 22*, 8–151.

2. Pearson, P. D., Hansen, J., & Gordon, C. (1979). The effect of background knowledge on young children's comprehension of explicit and implicit information. *Journal of Literacy Research, 11*(3), 201–209 ; Hirsch Jr., E. D., Kett, J. F., & Trefil, J. S. (1987). *Cultural literacy: What every American needs to know*. New York: Random House Digital; Hirsch Jr., E. D. (2006). *The knowledge deficit: Closing the shocking education gap for American children*. New York: Houghton Mifflin; Hirsch Jr, E. D., & Holden, J. (Eds.) (2009). *Books to build on: A grade-by-grade resource guide for parents and teachers*. New York: Random House Digital.

3. Stanovich, K. E. (1986). Matthew effects in reading: Some consequences of individual differences in the acquisition of literacy. *Reading Research Quarterly, 21*, 360–407. doi:10.1598/RRQ.21.4.1; Walberg, H. J., & Tsai, S. (1983). Matthew effects in education. *American Educational Research Journal, 20*, 359–373. doi:10.2307/1162605

4. Cunningham, A. E., & O'Donnell, C. R. (2012). Independent reading and vocabulary growth. In J. Baumann, & E. Kame'enui (Eds.), *Vocabulary Instruction: Research to Practice,* 2nd ed. New York: Guilford.

5. Beck, I. L., Perfetti, C. A., & McKeown, M. G. (1982). Effects of long-term vocabulary instruction on lexical access and reading comprehension. *Journal of Educational Psychology, 74*, 506–521. doi:10.1037/0022-0663.74.4.506

6. Hayes, D. P., & Ahrens, M. G. (1988). Vocabulary simplification for children: A special case of "motherese"? *Journal of Child Language, 15*, 395–410. doi:10.1017/S0305000900012411; Nagy, W. E., & Herman, P. A. (1985). Incidental vs. instructional approaches to increasing reading vocabulary. *Educational Perspectives, 23*, 16–21; Nagy, W. E., Herman, P. A., & Anderson, R. C. (1985). Learning words from context. *Reading Research Quarterly, 20*, 233–253. doi:10.2307/747758

7. Hayes & Ahrens (1988); Nagy, W. E., & Herman, P. A. (1985). Nagy, W. E., Herman, P. A., & Anderson, R. C. (1985). Learning words from context. *Reading Research Quarterly, 20*, 233–253. doi:10.2307/747758

8. Sénéchal, M., & Cornell, E. H. (1993). Vocabulary acquisition through shared reading experiences. *Reading Research Quarterly, 28*, 360–374. doi:10.2307/747933

9. Nagy & Herman (1985).

10. Nation, I. S. P. (2006). How large a vocabulary is needed for reading and listening? *The Canadian Modern Language Review, 63*, 59–81.

11. Hayes & Ahrens (1988).

12. Leaf, M. (1979). *Aesop's Fables*. Norwalk, CT: Easton.

13. Anderson, R. C., Wilson, P. T., & Fielding, L. G. (1988). Growth in reading and how children spend their time outside of school. *Reading Research Quarterly*, *23*, 285–303. doi:10.1598/RRQ.23.3.2

14. Cunningham, A. E., & Stanovich, K. E. (1991). Tracking the unique effects of print exposure in children: Associations with vocabulary, general knowledge, and spelling. *Journal of Educational Psychology*, *83*(2), 264–274. doi:10.1037/0022-0663.83.2.264; Stanovich, K. E., & Cunningham, A. E. (1992). Studying the consequences of literacy within a literate society: The cognitive correlates of print exposure. *Memory & Cognition*, *20*(1), 51–68; Stanovich, K. E., & Cunningham, A. E. (1993). Where does knowledge come from? specific associations between print exposure and information acquisition. *Journal of Educational Psychology*, *85*(2), 211–229. doi:10.1037/0022-0663.85.2.211

15. Chall, J. S. (1993). *Stages of Reading Development*. New York: McGraw-Hill.

16. Dochy, F., Segers, M., & Buehl, M. M. (1999). The relation between assessment practices and outcomes of studies: The case of research on prior knowledge. *Review of Educational Research*, *69*, 145–186.

17. Cunningham, A. E., & Stanovich, K. E. (1991); Stanovich, K. E., & Cunningham, A. E. (1992); Stanovich, K. E., & Cunningham, A. E. (1993).

18. Cunningham & Stanovich (1991).

19. Stanovich & Cunningham (1992).

20. Stanovich & Cunningham (1993).

21. Ibid., 31–33.

22. Beers, K. (1998). Choosing not to read: Understanding why some middle schoolers just say no. In Beers, K. (Eds.), *Into Focus: Understanding and Creating Middle School Readers* (pp. 37–64). Norwood, MA: Christopher-Gordon.

23. Slater, T. (2002). *Beauty and the Beast*. New York: Random House Disney.

24. Cunningham, A. E., & Stanovich, K. E. (1997). Early reading acquisition and its relation to reading experience and ability 10 years later. *Developmental Psychology*, *33*(6), 934–945. doi:10.1037/0012-1649.33.6.934

25. Morrow, L. M. (1983). Home and school correlates of early interest in literature. *Journal of Educational Research*, *76*(4), 221–230.

26. Hirsch (1988; 2006).

27. Hirsch (1988; 2006).

28. Hirsch (1988; 2006); Neuman, S. B. (2007). The knowledge gap: Implications for early education. In Dickinson, D. K. & Neuman, S. B. (Eds), *Handbook*

of early literacy research (Vol. 2, pp. 29–40). New York: Guilford; Neuman, S. B. (2001). The role of knowledge in early literacy. *Reading Research Quarterly, 36*(4), 468-475.

29. Beers (1998); Beers, Kylene (1996). No time, no interest, no way! The 3 voices of aliteracy. *School Library Journal 42*(2), 30–33.

30. Lester, H. (1990). *Tacky the Penguin.* New York: Sandpiper.

31. DK Publishing. (2007). *See How They Grow: Penguin.* New York: DK Preschool.

32. Cunningham & Stanovich (1997).

33. O'Donnell, C. R. (2006). *Personality as a Predictor of Independent Reading Behavior* (doctoral dissertation, University of California, Berkeley). *ProQuest Dissertations and Theses database,* UMI No. 3228445.

34. Tompkins, G. E. (2007). *Literacy for the 21st Century: Teaching Reading and Writing in Prekindergarten Through Grade 4.* Upper Saddle River, NJ: Merrill Prentice-Hall.

35. Hayden, H. M., & Fagan, W. T. (1987). Keeping it in context: Strategies for enhancing literacy awareness. *First Language,* 7, 159–171. doi:10.1177/014272378700702007

36. Cech, J., & Hargreaves, M. (2009). *Rumpelstiltskin.* New York: Sterling; Hirsch (1988; 2006).

37. Hayden & Fagan (1987).

38. Cole, J., & Degen, B. (1992). *The Magic School Bus Lost in the Solar System.* New York: Scholastic.

39. Gibbons, G. (1999). *Stargazers.* New York: Holiday House.

40. Reigot, B. P. (1988). *A Book about Planets and Stars.* New York: Scholastic.

41. Carle, E. (1991). *Papa, Please Get the Moon for Me.* New York: Simon & Schuster.

42. See Hirsch (2009) for further suggestions.

43. Graves, M. (2006). *The Vocabulary Book: Learning and Instruction.* Newark, DE: International Reading Association.

44. Cain, J. (2000). *The Way I Feel.* Seattle, WA: Parenting Press.

45. Ogle, D. M. (1986). (1986). K-W-L: A teaching model that develops active reading of expository text. *The Reading Teacher, 39,* 564–570; Hirsch (1988; 2006).

46. Seuss, Dr. (1978). *I Can Read with My Eyes Shut.* New York: Random House.

47. Wallis, C. (1998). *How to Make a Better Student. Time,* October 19, 1998, 78–86.

Chapter 6

The Social and Emotional Benefits of Reading Together

Given all that you have read in this book about how children learn to read, it probably will not surprise you that *reading together,* something we have suggested over and over, provides both social and emotional benefits to your child. Throughout much of this book, we have focused on the academic benefits of reading, but shared reading also provides an opportunity to help your child develop a variety of social-emotional skills too, both through the interactions between the two of you and through exploring the emotional lives of characters in the books you read. Our goal in each chapter of this book has been to help you focus on one particular aspect of reading development, but in this chapter we will introduce a new goal that connects your child's reading skills with other important skills. Our ultimate goal is to ensure that your child is a lifelong, motivated reader. This bigger goal means that we cannot talk only about the nitty-gritty reading skills your child needs to acquire, but also the psychological challenges your child will face when becoming a reader, a persistent learner, and an empathetic person. In this chapter, we will focus on these social and emotional skills and explain how they can be fostered through shared reading activities and why they are essential components of reading success. As you first read about some of these skills, they may seem far afield from the topics we discussed earlier, but it is important to remember that your child will have many new adventures and face many new challenges when she begins going to school. The social and emotional skills we discuss in this chapter not only foster reading success, but also help children demonstrate resiliency when transitioning into the school environment.

When we thought about how to describe the activity of shared book reading vividly enough that everyone would see its importance for overall development, we started to fall back on analogies about food. Shared reading is delicious. It is an activity families engage in together naturally, from which they can get much pleasure and derive health benefits. In many ways, it is like a superfood that confers all sorts of different benefits upon the person who eats it because it contains so many diverse nutrients. Not only is shared book reading an effective strategy for building the reading skills we have talked about throughout the book, but it also gives you and your child many other advantages by providing opportunities for trusting conversations, snuggling together, praising your child's effort and ideas, and talking about life—all aspects of social and emotional growth!

When discussing pragmatic language development, we spoke of how stories provide us with models for dealing with difficult situations.[1] Often, when we experience a difficult situation ourselves, we are too emotionally involved to make a rational decision about how to act. Yet, when we ask children questions about abstract social situations and pick the hypothetical *right* answer, they are too far removed from the situation to do anything but give the right answer. Of course, your child knows that hitting and name-calling is wrong—it is just that applying this knowledge is difficult. When reading a book, however, we can empathize with the characters while maintaining objectivity. You can help your child examine how characters feel, and ask your child's opinion about how the characters decided to act. Helping children recognize that thoughts, feelings, and behaviors are interrelated is an early step toward self-awareness and empathy for others, the basic building blocks of social and emotional development. Figure 6-1 provides an example of the interaction between thoughts, feelings, and behaviors that might sound familiar to parents who have children who are close in age.

By allowing children to focus on the way that thoughts and feelings influence actions, shared reading helps them better understand their own

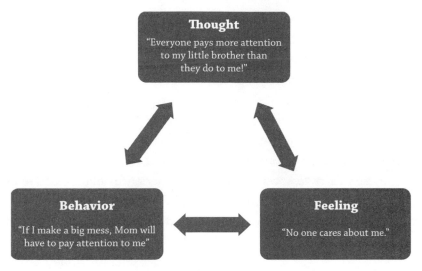

Figure 6-1. How thoughts, feelings, and behaviors are connected.

reasons for acting as they do, and why others may act differently. Our goal throughout this chapter is to highlight for you many of the social and emotional benefits that shared reading can have, and to provide you with strategies for building your child's social and emotional strengths. These strengths include developing a positive sense of self, staying motivated and having a mastery mindset, and being able to take the perspective of others and display empathy. When you send your child off to school, these are skills that you want to be sure he is already developing, because they are all associated with academic success.

A Healthy Sense of Self

What Does It Mean to Have a Healthy Sense of Self?

We are beginning to talk about what seems like an entirely different topic now: psychology. And when you think about psychological challenges that all children face and try to remember the psychology class you took in high school or college, the first person who jumps into your mind might be Sigmund Freud. His ideas about how early childhood issues affect personality development have influenced popular culture in many ways. Nail biters talk about their oral fixations, very organized people talk about their anal-retentive personalities, and we all love to point out the "Freudian slip" that occurs when someone calls somebody else by the wrong name or uses the wrong word to describe how he is feeling.

Fewer people are familiar with the theory of Erik Erikson, who expanded on Freud's work and focused on the social-emotional skills that children acquire throughout their development. While Freud focused on how children react to specific childhood experiences like breastfeeding and toilet training, Erikson thought more broadly about how children respond to all sorts of events that occur during those early years. His theory, an expansion of Freud's, has become an influential theory of child development and is used to explain children's personality and identity development. This theory explains how children develop a healthy **sense of self** (what some people might call *ego* or a personality), rather than focusing on children's unconscious desires (what Freud called the *id*). This sense of self develops throughout a person's entire life, although we will only focus on the early stages of psychosocial development in this chapter. In each of these stages, a person deals with a major issue that all people his or her age experience.

> **SENSE OF SELF**
> A person's perception of his skills and abilities, and of how these skills and abilities are valued by others around him. A child with a healthy sense of self generally trusts the world around him, asks for help when needed but takes pleasure in completing tasks independently, and feels purposeful and competent.

For instance, over time, newborns must learn how to trust their caregivers. The way that each child progresses through each stage of development predicts whether or not he will possess the characteristic (or ego strength) associated with successfully completing that stage. So, infants who learn to be adequately trusting—who know that their caregivers will respond to crying and change diapers as needed, but are less comfortable with unfamiliar adults—are said to be *hopeful*. Hopefulness is a characteristic that these children will carry with them throughout their lives and apply to new situations as they arise. Throughout this chapter, we will explain how children tackle these challenges—needing to trust parents and other caregivers, to become more independent, and to face new and difficult situations—and develop feelings of hope, will, purpose, and competence. We will also explain how developing this strong sense of self is important for academic development and motivation to complete academic tasks, like reading.

Why Is Developing a Sense of Self Important for Future Reading Development?

These character traits contribute to the type of reading experience you have when sitting down with your child, and to the way that your child approaches schoolwork, teachers, and many other life experiences. Children's beliefs about their own capabilities and the world around them play an important role in how they tackle new tasks. We know that children who have secure attachment relationships with their parents— that is, children who are trusting—also engage in higher quality and more frequent book-reading sessions with their parents.[2] This stands to reason because it is easier and more enjoyable to read together when you have a strong relationship. This initial trust, and having a secure relationship that allows children to safely explore on their own, can lead to more independent reading skills over time. Children who develop these strong relationships and feel comfortable exploring then learn to do things independently and be proud of their own efforts, rather than ashamed of their mistakes, because important adults have made them feel comfortable attempting to be independent. As you read more about Erikson's theory, you will begin to see why taking pride in their own work leads these children to develop their own interests, follow through on projects that require persistence, and acquire the skills to become lifelong, motivated readers. Reading continues to become more closely intertwined with children's social and emotional development throughout elementary school, and each earlier stage in Erikson's model lays the groundwork for eventual success in this area. You have so many opportunities to influence your child's progress through these early stages and make sure that she enters elementary school with these important skills, both academic and social-emotional, in place.

We cannot guarantee that your child will be an enthusiastic and engaged reader just because he possesses the skills needed to read accurately. In fact, many strong readers do not possess the motivation to read frequently.[3] Good readers also need to believe in themselves and the people who help them along the path to success. Although these social skills may seem less tangible than the other skills we discuss, we will give you some concrete examples of what they look like and how they affect reading development in the following explanations of each developmental stage.

How Does a Child's Sense of Self Develop Over Time?

We've already begun to talk about the importance of trust for children's early development, and in the following section we will describe each of the early stages in Erikson's model of personality development. These stages are described in order to provide you with a general sense of the psychosocial issues that children commonly cope with during childhood and how these issues affect the way children approach people and tasks, including reading. Because this is a broad theory, we suggest that you use Erikson's ideas as background information to help organize the more specific research findings discussed later in the chapter. All children do not experience the stages described below in precisely the same way, and children do not proceed through these stages on a strict timeline. The information about these stages highlights some of the big themes that influence children's developing sense of self.

> **TRUST AND MISTRUST**
> Children conquer the first developmental crisis of psychosocial development by learning when to be trusting and when to be mistrustful. Successful completion of this stage of development fosters *hopefulness*.

Trust and mistrust. The first stage in Erikson's theory focuses on the resolution of the issue **trust and mistrust**

during the first 18 months of a child's life. Being fed is one of the primary activities that allow children to build trust with their parents, but Erikson considered more than just children's reactions to initial milestones such as breast- or bottle-feeding (the issues that Freud focused on). A trusting child knows that her parents generally respond in a consistent and fair way to her actions and even to her misbehavior. If we always know that our needs are going to be met, then our lives are predictable. But if we have no idea how someone will respond to us, we are less trusting and become more suspicious. We have just described the two ends of the spectrum, but it is important to realize that Erikson did not intend for these stages to be thought about in an "all or nothing" way. No parent, no matter how wonderful, can always respond to a child's needs immediately and every parent, no matter how wonderful, gets frustrated sometimes. What Erikson focused upon was not each individual interaction that a parent and child have, but the sum total of those interactions over a period of time. When children's needs are more often than not met in a consistent and fair way, they are more likely to develop into trusting and hopeful people.

This idea, that we respond differently in environments where people react consistently and inconsistently, doesn't apply only to babies—think about the best boss that you've ever had, as well as the most intimidating boss you've ever had. A great boss is generally someone who wants to nurture and support you. You know how she will respond when you do a great job, and you know how she will respond when you experience difficulty. Even when she is not happy with your performance, you know she will be fair and that the issue will be resolved. In contrast, the other boss that you pictured may have been somebody who flew off the handle without warning. There were probably times when you expected her to react one way and were surprised when she did something different. Some days, you walked into her office expecting to be yelled at and nothing bad happened. Other days, you thought you were doing great work and ended up in trouble. All of this uncertainty probably made you less comfortable, and you may have started acting differently—talking less during meetings, avoiding sharing your opinion—so that you didn't risk setting her off.

We provided this example to illustrate why Erikson says that children who adequately resolve this stage of trust and mistrust are hopeful. If children believe the world around them is fairly predictable and that people are going to treat them kindly, they will hope for the best when in new situations. But if their experiences teach them that the world is unpredictable and you can't expect people to act fairly, they will become hopeless. These early experiences color the way we respond to future events. For example, when they get older, hopeful people who experience a situation like the one we just described—the intimidating boss—will be more likely to recognize that the intimidating boss has her own personality issues that affect her behavior and come up with ways to manage the situation. In contrast, people who have had more experiences that have made them feel hopeless will be more likely to give up when faced with the intimidating boss and believe there is no way they can resolve the situation.

These early experiences also influence how willing children are to engage in day-to-day interactions such as the activities and strategies we have described throughout the book. Hopeful children want to read another book with their parents, because they assume that this new experience will be another great moment in a life that is full of happy times. Shared reading time together facilitates this sort of trust, and also happens more frequently as a function of trust. For many young children, shared reading is just as predictable and soothing a part of their daily bedtime ritual as taking a bath or getting a bottle.

We also want to be sure to explain that this idea of trust doesn't mean that healthy kids are *always* trusting or that their lives are *always* great. Healthy kids are trusting when they should be—when they are with their parents or other trusted caregivers—and mistrustful when a stranger shows up at their house for the first time. And bad things do happen in their lives, but they possess the skills to deal with them (and can acquire these skills through shared reading).

Autonomy and shame/doubt. Once children resolve this initial issue of trust, Erikson believed they went on to spend the next eighteen months of their lives primarily learning about independence and the

AUTONOMY AND SHAME/ DOUBT

Children conquer the second developmental crisis of psychosocial development by trying to complete tasks independently and seeing how others (primarily parents) respond to their successes and mistakes. Successful completion of this stage of development fosters *will*.

feelings of shame and doubt that arise if the quest for independence does not go well. When many parents think back on the biggest challenges they had to deal with when their children were between the ages of eighteen months and three years old, they tend to focus on activities that their children were newly able to participate in because of the fine and gross motor developmental milestones they had recently experienced, which made it easier for them to try to explore new places, put on clothes, use the bathroom, and eat independently. Erikson thinks about toilet-training as either a primary activity that can help children develop a sense of *autonomy* and a belief that they can do things independently or as a source of *shame and doubt*, although the other examples described above can also serve this same purpose. As we were writing this book, Jamie's niece Regan was learning to use the toilet by herself. Jamie was video-chatting with her in-laws by computer, and little Regan wandered into the room where everyone was talking. Upon seeing her aunt and uncle on the screen of her computer, Regan gleefully announced, "Poo-poo on the potty! Poo-poo on the potty!" This accomplishment was a huge source of pride for her, and she wanted to broadcast the good news to everyone—she was able to do something by herself.

We call this age the "terrible twos" precisely because children are learning to exercise their autonomy. Toilet-training might be the most primal example of autonomy we can provide, but children of this age may also begin to insist on walking everywhere by themselves, getting dressed independently, and playing games according to their own rules. This desire to do everything "my way" is natural. A big part of what determines how children progress through this stage, and their eventual approach to new tasks, is how parents generally respond to mistakes or struggles. For instance, if Regan were to have an accident, her mother might say, "That's okay, sweetie! You *almost* made it to the toilet but we had a long drive. I know that you'll have another chance to make it to the potty next time, and you can tell me right when you know you need to go." This support and feedback would help Regan maintain her new sense of autonomy, even in the face of a setback. But if she had an accident and was scolded for it, or told that big girls don't have accidents, she would most likely feel ashamed and could begin to doubt herself. Some children are very eager to begin to do things independently and other children relish their parents' support, so it is helpful when parents try to strike the right balance and respond in ways, from coaxing to praising, that help your unique child develop autonomy. Because these early experiences help inform how people will respond to later events, helping your child develop autonomy when she is young makes it more likely that she will feel comfortable trying new things and asking for help as she gets older.

Now, just like with the idea of trust, we don't want children to be 100 percent autonomous. There are times when it may be appropriate to be embarrassed by how we behave, and there are times when it is helpful and necessary to doubt our own abilities and seek the help of others. Being autonomous does not mean that a child takes care of all of her needs by herself. Instead, an autonomous child will recognize when she should ask for help (such as when a ball she is playing with rolls into the street) and when she can help herself (such as when the ball rolls near the next group of picnickers in the park). But your goal at this stage of development is to provide your child with choices, and to strike the right balance between encouraging independence and letting your child know when she needs guidance. You can strike this balance by thinking about what will keep your child safe and what will provide her with an appropriate amount of challenge, as illustrated by the example about retrieving her ball.

Again, providing this type of support has important implications for later development. If she thinks she should only try to do things on her own when she can do them perfectly, then she won't get practice dressing herself or picking out books to read, because she will always look to you to make those decisions. If she is afraid of your judgment, then taking risks will seem scary. Erikson talks about children who conquer this stage successfully as children with *will*. We want children to recognize that part of becoming independent and making decisions is making mistakes, and that even independent people need to ask for help sometimes. You may already be realizing how each of these stages feeds into the next—children who develop a trusting relationship with their parents are well prepared to begin coping with this issue of autonomy. As we said earlier, these stages are not meant to be "all or nothing," and children who have difficulty trusting people can still go on to become appropriately autonomous, although they—like everyone else—carry their past experiences with them into the next phase of development.

This new skill of autonomy is one that you can develop through shared reading. Perhaps your child always knows exactly which book he wants to read, how many times he wants you to read it, and which parts of the story he wants to tell himself. Encouraging these early acts of a motivated reader makes it more likely that your child will continue to seek out reading experiences willingly. If your child is more reticent, creating opportunities for him to be autonomous by providing choices—like "Would you rather read *Goodnight Moon*[4] or *The Very Hungry Caterpillar?*[5]" or "Would you rather tell me the story on this page or on that page?"—can help him safely attempt to be more independent.

Initiative and guilt. Once children are able to act independently, they begin to take *initiative* by embarking on projects and following up on the tasks that they begin. Between the ages of three and six years old, children exercise this new ability, developing what Erikson calls a sense of *purpose*. And just as younger children who are

> **INITIATIVE AND GUILT**
> Children conquer the third developmental crisis of psychosocial development by exploring new situations or tasks and seeing how others (primarily parents) respond to their successes and mistakes. Successful completion of this stage of development fosters *purpose*.

often criticized for attempting to do things independently may end up feeling ashamed, children of this age who are not generally supported in their efforts may develop feelings of guilt. In this stage, Erikson thinks about children's interactions with the wider world around them, and their exploration of anything new, unfamiliar, or forbidden. It might be that when you go to the grocery store with your son, he wants to pick out all of the fruits that you will use to make a fruit salad. Or that he wants to make a sandwich for you, filled only with mustard and mayo. This doesn't mean that you need to let him do whatever he wants in order to foster this sense of initiative. Children are generally proud of these early attempts to demonstrate that they can serve a purpose and complete a task, unless they hear comments like, "Now you've wasted all the mustard! No one would eat this." If you want to dissuade your son from adding tomatoes to the fruit salad or making that sandwich, you can help him learn to engage in these behaviors more independently without bringing about a feeling of guilt, perhaps by saying something like, "Wow! I'm so excited that you're making a meal for me. You are such a great chef. Do you think you could add in a few more ingredients for me, because I'm a picky customer?" or even, "This is a busy day for you to be the chef, and I need to make my own sandwich right now. I'd really like you to make me a sandwich this weekend, though, and you can watch what I'm d oing right now if that will help you get ready to be the cook next time!" There are many ways that you can set clear limits while still encouraging your child to gain independence.

We expect children to engage in these types of purposeful behaviors not only at home, but also when they go to daycare or preschool. At this age, they begin to receive messages about what they can and can't do not only from parents, but also from teachers and other caregivers. Often, children this age request homework and like to show how ready they are to be grown-ups, whether that means reading a book aloud by making up their own story, dressing up, or making meals. Praising their purposeful efforts sets them up for a lifetime of goal-directed behavior. Depending on where your child currently is in the process of reading development, picking out a new book, playing a phonemic awareness game, sounding out a new word, or reading a whole page can be a purposeful activity that he takes pride in.

Industry and inferiority. Elementary school children spend several years developing a sense of *industry* and learning to keep feelings of *inferiority* at bay. Erikson explains that children who develop a healthy amount of industry experience feelings of *competence*. Again, you can probably see how natural it is for each of the positive attributes associated with these stages to feed into the next, as well as how natural it is for each of the negative attributes to do the same. A child who

> **INDUSTRY AND INFERIORITY**
> Children conquer the fourth developmental crisis of psychosocial development by working on tasks that often are completed over long periods of time, and seeing how others (including parents, teachers, and peers) respond to their successes and mistakes. Successful completion of this stage of development fosters *competence*.

is relatively trusting will attempt more things independently, and then develop a sense of purpose that allows her to flourish in elementary school by eagerly approaching new tasks, confidently asking her teacher for help when needed, and staying enthusiastic in the face of setbacks.

Although your child's progress through the first two stages in this model is heavily dependent on you and your reactions, it is in the third stage that the opinions of others begin to color your child's thinking. But it is not until this fourth stage of development that the balance of power really shifts. Now, once your child is in elementary school, he spends most of his day with his teachers and peers. Many of the most consequential tasks are the ones he engages in during school. So, it stands to reason that he learns to develop persistent, industrious behaviors in the school setting. And if he can't complete what he wanted to and feels that he doesn't compare well against other students, he may go on to develop feelings of inferiority in this setting as well.

It is in elementary school that reading becomes so closely intertwined with children's social development. Because being able to read is the bedrock of classroom activities, children who are able to read as well as their peers get frequent opportunities to demonstrate how competent they are—when reading aloud, writing a story, answering comprehension questions, taking a spelling test. In contrast, struggling readers have school days filled with moments that can induce feelings of inferiority. It is no wonder that many children's intrinsic motivation to read declines throughout the elementary school years.[6] Of course, all students are going to have some academic struggles, and our hope is that they are resilient enough to cope with challenges without beginning to feel inferior. Throughout the rest of this chapter, we will discuss ways that adults can help children deal with challenges to prevent this disengagement from reading from happening.

But first, we would like to talk a bit more about how the sense of competence that children develop in this stage has the most enduring influence on children's overall growth. Elementary school students who believe that they are competent readers often receive higher scores on reading comprehension tests than students who do not believe they are competent, even controlling for their actual reading abilities—like Dumbo's feather, this belief is often what helps children soar.[7] Although Erikson's work extends to psychosocial development throughout adolescence and adulthood, this feeling of competence is crucial for lifelong growth, because a child who believes that he is capable of success has many more opportunities to achieve this success and overcome challenges. Table 6-1 highlights the relationship between psychosocial skills and reading-related behaviors. Studies have shown that children who believe that they are capable and exhibit adaptive learning skills—like asking for help when it is needed and persisting with a difficult task—do better academically than students with stronger innate cognitive abilities who lack these traits.[8]

Children who believe they are competent are more likely to persist when working on a difficult task because they are also hopeful, willful, and purposeful, thinking, "I'll be able to solve it eventually!" They are more likely to ask for help when they need it because they see asking for help as an indication that they are working towards their goals, and do not fear that adults will make them feel ashamed, guilty, or inferior for needing assistance. It is this feeling of competence that serves as the foundation for a child's sense of self during his academic career, and parents who feel their child often struggles with feelings of inferiority can use the strategies outlined later in this chapter to build their child's confidence.

TABLE 6-1. HOW ONE'S GROWING SENSE OF SELF AFFECTS READING-RELATED BEHAVIOR

Age	Stage	Attitude	Reading-Related Behavior
0–18 Months	Trust and Mistrust	People take good care of me. I have **hope** for the world and the future.	I like to snuggle with my parents while they read to me. I sit and listen to the books they pick out, and I know no one will be mad when I play with the pages or stop paying attention.
18–36 Months	Autonomy and Shame/Doubt	I take good care of myself, and other people are proud of me. I have the **will** to succeed.	I like to snuggle with my parents while they read to me, as long as I get to pick out the books that we read. If they tell the story differently than the way I remember it or if they skip a page, I'm going to correct them! I may want to tell my own story while I look at the pictures in the book, instead of listening to what they say.
3–6 Years	Initiative and Guilt	I have good ideas, and people are proud of what I do. I have a **purpose** in this world.	I like to snuggle with my parents while we read together, and I get really excited to read books that I picked out myself. There are some topics I really care about, and I like it when we can pick out books about things that are interesting to me. Also, I am getting to be a good reader! I like it when I get to read the book to my parents, and when they ask me the names of letters on the page.

continues

TABLE 6-1. CONTINUED

Age	Stage	Attitude	Reading-Related Behavior
6–12 Years	Industry and Inferiority	I am good at what I do, and people are proud of my accomplishments. I am **competent**.	I like to snuggle with my parents while we read together or I read to them. We read some really long books that take weeks and weeks to finish. I like to talk about the ideas in books, why characters act the way they do, and what I think will happen next.

What Is the Role of Parents in Children's Developing Sense of Self?

Our goal in this chapter is to highlight for you the many ways that parents contribute to their children's social and emotional development. However, it is also very important to note that parents do not have the sole responsibility, or the power, to ensure that their children develop all of these skills, because there are many complex variables that affect a child's sense of self. Although we want to share all of the information we can about how you can contribute to your child's growth in this area, we want to be sure to recognize that no one can give you a prescription for making sure your child resolves all of these issues easily, and that the task is not entirely up to you. Despite the fact that you cannot control all of the experiences your children will have, the strategies in this chapter will talk about effective ways for handling the ones that you can exert control over.

> **Parents do not have the sole responsibility, or the power, to ensure that their children develop all of these skills.**

Helping your child become more independent is challenging because it requires really separating your own needs and desires from those of your child. This can be difficult at each of the stages that we discussed above for many different reasons. The basis for trust is providing responsive and consistent caregiving, which means responding to your child in the same way when you are in a good or bad mood. When times are tough—if your job is stressful, a family member is sick, you are worried about finances, or you are just having a bad day—responding calmly to a crying infant can be challenging for anyone. That is why the first thing that parents need to do to ensure that children develop a healthy sense of self is to take care of themselves. It may sound counterintuitive, since we are talking about responding to your child's needs, but you can't help others until you have helped yourself. You may have heard this analogy before, but it bears repeating. When you get onto an airplane and listen to the safety instructions, you are always told to put your own mask on first in the case of an emergency, and then to help your child. The same idea applies in day-to-day life as well. Although it is beyond the scope of this book to talk much about strategies for managing your stress, there are many other wonderful resources that can help you address these issues. If you think you need some additional support before you can respond to your child calmly and consistently, please look into some of the supports listed in Box 6-1.

Once you have established this trusting relationship with your child, supporting the development of autonomy can be a big challenge. This is one of the skills that requires a great deal of scaffolding, because you are trying to preserve your child's pride in her independence at the same time that you are helping her recognize that leaving the house in only a tutu is not appropriate in cold January weather. The type of scaffolding required in these situations often takes the form of giving praise, along with offering a **forced choice.** For example, you might say, "You picked out such a beautiful outfit today! Do you want to wear your red coat or your blue coat so that you don't get too cold outside?"

> The first thing that parents need to do to ensure that children develop a healthy sense of self is to take care of themselves.

BOX 6.1. RESOURCES FOR COPING WITH PARENTING STRESS

- If you need to revamp the discipline strategies you use at home, consider reading about or getting coached to use Parent Management Training. You can read more about this approach in Alan Kazdin's *The Kazdin Method for Parenting the Defiant Child* and find clinicians who use it at http://childconductclinic.yale.edu/parents.
- It is probably no surprise to you that healthy living is a key to stress reduction. Although it can be hard to make time for any of these things, consider
  - Whether you are getting a full night of sleep, and if you could get to sleep earlier, put away electronic devices earlier, and so on.
  - Whether you are eating well.
  - Whether you are getting enough exercise.
  - Whether you can increase your ability to be mindful in the moment through practices like yoga or meditation.
  - Whether talking with a professional might help you incorporate these strategies into your life. If so, find out what stress reduction services are offered by your insurance company and make an appointment to get some support.
- If you are feeling isolated, finding other parents in your area may be an excellent way to reduce stress and loneliness. Website like http://parents.meetup.com/ or information posted in your local library or grocery store may help.

Because your goal is to increase your child's capacity for independence, just grabbing a coat from the closet and putting it on her—although definitely the faster option—does not give her the same opportunity to feel capable.

As your child begins to develop independent interests and to take initiative, you can continue to encourage her growth by praising this newfound sense of purpose and supporting her efforts. When something sparks her interest—whether it is picking out a book to read, deciding

FORCED CHOICE
Presenting someone with two acceptable options for resolving a situation and allowing him to choose between them, with the goal of eliciting appropriate behavior while allowing that person to maintain a feeling of independence.

to open a play restaurant in your house, learning the lyrics to all of the songs by a particular musician, or practicing her bike-riding skills—encourage these efforts. You can also model this same behavior for your child by talking about times that you have acted with purpose and followed up on something that excited you—signing up for a boot camp training program, reading a book that you heard reviewed, or learning to cook a new dish. At this age, your child is learning to become an active and engaged learner, so showing her all of the different ways one can maintain these purposeful behaviors helps sets a good example.

This focus on learning becomes even more pronounced during the elementary school years, of course. As your child begins to focus much of her energy on completing tasks and begins to derive feelings of competence from doing good work, you can help her learn to set long-term goals and break them down into manageable tasks. For instance, if she has a book report project that needs to be completed in three weeks, taking out a calendar and working backwards from the due date to set daily goals can help her learn how to organize her time. Moreover, by setting these daily goals, she will have a chance to feel competent each day, when she meets her goal. Again, you can model this behavior by writing your own to-do lists or sharing aloud how you plan for big projects at work.

When your child reaches these goals, you will want to reward her efforts and the fact that she has met the goal, but not in a way that will overshadow her own initial interest in completing the project for its own sake. When we talk about motivation, later in this chapter, we will talk more about how rewards can be helpful or harmful. For now, though, it is important to remember that your child is naturally inclined to seek out experiences that make her feel competent. Unless people convince her that she cannot do a good job in school, each assignment she has to complete and each chance she has to read allows her another opportunity to feel good about herself. By setting realistic goals and praising her effort (that is, the work towards the goal, rather than just the finished product), you can foster feelings of competence even when the work is difficult.

Developing a Healthy Sense of Self: How Can I Support My Child's Individual Needs?

It can be difficult to figure out how to foster these qualities in a child who is struggling to learn to read. The most important thing to keep in mind is that competence is always in the eye of the beholder, and it is always relative. Compared to LeBron James, the forward for the Miami Heat and, as of this writing, one of the best basketball players in history, everyone else on his team probably feels inferior, even though they are all remarkable athletes. But at some level, they all know they are competent.

The same thing is true for kids. Some children are able to accept themselves and their weaknesses, and celebrate what they are good at doing. Others have more trouble celebrating their strengths, and may focus only on their weaknesses. If reading is not an activity that makes your child feel particularly competent, it can be helpful to try to shift his thinking about reading. This perceived lack of competence likely comes from a comparison he is making between himself and others, but what is best for him is to focus on his own progress and effort, rather than his initial skill level (especially because studies show that effort may be a better indicator of success than initial skill level).[9] This is another time when it can be very helpful to model the behavior you would like your child to display, especially because, as we said earlier, you do not have full control over everything that happens to your child.

Everyone has areas in which she struggles, but learning to deal with those struggles positively is an important skill that can be learned. Think about something that's been hard for you, a goal you needed to struggle to achieve, and share this story with your child. For example, one of Anne's graduate students has a son in the second grade who was having some difficulty in school. Putting in extra study time and work was making him feel like he must not be very smart, until his mother showed him all of the work that she was doing to study for one of her final exams. As he watched her put in a lot of time and effort to get a grade she was proud of, his feelings about his own need to study changed. These types of discussions, and providing ongoing support and specific praise as your child works to reach his next goal, can boost his feelings of competence. If reading is an area where your child struggles, helping him focus on his own effort and progress, rather than focusing on how he compares to other readers in his class, can be beneficial.

What Activities and Strategies Can I Use to Help My Child Develop a Healthy Sense of Self?

All of these stages of development feed into one another, so the strategies that you will use to foster a healthy sense of self are similar, but can be adapted, as your child gets older and becomes more independent. See Table 6-2 for even more strategies.

TABLE 6-2. FOSTERING A HEALTHY SENSE OF SELF: STRATEGIES FOR PARENTS

What to Do	How to Do It	Age(s)
Consider the Zone of Proximal Development	Provide your child with clues or hints, rather than the right answer, when she is working on a new task. Tailor how big a clue you give to your child's frustration level, giving more help when she seems ready to give up and less help when she is engaged.	

continues

TABLE 6-2. CONTINUED

What to Do	How to Do It	Age(s)
Allow Age-Appropriate Independence	You know your child best, so use this knowledge to help her tackle new skills that are developmentally appropriate such as tying her shoes or having a sleepover. Succeeding in such achievements encourages the development of a healthy sense of self!	
Take Time for Yourself, and Make Time Together quality Time	Take the time that you need to ensure that you can interact with your child calmly and patiently. Pick times to play and read together when you know you will not be distracted, and you can be consistent and responsive.	
Give Your Child Forced Choices	When possible, give your child forced choices, rather than just saying no, when you want to encourage a different behavior. For example, if your child is "helping" you cook but making a big mess, you can say "You can either help me fold the napkins or you can set the timer and let me know when the rice is ready" instead of "Stop making a mess." If there is a job that he really wants to do, you can make a date to let him help you with that task when you have more time.	

What to Do	How to Do It	Age(s)
Give Specific and Positive Feedback	Give feedback in ways that encourage growth rather than disparage the current behavior. For example, when reading together, you can say, "You did such a nice job sounding out the first word" instead of "You rushed through almost every word!"	
Give Your Child Opportunities to Shine	Turn everyday activities, like doing chores or taking a bath, into opportunities for your child to showcase competence. Each new skill she learns can be celebrated.	

Consider the zone of proximal development. The idea behind the zone of proximal development is that the answer to the question "What is this child capable of?" is not as straightforward as we think. If you are playing a spelling game with your child and ask him to spell the word *hot*, he may spell it correctly with no assistance at all. But then, when you ask him to spell the word *shot*, he pauses. If you

> **ZONE OF PROXIMAL DEVELOPMENT**
> The area of growth and change that exists between Point A, what a child can do independently, and Point B, what a child can do with the assistance of a more capable peer or adult. Providing experiences within this zone allows children to enhance their learning capacities.

stopped the interaction right there, we might say that your son was not yet capable of spelling the word *shot*. But, if you then sounded the word out for him slowly (*ssshh-oh-t*), you might see recognition dawn on his face. "Oh, I know how to spell that! S-H-O-T!" Now we know that, with guidance, he is able to spell that new word. Furthermore, if you then asked him to spell *shut,* he might pause again. But instead of sounding this word out for him as well, you might merely suggest that he sound the word out, just like you did before. And again, with your hint, he might be able to spell a word that had seemed beyond his ability level. The zone, in this example, includes your son's independent ability to spell the word *hot* and his ability, with help, to spell the word *shut*. We know that children are capable of surprising us, and that with just a small push, can often achieve things we thought were out of their grasp. We also know that the clues we give them can actually help them learn. Because, in this example, you suggested that your son sound out new words, you have now shifted his zone of proximal development (as shown in Figure 6-2). Words like *shut* and *shot* are now words he can spell independently, and the words he will need help with will become more complex.

The clues, or scaffolding, you provide to your child throughout this interaction ensure that he continues to build a healthy sense of self, regardless of what stage of development he is currently in. If you think

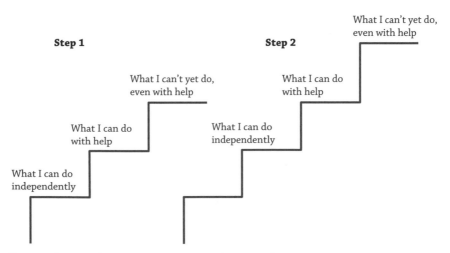

Figure 6-2: How the zone of proximal development shifts over time.

about helping your child in this way, whether you are helping with the "tutu in the winter" incident or with spelling a new word, your interaction is more likely to build feelings of hope, will, purpose, and competence.

Allow age-appropriate independence. Because all of these developmental stages are interconnected, they work together to help your child build what we've been calling a sense of self. And what that really means is that children, over time, learn who they are and what they are capable of doing. As a parent, you have a better sense than anyone else of what your child is capable of and where his zone of proximal development begins and ends. Using this knowledge to help your child tackle the next skill in a trajectory—whether that means learning to tie his shoes, sound out a new word, or have a sleepover—helps this sense of self flourish.

Motivation and Mastery Mindset

What Is Motivation?

Defined most simply, **motivation** is a force that causes people to act, but the definition can get much more complicated! We are motivated by all sorts of things—money, power, praise from others, innate interest in an activity, promises of a later reward. We generally talk about two different kinds of motivation—intrinsic motivation and extrinsic motivation. **Intrinsic motivation** comes from within and occurs when we spontaneously want to do something because we find it inherently interesting or rewarding. In contrast, **extrinsic motivation** comes from outside, in the form of tangible rewards (like money, candy,

MOTIVATION
A force that causes people to act.

INTRINSIC MOTIVATION
An internal force, generated by a genuine desire to complete a task for its own sake.

EXTERNAL MOTIVATION
An external force, generated by the praise or rewards provided by other people for completing a task.

promotions at work) or more ethereal rewards (like verbal praise, smiles and hugs, and being well-regarded). People often think of these two forms of motivation as opposites.

It's not quite as simple as that, though. If you are someone who works out regularly, think about why you go to the gym or go jogging. One big reason may be because it makes you feel good to exercise. If you feel better when you exercise than when you do not and work out just because it makes you feel good, you are intrinsically motivated to exercise. But you also probably like to stay in shape because other people compliment you on how you look or on your hard work. And maybe you see friends when you go to the gym or out for a run, making exercise a social activity. These extrinsic motivators play a role as well. If you think about any activity that you do regularly, you can probably come up with several different reasons that you are motivated to do it. Kids are no different—they may have many different motives for reading. Moreover, their motivations may vary from book to book or year to year. Some children, considered *ambivalent* readers, may be highly motivated to read some materials—like comic books and magazines—but reluctant to read school books, even though they possess all the necessary reading skills for school success.[10] It is probably not surprising to learn that researchers have found a relationship between intrinsic motivation and reading achievement for elementary school students.[11]

Because they were not satisfied that all acts are solely motivated for just intrinsic or extrinsic reasons, two researchers—Edward Deci and Richard Ryan, who have studied the field of motivation for a long time— worked to better understand the different reasons people are motivated to act. They came up with a continuum of motivation that includes six different stages.[12] The names of these stages are academic, but bear with us because we'll show you how they relate to reading development.

1. *Amotivation* occurs when a person has no desire or intention to act.
2. *External regulation* of motivation occurs when a person acts to receive a reward or please someone else (in other words, when someone else is regulating his or her behavior).

3. *Introjected regulation* occurs when a person begins to agree with the person who was externally regulating them, but still needs some pressure from outside in order to act. She or he engages in the behavior to avoid feelings of guilt or inferiority, or to maintain self-esteem.

4. *Regulation through identification* occurs when the person begins seeing the act as important and identifies with it, but still requires some external reward in order to act.

5. *Integrated regulation* occurs when the person truly sees the act as aligned with his or her values, but still requires some external reward in order to act.

6. *Intrinsic motivation* occurs when a person acts because of innate interest in the act.

Stages 3 to 5 in this continuum may seem similar to one another and they are supposed to, because each of these stages represents a slight shift in a person's motivation. We receive some form of extrinsic motivation for almost everything we do, even if it is as subtle as a smile. In Table 6-3, you will see that we illustrate this by showing that children

TABLE 6-3. HOW ONE'S MOTIVATION AFFECTS READING-RELATED BEHAVIOR

Stage	Attitude	Reading-Related Behavior
Amotivation	I hate reading. I am an unmotivated (and likely unskilled) reader.	I am squirmy when my parents try to read with me and I have tantrums when people tell me it is time to read. In school, I try to avoid reading.
External Regulation	My parents and teachers make me read. I am an uncommitted reader.	I read when my teacher tells me I have to, or when my parents set a timer at home so that I don't get into trouble. I get a sticker on my chart if I read 30 minutes each night, and my teacher tells my parents if I did a good job each day.

continues

TABLE 6-3. CONTINUED

Stage	Attitude	Reading-Related Behavior
Introjected Regulation	People need to read in order to do well in school. I am an uncommitted reader.	I read when my teacher tells me I have to, or when my parents set a timer at home because I want them to think I am a good kid. I get a sticker on my chart if I read 30 minutes each night, and my teacher tells my parents if I did a good job each day.
Regulation through Identification	I should read at home and on weekends, but sometimes there are other things I want to do. I am an uncommitted reader.	I am a good reader at school. I like to go to the library and pick out books to read, but it is hard to find time to read at home because there are so many other things I like to do! My family has reading time together some nights, and I like it when my parents tell me that we are all readers.
Integrated Regulation	I really like to read at home and on the weekends, but sometimes there are other things I want to do. I am an avid or dormant reader.	I am a good reader at school. I like to go to the library and pick out books to read, but it is hard to find time to read at home because there are so many other things I like to do! My family has reading time together some nights, and I like it when my parents tell me that we are all readers. Sometimes I tell everyone that I want to have a reading night, even if no one else has suggested it.
Intrinsic Motivation	I love reading! I am an avid reader.	I am a good reader at school, and I love to go to the library and read at home. You can find me reading before school, in the car, and all weekend long.

gradually move from needing tangible rewards, like stickers or points, to needing verbal praise. No matter how motivated a reader your child is, providing some sort of reinforcement for engaging in this behavior is important, although we want to be cautious of how we deal with children when they are amotivated or externally regulated for any particular act—especially reading! When dispensing tangible rewards, moderation is key, but you can be very generous in giving frequent verbal and nonverbal praise for positive behaviors.

We'll talk more about how to help amotivated or externally regulated readers, but first let's examine another important concept that helps explain whether or not someone will be motivated to try something new or difficult. Carol Dweck, a developmental and social psychologist who wrote the book *Mindset,* popularized the idea that people tend to have an overarching viewpoint on achievement.[13] Some people believe their intelligence is fixed and unchanging, determined by biological forces beyond their control. Other people believe that their intelligence is malleable and that effort predicts success. **Mindset** plays an important role in explaining why people might be likely to try certain new or difficult tasks and to shy away from others. Our willingness to attempt tasks is closely connected to the sense of self we talked about earlier, and our basic need to feel competent. People are likely to engage in behaviors that will enhance this feeling of competence and to avoid behaviors that diminish this feeling of competence. Similarly, people are more likely to engage in behaviors that enhance their autonomy and allow them choice than to engage in activities they feel coerced into trying.[14]

> **MINDSET**
>
> The beliefs a person holds about his abilities, either maintaining a *fixed mindset* (believing that abilities are genetically determined and unchangeable) or holding a *growth mindset* (believing that abilities can be changed through hard work).

So, if you think about someone who has a fixed mindset—who believes that his abilities are already formed and cannot be changed—it stands to reason that trying new tasks will feel scary for him. Let's consider Marco, a second grader, who has always been a good student. He was able to spell

his name and count to 20 in kindergarten, he learned his sight words easily, and he continued to excel in math during first grade. His parents and
teachers often said to him, "Marco, you are such a smart boy!" without
realizing that this statement could have anything but a positive effect on
his development. But reading fluently has been more of a challenge for
Marco. No one is particularly worried about his reading development,
because his parents and teachers know that learning to decode can take
practice and that Marco is getting good instruction and plenty of attention at home. But for Marco, who has always had an easy time picking up
new skills, this challenge feels scary. In the past, people have always told
him how smart he is because he has an easy time in school. So, he won-
ders, if I am having a hard time in school now, does that make me stupid?
People with these types of fixed viewpoints believe that putting in effort
is a sign of weakness, and would prefer to take on tasks that they know
will be easy for them—because these easy tasks reinforce the idea that
they are intelligent.

In contrast, Mira—one of Marco's classmates—has always had to
work hard to learn new things. She remembers practicing writing her
name over and over back in kindergarten and spending extra time with
flashcards in order to learn her sight words. Mira has a malleable view of
intelligence and does not avoid difficult reading tasks. She knows that
her hard work pays off and that once she puts in the time, she can do as
well or better than her classmates.[15] So when reading fluently is initially
challenging for her, Mira thinks to herself, "If I keep working at it, I'll
become a great reader!" People with these malleable viewpoints believe
that putting in effort is a sign of intelligence and prefer to take on
tasks that will challenge them and help them meet their own learning goals—because working hard to achieve reinforces the idea that
they are intelligent.

PERFORMANCE GOAL
Striving to achieve for the
purpose of demonstrating to
others that one can avoid failure.

MASTERY GOAL
Striving to achieve for the
purpose of becoming more
proficient at a task and approach
success.

The type of mindset you have is also related to the types of goals you set for yourself. Some people set **performance goals,** meaning that they want to get a certain grade or complete a task in a way that will be valued by others, who will judge them on their performance. Other people set **mastery goals,** meaning that they want to become proficient at doing whatever they have set out to do, and will judge their success based on their own mastery of the task, rather than by comparing themselves to others.

Mindset is also related to the way in which one seeks to fulfill those goals, either through trying to approach success or trying to avoid failure. Those people who believe that intelligence is malleable and want to master new tasks work hard to approach success and do as much as they can to reach their goals, because effort feels good to them. By the same token, those who believe that intelligence is fixed generally want set performance goals—to show others how smart they are—and work hard to avoid failure, because demonstrating how well they can do without effort feels good to them. It is important to recognize that people can have different mindsets and set different types of goals in different areas. Remember, all of these ideas about motivation are connected to one another, and all of them stem from children's need for autonomy and competence.

Why Is Motivation Important for Future Reading Development?

Learning to read is arguably the most difficult task that children need to accomplish during their school careers and takes years to accomplish. Moreover, there are many challenges that arise throughout the process. Some children have great phonemic awareness, but struggle with aspects of reading comprehension. Others practice the same spelling words over and over again and still make the same mistakes. The research described in this section illustrates why we want children to have some autonomous motivation to read. In addition, we want them to know that the effort that they put into tasks matters and that the goals they set should be for themselves and not just to win approval from others. Approximately

5 percent of children learn to read relatively independently and approximately 20 to 30 percent learn through the type of instruction provided in just about any classroom, which means that the majority of students need to put much more effort into this difficult task.[16] Keeping these statistics in mind, then, you can probably see why we want children to embrace the idea that effort pays off and why providing some extrinsic motivators, especially to struggling students, may be necessary.

How Does Children's Motivation Develop Over Time?

The rules that we set for young children are often more clear and concrete than the rules we set for older children, because we assume that younger children need more guidance in order to act as we expect. Similarly, parents generally give young children more frequent and tangible extrinsic reinforcers, because these rewards can help children recognize what type of behavior is valued and become more likely to exhibit such behaviors independently in the future. Thus, there are many behaviors that we expect young children to need external regulation in order to engage in—like not hitting a sibling, brushing teeth before bedtime, or cleaning up after playtime. But over time, as children develop more sophisticated cognitive and social skills, they begin to identify these same behaviors as part of their own value system. So, we generally expect to see these behaviors that were once at a low point on the motivation continuum become more valued over time.

However, not all behaviors enter at a low point on the motivation continuum. As we have discussed throughout this book, most young children greatly enjoy reading with their parents and do not need a reward beyond being able to cuddle and have fun together. There are many activities and behaviors that children feel intrinsically motivated to engage in from a young age. But, it is also important to remember that behaviors do not only travel in one direction on this continuum. A child who has always loved reading with his parents can become amotivated to read when he enters elementary school and begins to feel incompetent, and many studies have shown that enthusiasm for reading does indeed drop upon entry into formal schooling and continues to drop over time.[17] This drop may occur because the day feels so busy that reading time would prevent a child from engaging in a preferred activity, because reading is a struggle, or because reading is not rewarded or reinforced. For these reasons, and unlike other skills discussed in this book, the development of motivation does not follow a clear linear path. But, interacting with parents and teachers who value books and scaffold children's reading experiences has been shown to support ongoing intrinsic motivation to read.[18]

Moreover, the building blocks of motivation include all of the character traits we talked about in the section on developing a healthy sense of self. Our need to feel competent drives us to engage in behaviors that garner us attention and praise and that hold our interest. But the specific things that motivate us, and the mindset that we have, is influenced by the world around us. What does society tell us competent people do? Do teachers praise students for being smart or for working hard? Do we tell children that we are proud of them for getting a good grade or for being such thoughtful readers? The messages children receive shape the way they act, and children who are exposed to environments that support feelings of autonomy (through a choice of reading materials that have relevance to students) and competence (through a focus on mastery, rather than grades) gain and maintain intrinsic motivation to read.[19]

What Is the Role of Parents in Fostering Motivation?

As the three important questions in the prior paragraph suggest, the way that you interact with your child during shared reading experiences can influence how she will respond when faced with challenges. Children who believe that effort pays off and who set mastery goals will continue to persist even when a book is difficult. In contrast, children who expect success to come easily and see making mistakes as a sign of failure may not try hard when faced with a challenging book. Children who are praised for their efforts ("You worked so hard to sound out that new word. Great job!") are more likely to seek help from others when they need it, because they know that looking to others for assistance will help them meet their goals. Children who are praised only for their innate skills ("You are a great reader!") are more likely to avoid seeking help when they need it, because they believe that praise will come when

they do things perfectly and that having to expend effort is a sign of inferiority.[20] As your child embarks upon the long and sometimes arduous
process of becoming a reader, you can help him value effort.

The way to do this is to provide an appropriate level and variety of
verbal and nonverbal praise, as well as—when appropriate—tangible
rewards. It is important to use tangible rewards sparingly, because in
the long run, you want to cultivate an enthusiastic reader, rather than
a child who reads on demand for candy. And children who already like
reading, but who are given frequent tangible rewards for doing it, may
actually lose some of their intrinsic motivation to read because of what
is known as the **overjustification effect,** when receiving an extrinsic
reward leads to a drop in intrinsic motivation.[21] Despite this effect, however, there may be times when giv-
ing tangible rewards to your child
is appropriate, and we will provide
guidance on how and when to do
so next. In general, an easy rule of
thumb to use when determining if
tangible rewards are appropriate
might be, "If it ain't broke, don't fix
it." We only give tangible rewards to encourage behaviors that a child
does not exhibit independently and does not seem motivated to exhibit
even when provided with frequent and specific praise.

> **OVERJUSTIFICATION
> EFFECT**
> A phenomena in which an
> extrinsic motivator leads to a
> decrease in intrinsic motivation
> to engage in a task.

Your motivational goals for your child's learning are likely two-tiered.
First, you want your child to learn. And second, you want your child to
love learning. Ideally, just spending time with you and getting to show
off new reading skills should be motivation enough for your child. But, if
he is very reluctant to engage in reading activities, making reading time
more enticing for him may be necessary. Remember, our long-term goal
is to move your child's motivation up along the continuum.

So, if your child is initially amotivated, even after you have created
a safe and nurturing reading environment, the next step on the continuum is external regulation. We would rather see your child engage
in 30 minutes of reading each night, and then be rewarded with a dessert or 30 minutes of television time, than not read at all (or scream and

yell when you make him read!), because we know that the act of reading has so many cognitive benefits. You may not like the idea of providing rewards like these for engaging in reading, and we would hope that you did not need to do so for very long. But the hope is that, as you continue to read together and help him develop stronger reading skills, the feeling of competence becomes more important than the reward, and you can begin to wean him off receiving tangible reinforcers for this activity. Allowing your child television or other screen time after reading may also help reassure him that reading time is not taking the place of these other activities.

As reading together becomes an activity that your child is more willing to engage in without receiving rewards, you can also transition the reward to a more challenging activity and make your child feel proud of working towards this new challenge. For instance, you can say, "Now that you can read for 15 minutes without getting frustrated, I know you can read for 20 minutes. After you spend 20 minutes reading, you can pick a treat." Eventually, each of these activities you focus on—even if they are never intrinsically motivated—will become goals that your child identifies with, and can motivate himself to complete (just like you reward yourself with a snack, a trip to the movies, or a new purchase you've had your eye on when you complete a tough project).[22]

Speaking of how you reward yourself, it is also important to model for your child how to set mastery goals, monitor progress towards goals, aim to approach success rather than avoid failure, and take pride in effort. Think about a new thing you have been motivated to do recently, whether that is cooking dinner rather than ordering out, going to bed earlier, or running a 5K race. Talk about your own goals with your children, and make sure they know that you can accept less than perfection from yourself, as long as you try hard. You want to demonstrate to children how to be persistent, so that they are motivated to work hard even when a task seems challenging.

Developing Motivation and a Mastery Mindset:
How Can I Support My Child's Individual Needs?

Sometimes it can be difficult to figure out how to praise a child who is struggling, and who does not feel competent. When Jamie was growing up, her mother always told her, "You are the best Jamie I could ever have." This simple statement was always a source of comfort to Jamie. Years later, when she was completing one of her internships in graduate school, Jamie worked as a therapist for young children. One of her clients, Jane, was always very concerned that Jamie liked other children better than her and did not think that she was good at anything. After months of trying to address this child's insecurities using all of the methods her professors suggested, and failing to make things better, Jamie looked at Jane one day and said, "You know what, Jane? You are the best Jane I could ever know." Jane beamed. For the first time, she felt secure in herself and their relationship. Your child is not going to excel at everything he does, but he is always going to be the best him you know. Celebrating his achievements and his effort is the best way to let him know that.

What Activities and Strategies Can I Use to Help My
Child Get and Stay Motivated?

One of the reasons we described the continuum of motivation in such detail was to help you recognize that motivation is not something you have or don't have. We often think that people are either motivated or not and that the distinction between being enthusiastic about something and being unenthusiastic is black and white. But realizing that there are many different types of motivation, and many ways to support motivation, may help you be especially creative as you try to cultivate young readers.

Cultivate your child's interests. As we've said earlier, reading can take many forms and you can read about a wide variety of topics, from bugs to trains to princesses, that may be more or less interesting to your child. Young children may be highly motivated to interact with lift-the-flap books or books with pages that have cut-outs. Take note of your child's interests and help her explore them further, building on her sense of autonomy and initiative. Many children become intrinsically motivated readers through what was at first a situational interest in one particular book, topic, or storyteller at the library.[23] There will be ways that the printed word relates to your child's interest that you can build on.

Develop menus of reinforcement options. Because we know that not all activities are inherently interesting to all children, and that reading requires hard work and skill development that may sometimes feel frustrating, developing a list of rewards that you are willing to give for engaging in particular behaviors can be very helpful. These rewards should be inversely related to how frustrating the task is for your child— if she is almost ready to do something independently, a thumbs up may be all she needs. But if she is about to quit because she is so frustrated,

---

WAYS TO PRAISE
- Hug
- High five
- Thumbs up
- Smile
- Wink
- Kiss
- Backrub or shoulder squeeze
- Ruffling hair
- "You are working so hard!"
- "You are trying so hard!"
- "You did such a good job solving that last problem!"
- "You did such a good job sounding out that word!"
- "I can see you really understand _____."
- "I can see you really enjoyed learning about _____."
- "You did a great job explaining _____."
- "I can tell you worked so hard on your project/essay/assignment."

POSSIBLE TANGIBLE REINFORCEMENT OPTIONS
- Getting to pick a game that parent will play with child for 15 or 30 minutes
- Getting to play hide and seek with parent
- Doing something silly that's the child's choice (singing a song, wearing a funny outfit, etc.)
- Getting choice of dessert or beverage
- Getting 15 or 30 minutes of television time
- Getting 15 or 30 minutes of video game time
- Getting to stay up 15 or 30 minutes later than usual
- Taking a bubble bath with fancy soaps
- Getting to pick what the family eats for dinner
- Downloading a song or app
- Visiting a local park or skating rink

letting her know that she will get to pick a tangible reward from the list if she works for 10 more minutes might save the day.

You can see that not all of these rewards cost money and that you can be very creative in thinking up rewards that will be exciting to your child. The key is to consider what motivates your child and to use it. If you want to have your child work towards a longer-term goal, you can also think of a reward that he will gain points towards over time (like renting or buying a video game or movie, going out for pizza, or taking a trip to the zoo, museum, arcade, or amusement park). Remember to tailor the reward to your child's needs—you should only provide enough extrinsic motivation to make up for a lack of intrinsic motivation!

Find opportunities to praise effort. In the list of ways to praise that we included, you can see that we phrased our verbal praise in very particular ways. Rather than praising an attribute about your child (his intelligence, kindness, or athletic ability), praise the specific behavior that he just displayed (studying hard for a test, being patient with his sister, passing the basketball to a teammate). Remember, a child who believes he is so smart because he read a story accurately may believe that he is no longer smart when the next story is more difficult. But a child who knows that he worked so hard to sound out new words, and that taking time to look at words closely pays off, will feel just as smart when he gets to that next story.

Highlight areas where effort has already paid off. It may be that your child believes that intelligence is fixed (even if he could not yet express the idea in those terms), but that there are other areas of his life where he sees that effort pays off. Help him think about the similarities between these other areas and academic development. For instance, if your child has worked up to a brown belt in karate, ask him how he accomplished this. Was he always good at karate? Were there times when other kids were better at karate than him? How did he move from a white belt to a yellow belt? How did it feel to put in all of that time and effort? Share with your child the fact that the brain is like a muscle, and just like any muscle in our body, and we can strengthen it through hard work.[24] This strategy, as well as the others included in Table 6-4, can help your child become more mastery oriented.

Perspective-Taking and Empathy

Helping young children get in touch with their own feelings and those of others can be difficult. Perhaps the most common question that parents and teachers ask when a child acts unkindly to another child is, "How do you think you would feel if someone did that to you?" Why do we ask the question that way, rather than saying, "How do you think you made him feel?" One of the reasons is that we know that young children have limited perspective-taking abilities and are still developing their sense of empathy. When we ask a question about themselves and how they feel, it is easier for them to answer than when we ask them to consider how somebody else feels. Yet, the ability to mentally walk in someone else's shoes is an essential skill for social development and an important reading (and writing) skill as well. And reading together can provide you with wonderful insights into how your child responds spontaneously to the emotions of others. This was true for Anne, who has always treasured her son Michael's heart of gold. This characteristic

TABLE 6-4. FOSTERING MOTIVATION AND A MASTERY MINDSET: STRATEGIES FOR PARENTS

What to Do	How to Do It	Age(s)
Cultivate Your Child's Interests	Take note of your child's interests and help her explore them further, building on her sense of autonomy and initiative. Reading about topics that are intrinsically motivating can create positive associations with the reading process and help instill confidence.	
Find Opportunities to Praise Effort	Throughout the day, praise specific behaviors that your child displays, such as showing patience with a younger sibling or studying hard for a test. When your child knows she has worked hard at a difficult task or situation, she will have more confidence when she encounters another difficult one.	
Highlight Areas Where Effort Has Already Paid Off	Highlight areas where your child has demonstrated success in the past, in order to help him to remain persistent in other challenging endeavors. For example, just as he worked up the ranks of karate through hard work and dedication, he can become a better reader or speller. With effort, the sky's the limit!	
Choose Rewards Together	Brainstorm with your child about small, appropriate rewards to help motivate her to complete difficult or frustrating tasks.	

What to Do	How to Do It	Age(s)
Increase Motivation for Specific Behaviors	Determine where your child falls on the motivation continuum for any specific behavior, and help him move just one stage higher by making the task relevant to him, giving him some autonomy in deciding how and when to complete it, helping him feel competent, and providing an appropriate extrinsic motivator (if needed).	
Praise Effort	Praise effort, instead of ability. Highlight the attempt your child made, rather than the outcome of that attempt.	
Give Specific Praise	Give specific, rather than global, praise. Highlight the specific behavior that you are proud of, rather than labeling your child as smart, kind, or a good athlete.	
Praise Attempts at Mastery	Praise mastery goals, rather than performance. Focus on the new knowledge your child has acquired, rather than the grade she has received.	

continues

TABLE 6-4. CONTINUED

What to Do	How to Do It	Age(s)
Model Behaviors That Encourage Motivation	Model the behaviors you want to see— like goal-setting, taking pride in effort, and trying to approach success.	

developed early on and was quite evident during their special story time together. Whenever one of the characters would get hurt in a story they were reading together, Michael, even as a toddler, would say things like, "Oh no! They need help." Anne enjoyed seeing how his concern for others was unfolding in all of their daily interactions but especially through the world of literature. You can use reading time not just to observe how your child responds to these situations, but also to actively help him build perspective-taking skills.

> **PERSPECTIVE-TAKING**
> The ability to see a situation from someone else's point of view.

What Is Perspective-Taking?

Put simply, **perspective-taking** involves understanding somebody else's point of view and actions, including trying to understand what someone else knows about a situation, why somebody else acted the way that he did, how he feels about a situation, and how to resolve a dispute when two people have different points of view.[25] Young children have a hard time differentiating themselves from the other people around them and tend to see everything from their own perspective. Sometimes, we get very literal examples of that limited perspective—your two-year-old may ask you a question about an illustration in a book that he is looking at but is facing away from you, or your three-year-old may ask you to explain what is happening in a television program he is watching while you are in another room. When you ask a question about what happened at preschool, your daughter may say, "We ate cake for his birthday," without recognizing that you won't know whose birthday it was unless she tells you.

When young children do not take the perspective of someone else, they are not trying to be rude or inconsiderate (whereas an adult who acted similarly might be willfully ignoring someone else's perspective). The ability to understand things from someone else's point of view requires cognitive abilities that children develop over time. One of the ways that children's skill development in this area has been studied is through "false belief" tasks.[26] In these scenarios, children learn that something they believed is not actually true, and then need to think about how someone else would respond to the same situation. For example, a child will be shown a crayon box and asked what he thinks is inside. After saying, "Crayons!" he will open the box to find it filled with something else, like chocolate chips. If he were asked what somebody else would think

> **THEORY OF MIND**
> The ability to understand that others have thoughts, feelings, and beliefs that may differ from one's own thoughts, feelings, and beliefs.

is in that same box, what would he say? Around the age of four or five years old, children begin to recognize that someone else would be just as confused as they were at first. But before they develop this skill, what researchers call a **theory of mind**, they assume that the next person who is asked will think that the box is filled with chocolate chips, just as they do.[27] This false belief that others see the world exactly as they do means that young children do not yet possess the skills to contend with many social situations that older people can respond to easily. Moreover, this lack of perspective-taking may make it difficult for young children to understand a character's feelings or actions, or an author's intentions, when reading. Interestingly, though, book reading itself can help develop theory of mind, and the ability to take

> **EMPATHY**
> The ability to put oneself
> in another person's shoes
> and deeply understand their
> thoughts, feelings, and behaviors.

perspective, because of the ways that written narratives explain to us how different people feel and perceive the world.

What Is Empathy?

When we can commiserate with someone, we are being *sympathetic*. When we are able to really imagine how that person is feeling and have a vicarious sense of the emotion ourselves, we are being *empathetic*. There are both cognitive and emotional components to **empathy**. True empathy requires that we both intellectually understand how someone else is feeling, similar to the idea of perspective-taking, and that we respond emotionally to someone else's signs of sadness, anger, or distress. Although it was long believed that empathy was a sophisticated skill beyond the grasp of young children, we now know that even infants possess rudimentary attributes of emotional empathy.[28] For example, babies cry when they hear other babies crying and respond to this sound more vigorously than they respond to other loud noises.[29] By the age of two, we can see many children exhibiting concern for others through sharing or trying to provide physical comfort, rather than just displaying distress when others are distressed.[30] Between the ages of two and three, children become increasingly more aware of how others are feeling and more likely to try to help.

Showing this type of concern for others is the glue that binds interpersonal relationships. Not only does being empathetic enrich our social experiences in day-to-day life, it also enriches our understanding of works of art and expression, such as books, movies, music, and paintings. Once we are proficient readers, a main impetus for reading fiction is to explore the life, and feelings, of someone unfamiliar to us.[31] This same desire may also compel us to read biographies, memoirs, and works of historical fiction.

Why Are Perspective-taking and Empathy Important for Future Reading Development?

By the time children are in late elementary school, there is an expectation that they will be able to identify an author's reason for writing a descriptive essay, a persuasive editorial, an informational text, or a narrative story. They are expected to understand the rich emotional life of characters in the stories they read, and why these characters respond to various situations in the ways that they do. The ability to perspective-take is an essential component of reading comprehension. Thus, it is a necessary skill for reading development and also contributes substantially to creating lifelong, motivated readers. Children who struggle to understand the opinions of characters, and who have limited empathy for the situations these characters find themselves in, lack investment in the reading process as well as opportunities to demonstrate competence.

Reading will not be enjoyable under these circumstances. Think about times you have read a book with unsympathetic characters, whose feelings didn't interest you. You probably were not enthusiastic about finishing the book and didn't pick it up with the same eagerness as a book in which you were really rooting for the characters. Similarly, if you've read nonfiction essays in which the author was writing from a perspective that did not make sense to you, you probably found the essay alienating. Being able to empathize with others and perspective-take are key components of what make life, and literature, enjoyable. These skills also help children talk about books with others, and understand that not everyone shares the same opinions about what they read.

How Do Children's Perspective-Taking and Empathy Skills Develop Over Time?

As you might suspect, both perspective-taking and empathy are nuanced and sophisticated skills that continue to develop over a person's entire life. Often, as we get older, we possess the cognitive skills to understand another person's perspective, but don't activate these skills in all circumstances. We may struggle to empathize with the feelings of people whose beliefs are very different from our own. It is important to remember that although we see considerable development in these skills throughout the preschool and elementary school years, this does not mean that children fully possess both skills by the time they move on to middle school. Even as adults, being exposed to new information—often through literature—can help us build these skills. For example, reading a historical account of how Japanese Americans were treated during World War II may help us recognize how prejudice and discrimination has affected, and continues to affect, those around us. Marcia Savin addresses this period of American history in her book, *The Moon Bridge*,[32] which is appropriate for older elementary school readers. This same issue is also addressed, in a developmentally appropriate way for younger children, in picture books like *Flowers from Mariko*[33] by Rick Noguchi and Deneen Jenks. There are many excellent books for children written about specific times in history (the Civil Rights movement, natural disasters like the tsunami that hit Japan in 2011) and issues that can affect any community (bullying, moving to a new home, losing a friend or family member) that can inspire a deeper understanding of the experiences that other people have had and increase empathy for their plights.

At all ages, having the opportunity to hear about an issue from multiple points of view can build empathy. For example, reading stories about how unsafe victims of burglaries can feel for years afterwards as well as the circumstances that could lead a normally law abiding person to commit a crime can help both people who support harsh prison sentences and those who support alternatives to incarceration empathize with the other point of view. Researchers have found that adults who are more engaged in the stories they read have more empathy towards the characters and display more helpful behavior to the people around them, upon completion of the story.[34]

Children build these social skills through watching the adults around them exercise these same skills; they learn to apply their new knowledge through watching others act. They also acquire an understanding and appreciation for other people's perspectives by engaging in shared and independent reading.[35] Although there is a great deal of variation in how people apply these skills in the situations they face, there are some common changes, as highlighted in Table 6-5, we can expect to see as children get older.[36]

What Is the Role of Parents in Fostering the Development of Perspective-Taking and Empathy?

The best way that you can help your child develop these skills is to talk frequently about the thoughts, feelings, and behaviors of people your child encounters in everyday life, as well as the characters in books you read together (or movies or television shows you watch together). Because stories follow the narrative arc that we talked about in the chapter on reading comprehension, all fictional books include some issue or conflict that needs to be resolved. That issue almost always involves an interpersonal problem between two or more characters, whether they are people, animals, or space creatures. For this reason, storybooks offer great opportunities to discuss the internal states of characters, as well as their intentions or motives. Researchers who examined a wide variety of children's books found that, on average, stories focused on the emotions of characters or other aspects of social interactions every three sentences.[37] Unless your life often feels like a soap opera, the conversations that you have with your child—when they are not about books—probably include many fewer emotion-focused statements!

Being able to talk about a character's internal state—the feelings and thoughts going on within a person that others can't actually see happening—is an indicator of social perspective-taking ability. Preschoolers who engage in dialogic reading at home and school have been shown to talk more about characters' thoughts and beliefs, and make inferences about why those characters acted and felt particular ways, than children who did not engage in shared reading as regularly.[38] In fact, the frequency of shared reading at home has been shown to support the development of a theory of mind.[39] Even when mothers and children talked about

TABLE 6-5. INDICATORS OF PERSPECTIVE-TAKING AND EMPATHY DEVELOPMENT

Age	Indicators of Perspective-Taking Abilities	Indicators of Empathy	Reading-Related Behaviors
Preschool and Younger	• Children are likely to act on their feelings impulsively, without trying to regulate them or consider the perspectives of others. • 4–5-year-olds are usually able to correctly state what others might be thinking during "false belief" tasks.	• 0–1-year-olds may cry when they hear others cry. • 1–2-year-olds may offer comfort when others are distressed. • 2–3-year-olds may understand, or try to understand, why others are distressed and attempt to provide help. • 3–5-year-olds continue to offer comfort and help, often offering what they themselves would want if upset.	• Children may focus on the faces depicted in a book's illustrations, particularly faces expressing strong emotions. • Children may be able to use picture and context clues to identify how a character feels, and suggest simple resolutions to problems.
Early Elementary School	• Children are able to recognize that other people's thoughts and feelings may differ from their own. • Children can draw simple inferences about how others are feeling (e.g., sad, happy, mad). • Children can resolve conflicts (perhaps imperfectly) by recognizing that there are two perspectives on the situation, and valuing one over the other.	• Children develop an increased capacity to understand another's perspective, and can apply this skill by providing comfort and help that is more appropriate to the person's needs. • Children may use active perspective-taking or similar strategies to increase their feelings of empathy. • Feelings of empathy are generally exhibited toward individuals that children come into contact with most regularly.	• Children may more readily describe the thoughts and feelings of characters in books, and provide more sophisticated resolutions to problems.

Age	Indicators of Perspective-Taking Abilities	Indicators of Empathy	Reading-Related Behaviors
Late Elementary School	• Children are able to recognize that people may act in ways that mask their true thoughts or feelings. • Children are able to recognize that people remember and interpret events differently from one another. • Children can resolve conflicts by recognizing that there are two perspectives on the situation, and seeking a solution that can satisfy both perspectives.	• Feelings of empathy may extend beyond the child's individual social network, and include people affected by global and abstract issues (e.g., war, poverty).	• Children may be able to express thoughts and feelings of two characters with opposing points of view. • Children may be able to explain why a solution that is satisfactory for one character may not work for another character, and be able to suggest a compromise.

wordless picture books together and could not rely on the text on the page to tell the story, mothers who made more empathetic statements about the characters and discussed the causes and consequences of characters' emotions had children who performed better on tasks of social perspective-taking.[40] Moreover, researchers have found that a mother's ability to select appropriate children's books is related to kindergarten teachers' ratings of children's empathy skills and overall social adjustment.[41] All of these scientific studies provide further evidence that we can think of shared reading as a superfood. Talking about books together provides so many different types of nutrients, including this dose of emotion-rich language.

Beyond helping build your child's emotional vocabulary, you will also begin to help your child recognize that there is a connection between what someone thinks, how he feels, and how he acts. A person's perspective on a situation is informed by his thoughts and feelings, and his actions stem from this perspective. Gradually beginning to understand why others act the way that they do can also increase your child's capacity for empathy.

For example, let's say that there is a child, Nora, who often plays by herself at recess and sometimes says mean things to your daughter and her group of friends. Your daughter, Jill, may think that Nora is just a mean kid who doesn't deserve to have any friends because she treats other people so poorly. But when you go to visit the school, you see how Nora looks wistfully at the other children at the beginning of recess and seems clueless when it comes to joining others in a game. You can empathize with Nora, because you have a good guess about why she is being so

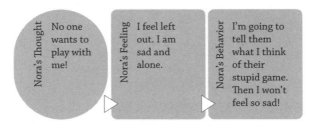

Figure 6-3. How thoughts influence feelings and behaviors.

mean. Figure 6-3 explains how Nora's thoughts and feelings may affect her behavior.

Once you are able to help Jill think about Nora's thoughts and feelings, she may be better able to understand Nora's perspective. Now, as we said before, just because someone can perspective-take doesn't necessarily mean that they will apply these skills, or demonstrate empathy towards the other person. Jill may still not feel like Nora deserves much empathy, because she knows that she herself has felt left out on other occasions and did not respond the same way! But by helping your child begin to put these puzzle pieces together, you are helping her understand the complex emotional life of herself and others. If Jill becomes more able to recognize the Nora's behavior stems from feelings of sadness and loneliness, she may be able to help Nora break this cycle. This understanding that thoughts, feelings, and behaviors are connected can take time to develop—children often read or request stories repeatedly, in order to make sense of their own life experiences and to problem-solve about new or unfamiliar events.[42]

Earlier in the chapter, we mentioned that talking about the emotions of book characters may be helpful because it allows children to talk about how people feel and act in a more objective way. Although Nora may make your daughter's blood boil, reading a story about a sad bully may help Jill better understand Nora's perspective. As you read together, remember to ask many questions about how the characters are thinking and feeling about the situations they find themselves in, and why they respond the way they do. You can ask your child to think about other ways they could have perceived the situation instead, and how that might have led to different outcomes. As your child's understanding of these issues becomes more sophisticated, your questions can become more complex as well. And rather than reading books about events that are familiar to your child, like the sad bully at recess, you can begin to read about more abstract topics and events that occur in places further from home.

Developing Perspective-Taking and Empathy: How Can I Support My Child's Individual Needs?

For almost all children, these social skills develop naturally as long as children are provided with a nurturing environment and the types of experiences that are described in this chapter. However, some children struggle to develop them. Children with pervasive developmental delays, like autism, can lack the social-cognitive capacity to take another person's perspective. They may lack a theory of mind, and have trouble putting themselves in somebody else's position. In contrast, children who have conduct problems, who act unkindly toward others without provocation, often possess the necessary cognitive skills to understand how someone else is feeling, but lack the emotional component of empathy needed to curb their behavior.[43] The reasons that infants cry when they hear others crying is because recognizing that someone else is sad makes them feel distressed; the same is true for most adults. Watching someone else being sad stirs our own emotions, and we instinctively want to reduce the other person's sadness, so that we feel better, too. But some children have less of this instinctual urge to help others, because those sights and sounds of distress don't affect them the way they affect the rest of us. If you recognize that your child consistently struggles to understand how others are feeling or to act kindly to most people, and in a manner that does not seem comparable to his or her peers, talk with your pediatrician. Remember, we all have trouble displaying these skills in certain situations; the fact that your son is often unkind to his younger brother may be frustrating, but it should not make you concerned that he lacks these skills entirely, unless he also treats most other people in this same way.

What Activities and Strategies Can I Use to Help My Child Develop Perspective-Taking and Empathy?

Throughout this section, we've repeatedly said that talking about these issues is the best way to help your child. But because beginning to think differently about how others feel and act requires thoughtful reflection, it can also be helpful for your child to engage in activities that allow time

TABLE 6-6. FOSTERING PERSPECTIVE-TAKING AND EMPATHY: STRATEGIES FOR PARENTS

What to Do	How to Do It	Age(s)
Act Out Scenes from Books and Hold Debates	During shared reading, verbalize things from a character's perspective to help your child better understand how that person is thinking or feeling or to better understand the character's behavior. You can act out scenes from the book and, when relevant, delve deeper into those that are conducive to the examination of a character's perspective. In books in which a conflict exists between characters, you and your child can each take sides and hold a debate, where each character gets to share her point of view.	
Keep a Book Journal	Encourage your child to keep a book journal where he can keep track of how favorite books affected him. This will encourage him to reflect on the kinds of emotions and feelings the book created. Through the act of writing, your child may discover ideas that weren't obvious immediately after completing the story.	
Write Letters to Characters	Encourage your child to connect with her favorite characters through letter writing. By articulating her feelings and understanding of a character's behavior and the reasons for it, your child will gain important experience applying perspective-taking skills.	
Model Perspective-Taking and Empathy	Model these skills by talking about your understanding of other people's perspective, and describing why, when, and how you show empathy for others.	

continues

TABLE 6-6. CONTINUED

What to Do	How to Do It	Age(s)
Ask Questions about Thoughts and Feelings	Ask your child how she thinks others think and feel, and why they act the way that they do. Ask these questions during book reading sessions, when you are watching movies or TV shows, about people you see every day...and whenever else you can!	
Act Out Situations	Create playful situations that let your child explore other people's perspectives by acting together, staging debates or puppet shows, or writing your own plays or movies.	
Write about Experiences	Encourage your child to write about his reading experiences by keeping a book journal of his own thoughts and feelings and by writing letters to characters to connect his own experiences to what happened in the book.	

for reflection, rather than just giving immediate answers to the questions you ask. Table 6-6 provides a list of strategies that will further this goal.

Act out scenes from books and hold debates. Actually verbalizing things from a character's perspective can help your child better understand how a character—like Goldilocks—is thinking or feeling, and then make sense of that character's behavior. Acting out scenes from a book together can be a fun way to delve deeper into the emotional lives of characters, as can acting out "deleted scenes" that did not make it into the book. Use your imagination to come up with other scenarios that could have happened, like what Goldilocks might do on her first day of camp or school, and act out those scenes as well. In books where a conflict exists between characters, you and your child can each take sides and hold a debate, giving each character the chance to share her point of view. Some books even do this for you. For example, you can read *The True Story of the Three Little Pigs,*[44] told by Jon Scieszka from the wolf's point of view, or *Honestly, Red Riding Hood was Rotten!; The Story of Little Red Riding Hood as Told by the Wolf*[45] by Trisha Speed Shaskan, another story where a villainous wolf gets a chance to set the record straight.

Keep a book journal. The books that are most memorable to us are usually books that made us think about issues in a new way, or that evoked strong feelings. To help your child reflect on the books that he reads, encourage him to keep a book journal. Rather than just focusing on discussing details of the plot in this journal, help him think about how the book affected him. You can use prompts that ask about the following topics:

- Your child's thoughts and feelings
  - "The part of this book that made me laugh out loud was . . . ."
  - "I was SO scared when . . . "
  - "It made me sad when . . . ."
  - "If I were _____, I would have been really angry . . . "
  - "After I finished the first chapter, I felt . . . "
- The characters' thoughts and feelings
  - "I think _____ was thinking . . . ."
  - "The reason _____ acted that way was because . . . "
  - "_____ felt . . . because . . . "

As we discussed in chapter 3, we often discover our own ideas through the act of writing. Taking the time to really think about a book he read, with you or independently, will allow your child to learn more from this book than merely closing it once he has reached the last page.

Write letters to characters. The strategies just discussed have mainly focused on helping your child gain perspective-taking skills. To help build empathy as well, it can be beneficial to have your child try to connect with a character by writing a letter. Writing to a fictional character will give your child practice making sense of another person's emotions. This activity will give him a chance to express that he understands how the character is feeling, relate a situation in which he felt similar, and offer suggestions for ways to feel better. By helping him articulate these three things, you will give him practice applying his perspective-taking skills.

Additional Benefits for You

The benefits of cultivating a rich shared reading practice extend to you, too, in ways that are most relevant to discuss in this chapter. Studies have shown that using strategies for scaffolding reading time, like dialogic reading, may reduce parent stress.[46] Additionally, by focusing on your child's growing competence and engaged behaviors, and ignoring fidgety behavior or silly comments, you will begin to reinforce these reading and social skills.[47] For reading time with your child to feel fun for both of you, there are behavioral skills that you can use to make sure your child stays calm and focused. These same skills—attending to positive behavior and ignoring minor misbehavior, praising effort over ability—can be used throughout the day to help your child complete other tasks and to keep your household calm.

Of course, the biggest benefit for you will be the pride you feel in your successful, motivated reader! We hope that the earlier chapters in this book provided *you* with the confidence to help your child learn to read, and that this chapter includes strategies that help *your child* gain the same level of confidence. As we said earlier in this chapter, first you want your child to learn. And second, you want your child to love learning. You now have the skills and strategies to make both those things happen!

Conclusion

We dubbed shared reading a "superfood" earlier in this chapter because of its remarkable powers to help your child in so many different ways. Teaching your child to ride a bike can build perseverance and confidence, but probably does very little to help with academic development or building empathy. Working on math problems together is an important academic task, may strengthen your relationship with your child, and may help your child feel competent, but it does not give her an opportunity to explore the emotional lives of others and relate them to her own life.

Talking with your child about the rich world of books awakens her mind—to her own opinion, to yours, to those of the characters. Helping her sound out words strengthens her will to succeed, and sets her on the path to feeling like a purposeful and competent reader. Praising her

TABLE 6-7. TECH TIPS FOR PARENTS: SOCIAL AND EMOTIONAL DEVELOPMENT

Tech Tips: Social and Emotional Development

Concerned parents and researchers are involved in an ongoing discussion about the potential problems technology can present for children, particularly in terms of social development. It is difficult to make a universal statement about the negative effects that technology can have on children because the research is mixed—and still being conducted—on the ways that technology can affect a wide range of social skills. However, it is certainly a reality that these technology tools—like laptops, smartphones, and tablets—are increasingly present in homes and turned on many hours of the day. Just as frequent use of technology can lead to less time spent building new vocabulary words through interpersonal communication, it can also lead to less time spent engaging in activities that foster autonomy and competence or talking about issues that help develop perspective-taking skills. In addition, becoming reliant on these tools can teach children that immediate gratification is always possible, making it more difficult for them to tolerate frustration and deeply reflect on something they want to learn or resolve. We have tried to provide tips for using these tools responsibly throughout the book and below, but our parting message is that when in doubt, moderation is key.

What to Do	How to Do It	Appropriate Age Group(s)
Use Technology to Offer Choice	By offering multiple ways to complete many academic tasks, technology tools can help children feel autonomous and competent. For example, if you were hoping that your child would write down a story at home and she is reluctant to do so, you can offer a choice between writing the story on paper, dictating the story into the smartphone's microphone, or drawing a picture of the beginning, middle, and end of the story using an electronic illustrator. Offering this choice will let you focus on the skill you want to build and give your child a chance to feel in control.	

What to Do	How to Do It	Appropriate Age Group(s)
Create Finished Products	Completing a project (like making a printed book or keeping track of books read as a family, as we discussed in previous sections) can help children develop a long-term investment in reading because it allows them an opportunity to feel like competent authors and readers, and be proud of their work. Technology tools facilitate projects like these because they allow children fun and unique ways to express themselves and create a finished product.	
Track Progress Toward Goals	Technology tools can foster a growth-oriented mindset for the reading skills discussed in other chapters insofar as they allow children to track their own progress and see it represented visually. Many educational games provide children with a "score" and set of strengths and areas for growth. You can use computer programs to help your child keep track of activities, such as the number of minutes he spends reading every day, and help him graph his progress toward the number he hopes to reach.	
Use Technology to build Perspective-Taking Skills	Because technology has the capacity to let us interact with people we wouldn't come into contact with otherwise (through learning about an issue in another part of the country or world from the Internet, or through having a pen pal), it can increase our capacity for understanding situations that we have not been in personally. For example, having an electronic pen pal (or text message buddy) from another part of the state, country, or world can help a child understand that customs are different in other parts of the world (for example, how people dress, eat, get to school) and that good people may experience difficulties that people in their family may not experience.	

TABLE 6-8. ENGLISH LANGUAGE LEARNER TIPS FOR PARENTS: SOCIAL AND EMOTIONAL DEVELOPMENT

English Language Learner Tips: Social and Emotional Development

One of the most important things in life besides acquiring knowledge is the development of social relationships. In this chapter we talked about the importance of acquiring a positive sense of self, motivation and a mastery mindset, as well as developing perspective taking and empathy skills. We want to commend you if you are raising your child in a multilingual environment. Mastering two or more languages not only allows your child to connect with your cultural background in a meaningful way, it can also foster a deeper understanding of language systems which will serve your child well as she progresses through school. Moreover, your child may acquire a deeper understanding of perspective taking and empathy at a young age,[48] and develop a stronger sense of self, because of the opportunity to explore different cultures through learning L2. That being said, it is not unusual for a child to go through phases during which she may appear to reject your home language and culture or your adopted language and culture, or to become frustrated and lack motivation when learning L2. As your child develops her identity, she will need the freedom and opportunity to explore both cultures with your loving support and guidance. In this way she can continue to value your home language and culture while learning a new one. In this table, we provide some ideas to help your child's social and emotional development as an English language learner.

What to Do	How to Do It	Appropriate Age Group(s)
Encourage Your Child in Learning Both Languages	Learning to speak, read, and write in a second language is an opportunity and a challenge! Remember to provide specific praise for your child, highlighting how well she is doing in each language. This will help your child develop her feelings of competence rather than inferiority. For example, if your child makes a grammatical error and then attempts to correct herself, you might want to let her know that she has done something great. You might say, "Hey! That's so great that you were able to notice the difference between what you said and what you wanted to say, and then came up with better words to use. I need to remember to do that the next time I make that mistake."	

What to Do	How to Do It	Appropriate Age Group(s)
Model a Mastery Mindset When Learning a Second Language	When you become frustrated while navigating two languages, try to model for your child the use of a mastery mindset. Instead of focusing on being correct so that you aren't embarrassed if someone notices your mistake, reframe your frustration as an opportunity to learn. For example, if you come across a new word in a book you are reading to your child, demonstrate excitement at the opportunity to learn the new word and illustrate to your child the methods you use to define the word (for example, using a dictionary, looking it up online, using context clues).	
Support Perspective-Taking	Learning multiple languages offers children the opportunity to build important social skills. For example, to determine if a conversation partner speaks L1 or L2, your child can practice paying attention to both verbal and non-verbal cues. This increased awareness of others, and to different levels of interaction, are assets in our global world, which values interpersonal skills and a cross-cultural perspective. You can support perspective-taking by encouraging your child to describe scenes in a book and what she thinks the characters are thinking and why.	

continues

TABLE 6-8. CONTINUED

What to Do	How to Do It	Appropriate Age Group(s)
Arrange Play Dates with Children Who Speak Either L1 or L2	Children's play with peers provides rich experiences in using language. Setting up play dates with peers who speak your first language and English can motivate your child in learning both languages. In addition to children's natural communication in play, you can take a more active role at times. For example, you can organize a game of sorting objects, having the children switch between your first language and English. If they enjoy drama, ask them to present a song or dance show for a bilingual audience! For information on local playgroups with a specific language or cultural focus, check online or in parent newspapers.	
Be Sensitive of Phases in Speaking a New Language	Children can go through predictable phases when learning a second language. In the first phase, a child relies on L1 to communicate in all contexts. As the child becomes more aware of others speaking L2, he may begin a nonverbal period, watching and listening, but not talking as much. He will then move on to using basic words and phrases to communicate. In the final phase, a child practices more complex grammar with increased vocabulary. The unique personality of your child and the contexts will also affect his comfort level in speaking a new language. Give your child encouragement without forcing language use.	

effort, rather than her ability, instills in her the idea that working hard is valued. And getting to know characters deeply can help her reflect on their perspectives and even change her beliefs about the world around her. There really is no comparable activity that changes in its focus over the years of your child's development, but continues to be so important for school and life success. If you are able to keep in mind the goal of supporting the development of a motivated, lifelong reader in mind when reading with your child, we are sure that you will provide the type of support that helps achieve this goal.

Notes

1. Alexander, K. J., Miller, P. J. & Hengst, J. A. (2001). Young children's emotional attachments to stories. *Social Development*, *10*(3), 374–398.

2. Bus, A. G., & van IJzendoorn, M. H. (1997). Affective dimension of mother-infant picturebook reading. *Journal of School Psychology*, *35*, 46–61; Clingenpeel, B. T., & Pianta, R. C. (2007). Mothers' sensitivity and book-reading interactions with first graders. *Early education and development*, *18*(1), 1–22.

3. Wigfield, A. & Guthrie, J. T. (1997). Relation of children's motivation for reading to the amount and breadth of their reading. *Journal of Educational Psychology*, *89*, 420–432.

4. Brown, M. W. (1947). *Goodnight Moon*. New York: Harper.

5. Carle, E. (1969). *The Very Hungry Caterpillar*. New York: World.

6. Eccles, J. S. & Wigfield, A. (2002). Motivational beliefs, values and goals. *Annual Review of Psychology*, *53*, 109–132.

7. Chapman, J. W., & Tunmer, W. E. (1995). Development of young children's reading self-concepts: An examination of emerging subcomponents and their relationship with reading achievement. *Journal of Educational Psychology*, *87*, 154–167.

8. Guthrie, J. T., Coddington, C. S., & Wigfield, A. (2009). Profiles of motivation for reading among African American and Caucasian students. *Journal of Literacy Research*, *41*, 317–353; McClelland, M. M., Acock, A. C., & Morrison, F. J. (2006). The impact of kindergarten learning-related skills on academic trajectories at the end of elementary school. *Early Childhood Research Quarterly*, *21*, 471–490; Schaefer, B. A., & McDermott, P. A. (1999). Learning behavior and intelligence as explanations for children's scholastic achievement. *Journal of School Psychology*, *37*, 299–313; Yen, C., Konold, T. R., & McDermott, P. A. (2004). Does learning behavior augment cognitive ability as an indicator of academic achievement? *Journal of School Psychology*, *42*, 157–169.

9. Dweck, C. S. (2006). *Mindset*. New York: Random House.

10. Guthrie, J. T., Coddington, C. S., & Wigfield, A. (2009). Profiles of motivation for reading among African American and Caucasian students. *Journal of Literacy Research, 41,* 317–353.

11. Baker, L., & Wigfield, A. (1999). Dimensions of children's motivation for reading and their relations to reading activity and reading achievement. *Reading Research Quarterly, 34,* 452–477; Cox, K. E., & Guthrie, J. T. (2001). Motivational and cognitive contributions to students' amount of reading. *Contemporary Educational Psychology, 26,* 116–131; Wigfield, A., & Guthrie, J. T. (1997). Relations of children's motivation for reading to the amount and breadth of their reading. *Journal of Educational Psychology, 89,* 420–432.

12. Ryan, R. M., & Deci, E. L. (2000). Intrinsic and extrinsic motivations: Classic definitions and new directions. *Contemporary Educational Psychology, 25,* 54–67.

13. Dweck (2006).

14. Wigfield, A., Guthrie, J. T., Tonks, S., & Perencevich, K. C. (2004). Children's motivation for reading: Domain specificity and instructional influences. *The Journal of Educational Research, 97*(6), 299–309.

15. Guthrie, Coddington, & Wigfield (2009).

16. Lyon, G. R (Speaker). (1998). *Statement of Dr. G. Reid Lyon. April 28, 1998: Overview of Reading and Literacy Initiatives.* Retrieved from http://langsfordcenter.com/uploads/LAC-Docs/Publications/RLyon%20-%20Statement%20to%20Committee%20on%20Labor%20and%20Human%20Resources.pdf

17. Eccles, J. S., & Wigfield, A. (2002). Motivational beliefs, values and goals. *Annual Review of Psychology, 53,* 109–132; Gottfried, A. E., Fleming, J. S., & Gottfried, A. W. (2001). Continuity of academic intrinsic motivation from childhood through late adolescence: A longitudinal study. *Journal of Educational Psychology, 93,* 3–13.

18. Edmunds, K., & Bauserman, K. (2006). What teachers can learn about reading motivation through conversations with children. *The Reading Teacher, 59,* 414–426; Worthy, J., Patterson, E., Salas, R., Prater, S., & Turner, M. (2002). More than just reading: The human factor is reaching resistant readers. *Reading Research & Instruction, 41,* 177–202.

19. Guthrie, J. T., Hoa, L. W., Wigfield, A., Tonks, S. M., & Perencevich, K. C. (2006). From spark to fire: Can situational reading interest lead to long-term reading motivation? *Reading Research and Instruction, 45,* 91–117.

20. Ryan, A. M., Pintrich, P. R., & Midgley, C. (2001). Avoiding seeking help in the classroom: Who and why? *Educational Psychology Review, 13*(2), 93–114.

21. Lepper, M. R., Greene, D., & Nisbett, R. E. (1973). Undermining children's intrinsic interest with extrinsic reward: A test of the "overjustification" hypothesis. *Journal of Personality and Social Psychology*, 28(1), 129–137; Ryan, R. M., & Deci, E. L. (2000). Intrinsic and extrinsic motivations: Classic definitions and new directions. *Contemporary Educational Psychology*, 25, 54–67.

22. Guthrie, J. T., Hoa, L. W., Wigfield, A., Tonks, S. M., & Perencevich, K. C. (2006).

23. Ibid.

24. You Can Grow Your Intelligence. Internet posting, unauthored.]www.brainology.us/websitemedia/youcangrowyourintelligence.pdf

25. Edwards, C. P. (1986). *Promoting Social and Moral Development in Young Children: Creative Approaches for the Alassroom*. New York: Teachers College, Columbia University.

26. Wellman, H. M., & Liu, D. (2004). Scaling of theory-of-mind tasks. *Child Development*, 75, 523–541.

27. Astington, J. W., Harris, P. L., & Olson, D. R. (1988). *Developing theories of mind*. New York: Cambridge University Press.

28. Zahn-Waxler, C., Radke-Yarrow, M., Wagner, E., & Chapman, M. (1992). Development of concern for others. *Developmental Psychology*, 28, 126–136; Zahn-Waxler, C., Robinson, J. L., & Emde, R. N. (1992). The development of empathy in twins. *Developmental Psychology*, 28, 1038–1047.

29. Hoffman, M.L. (2000). *Empathy and moral development: Implications for caring and justice*. New York: Cambridge University Press.

30. Kanfo, A., Zahn-Waxler, C., Van Hulle, C., Robinson, J. L., & Rhee, S. H. (2008). The developmental origins of a disposition toward empathy: Genetic and environmental contributions. *Emotion*, 8, 737–752; Zahn-Waxler, C., Radke-Yarrow, M., Wagner, E., & Chapman, M. (1992). Development of concern for others. *Developmental Psychology*, 28, 126–136.

31. Mar, R. A., & Oatley, K. (2008). The function of fiction is the abstraction and simulation of social experience. *Perspectives on Psychological Science*, 3, 173–192.

32. Savin, M. (1992). *The Moon Bridge*.New York: Scholastic.

33. Noguchi, R., & Jenks, D. (2001). *Flowers from Mariko*. New York: Lee & Low Books.

34. Johnson, D. R. (2012). Transportation into a story increases empathy, prosocial behavior, and perceptual bias toward fearful expressions. *Personality and Individual Differences*, 52, 150–155.

35. Zevenberger, A. A., Whitehurst, G. J., & Zevenberger, J. A. (2003). Effects of a shared-reading intervention on the inclusion of evaluative devices in narratives of children from low income families. *Applied Developmental Psychology*, *24*, 1–15.

36. Brophy, J., & Alleman, J. (2007). *Powerful social studies for elementary students,* 2nd ed. Belmont, CA: Wadsworth; Eisenberg, N., & Fabes, R. A. (1998). Prosocial development. In W. Damon (Series Ed.) & N. Eisenberg (Vol. Ed.), *Handbook of Child Psychology,* Vol. 3: *Social, Emotional, and Personality Development* 5th ed., pp. 701–778. New York: John Wiley; Ormrod, J. E. (2008). *Educational Psychology: Developing Learners*, 8th ed. New York: Prentice Hall; Selman, R. L. (1980). *The Growth of Interpersonal Understanding*. New York: Academic Press.

37. Dyer, J. R., Shatz, M., & Wellman, H. M. (2000). Young children's storybooks as a source of mental state information. *Cognitive Development, 15*, 17–37.

38. Zevenberger, A. A., Whitehurst, G. J., & Zevenberger, J. A. (2003).

39. Mar., R. A., Tackett, J. L., & Moore, C. (2010). Exposure to media and theory-of-mind development in preschoolers. *Cognitive Development, 25*, 69–78.

40. Garner, P. W., Jones, D. C., Gaddy, G., & Rennie, K. M. (1997). Low-income mothers' conversations about emotions and their children's emotional competence. *Social Development, 6*(1), 37–52.

41. Aram, D., & Aviram, S. (2009). Mother's storybook reading and kindergartners' socioemotional and literacy development. *Reading Psychology, 30*, 175–194.

42. Alexander, K. J., Miller, P. J., & Hengst, J. A. (2001). Young children's emotional attachments to stories. *Social Development, 10*(3), 374–398.

43. Jones, A. P., Happé, F. G., Gilbert, F., Burnett, S., & Viding, E. (2010). Feeling, caring, knowing: Different types of empathy deficit in boys with psychopathic tendencies and autism spectrum disorder. *Journal of Child Psychology and Psychiatry, 5*(11), 1188–1197.

44. Schieszka, J. (1989). *The True Story of the Three Little Pigs*. New York: Viking Kestrel.

45. Shaskan, T. S. (2011). *Honestly, Red Riding Hood Was Rotten!; The Story of Little Red Riding Hood as Told by the Wolf*. North Mankato, MN: Picture Window Books.

46. Huebner, C. E. (2000). Promoting toddlers' language development through community-based intervention. *Journal of Applied Developmental Psychology, 21*(5), 513–535.

47. Kazdin, A. E. (2008). *Parent Management Training: Treatment for Oppositional, Aggressive, and Antisocial Behaviors in Children and Adolescents*. New York: Oxford University Press.

48. Goetz, P. J. (2003). The effects of bilingualism on theory of mind development. *Bilingualism: Language and Cognition, 6*(1), 1–15. http://dx.doi.org/10.1017/S1366728903001007

Chapter 7

Conclusion

In 1965, Orville Prescott wrote *A Father Reads to His Children: An Anthology of Prose and Poetry*. His goal was to pick a wide variety of stories and poems that could introduce young readers to new situations and new worlds, and to encourage fathers—who, he thought, might spend less time engaging in shared reading with their children than mothers did—to serve as their children's guides. Prescott stated that shared reading "offers fathers an opportunity to answer questions, to comment and to explain,"[1] describing the idea of dialogic reading even before it was in vogue. He recognized the incredible support that parents could provide children who were learning to read.

However, as a writer himself, Prescott also recognized how parents could help children read to learn. In explaining the role that parents could play in cultivating skills like critical thinking and reflection, he said, "Few children learn to read books by themselves. Someone has to lure them into the wonderful world of the written word; someone has to show them the way." Shared reading, in its many forms, provides you with this fantastic opportunity to show your child the way to read and think about reading.

We hope that we've illustrated this idea throughout the book and demonstrated that, through reading together, you've helped your child develop a wide variety of skills that are important for reading development. Some of these skills may have been the ones that you were hoping to learn more about when you first picked up this book, such as recognizing letters, sounding out simple words, and comprehending longer passages. Others may have once seemed less connected to reading, like building oral language skills, learning how to express oneself in writing, and developing a healthy sense of self. But now that you understand how all of these skills are related to one another and to reading development, we hope you see the value and importance of guiding your child down this path.

Each chapter in this book highlights a specific aspect of reading development, because what it means to "show them the way" can mean so many different things for different types of children, and for children of different ages. Your child may benefit most from playing rhyming games and with letter magnets as you help her learn to pair letters and their sounds, or from creating semantic webs by drawing upon background information you provide. It is because each child's needs vary that we keep returning to the idea of the zone of proximal development, and the support you can provide by scaffolding, in each chapter of this book. You know your child best. You know what she is interested in, and you know what tasks are easy or difficult for her. As you page back through this book and turn your attention to different sections when they become most appropriate, reviewing the information about the reading skills that your child is in the midst of developing will help you pinpoint where she is in the process and be more able to help her grow. Remember that our intention is not for you to use every suggested strategy in the book. We want you to pick and choose those activities that work best for you and your child, so that you can help advance her development. Some activities you've read about may be ones that you will use regularly in daily life, whereas others may make an appearance for just a week or a month, until they have served their purpose and you have moved on to other things.

Of course, each child is unique and does not develop in exactly the same way or at exactly the same time as other children. There are many different issues that may have driven you to first pick up this book. Your child may already be a reader, but not a motivated reader. Your child may have some academic challenges that will keep him from being as sophisticated a reader as you would have imagined, but that doesn't mean you cannot keep reading together and building his skills. We hope that this book has illustrated that there is not a "one size fits all" approach to becoming a fluent and motivated reader. There are many different ways to get children engaged in language and literature, and you can pick those strategies that work best for your child.

Prescott's quote is powerful in part because it can be applied so widely. This idea of showing your child the way is probably not a new idea to you. In almost all aspects of life, you act as your child's guide. You give advice, model the right way to do things, and help her reach new heights that she could not reach independently. You praise her for her efforts when she works hard in school, has a good day on the soccer field, or plays well with her peers. In this book, we highlight the ways in which you can treat reading like any of these other activities.

Keeping your child's zone of proximal development in mind and providing praise and scaffolding are strategies that will serve you well in many different situations and help you to tailor the reading activities discussed throughout the book to your child's individual needs. Remember to watch your child so you can recognize what he can do on his own and what he needs a little help to do. Can he turn the pages of the book? Is he able to finish the sentence as you read a familiar story? Has he started sounding out words? When you see your son completing a task independently, sit back proudly and let him. Moreover, help him recognize what amazing leaps he is making by offering specific praise like "Wow, only a big kid knows how to find letters!" rather than general praise like "Great job! You're so smart!" This type of support not only helps your child build important reading skills, but also paves the way for staying engaged and motivated in the world of books.

Prescott's quote is also powerful because it highlights how important shared reading can be and the fact that reading is an act people engage in together. You serve as a guide as you read with your child in so many ways, from talking about the language in books to pointing out print cues to chatting about a character's reason for acting a particular way. Moreover, books are effective tools for bringing you and your child closer and creating avenues for dialogue about those moments that might otherwise not be discussed or may be difficult to broach, like having a new sibling or preparing for the first day of school. Even as your child is able to read independently, reading together remains important. You can help your older elementary school child or adolescent make sense of new vocabulary words, understand issues that are being debated in a text, and use situations in stories as springboards for discussing events happening in your own family or community.

To raise a reader, you need to keep providing guidance as your child continues down the path. Books are vehicles for learning to make inferences, developing perseverance, talking about imaginary worlds, and discussing difficult situations. Your child's world will become more complicated as he gets older, but you will continue to show him the way through new adventures and challenges. And there will be books suited to each of these new situations for you to enjoy together. As you continue to explore together, remember that reading really is like helping your child learn to ride a bicycle. You'll adjust the level of support you provide over time, as your child begins to become more independent and wobble less as he makes his way down the street, but you will always keep your eyes on him and be ready to help if he hits a bump in the road.

Note

1. Prescott, O. (1965). *A Father Reads to His Children: An Anthology of Prose and Poetry*. New York: E. P. Dutton, p. 13.

Create Your Own Letter and Phoneme Tiles!

Copy these pages and cut the blocks apart for a quick and easy set of letter and phoneme tiles! Arrange and rearrange them with your child to make words and practice letter sounds. Make sure to copy more than one set so that you can use each sound more than once.

b	c	d	f
f	g	h	j
k	l	l	m
n	p	qu	r
s	s	t	t
u	v	w	x
y	z	th	sh
ch	wh	ck	ph

ar	er	ir	ur
or	tch	dge	ge
mn	kn	mb	kn
wr	a	ai	ay
e	ee	ea	i
o	oo	oa	ie
igh	u	ue	y
oi	oy	ow	ou
aw	au	ui	eu
eigh	ue		

Help Your Child Build Letter and Word Knowledge

Alphabet Scavenger Hunt

Draw a two-column table on a piece of paper or cardstock. The left column will be labeled "Letter/Phoneme" and the right column should be labeled "Picture Match." Make a copy of the tiles provided in appendix A and cut them out or make your own letter tiles by writing each letter of the alphabet on a small piece of paper. Have your child pick one letter from a bowl, hat, or pile and place it in the left column of the table. Tell him he is going to go on a scavenger hunt to find an item that begins with that letter or phoneme. Then have him find a match from pictures of objects with the same letter sound. Pictures can be hand drawn or cut out from magazines. As your child becomes more proficient at recognizing letters, sounds, and words, this activity can be made more challenging by:

- using upper and lowercase letters
- picking objects that end, rather than begin, with the same consonant sound
- finding pictures of words with different vowel sounds within them (for example, pictures of words like *lip* that include the short "i" sound or words like *mane* that include the long "a" sound)

Letter/Phoneme	Picture Match

Bingo with Letter Tiles

Make a nine-square grid (three squares across, and three down), and write nine different uppercase letters, one in each box. Using the tiles from appendix A, put matching
lowercase letters into a bowl or box. Have your child close her eyes and pick one of the
lowercase letters out of the bowl. Have her match the letter to its uppercase match by
placing it on top of the uppercase letter. Then you can take a turn. Three in a row makes
Bingo! To practice more letters, try making a 16- or 25-square grid.

Letter/Sound Blending

Create a few consonant/vowel/consonant (CVC) words (for example, *cat, pot,* and *tin*)
with the letter tiles or by writing the words on a small whiteboard. Then—using your
finger or a marker—connect, or "swoop" under, the first two letters (while blending
together the first two sounds), and continue to "swoop" to the third letter as you blend
the final sound. In this way, your child can begin to recognize how letters and sounds are
combined to create words.

You can connect these letter sounds solely by using your finger, but younger children may
benefit from seeing the connections more clearly. You can place the letter tiles on a piece
of paper and then connect the letters using a marker, or do the same on a whiteboard.

Word Building Made Easy

Children learn the letters of the alphabet in a typical sequence based on each letter's
frequency, sound, and the way it is formed in the mouth. Listed below is an easy way
to divide the alphabet into smaller, more manageable chunks. Several simple words, for
example, can be created using just Group 1 letters. Using the tiles from Group 1, explore
with your child how to make simple CVC words. Point out that the colors of the tiles
are different (in that consonant tiles are grey and vowel tiles are white). You don't need
to explain the meanings of consonants and vowels, but you may want to point out that
every word you make has a white tile. Once those are somewhat mastered, your child can
continue to add groups to make even more words using the letters from all earlier groups.

> Group 1: A, L, M, S, F,
> Group 2: H, C, N, R, O
> Group 3: B, P, J, T, I, D
> Group 4: G, K, V, U, Z
> Group 5: E, X, Y, W, Q

Rhyming

For this activity, you will need pictures of objects that rhyme (see suggestions below). Choose two pictures that rhyme and one that does not. Lay them in front of your child and have him choose the two pictures that rhyme. Then, using the tiles included, have your child build one of the words in the pair. Note: this does not require perfect spelling! Next, have him change just one or two sounds to spell the other rhyming word in the pair. Rhyming words might include:

- cat, rat, bat, hat
- dog, hog, log, frog
- goat coat, note, boat
- cap, tap, map, clap
- fly, tie, pie, cry

You can see that we begin with rhyming words that share the same spelling pattern, and end with rhyming words that do not. As children become more familiar with the different ways that sounds can be represented, asking them to spell words that sound similar but are spelled differently can help them grasp the many different spelling patterns in our language.

Word Manipulation

Gather several letters from the tiles, including vowels and various consonants. Choose three letters to begin with a simple CVC word like *hat*. Explain to your child, "Now I want to change that word to '*cat*'—how can I do that?" Or, "Now I want to make '*cap*'—what letter do I need to change?" "Can I change this word to '*cup*'?" Meanwhile, your child will find the appropriate letter tile and replace the previous one as needed, in order to make the new words. Other simple CVC words and manipulations are indicated below:

tin	tan → man → pan → pin → fin → fun
dot	pot → pit → bit → big → bag → bat
far	car → cat → cut → nut → net → met

As your child becomes more familiar with these simple CVC words and common spelling patterns, you can begin to experiment with lengthier words and sounds that are represented by more than one letter. For example, you can cut out the letter tiles for the vowels **a** and **e**, as well as the **b, ch,** and **t** consonant tiles. Then display the tiles for your child and ask him to make the word *at*. Next, you can ask him which letter he needs to make the word *eat*. You can continue on in this way, creating the words *beat* and even *beach* by adding and taking away letters. Similarly, you can use the letters **a, e, t,** and **ch** to create words like *at, tea, eat, each,* and *teach.* The possibilities are almost endless, so get creative with your letter combinations!

Explore Orthographic Patterns

Another strategy that can be used to familiarize your child with the unique letter patterns in words is focusing on a particular combination and building as many words as you can from that base. This strategy can be used with myriad letters and patterns. For example, you can focus on the final consonant patterns *–ch* and *–tch* and work toward contrasting short-vowel and long-vowel patterns.

To do so, you will want to provide your child with words written on index cards that end with the final consonant sound *–ch* (giving him the example word *teach*) and *–tch* (giving him the example word *itch*). Using the example word to illustrate the orthographic pattern to focus on, ask your child to sort the remaining word cards into two piles, consistent with the spelling pattern in which it fits. In other words, have your child sort the words into the two columns, making note of the ending sound and its corresponding spelling.

Tea**ch**	I**tch**
Each	Match
Beach	Catch
Reach	Fetch
Speech	Stretch
Coach	Hatch
Pooch	Pitch

After sorting the words into two categories, perhaps you can try other patterns, such as the ending letters *–ck* (as in *tack* and *lick*) and *–ke* (as in *take* and *like*).

APPENDIX C

Print Your Own Sight Word Tiles!

Print these pages and cut the blocks apart for a quick and easy set of sight words! Arrange and rearrange them with your child to make words. Make sure to print more than one set so that you can use each word more than once as you play games such as those listed in Appendix D.

were	said	does	the
know	you	his	was
they	there	some	your
here	in	is	it
what	who	whose	would
any	give	off	only
have	four	where	though
through	from	come	been

Help Your Child Learn High-Frequency Words

There are many words in the English language that are written frequently and that children learn to recognize by sight in their early elementary school years. Some of these words are difficult to sound out because they do not follow regular spelling rules, and recognizing them by sight is the most efficient way to read these words. Have your child look over the list of high-frequency words in appendix C and begin by seeing which words he can read. You can cut out all of the words included in appendix C, or just write the words that he does not recognize on index cards. There are several simple games that can be played with these words, rather than just using them as flash cards. Once all of these words are mastered, you can create your own word tiles for other high-frequency words you come across while reading together. Here are some of the games that you can play to increase recognition of these words.

Bingo

Many common games can be turned into fun and informative ways for your child to identify words and recognize how they are spelled. In order to play this version of Bingo, cut out nine word cards and place them in a nine-square grid (three squares across, and three down). Using two different colored markers (coins, cereal Os or squares, or board game pieces can serve as markers), you can take turns each placing a marker on the board, while reading a word aloud. The first to get three in a row wins. In this playful way, your child will read these high-frequency words and begin to recognize their spelling multiple times without being drilled.

Example:

were	said	does
the	know	you
his	was	they

Concentration

Make a duplicate set of sight word cards and lay them in 12-square grid (3 squares across, and 4 down). Play Concentration by flipping over two word cards at a time to look for matches for the sight words.

Recommended Children's Books

The following lists of recommended children's books include many wonderful resources that can help you foster the specific reading skills we discussed in this book. We hope these lists help you identify many books that are appropriate for your developing reader. However, we want to make sure that you know that these lists are in no way meant to be exhaustive. There are so many excellent books that are out there for you to chose from, and more are published every day. Browsing through your local library or bookstore is one of the best ways for you to discover which books will most excite your child, and asking for specific recommendations from librarians and teachers can be a great way to select books at the right difficulty level for your child. There are many other books (like *A Parent's Guide to Reading with Your Young Child* by Susan Neuman, *What to Read When: The Books and Stories to Read with Your Child--and All the Best Times to Read Them* by Pam Allyn and *The Read-Aloud Handbook* by Jim Trelease) which provide much more comprehensive information to help you with book selection, and we would recommend that you refer to them for more support in this area. Included on the next few pages is just a small sample to get you started!

Chapter 1: The Role of Oral Language in Reading Development

Wordless Picture Books

These picture books use illustrations to reveal a clear storyline with little or no text. Through making sense of the stories depicted in wordless

A Ball for Daisy	Chris Raschka
Bow-Wow Bugs a Bug	Mark Newgarden & Megan Montague
Chicken and Cat	Sara Varon
Flotsam	David Wiesner
Goodnight, Gorilla	Peggy Rathman
Home	Jeannie Baker
Ice	Arthur Geisert
Oops!	Arthur Geisert
Peep!	Kevin Luthardt
Sea of Dreams	Dennis Nolan
The Boy, The Bear, The Baron, The Bard	Gregory Rogers
The Lion and the Mouse	Jerry Pinkney
The Red Book	Barbara Lehman
The Surprise	Sylvia Van Ommen
The Treasure Bath	Dan Andreasen
The Yellow Balloon	Charlotte Dematons
Wave	Suzy Lee
You Can't Take a Balloon into the Metropolitan Museum	Jacqueline Preiss Weitzman

picture books, children develop their oral narrative skills by following the sequence of events and becoming familiar with key story elements.

Songs, Poems, And Rhyming Books

These are books which allow children to focus on the sounds and rhythm, of the English language. By hearing poems read aloud and singing along with their favorite songs in print, children can begin to recognize the relationship between written and spoken language.

*Poetry for Young People (series) Includes Robert Frost, Emily Dickinson, and Langston Hughes	various authors by Sterling Children's Books
Baby Beluga: The Famous Raffi Songs, Learning Activities, Patterns, Props and Creative-play Ideas	Sherrill B. Flora & Val Larsen

Demolition	Sally Sutton
Goodnight, Goodnight Construction Site	Sherri Duskey Rinker
I Know a Lot!	Stephen Krensky
I Spy Little Letters (and other books from the *I Spy* series)	Jean Marzollo
Joyful Noise: Poems for Two Voices	Paul Fleischman
My Very First Mother Goose	Lona Opie
Nursery Rhymes	Kate Toms
One, Two Buckle my Shoe	Salina Yoon
Over in the Meadow	John Langstaff
Switching on the Moon: A Very First Book of Bedtime Poems	Jane Yolen & Andrew Fusek Peters (Eds.)
The Random House Book of Poetry for Young Children	Jack Prelutsky & Arnold Lobel (Eds.)
We Are Going on a Bear Hunt	Helen Oxenbury

Idioms

These are books that teach children about the concept of idioms. An idiom or idiomatic expression has a special meaning, which is different from the literal interpretation, and these playful books provide great examples of how we use idioms in daily life.

A Little Pigeon Toad	Fred Gwynne
Amelia Bedelia	Peggy Parish
Butterflies in My Stomach and Other School Hazards	Serge Bloch
In a Pickle: And Other Funny Idioms	Marvin Terban
Raining Cats and Dogs: A Collection of Irresistible Idioms and Illustrations to Tickle the Funny Bones of Young People	Will Moses
There's a Frog in my Throat!	Loreen Leedy & Pat Street

Chapter 2: Emergent Literacy

Books To Support Phonological Awareness

These are books that incorporate word play that allows children to explore and understand the ways spoken language can be manipulated. They support the development of phonological awareness.

Amelia Bedelia	Peggy Parish
Bark, George!	Jules Feiffer
Chugga Chugga Choo Choo	Kevin Lewis
Clip-Clop	Nicola Smee
Flip, Flap, Fly!: A Book for Babies Everywhere	Phyllis Root
Giraffes Can't Dance	Giles Andreae
Green Eggs and Ham	Dr. Seuss
Henny Penny	Paul Galdone
I Love You, Good Night	Jon Buller
Is Your Mama a Llama?	Deborah Guarino
Jamberry	Bruce Degen
Madeline	Ludwig Bemelmans
Moo, Baa, La La La!	Sandra Boynton
Rhyming Dust Bunnies	Jan Thomas
Sheep in a Jeep	Nancy E. Shaw
Sheep on a Ship	Nancy E. Shaw
Silly Sally	Audrey Wood
The Berenstain's B Book	Stan & Jan Berenstain
The Cow Loves Cookies	Karma Wilson
Where Is the Green Sheep?	Mem Fox

Abc Books

These are books that emphasize developing knowledge of letter name and their corresponding sounds in the English language.

AlphaOops!: The Day Z Went First	Alethea Kontis
Animalia	Graeme Base
B Is for Bulldozer: A Construction ABC	June Sobel
Chicka Chicka Boom Boom	Bill Martin, Jr. and John Archambault
Click, Clack, Quackity-Quack: An Alphabetical Adventure	Doreen Cronin
Dr. Seuss's ABC	Dr. Seuss
Eric Carle's ABC	Eric Carle
Flora McDonnell's ABC	Flora McDonnell
The Hidden Alphabet	Laura Voccaro Seeger
Z Is for Moose	Kelly Bingham

Decodable Books

These are books that contain words that are easily sounded out by children, based on their early grasp of letter–sound relationships. Many decodable books include words that children often are able to sound out at a young age while also maintaining an entertaining storyline.

And to Think That I Saw It on Mulberry Street	Dr. Seuss
Bob Books	Lynn Maslen
Decodable Little Books	Chrisitine McCormick
Green Eggs and Ham	Dr. Seuss
Hot Rods (Phonics Practice Readers)	Janis Asad Raabe
Playful Pals (Set)	Nora Gaydos
Primary Phonics (Set)	Barbara Makar
The Cat in the Hat	Dr. Seuss

Print Salient Books

These are books that have just a few words on each page, and allow your child to focus on the print itself. The page may have an embedded picture to support the text, but by making the words very obvious, books like these support children's growing awareness of a word as a single unit in text.

A Frog in the Bog	Karma Wilson & Joan Rankin
Big Dog . . . Little Dog	Philip D. Eastman
Hop on Pop	Dr. Seuss
Is it Big or is it Little?	Claudia Rueda
Knuffle Bunny Too: A Case of Mistaken Identity	Mo Wilems
Pigeon Finds a Hot Dog!	Mo Wilems
Polar Bear Morning.	Lauren Thompson
Pomelo's Opposites	Ramona Badescu
Punctuation Takes a Vacation	Robin Pulver
Rocket's Mighty Words	Tad Hills
Tails Chasing Tails	Matthew Porter
The Monster at the End of this Book	Jon. Stone
Where Is Spot?	Eric Hill
Who's Hiding	Sebastien Braun
Wild About Books	Judy Sierra

Chapter 3: Learning to Write

Books for Writing

These are books in which characters engage in writing activities, and provide examples for your child of how writing can be useful and fun.

A Book of Letters	Ken Wilson-Max
A Nap in a Lap	Sarah Wilson
Beatrice Spells Some Lulus and Learns to Write a Letter	Cari Best
Click, Clack, Moo: Cows That Type	Doreen Cronin
Dear Miss LaRue	Mark Teague
Dear Tyrannosaurus Rex	Lisa McClatchy
Desperate Dog Writes Again	Eileen Christelow
Diary of a Spider	Doreen Cronin
Diary of a Wombat	Jackie French
Dumpy LaRue	Elizabeth Winthrop
From Pictures to Words: A Book About Making a Book	Janet Stevens
Jolly Postman	Janet Ahlberg
Kids Are Authors: A Band of Coyotes	Scholastic Books
Kindergarten Diary	Antoinette Portis
Memoirs of a Goldfish	Devin Scillian
Messages in the Mailbox: How to Write a Letter	Loreen Leedy
Miss Alaineus: A Vocabulary Disaster	Debra Fraiser
My Grandma Lived in Gooligulch	Graeme Base
Nothing Ever Happens On 90th Street	Ronnie Schotter
Nouns and Verbs Have a Field Day	Robin Pulver
Rocket Writes a Story	Tad Hills
Thank You, Miss Doover	Robin Pulver
T. F. Letters	Karen Ray
The Important Book	Margaret Wise Brown
The Noisy Book	Margaret Wise Brown
Time For Bed	Mem Fox
What Do Authors Do?	Eileen Christelow
Written Anything Good Lately?	Susan Allen & Jane Lindaman

Books To Teach Writing

These are books that emphasize specific aspects of written language, helping children recognize parts of speech, understand when to use punctuation marks, and develop a voice as a writer.

A Dictionary of Homophones	Leslie Presson
Best Word Book Ever	Richard Scarry
Checking Your Grammar	Marvin Terban
Dictionary of Idioms	Marvin Terban
Eight Ate: A Feast of Homonym Riddles	Leslie Presson
Punctuation Power	Marvin Terban
Punctuation Takes a Vacation	Robin Pulver
Rip the Page!: Adventures in Creative Writing	Karen Benke
Scholastic Children's Dictionary	Scholastic, Inc.
The Amazing Pop-up Grammar Book	Jennie Maizels and Kate Petty
The Journey of English	Donna Brook
The Scholastic Dictionary of Spelling	Marvin Terban
Time to Rhyme	Marvin Terban
To Root, To Toot, To Parachute: What is a Verb? and other books from the *Words are Categorical* series	Brian Cleary
What in the World Is a Homophone?	Leslie Presson
Write Away: A Handbook for Young Writers and Learners	Dave Kemper, Ruth Nathan, and Patrick Sebranek

Chapter 4: Story Comprehension

Books That Utilize Background Knowledge

These are books that allow children to draw upon their own experiences to facilitate comprehension of stories. By describing situations that are familiar to most children, these books make it simple to prompt children to use their relevant prior knowledge before, during, and after reading in order to develop a simple story schema.

Before I Was Born	Harriet Ziefert
Birthday Presents	Cynthia Rylant
Flying Solo	Ralph Fletcher
Hey Daddy: Animal Fathers and Their Babies	Mary Batten & Higgins Bond
Hooway for Wodney Wat	Helen Lester
Ira Sleeps Over	Bernard Waber
Julius, the Baby of the World	Kevin Henkes
Listen Buddy	Helen Lester
Some Things are Scary	Florence Parry Heide

Inferential Thinking

These are books that present the reader with frequent opportunities to draw inferences. In these books, readers are often provided information by the author that is not "on the page." Inferring is a strategy that requires the reader to predict upcoming events in a story, empathize with characters' feelings, or draw conclusions.

Anna Banana and Me	Erik Lenore Blegvad
Anno's Hat Tricks	Akihiro Nozaki & Mitsumasa Anno
Cloudy With a Chance of Meatballs	Judi Barrett
Do You Know Which Ones Will Grow?	Susan A. Shea
Frog & Toad Are Friends	Arnold Lobel
Good Dog Carl	Alexandra Day
Hattie and the Fox	Mem Fox
Teammates	Peter Golenbock
Tuesday	David Weisner

Causal Reasoning

These are books in which children are given frequent opportunities to understand the relationship between cause and effect; to find meaningful, cohesive order in events; and to help predict what is going to happen next in a story.

Comet's Nine Lives	Jan Brett
Don't Slam the Door	Dori Chaconas
If You Give a Mouse a Cookie	Laura Numeroff
Jimmy's Boa and the Big Birthday Bash	Trinka Hakes Noble
That's Good, That's Bad	Margery Cuyler
The Giving Tree	Shel Silverstein
The Runaway Bunny	Margaret Wise Brown
The Stray Dog	Marc Simont

Visualizing

These are books in which children can incorporate the skills of visualizing, or creating a mental movie while reading text. Mental imagery is a critical component to understanding and remembering what is read. Through these stories, children can become more involved in the text and attempt to visualize, making the story come to life.

Barn Dance!	Bill Martin
Fireflies	Julie Brinklow
Harold and the Purple Crayon	Crockett Johnson
Miss Rumphius	Barbara Cooney
Night in the Country	Cynthia Rylant
The Lotus Seed	Sherry Garland
The Seashore Book	Charlotte Zolotow
The Stories Julian Tells	Ann Cameron
Time for Bed	Mem Fox
When I Was Young in the Mountains	Cynthia Rylant

Predicting

These books allow children to learn the power of prediction through engaging with the text and monitoring their understanding of what might happen next. These books can engage the inquisitive reader as they attempt to accurately predict the next steps while learning to modify their predictions along the way.

Are You My Mother?	P. D. Eastman
Bark, George	Jules Feiffer
Click, Clack, Moo: Cows That Type	Doreen Cronin
Dear Miss LaRue: Letters from Obedience School	Mark Teague
Mr. Grumpy's Outing	John Burningham
The Enormous Crocodile	Roald Dahl
Who Took the Farmer's Hat?	Joan L. Nodset

Questioning

All of these stories focus on aspects of questioning, so that children can learn to clarify meaning and focus on important components of the text. These books will help children read with purpose, as they attempt to find the answers to thought-provoking questions.

Big Al	Andrew Clements
Charlie Anderson	Barbara Abercrombie
Fly Away Home	Eve Bunting
May I Bring a Friend?	Beatrice Schenk deReginiers
The Sick Day	Patricia MacLachlan
The Stranger	Chris Van Allsburg
The Wednesday Surprise	Eve Bunting

Books That Faciliate Narrative Retelling And Summarizing

These are books with simple themes and repetitive language that makes it easy for children to retell and summarize the stories they read and hear. By retelling and summarizing, they can extract important ideas from what they have read, while coming to understand the text more deeply.

Koala Lou	Mem Fox
Sylvester and the Magic Pebble	William Steig
The Napping House	Audrey & Don Wood
The Snowy Day	Erza Jack Keats
The Tiny Seed	Eric Carle
The Very Hungry Caterpillar	Eric Carle
Where the Wild Things Are	Maurice Sendak

Synthesizing

These are books in which children can utilize the strategy of synthesizing. This strategy is one of the most sophisticated comprehension strategies because it requires the reader to bring new information and his or her own experiences together to reach a deeper understanding of the story or text. All of these books require the reader to employ techniques such as questioning, inferring, and causal reasoning to more deeply understand the text.

Annie and the Wild Animals	Jan Brett
A Rainbow of My Own	Don Freeman
Cookie's Week	Cindy Ward
Don't Let the Pigeon Drive the Bus!	Mo Willlems
Fireflies in the Night	Judy Hawes
Leo the Late Bloomer	Robert Kraus
Meanwhile...	Jules Feiffer
The Mitten	Jan Brett
Rachel's Journal	Marissa Moss
Shortcut	David Macaulay
The Widow's Broom	Chris Van Allsburg
Two Bad Ants	Chris Van Allsburg

Chapter 5: The Effects of Reading Volume

In the chapter on reading volume, we discuss the importance of selecting books focused on topics that are highly interesting to your child. However, it is very difficult to create a recommended list of interest-based books because these suggestions need to be tailored so specifically to you and your emerging reader, and are therefore beyond the scope of recommendations we can provide here. These types of books are best discovered by taking the opportunity to browse in a library or bookstore at a leisurely rate and seeing which books spark your child's interest. Although it is beyond the scope of this book to recommend books for strengthening background knowledge, two resources for parents are E. D. Hirsch's Core Knowledge Grader Series *and* The New Dictionary of Cultural Literacy, 3rd Edition.

Books To Support Vocabulary Development

These are books that include rare or sophisticated words that we do not commonly use in everyday conversations. They contain words like *perplexed, route,* and *creatures,* vocabulary essential for comprehending text in school. There are so many wonderful books that include sophisticated language, so do not limit yourself to this or any list! In general, written materials expose children to words they would not learn otherwise.

A Visitor for Bear	Bonny Becker
Alexander and the Terrible, Horrible, No Good, Very Bad Day	Judith Viorst
Chrysanthemum	Kevin Henkes
Corduroy	Don Freeman
Fancy Nancy	Jane O'Connor
Grandfather's Journey	Allen Say
James and the Giant Peach	Roald Dahl
One Grain of Rice: A Mathematical Folktale	Demi
Magic Tree House Boxed Set	Mary Pope Osborne
Stellaluna	Janelle Cannon
Sylvester and the Magic Pebble	Willliam Steig

Chapter 6: The Social and Emotional Benefits of Reading Together

These are books in which characters make friends, experience varied emotions, and experience changes in their home life or the world around them. These books help to provide perspective on emotional experiences that your child may have; they give you the opportunity to discuss these events in a neutral way with your child as well as provide answers to questions they may have as well as share information about the topic. By reading and discussing the experiences of the characters in these books, your child has a chance to share his or her own experiences, develop strategies for coping with such situations, and foster empathy for others who may be experiencing similar events.

Books That Support Perspective-Taking

These are books that help children think about events from the perspective of others, and sensitize them to the many differences among individuals.

A Rainbow of Friends	P. K. Hallinan
Don't Call Me Special: A First Look at Disability	Pat Thomas
Honestly, Red Riding Hood Was Rotten	Trisha Speed Shaskan
Leo the Late Bloomer	Robert Kraus
The True Story of the Three Little Pigs	Jon Scieszka

Books That Discuss Friendship or Relationship Conflict

These are books in which children learn about developing and maintaining friendships, strategies for conflict resolution and anger management, and how to contend with bullies.

A Visitor for Bear	Bonny Becker
Arthur's April Fool	Marc Brown
Bad Apple: A Tale of Friendship	Edward Hemingway
Bullies Never Win	Margery Cuyler
Bully	Patricia Polacco
Elmer	David McKee
Flabbersmashed About You	Rachel Vail
Help!: A Story of Friendship	Holly Keller
Here's to You, Rachel Robinson	July Blume
Horace and Morris Join the Chorus (But What about Dolores?)	James Howe
Hurty Feelings	Helen Lester
I Am Not Sleepy and I Will Not Go to Bed	Lauren Child
Jake Drake, Bully Buster	Andrew Clements
Shredderman	Wendelin Van Draanen
The Juice Box Bully: Empowering Kids to Stand up for Others	Bob Sornson and Maria Dismondy
The Moon Bridge	Marcia Savin
Walk Two Moons	Sharon Creech

Books That Discuss New Events and Life Transitions

These are books in which children share their feelings about upcoming life events, such as becoming an older sibling, going to school for the first time, or having parents separate. Children's reactions range from excitement to sadness and worry, and these books help the reader recognize that such reactions are normal. Throughout the stories, other characters help children develop effective ways of coping with life transitions and provide answers to important questions, helping young readers to be resilient in the face of these big changes.

| Brand-New Pencils, Brand-New Books | Diane deGroat |
| Bunny Bungalow | Cynthia Rylant |

Dinosaur's Divorce	L. Brown & M. Brown
I Am Too Absolutely Small for School	Lauren Child
I'm a Big Brother	Joanna Cole
I'm a Big Sister	Joanna Cole
Mama and Daddy Bear's Divorce	Cornelia Maude Spelman
My Brave Year of Firsts: Tries, Sighs, and High Fives	Jamie Lee Curtis & Laura Cornell
One Special Day (A Story for Big Brothers and Sisters)	Lola M. Schaefer
Samuel's Baby	Mark Elkin
Sarah, Plain and Tall	Patricia MacLachlan
Spot's Baby Sister	Eric Hill
The Last Day of Kindergarten	Nancy Loewen
Wemberly Worried	Kevin Henkes
When My Parents Forgot How to Be Friends	J. Moore-Malinos

Books That Discuss Emotions:

These are books that focus on the common emotions that people feel, including happiness, sadness or grumpiness, fear, and anger. Several of these books focus on the identification of emotions, while the more sophisticated books focus on how characters learn to cope with and regulate their feelings.

Alexander and the Terrible, Horrible, No Good, Very Bad Day	Judith Viorst
Don't Worry Bear	Greg Foley
Happy	Mies Van Hout
Lizzy's Ups and Downs	Jessica Harper
Mean Soup	Betsy Everitt
My Many Colored Days	Dr. Seuss
On Monday When It Rained	Cherryl Kachenmeiste

Sometimes I'm Bombaloo	Rachel Vail
The Dark	Lemony Snicket
The Dark, Dark Night	M. Christina Butler
The Feelings Book	Todd Parr
The Grouchies	Debbie Wagenbach
The Way I Feel	Janan Cain
There's a Nightmare in My Closet	Mercer Mayer
Today I Feel Silly: And Other Moods That Make My Day	Jamie Lee Curtis & Laura Cornell
When I Feel Scared (and other books from *The Way I Feel* series)	Cornelia Maude Spelman
When Sophie Gets Angry—Really, Really Angry	Molly Bang
Where the Wild Things Are	Maurice Sendak

Books That Discuss Loss

These are books in which characters experience the loss of pets, friends, and extended family members. In these stories, characters learn to understand death and cope with feelings of grief and loss. Some books focus on a particular character's story, while others provide more general information about what happens when people or animals pass away. *These books provide general information about losses that children commonly experience or include stories about characters who experience these common losses. If your family experiences a particularly sudden or traumatic loss, or the loss of an immediate family member, please seek out other resources to ensure that your child gets the appropriate information and support.*

A Gift for Tia Rosa	Karen Taha
A Terrible Thing Happened	Margaret Holmes
Always and Forever	Alan Durant
Blackberries in the Dark	Mavis Jukes
Bridge to Terabithia	Katherine Paterson

I Miss You—A First Look at Death	P. Thomas
Nana Upstairs and Nana Downstairs	Tomie dePaolo
Saying Goodbye	Jim Boulden
Tear Soup	Pat Schwiebert
The Invisible String	Patrice Karst
The Saddest Time	Norma Simon
The Tenth Good Thing About Barney	Judith Viorst
When Dinosaurs Die	Laurie Krasny Brown

All the Books We've Mentioned

Abercrombie, Barbara, & Mark Graham. *Charlie Anderson*. New York: M.K. McElderry, 1990. Print.

Ahlberg, Janet, & Allan Ahlberg. *The Jolly Postman, Or, Other People's Letters*. Boston: Little, Brown, 1986. Print.

Allen, Susan, Jane Lindaman, & Vicky Enright. *Written Anything Good Lately?* Minneapolis, MN: Millbrook, 2006. Print.

Andreae, Giles, & Guy Parker-Rees. *Giraffes Can't Dance*. New York: Orchard, 2001. Print.

Andreasen, Dan. *The Treasure Bath*. New York: Henry Holt, 2009. Print.

Badescu, Ramona. *Pomelo's Opposites*. New York: Enchanted Lion Books, 2013. Print.

Baker, Jeannie. *Home*. New York: Greenwillow, 2004. Print.

Bang, Molly. *When Sophie Gets Angry: Really, Really Angry*. New York: Scholastic, 2004. Print.

Barrett, Judi, & Ron Barrett. *Cloudy with a Chance of Meatballs*. New York: Atheneum, 1988. Print.

Base, Graeme. *Animalia*. London: HN Abrams, 1987. Print

Base, Graeme. *My Grandma Lived in Gooligulch*. New York: Abrams, 1990. Print

Batten, Mary, & Higgins Bond. *Hey, Daddy!: Animal Fathers and Their Babies*. Atlanta: Peachtree, 2002. Print.

Becker, Bonny. *A Visitor for Bear*. Cambridge: Candlewick Press, 2008. Print.

Bemelmans, Ludwig. *Madeline*. New York: Viking, 1967. Print.

Benke, Karen. *Rip the Page!: Adventures in Creative Writing*. Boston: Trumpeter, 2010. Print.

Berenstain, Stan, & Jan Berenstain. *The Berenstains' B Book.* New York: Random House, 1971. Print.

Best, Cari, & Giselle Potter. *Beatrice Spells Some Lulus and Learns to Write a Letter.* New York: Margaret Ferguson, 2013. Print.

Bingham, Kelly L., & Paul O. Zelinsky. *Z Is for Moose.* New York: Greenwillow, 2012. Print.

Blegvad, Lenore, & Erik Blegvad. *Anna Banana and Me.* New York: Atheneum, 1985. Print.

Bloch, Serge. *Butterflies in My Stomach and Other School Hazards.* New York: Sterling, 2008. Print.

Blume, Judy. *Here's to You, Rachel Robinson.* New York: Orchard, 1993. Print.

Boynton, Sandra. *Moo, Baa, La La La!* New York: Little Simon, 1995. Print.

Braun, Sebastien. *Who's Hiding.* New York: Candlewick Press, 2013. Print.

Brett, Jan. *Annie and the Wild Animals.* Boston: Houghton Mifflin, 1985. Print.

Brett, Jan. *Comet's Nine Lives.* New York: Putnam, 1996. Print.

Brett, Jan. *The Mitten.* New York: Simon & Schuster, 1990. Print.

Brinckloe, Julie. *Fireflies!: Story and Pictures.* New York: Aladdin, 1986. Print

Brook, Donna. *The Journey of English.* New York: Clarion Books. 1998. Print.

Brown, L., & Brown, M. *Dinosaur's Divorce.* New York: Little, Brown, 1988.

Brown, L., & Brown, M. *When Dinosaurs Die.* Canada: Little, Brown and Company, 1996. Print.

Brown, Marc Tolon. *Arthur's April Fool.* Little Rock. Arkansas: Little, Brown Books for Young, 1995. Print.

Brown, Margaret Wise, & Clement Hurd. *The Runaway Bunny.* New York: Harper & Row, 1972. Print.

Brown, Margaret Wise, & Leonard Weisgard. *Noisy Book.* New York: Harper & Row, 1939. Print.

Brown, Margaret Wise, & Leonard Weisgard. *The Important Book.* New York: Harper, 1949. Print.

Buller, Jon, Susan Schade, & Bernadette Pons. *I Love You, Good Night.* New York: Little Simon, 2006. Print.

Bunting, E. *How Many Days to America?: A Thanksgiving Story.* New York: Houghton Mifflin Company, 1990.

Bunting, Eve, & Donald Carrick. *The Wednesday Surprise.* New York: Clarion, 1989. Print.

Bunting, Eve, & Ronald Himler. *Fly Away Home.* New York: Clarion, 1991. Print.

Burningham, John. *Mr Grumpy's Outing.* London: Red Fox, 2001. Print.

Butler, M. Christina. *The Dark, Dark Night.* London: Magi Publications, 2008. Print.

Cain, J. *The Way I Feel.* Seattle, WA: Parenting Press Inc, 2004. Print.

Cameron, Ann, & Ann Strugnell. *The Stories Julian Tells.* New York: Pantheon, 1981. Print.

Cannon, Janelle. *Stellaluna.* Orlando, FL: Harcourt Brace & Company. 1993. Print.

Carle, Eric. *Eric Carle's ABC*. New York: Grossett & Dunlap, 2007. Print.

Carle, Eric. *The Tiny Seed*. Natick, MA: Picture Book Studio, 1987. Print.

Carle, Eric. *The Very Hungry Caterpillar*. New York: Philomel, 1987. Print.

Chaconas, Dori, & Will Hillenbrand. *Don't Slam the Door!* Somerville, MA: Candlewick, 2010. Print.

Child, Lauren. *I Am Not Sleepy and I Will Not Go to Bed*. Cambridge, MA: Candlewick, 2001. Print.

Child, Lauren. *I Am Too Absolutely Small for School: Featuring Charlie and Lola*. London: Orchard, 2003. Print.

Christelow, Eileen. *The Desperate Dog Writes Again*. Boston: Clarion, 2010. Print.

Christelow, Eileen. *What Do Authors Do?* New York: Clarion, 1995. Print.

Cleary, Brian P., & Jenya Prosmitsky. *To Root, to Toot, to Parachute: What Is a Verb?* Minneapolis, MN: Carolrhoda, 2001. Print.

Clements, Andrew, & Yoshi. *Big Al*. Saxonville, MA: Picture Book Studio, 1988. Print.

Clements, Andrew. *Jake Drake, Bully Buster*. New York: Athenum Books for Young Readers, 2007. Print.

Cole, Joanna, & Maxie Chambliss. *I'm a Big Brother*. New York: Morrow Junior, 1997.

Cole, Joanna, & Maxie Chambliss. *I'm a Big Sister*. New York: Morrow Junior, 1997. Print.

Cooney, Barbara. *Miss Rumphius*. New York: Viking, 1982. Print.

Creech, Sharon. *Walk Two Moons*. New York: HarperTeen, 2003. Print.

Crews, Donald. *Shortcut*. New York: Greenwillow, 1992. Print.

Cronin, Doreen, & Betsy Lewin. *Click Clack, Quackity-quack: An Alphabet Adventure*. New York: Atheneum for Young Readers, 2006. Print.

Cronin, Doreen, & Betsy Lewin. *Click, Clack, Moo: Cows That Type*. New York: Simon & Schuster for Young Readers, 2000. Print.

Cronin, Doreen. *Diary of a Spider*. New York: HarperCollins, 2005. Print.

Curtis, Jamie Lee, & Laura Cornell. *My Brave Year of Firsts: Tries, Sighs, and High Fives*. New York: Joanna Cotler, 2012. Print.

Curtis, Jamie Lee, & Laura Cornell. *Today I Feel Silly & Other Moods That Make My Day*. New York: HarperCollins, 1998. Print.

Cuyler, Margery, & David Catrow. *That's Good! That's Bad!* New York: H. Holt, 1991. Print.

Cuyler, Margery. *Bullies Never Win*. New York: Simon & Schuster Books for YoungReaders, 2009. Print.

Dahl, Roald, & Quentin Blake. *The Enormous Crocodile*. New York: Knopf, 1978. Print.

Dahl, Roald. *James and the Giant Peach: A Children's Story*. New York: Knopf, 1961. Print.

Day, Alexandra. *Good Dog Carl*. New York: Simon & Schuster. 1986. Print.

De, Regniers Beatrice Schenk, & Beni Montresor. *May I Bring a Friend?* New York: Atheneum, 1964. Print.

Degen, Bruce. *Jamberry*. New York: HarperCollins, 2000. Print.

deGroat, Diane. *Brand-new Pencils, Brand-new Books*. New York: HarperCollins, 2005. Print.

Dematons, Charlotte. *The Yellow Balloon*. Asheville, NC: Front Street/Lemniscaat, 2003. Print.

Demi. *One Grain of Rice: A Mathematical Folktale*. New York: Scholastic Press, 1997. Print.

dePaola, Tomie. *Nana Upstairs & Nana Downstairs*. New York: Penguin Books, 1973. Print

Dr. Seuss. *My Many Colored Days*. New York: Alfred A. Knopf, 1996. Print.

Durant, Alan. *Always and Forever*. New York: Harcourt, 2003. Print.

Eastman, Philip D. *Big Dog…Little Dog*. New York: Random House Books for Young Readers, 2010. Print.

Eastman, Philip. D. *Are You My Mother?* New York: Beginner, Distributed by Random House, 1960. Print.

Elkin, Mark. *Samuel's Baby*. Berkeley: Tricycle Pree, 2010. Print.

Elliott, David, & Randy Cecil. *And Here's to You!* Cambridge, MA: Candlewick, 2004. Print.

Emberley, Ed, & Anne Miranda. *Glad Monster, Sad Monster: A Book about Feelings*. Boston: Little, Brown, 1997. Print.

Everitt, Betsy. *Mean Soup*. Orlando, FL: Voyager Books, 1992. Print.

Feiffer, Jules. *Bark, George*. New York: HarperCollins, 1999. Print.

Feiffer, Jules. *Meanwhile--*. New York: HarperCollins, 1997. Print.

Fleischman, Paul, & Eric Beddows. *Joyful Noise: Poems for Two Voices*. New York: Harper & Row, 1988. Print.

Fletcher, Ralph J. *Flying Solo*. New York: Clarion, 1998. Print.

Flora, Sherrill B., & Val Larsen. *Baby Beluga: The Famous Raffi Songs, Learning Activities, Patterns, Props and Creative-play Ideas*. Grand Rapids, MI: Instructional Fair, TS Denison, 1997. Print.

Foley, Greg. *Don't Worry Bear*. New York: Penguin Group, 2008. Print.

Fox, Mem, & Jane Dyer. *Time for Bed*. San Diego: Harcourt Brace Jovanovich, 1993. Print.

Fox, Mem, & Judy Horacek. *Where Is the Green Sheep?* Orlando, FL: Harcourt, 2004. Print.

Fox, Mem, & Pamela Lofts. *Koala Lou*. San Diego: Harcourt Brace Jovanovich, 1989. Print.

Fox, Mem, & Patricia Mullins. *Hattie and the Fox*. New York: Bradbury, 1987. Print.

Frasier, Debra. *Miss Alaineus: A Vocabulary Disaster*. San Diego: Harcourt Brace, 2000. Print.

Freeman, Don. *A Rainbow of My Own*. New York: Viking, 1966. Print.

Freeman, Don. *Corduroy*. New York: Viking, 1968. Print.

French, Jackie, & Bruce Whatley. *Diary of a Wombat*. New York: Clarion, 2003. Print.

Galdone, Paul. *Henny Penny*. New York: Seabury, 1968. Print.

Garland, Sherry, & Tatsuro Kiuchi. *The Lotus Seed*. San Diego: Harcourt Brace Jovanovich, 1993. Print.

Gaydos, Nora, & B. B. Sams. *Playful Pals*. Norwalk, CT: Innovative Kids, 2003. Print.

Geisert, Arthur. *Ice*. Brooklyn, NY: Enchanted Lion, 2011. Print.

Geisert, Arthur. *Oops*. Boston: Houghton Mifflin, 2006. Print.

Golenbock, Peter, & Paul Bacon. *Teammates*. San Diego: Harcourt Brace Jovanovich, 1990. Print.

Guarino, Deborah. *Is Your Mama a Llama?* New York: Scholastic, 1991. Print.

Gwynne, Fred. *A Little Pigeon Toad*. New York: Aladdin, 1988. Print.

Hallinan, P. K. *A Rainbow of Friends*. Canada: Ideals Children's Books, 2006. Print.

Harper, Jessica. *Lizzy's Ups and Downs: Not an Ordinary School Day*. China: Harper.

Hawes, Judy, & Ellen Alexander. *Fireflies in the Night*. New York: HarperCollins, 1991. Print.

Heide, Florence Parry, & Jules Feiffer. *Some Things Are Scary*. Cambridge, MA: Candlewick, 2000. Print.

Hemingway, Edward. *Bad Apple: A Tale of Friendship*. New York: Penguin Group, 2012. Print.

Henkes, Kevin. *Chrysanthemum*. New York: Greenwillow, 1991. Print.

Henkes, Kevin. *Julius, the Baby of the World*. New York: Greenwillow, 1990. Print.

Herman, Gail, Lisa McCue, & Aesop. *The Lion and the Mouse*. New York: Random House, 1998. Print.

Hill, Eric. *Spot's Baby Sister*. New York: Putnam, 1989. Print.

Hill, Eric. *Where Is Spot?* New York: Putnam, 1980. Print.

Hills, Tad. *Rocket Writes a Story*. New York: Schwartz & Wade, 2012. Print.

Hills, Tad. *Rocket's Mighty Words*. New York: Schwartz & Wade Books, 2013. Print.

Holmes, Margaret. *A Terrible Think Happened—A Story for Children Who Have Witnessed Violence or Trauma*. Washington, DC: Magination Press, 2000. Print.

Howe, James, & Amy Walrod. *Horace and Morris but Mostly Dolores*. New York: Atheneum for Young Readers, 1999. Print.

Howe, James, & Amy Walrod. *Horace and Morris Join the Chorus: (But What about Dolores?)*. New York: Atheneum for Young Readers, 2005. Print.

Hutchins, Pat. *Llaman a La Puerta*. New York: Mulberry, 1994. Print.

Johnson, Crockett. *Harold and the Purple Crayon*. New York: HarperCollins, 1955. Print.

Jukes, Mavis. *Blackberries in the Dark*. Jukes, Mavis. New York: Random House, 1985. Print.

Kachenmeiste, Cherryl. *On Monday When it Rained*. New York: Houghton Mifflin. 2001. Print.

Karst, Patrice, & Geoff Stevenson. *The Invisible String*. Marina Del Rey, CA: DeVorss Publications, 2000. Print.

Keller, Holly. *Help!: A Story of Friendship*. New York: HarperCollins, 2007. Print.

Kemper, Dave, Nathan, Ruth, & Patrick Sebranek. *Write Away: A Handbook for Young Writers and Learners*. New York: Great Source/Houghton Mifflin. 2001. Print.

Kontis, Alethea, & Bob Kolar. *AlphaOops!: The Day Z Went First*. Somerville, MA: Candlewick, 2006. Print.

Kraus, Robert, & José Aruego. *Leo the Late Bloomer*. New York: Windmill, 1971. Print.

Krensky, Stephen. *I Know a Lot!* New York: Abrams Appleseed, 2013. Print.

Langstaff, John, & Marshall Woodbridge. *Over in the Meadow*. New York: Harcourt, Brace, 1957. Print.

Lee, Suzy. *Wave*. San Francisco: Chronicle, 2008. Print.

Leedy, Loreen, & Pat Street. *There's a Frog in My Throat!: 440 Animal Sayings a Little Bird Told Me*. New York: Holiday House, 2003. Print.

Leedy, Loreen. *Messages in the Mailbox: How to Write a Letter*. New York: Holiday House, 1994. Print.

Lehman, Barbara. *The Red Book*. Boston: Houghton Mifflin, 2004. Print.

Lester, Helen, & Lynn Munsinger. *Hooway for Wodney Wat*. Boston: Houghton Mifflin, 1999. Print.

Lester, Helen, & Lynn Munsinger. *Listen, Buddy*. Boston: Houghton Mifflin, 1995. Print.

Lester, Helen. *Hurty Feelings*. New York: Houghton Mifflin, 2004. Print.

Levi, Dorothy Hoffman, & Ethel Gold. *A Very Special Friend*. Washington, DC: Kendall Green, 1989. Print.

Lewis, Kevin. *Chugga Chugga Choo Choo*. New York: Hyperion, 1999. Print.

Lobel, Arnold. *Frog and Toad Are Friends*. New York: HarperCollins, 1979. Print.

Loewen, Nancy. *The Last Day of Kindergarten*. New York: Marshall Cavendish, 2011. Print.

Luthardt, Kevin. *Peep!* Atlanta: Peachtree, 2003. Print.

Lyons, D. *The Tree*. Bellevue, WA: Illumination Arts Publishing Company, 2002.

MacLachlan, Patricia, & Jane Dyer. *The Sick Day*. New York: Random House Children's, 2001. Print.

MacLachlan, Patricia. *Sarah, Plain and Tall*. New York: HarperCollins, 1985. Print.

Makar, Barbara W. *Primary Phonics*. Cambridge, MA: Educators Publishing Service, 1996. Print.

Martin, Bill, John Archambault, & Lois Ehlert. *Chicka Chicka Boom Boom*. New York: Simon & Schuster, 1989. Print.

Martin, Bill, John Archambault, & Ted Rand. *Barn Dance!* New York: Henry Holt, 1986. Print.

Marzollo, Jean. *I Spy Little Letters*. New York: Scholastic, 2000. Print.

Maslen, Bobby Lynn., & John R. Maslen. *Bob Books*. New York: Scholastic, 1987. Print.

Mayer, Mercer. *There's a Nightmare in My Closet*. New York: Dial, 1968. Print.

McClatchy, Lisa, & John Manders. *Dear Tyrannosaurus Rex*. New York: Random House, 2010. Print.

McCormick, Christine E., & Jill Dubin. *Decodable Little Books: 20 Reproducible Little Books for Short Vowel Sounds*. Parsippany, NJ: Good Year, 2000. Print.

McDonnell, Flora. *Flora McDonnell's ABC*. Cambridge, MA: Candlewick Press, 1997. Print.

McKee, David. *Elmer*. New York: Lothrop, Lee & Shepard, 1989. Print.

Moore-Malinos, J. *When My Parents Forgot How to Be Friends*. New York: Barron's Educational Series, 2005. Print.

Moses, Will. *Raining Cats & Dogs*. New York: Philomel, 2008. Print.

Moss, Marissa. *Amelia's Notebook*. Berkeley: Tricycle, 1995. Print.

Moss, Marissa. *Rachel's Journal: The Story of a Pioneer Girl*. San Diego: Harcourt Brace, 1998. Print.

Newgarden, Mark, & Megan Montague. Cash. *Bow-Wow Bugs a Bug*. Orlando, FL: Harcourt, 2007. Print.

Noble, Trinka Hakes., & Steven Kellogg. *Jimmy's Boa and the Big Splash Birthday Bash*. New York: Dial for Young Readers, 1989. Print.

Nodset, Joan L., & Fritz Siebel. *Who Took the Farmer's Hat?* New York: Harper & Row, 1963. Print.

Nolan, Dennis. *Sea of Dreams*. New York: Roaring Brook, 2011. Print.

Nozaki, Akihiro, & Mitsumasa Anno. *Anno's Hat Tricks*. New York: Philomel, 1985. Print.

Numeroff, Laura Joffe, & Felicia Bond. *If You Give a Mouse a Cookie*. New York: Harper & Row, 1985. Print.

O'Connor, Jane. *Fancy Nancy*. New York: HarperCollins, 2005. Print.

Ommen, Sylvia Van. *The Surprise*. Asheville, NC: Front Street, 2007. Print.

Opie, Lona. *My Very First Mother Goose*. Cambridge, MA: Candlewick, 1996. Print.

Parish, Peggy, & Fritz Siebel. *Amelia Bedelia*. New York: Harper & Row, 1963. Print.

Parr, Todd. *The Feelings Book*. Boston: Little, Brown, 2000. Print.

Paterson, Katherine. *Bridge to Terabithia*. New York: Harper Trophy, 1977. Print.

Pfister, Marcus. *The Rainbow Fish*. New York: North-South, 1992. Print.

Pinkney, Jerry, & Aesop. *The Lion and the Mouse*. New York: Little, Brown for Young Readers, 2009. Print.

Polacco, Patricia. *Bully*. New York: Putnam Juvenile, 2012. Print.

Pope Osborne, Mary. *Magic Tree House, Boxed Set, Books 1–4: Dinosaurs Before Dark, The Knight at Dawn, Mummies in the Morning, and Pirates Past Noon*. New York: Random House, 2001. Print.

Pope Osborne, Mary. *Magic Tree House, Boxed Set, Books 9–12: Dolphins at Daybreak, Ghost Town at Sundown, Lions at Lunchtime, and Polar Bears Past Bedtime*. New York: Random House, 2003. Print.

Pope Osborne, Mary, & Sal Murdocca. *Magic Tree House, Boxed Set, Books 5–8: Night of the Ninjas, Afternoon on the Amazon, and Sunset of the Sabertooth*. New York: Random House Books for Young Readers, 2002. Print.

Porter, Matthew. *Tails Chasing Tails*. New York: Sasquatch Books, 2013. Print.

Portis, Antoinette. *Kindergarten Diary*. New York: Harper, 2010. Print.

Prelutsky, Jack, & Lobel, Arnold (Eds.). *The Random House Book of Children's Poetry*. New York: Random House, 1983. Print.

Presson, Leslie. *A Dictionary of Homophones*. New York: Barron's Educational Series, 1997. Print.

Presson, Leslie. *What in the World Is a Homophone?* New York: Barron's Educational Series, 1996. Print.

Pulver, Robin. *Punctuation Takes a Vacation*. New York: Holiday House, 2004. Print.

Pulver, Robin, & Lynn Rowe Reed. *Nouns and Verbs Have a Field Day*. New York: Holiday House, 2006. Print.

Pulver, Robin, & Lynn Rowe Reed. *Punctuation Takes a Vacation*. New York: Holiday House, 2003. Print.

Pulver, Robin, & Stéphanie Roth Sisson. *Thank You, Miss Doover*. New York: Holiday House, 2010. Print.

Raabe, Janis Asad, & Emil Ian. *Hot Rods*. Cleveland, OH: Modern Curriculum, 1986. Print.

Raschka, Christopher. *A Ball for Daisy*. New York: Schwartz & Wade, 2011. Print.

Rathmann, Peggy. *Goodnight, Gorilla*. New York: Putnam, 1993. Print.

Ray, Karen. *The T.F. Letters*. New York: DK Publishers, 1998. Print.

Relf, Adam. *Fox Makes Friends*. New York: Sterling, 2005. Print.

Rinker, Sherri Duskey, & Tom Lichtenheld. *Goodnight, Goodnight, Construction Site*. San Francisco: Chronicle, 2011. Print.

Rogers, Gregory. *The Boy, the Bear, the Baron, the Bard*. Brookfield, CT: Roaring Brook, 2004. Print.

Rogers, M., & Gill Guile. *Clip! Clop!*. Newmarket, UK: Brimax, 1994. Print.

Root, Phyllis, & David Walker. *Flip, Flap, Fly!: A Book for Babies Everywhere*. London: Walker, 2009. Print.

Rosen, Michael, & Helen Oxenbury. *We Are Going on a Bear Hunt*. London: Walker, 1989. Print.

Rueda, Claudia. *Is It Big or Is it Little?* New York: Eerdmans, 2013. Print.

Rylant, Cynthia, & Mary Szilagyi. *Night in the Country*. New York: Bradbury, 1986. Print.

Rylant, Cynthia, & Nancy Hayashi. *Bunny Bungalow*. San Diego: Harcourt Brace, 1999. Print.

Rylant, Cynthia, & Suçie Stevenson. *Birthday Presents*. New York: Orchard, 1987. Print.

Rylant, Cynthia, Diane Goode, Ann Durell, & Riki Levinson. *When I Was Young in the Mountains*. New York: E. P. Dutton, 1982. Print.

Sandburg, Carl, & Steve Arcella. *Poetry for Young People*. New York: Sterling, 1995. Print.

Savin, Marcia. *The Moon Bridge*. New York: Scholastic, 1992. Print.

Say, Alan. *Grandfather's Journey*. New York: Houghton Mifflin, 1993. Print.

Scarry, Richard. *Best Word Book Ever*. Racine, WI: Western Publishing Company, 1980. Print.

Schaefer, Lola M. *One Special Day (A Story for Big Brothers and Sisters)*. New York: Hyperion Books, 2012. Print.

Scholastic Children's Dictionary. New York: Scholastic, 2013. Print.

Scholastic. *A Band of Coyotes*. New York: Scholastic, 2002. Print.

Schotter, Roni, & Kyrsten Brooker. *Nothing Ever Happens on 90th Street*. New York: Orchard, 1997. Print.

Schwiebert, Pat, Chuck DeKlyen, & Taylor Bills. *Tear Soup: A Recipe for Healing after Loss*. Portland, OR: Grief Watch, 1999. Print.

Scieszka, Jon, & Kurt Hoffman. *The True Story of the Three Little Pigs*. New York: Viking Kestrel, 1989. Print.

Scillian, Devin, & Tim Bowers. *Memoirs of a Goldfish*. Ann Arbor, MI: Sleeping Bear, 2010. Print.

Seeger, Laura Voccaro. *The Hidden Alphabet*. New York: Roaring Brook, 2010. Print.

Sendak, Maurice. *Where the Wild Things Are*. New York: Harper & Row, 1963. Print.

Seuss, Dr. (Theodore Geisel). *And to Think That I Saw It on Mulberry Street*. New York: Vanguard, 1937. Print.

Seuss, Dr. (Theodore Geisel). *Green Eggs and Ham*. New York: Beginner, 1960. Print.

Seuss, Dr. (Theodore Geisel). *Hop on Pop*. New York: Beginner, 1963. Print.

Seuss, Dr. (Theodore Geisel). *Seuss ABC*. London: HarperCollins, 2003. Print.

Seuss, Dr. (Theodore Geisel). *The Cat in The Hat*. New York: Random House, 1957. Print.

Shaskan, Trisha Speed, & Gerald Guerlais. *Honestly, Red Riding Hood Was Rotten!: The Story of Little Red Riding Hood as Told by the Wolf*. New York: Nonfiction Picture Books, 2011. Print

Shaw, Nancy E. *Sheep on a Ship*. New York: Houghton Mifflin Harcourt, 1992. Print.

Shaw, Nancy, & Margot Apple. *Sheep in a Jeep*. Boston: Houghton Mifflin, 1986. Print.

Shea, Susan A., & Tom Slaughter. *Do You Know Which Ones Will Grow?* Maplewood, NJ: Blue Apple, 2011. Print.

Sierra, Judy, & Marc Tolon Brown. *Wild about Books*. New York: Knopf, 2004. Print.

Silverstein, Shel. *The Giving Tree*. New York: Harper & Row, 1964. Print.

Simon, Norma. *The Saddest Time*. Park Ridge, IL: Albert Whitman, 1986. Print.

Simont, Marc, & Reiko Sassa. *The Stray Dog*. New York: Scholastic, 2002. Print.

Smee, Nicola. *Clip-clop*. London: Boxer, 2006. Print.

Snicket, Lemony. *The Dark*. New York: Little Brown, 2013. Print.

Sobel, June, & Melissa Iwai. *B Is for Bulldozer: A Construction ABC*. San Diego: Harcourt, 2003. Print.

Sornson, Bob, & Maria Dismondy. *The Juice Box Bully: Empowering Kids to Stand up for Others*. Northville, MI: Nelson, 2010. Print.

Spelman, Cornelia Maude. *When I Feel Scared*. Morton Grove, IL: Albert Whitman, 2002. Print.

Spelman, Cornelia. *Mama and Daddy Bear's Divorce.* Morton Grove, IL: Albert Whitman, 1998. Print.

Steig, William. *Sylvester and the Magic Pebble.* New York: Windmill, 1969. Print.

Stevens, Janet. *From Pictures to Words: A Book about Making a Book.* New York: Holiday House, 1995. Print.

Stone, Jon. *The Monster at the End of this Book.* Sesame Workshop, 2011. Print.

Sutton, Sally. *Demolition.* New York: Candlewick, 2012. Print.

Taha, Karen. *A Gift for Tia Rosa.* New York: Bantam Books, 1991. Print.

Teague, Mark. *Dear Mrs. LaRue: Letters from Obedience School.* New York: Scholastic, 2002. Print.

Terban, Marvin. *Checking Your Grammar.* New York: Scholastic, 1994. Print.

Terban, Marvin. *Dictionary of Idioms.* New York: Scholastic, 2006. Print.

Terban, Marvin. *Eight Ate: A Feast of Homonym Riddles.* New York: Houghton Mifflin, 2007. Print.

Terban, Marvin. *In a Pickle: And Other Funny Idioms.* New York: Houghton Mifflin, 1983. Print.

Terban, Marvin. *The Scholastic Dictionary of Spelling.* New York: Scholastic, 2006. Print.

Terban, Marvin. *Time to Rhyme: A Rhyming Dictionary.* Honesdale, PA: Wordsong, 1997. Print.

Thomas, Pat. *Don't Call Me Special: A First Look at Disability.* New York: Barron's Educational Series, 2000. Print.

Thomas, Pat. *I Miss You: A First Look at Death.* New York: Barron's Educational Series, 2000. Print.

Thompson, Lauren. *Polar Bear Morning.* New York: Scholastic, 2013. Print.

Toms, Kate. *Nursery Rhymes.* Hertfordshire, UK: Make Believe Ideas, 2010. Print.

Turner, Priscilla, & Whitney Turner. *The War Between the Vowels and the Consonants.* New York: Farrar, Straus and Giroux, 1996. Print.

Vail, Rachel. *Flabbersmashed About You.* New York: Feiwel and Friends, 2012. Print.

Vail, Rachel. *Sometimes I'm Bombaloo.* New York: Scholastic, 2002. Print.

Van Draanen, Wendelyn. *Shredderman.* New York: Yearling, 2006. Print.

Van Hout, Mies. *Happy.* La Vergne, TN: Lemniscaat, 2012. Print.

Van, Allsburg Chris. *The Stranger.* Boston: Houghton Mifflin, 1986. Print.

Van, Allsburg Chris. *The Widow's Broom.* Boston: Houghton Mifflin, 1992. Print.

Van, Allsburg Chris. *Two Bad Ants.* Boston: Houghton Mifflin, 1988. Print.

Varon, Sara. *Chicken and Cat.* New York: Scholastic, 2006. Print.

Viorst, Judith, & Ray Cruz. *Alexander and the Terrible, Horrible, No Good, Very Bad Day.* New York: Atheneum, 1972. Print.

Viorst, Judith. *The Tenth Good Thing about Barney.* New York: Simon & Schuster. 1988. Print.

Waber, Bernard. *Ira Sleeps over.* Boston: Houghton Mifflin, 1972. Print.

Wagenbach, Debbie. *The Grouchies.* Washington, DC: Magination Press, 2009. Print.

Ward, Cindy, & Tomie DePaola. *Cookie's Week*. New York: Putnam, 1988. Print.

Weitzman, Jacqueline Preiss, & Robin Preiss-Glasser. *You Can't Take a Balloon into the Metropolitan Museum*. New York: Dial for Young Readers, 1998. Print.

Wiesner, David. *Flotsam*. New York: Clarion, 2006. Print.

Wiesner, David. *Tuesday*. New York: Clarion, 1991. Print.

Willems, Mo. *Knuffle Bunny Too: A Case of Mistaken Identity*. New York: Hyperion for Children, 2007. Print.

Willems, Mo. *The Pigeon Finds a Hot Dog!* New York: Hyperion for Children, 2004. Print.

Wilson, Karma, & Joan Rankin. *A Frog in the Bog*. New York: Margaret K. McElderry, 2003. Print.

Wilson, Karma, & Marcellus Hall. *The Cow Loves Cookies*. New York: Margaret K. McElderry, 2010. Print.

Wilson, Sarah, & Akemi Gutierrez. *A Nap in a Lap*. New York: Henry Holt, 2003. Print.

Winthrop, Elizabeth, & Betsy Lewin. *Dumpy La Rue*. New York: Henry Holt, 2004. Print.

Wood, Audrey, Don Wood, Dalia Hartman, Ernest V. Troost, & Melissa Leebaert. *The Napping House*. San Diego: Harcourt Brace Jovanovich, 1984. Print.

Wood, Audrey. *Silly Sally*. San Diego: Harcourt Brace Jovanovich, 1992. Print.

Yolen, Jane, Andrew Peters, & G. Brian Karas. *Switching on the Moon: A Very First Book of Bedtime Poems*. Cambridge, MA: Candlewick, 2010. Print.

Yoon, Salina. *One, Two Buckle My Shoe*. New York: Robin Corey Books, 2011. Print.

Ziefert, Harriet, & Rufus Coes. *Before I Was Born*. New York: Knopf, 1989. Print.

Zolotow, Charlotte, & Wendell Minor. *The Seashore Book*. New York: HarperCollins, 1992. Print.

GLOSSARY

Alphabetic knowledge	Children's ability to recognize letters of the alphabet and their knowledge of lettersound relationships.
Alphabetic principle	The concept that letters and letter patterns represent the sounds of spoken language and can be applied to letter sequences to read words fluently, or the ability to pair sounds with the letters that represent them.
Amotivation	A lack of desire or intention to act.
Annotation	The act of writing on a text one is reading, for the purpose of remembering key points (underlining or highlighting, for example) or jotting down questions to be addressed in the future.
Automaticity	Refers to reading quickly, without having to analyze each individual word, because reading at the word level has become automatic; the ability to read words without having to sound them out.
Autonomy	Having or perceiving the free will to act, think, or feel as one wishes.

Autonomy and shame/ doubt:

Erikson's second stage of development	Children conquer the second developmental crisis of psychosocial development by trying to complete tasks independently and seeing how others (primarily parents) respond to their successes and mistakes. Successful completion of this stage of development fosters *will*.
Background knowledge	What a person knows from previous experiences.
Causal reasoning	The ability to think logically; to order facts, understand how people affect one another, and identify causes and consequences of events.
Clue words	Words or phrases that indicate some sort of relationship between events (for example, *because, so, that, next, before, after*).
Competence	Actual or perceived capabilities in a variety of areas, including reading and other academic domains, as well as areas such as social and physical development.
Composing	The act of writing, or selecting the appropriate written language to use when expressing oneself, as well as planning and executing a piece of writing carefully.
Comprehension	The ability to understand the meaning and intent of what is said or read.
Concepts of print	An understanding of the general conventions of text (for example, print carries meaning, in English is written from left-to-right, words are composed of letters).
Contextualize	To define or analyze a word in terms of the other words surrounding it, or within a specific situation.
Conventional writing	Legible writing that follows standard rules of grammar, syntax, spelling, and usage.
Conventions (of writing)	All of the basic aspects of writing that help convey meaning clearly, like proper spelling, punctuation, and indentation.

Decoding	Using spoken language to crack the code of written language and sound out words. These strategies can include sounding out, decoding by analogy (using knowledge of similar words to decode), breaking words into syllables, and using knowledge of prefixes and suffixes.
Descriptive writing	The type of written language that is used to make a story come to life; descriptive text includes vivid imagery, as well as similes and metaphors, to explain how people feel and act or to set the scene.
Emergent literacy skills	The first visible and predictive evidence that your child is beginning the process of learning to read. These skills, including phonological awareness, concepts of print, and alphabetic knowledge are considered precursors to conventional reading.
Emergent writing	Children's earliest attempts to explain their ideas in print, ranging from random squiggles to partial representations of words.
Empathy	The ability to put oneself in another person's shoes and deeply understand their thoughts, feelings, and behaviors.
Encoding	The act of translating spoken sounds into written letters, as is required in spelling out words; the opposite of decoding (see also *decoding*).
Expository writing	The type of written language that is used to provide a detailed explanation of an idea, like a recipe, a set of instructions, or a how-to guide.
Expressive language skills	The ability to communicate thoughts, needs, experiences, opinions, ideas, and feelings in a concise, grammatically correct, and fluent manner.
External regulation	The type of motivation where a person acts to receive a reward or to please someone else (in other words, when someone else is regulating his/her behavior).

Extrinsic motivation	An external force, generated by the praise or rewards provided by other people for completing a task, including tangible rewards (like money, candy, promotions at work) or social rewards (like verbal praise, smiles and hugs, and being well-regarded).
Fast mapping	Forming a simple, mental definition of a word after hearing it just once.
Forced choice	Presenting someone with two acceptable options for resolving a situation and allowing him to choose between them, with the goal of eliciting appropriate behavior while allowing that person to maintain a feeling of independence.
General knowledge	Knowledge about the world that a person can readily recall when reading. Also referred to as background knowledge or prior knowledge (see also *background knowledge*).
Grapheme	The written expression of a single sound of spoken language; may consist of one or more letters (for example, *shock* has three graphemes: *sh, -o-, -ck*).
Graphic organizers	Visual representations of information to be learned or expressed, presented in a simple format that aids organization.
Homophone	Words that sound the same when spoken aloud, but differ in meaning despite being spelled the same way (referred to as *homonyms* or *homographs*), or in meaning and spelling (referred to as *heterographs*).
Idiom	An expression whose meaning cannot be interpreted by examining the usual meaning of the words used in it; for example, "It's raining cats and dogs."
Inferential thinking	The ability to "read between the lines" to deduce or infer what the author is discussing and to explain how people or situations affect others, even when this is not explained directly.

Industry and inferiority: Erikson's fourth stage of development	Children conquer the fourth developmental crisis of psychosocial development by working on tasks that often are completed over long periods of time, and seeing how others (including parents, teachers, and peers) respond to their successes and mistakes. Successful completion of this stage of development fosters competence.
Initiative and guilt: Erikson's third stage of development	Children conquer the third developmental crisis of psychosocial development by actively seeking out new tasks to engage in, and seeing how others (primarily parents) respond to their attempts at task completion. Successful completion of this stage of development fosters *purpose*.
Intrinsic motivation	Motivation that comes from within and occurs when we spontaneously want to do something because we find it inherently interesting or rewarding.
Inventive spelling	Young children's natural tendency to experiment with letters and sounds, using a rudimentary understanding of the alphabetic principle to represent words in print.
K-W-L strategy	A technique for helping your child activate and expand his or her knowledge while reading. Ask your child to reflect on these questions: • What do I *know*? • What do I *want* to find out? • What did I *learn*?
Language	The many different components of spoken words that help us understand others (our *receptive* skills) and share our own thoughts (*expressive* skills).
Lexical level (of language)	The level of language that allows us to understanding the meaning of individual words; for example, understanding that "bed" is the place you sleep.

Lexicon	A collection of known words, similar to an internal dictionary, developed by each individual speaker of a language; the vocabulary of a language.
Letter–sound knowledge	The ability to connect printed letters to the sounds of spoken language; also referred to as alphabetic knowledge.
Listening comprehension	The ability to process and understand spoken language.
Literal elements	Ideas that are "right there" and are immediately accessible within the text and illustrations.
Mastery goals	Striving to achieve for the purpose of becoming more proficient at a task and approach success.
Matthew Effect	The theory that the "rich get richer and the poor get poorer"; children who start out with stronger initial reading skills will build their skills at a faster rate, while those with weaker skills will fall further and further behind.
Mindset	The beliefs a person holds about his abilities, either maintaining a fixed mindset and believing that abilities are genetically determined and unchangeable or holding a growth mindset and believing that abilities can be changed through hard work.
Morphology	Meaningful units that dictate word formation; a morpheme such as *-ed* indicates past tense.
Motivation	An external force or internal drive that causes people to act (see also *extrinsic motivation* and *intrinsic motivation*).
Narrative retellings	An exercise in which a reader (or listener) reconstructs a story. The goal is to remember important points in the story and to demonstrate an understanding of the story's structure.
Narrative text	Writing that tells a story rather than describing information or attempting to persuade the reader to a certain viewpoint.

Narrative writing	The type of written language that is used to tell a story; narrative text includes a starting point, events that typically lead up to a climax, and then a resolution.
Onset	The sounds that come before the vowel in a syllable, such as the /c/ in *cat*.
Onset-rime awareness	The component of phonological awareness that is acquired when one recognizes that spoken syllables can be broken down further to an onset (the sounds that precede the vowel sound) and a rime (the rest of the syllable).
Oral language skills	A set of skills that allow people to listen and respond to others, comprehend words heard or read, gather new information, and express their thoughts, feelings, and ideas. These skills include word knowledge (vocabulary), sentence structure (grammar), language structure (semantics and comprehension), social language (pragmatics), and higher order thinking that aids in organizing and sequencing thoughts.
Orthography	The study of rules that govern the representation of sounds by printed symbols (letters); a language's writing or spelling system that utilizes the correct pattern of letters, characters, and symbols. (see also *alphabetic principle* or *knowledge*).
Overjustification effect	A phenomenon in which an extrinsic motivator leads to a decrease in intrinsic motivation to engage in a task.
Performance goal	Striving to achieve an observable goal for the purpose of demonstrating to others that one can avoid failure.
Perspective-taking	The ability to see a situation from someone else's point of view; being able to recognize and understand another's thoughts, feelings, and motivations.

Persuasive writing	The type of written language that is used to make a point, take a side in a debate, and convince others of the validity of that viewpoint.
Phoneme	The smallest unit of sound that makes a difference to meaning. For example, changing the one vowel sound in *cat* to *cut* changes the meaning of the word.
Phoneme or phonemic awareness	The ability to perceive and manipulate the individual speech sounds, or phonemes, within words.
Phonics	An approach to teaching beginning reading that emphasizes letter-sound relationships as the path to efficient word recognition.
Phonological awareness	The ability to perceive and manipulate sounds. Phonological awareness includes four levels of sound: word awareness, syllable awareness, onset-rime awareness, and phoneme awareness. Because the focus is on sounds, it is not necessary to reference print to develop phonological awareness.
Phonology	The study of how sounds are organized and used in different languages.
Picture walk	Looking deliberately (that is, "walking") through a book you have not yet read, for the purpose of preparing to read, as well as making predictions and inferences.
Positive feedback loop	An ongoing process where one action has a positive result, which then creates a rewarding cycle, encouraging that action to continue and increase.
Pragmatic development	The ability to use language for social communication, including requests, refusals, assertions, denials, as well as using metaphors and idioms (see also *idiom*).
Pragmatics	The social aspect of language, which varies depending on social and cultural contexts.

Predictable books	Books that have a recurring structure, allowing a child to predict what words will come next. Such structures include cumulative stories, repetitive phrases, question and answer patterns, story patterns, familiar sequences, rhyming, and circular stories.
Predicting	A reading strategy in which guesses (based on background knowledge and story clues) are made about what will happen later in the story.
Presentation	How a child's writing appears, including whether the text is written neatly and words are spelled correctly.
Print referencing	Refers to using verbal and nonverbal cues to guide a child's attention to the written word. Nonverbal cues include gestures, such as pointing to words or drawing one's finger under the text one is reading to guides a child's attention to the written word. Verbal cues include questions, comments, or requests that draws a child's attention to the written word.
Print-rich environment	An environment that maximizes a child's exposure to the written word. Such environments include many books, but can also include written labels for important objects, toys that incorporate letters in writing, and opportunities to see adults using print in their daily lives (for example, reading a recipe or making a grocery list).
Print-salient storybooks	Books with prominent print features, such as text bubbles, print embedded in pictures, or emphases on certain words in the text (for example, POW!, ZZZZ, or STOP).
Prior knowledge	Knowledge about the world that a person can readily recall when reading. Also referred to as *background knowledge* or *general knowledge*.

Questioning	A strategy in which readers interact with the text and express wonder or confusion about a story and its events. By forming their own questions, readers understand more about the information in the text.
Reading comprehension	The ability to decode written words as well as derive meaning from what is read.
Reading fluency	Reading smoothly, accurately, quickly, with expression, and understanding the meaning of the text.
Reading volume	The cumulative amount of reading a person does over time.
Receptive language skills	The ability to understand what people are saying.
Reciprocal processes	Growth in particular areas that causes growth in other, related areas; for example, improved literacy nourishes growth in vocabulary and general knowledge, which in turn enables additional improvements in literacy via the Matthew Effects.
Rhyming	A type of onset–rime awareness wherein the individual identifies words that end in the same sound, for example, *chair* and *stair*.
Rime	The vowel and remaining parts of a syllable, such as the /at/ in *cat;* what is left over in a syllable after the onset (see also *onset*).
Scaffolding	A way of providing support to a child so that he can complete tasks with which he needs assistance.
Schema	An organizing mental framework.
Semantic development	The ability to understand the meaning of words and make connections between words, including finding a word's synonyms and antonyms (see also *semantics*).

Semantic web	A "web" depicting how ideas, words, or objects are connected to each other in various ways. It might start with one word or idea in the middle, with other connected ideas branching off, connected by lines; for example, leash, collar, and food might branch off from dog.
Semantics	The system of language focusing on word meaning. This system involves vocabulary including synonyms, antonyms, and homonyms (words that are spelled differently but sound similar).
Sense of self	A person's perception of his skills and abilities, and of how these skills and abilities are valued by others around him. A child with a healthy sense of self generally trusts the world around him, asks for help when needed but takes pleasure in completing tasks independently, and feels purposeful and competent.
Sentence fluency (in writing)	A writer's ability to readily use many different sentence structures when composing.
Social-emotional skills	A set of skills that allows children to develop close relationships with adults and peers, including: a positive sense of self, perspective-taking and empathy, self-management, self-awareness, awareness of those around them, relationship skills, and responsible decision making.
Specific feedback	A response to a child's behavior that includes praise ("Amazing job!") along with labeling the reason for that praise ("You found a rhyming word!").
Speech	The ability to express oneself orally, using language.
Spelling	The act of putting the alphabetic principle into action and encoding speech sounds into print; generating the correct written representation of a word.

Spelling development	Children's movement through a series of developmental stages, in which they progressively encode more of the sounds they hear into print using appropriate letter representations.
Story comprehension (or narrative competence)	The ability to understand and make sense of a narrative; consists of both listening and reading comprehension.
Story schema	An understanding of the general framework of stories including setting, characters, a main problem, climax, and a resolution.
Sublexical level (of language)	The level of language that allows us to understand the meaning of parts of words, including syllables, some grammatical morphemes, individual speech sounds or phonemes in words, and the word's onset and rime.
Summarizing	Identifying the most important ideas from a text and paraphrasing them, or restating the ideas in one's own words.
Syllable awareness	The component of phonological awareness that is acquired when one recognizes that spoken words can be broken down into syllables, which are generally no longer meaningful on their own.
Syntactic development	The ability to understand the structure of a sentence, including its tense, subject, and object (see also *syntax*).
Syntax	The system of language that governs language and guides how words should be combined into sentences. This involves capitalization and punctuation, using appropriate tenses, and being able to use simple, compound, and complex sentences.
Synthesizing	A reader's process of bringing new information from a text and her own experiences together to reach a deeper understanding of the text.

Taxonomy	A more sophisticated semantic web where items are organized by categories and subcategories; for example, dog, cat, and fish would be subcategories of "pets."
Telegraphic speech	The type of speech that emerges around two years of age in which children use just one or two words to communicate their needs (for example, "Mom go," or "Dad cookie").
Theory of mind	The ability to understand that others have thoughts, feelings, and beliefs that may differ from one's own thoughts, feelings, and beliefs.
Think-alouds	Activities in which an adult models inferential thinking and identification of story components by making observations out loud and asking questions while reading with a child, demonstrating what the internal monologue of a good reader sounds like.
Translexical level (of language)	The level of language that allows us to understand the meaning of sentences.
Trust and mistrust: Erikson's 1st stage of development	Children conquer the first developmental crisis of psychosocial development by learning when to be trusting and when to be mistrustful. Successful completion of this stage of development fosters *hopefulness.*
Visualizing	The ability to create mental images while reading text.
Voice (in writing)	The style that an author uses when writing.
Word awareness	The component of phonological awareness that is acquired when one recognizes that spoken sentences and compound words are divided into individual words.
Word consciousness	The awareness of and interest in words and their meanings.
Word recognition	The ability to recognize written words correctly and with little effort. This capacity develops when a child does not need not to sound out a word or depend on context, but instead recognizes it as a unit.

Word study   The practice of exploring the patterns of letter
                                use in words, including a focus on spelling
                                patterns that help explain, among other
                                things, which words use a letter's hard vs. soft
                                sound (e.g., *call* vs. *cell*).

Zone of proximal   The area of growth and change that exists
development   between Point A, what a child can do
                                independently, and Point B, what a child can
                                do with the assistance of a more capable peer
                                or adult. Providing experiences within this
                                zone allows children to enhance their learning
                                capacities.

INDEX